Open Minds

Open Minds

The Social Making of Agency and Intentionality

Wolfgang Prinz

The MIT Press
Cambridge, Massachusetts
London, England

For information about special quantity discounts, please email special_sales@ mitpress.mit.edu

This book was set in Stone Sans and Stone Serif by Toppan Best-set Premedia Limited. Printed and bound in the United States of America.

Library of Congress Cataloging-in-Publication Data

Prinz, Wolfgang, 1942–.
Open minds: the social making of agency and intentionality / Wolfgang Prinz.
   p.   cm.
Includes bibliographical references and index.
ISBN 978-0-262-01703-9 (hbk. : alk. paper)
1. Will. 2. Cognition. 3. Intentionalism. 4. Agent (Philosophy). 5. Intentionality (Philosophy). I. Title.
BF611.P75   2012
153.8—dc23

                                                                    2011028981

10 9 8 7 6 5 4 3 2 1

Contents

Preface

A book like this is always a collective endeavor. Collective action pertains to both intellectual foundations and practical realization. As regards intellectual foundations, the ideas laid out here have emerged over the past two decades from numerous discussions with scientists from various branches of cognitive science. Their ideas have helped me tremendously to shape my own views. Yet, while I am extremely grateful to all of them, I have decided to refrain from naming them here. Since a good deal of these discussions have actually yielded contrast rather than assimilation between their ideas and my views, I thought it would be both unfair and unwise to mention their names in connection with ideas that they may find strange or even somewhat absurd. There is one exception, though—one of the rare cases of assimilation. I would like to thank Pascal Mercier for allowing me to use a congenial passage from one of his novels as epigraph and helping with its translation.

As concerns practical realization, the work on the manuscript has extended over more than a decade. While it has been a painfully slow process for me, it must have been a painfully chaotic and patience-demanding process for all of those who supported me during that time. I am extremely grateful for their never-ending patience with my reiterative attempts at clarifying thoughts and shaping words accordingly. Angelika Gilbers, Heide John, Assja Metzger, and Claudia Pethke started working on the manuscript in my former Munich office, supported by Monika Nisslein, who coordinated their work. Later, Susanne Starke, Stefan Liebig, and Marion Schmidt took over in my Leipzig office and helped complete the project. I am deeply indebted to all of them for their friendly support and enduring patience. Special thanks go to Susanne Starke, Janette Studniczka, and Rosie Wallis for putting it all together in the end.

Last, but not least, I would like to thank Philip Laughlin and Judy Feldmann at the MIT Press for their constructive support. Without Phil's enthusiasm for the project and Judy's careful and sensitive editing, the book would not be what it is now.

Leipzig, July 2011

Prologue

The nature of all other beings is limited and constrained
within the bounds of laws prescribed by Us.
Thou, constrained by no limits,
in accordance with thine own free will, in whose hand We have placed thee,
shalt ordain for thyself the limits of thy nature.
. . .
We have made thee neither of heaven nor of earth,
neither mortal nor immortal,
so that with freedom of choice and with honor,
as though the maker and molder of thyself,
thou mayest fashion thyself in whatever shape thou shalt prefer.
—Giovanni Pico della Mirandola[1]

Autonomy from Heaven

In 1486, in the heyday of Renaissance humanism in Northern Italy, the Tuscan nobleman Giovanni Pico della Mirandola delivered to the Florentine intellectual elite an oration entitled "On the Dignity of Man." This oration was to become a manifesto of humanism—a programmatic document of a novel understanding of man's place in the world, remapping the human landscape to focus all attention on human talent and capacities and the human perspective. At the heart of the novel understanding lies the idea that man is not only God's creature but his own creator as well. God, after creating man in His own image and shaping him after His likeness, grants man creatorship to make and mold himself and freedom of choice to fashion himself in whatever shape he may prefer.

Rhetorically, Pico della Mirandola lets God speak to Adam, explaining to him that He has endowed him with the capacity to create himself and

1. Pico della Mirandola (1486/1948), pp. 3–4.

determine his own nature (". . . shalt ordain for thyself the limits of thy nature"). God's speech puts Adam into the role of an artist or engineer who invents and creates himself—in fact, a godlike role, as the same text addresses God as the supreme architect and craftsman of the world. Accordingly, since man is now endowed with the ability to fashion himself, facts about man's nature must, to a large extent, be facts about artifacts created by himself.

Today, more than 500 years later, we find Pico's message broadly received and widely implemented in various domains of life and branches of scholarship such as the arts, literature, politics, economics, and law. Modern theory and practice in these domains is very much grounded in the notion that human beings are autonomous agents, who are, at least to some extent, capable of inventing and creating themselves and designing their lives. Western, post-enlightenment modernity assumes that humans have the right and the necessary talent to determine their own way of life. We attribute such rights and talent not only to individuals but also to collectives such as families, tribes, cultures, and states. Yet, Pico's claim suggests that humanity's self-determination goes deeper than just scratching the surface of our way of life. It seems to posit that we humans can even self-create the talents and capacities through which we make and mold our way of life.

In a nutshell, Pico's account of human autonomy is as simple as it is radical: God gives man autonomy as a gift, and man, who is furnished with all the necessary talents for making use of that gift, thankfully accepts it and happily enjoys it.

Deterministic Science

On the one hand, the idea of human autonomy has been widely received and implemented in various branches of modern life and associated practices and discourses; however, on the other hand, it is fair to say that scientists concerned with the study of the mind and its workings have always been skeptical of the message of Pico's manifesto and have remained more or less immune to its constructivist spirit. Science has a hard time accommodating the notion that humans are capable of creating and designing their own minds and fashioning the way they themselves work. A famous pamphlet by the behaviorist B. F. Skinner, which also deals with man's freedom and dignity, may be considered a modern scientific counterpart to Pico's manifesto. For Skinner, the notion of autonomous man is, in scientific terms, useless and misleading. Autonomous man is for him "a center from which behavior emanates. He initiates, originates, and creates, and in doing so he remains, as he was for the Greeks, divine. We say that he is autonomous—and, so far as a science of behavior is concerned, that means miraculous."[2]

Rather than believing in humans as makers and molders of their own minds—as Pico suggests—cognitive and behavioral scientists believe that the workings of human minds are determined by the natural history of their makeup and the cultural and individual history in which they are formed. A deterministic blueprint like this is implicitly inherent in all branches of these sciences. On this view, the human mind is made and shaped by nature and culture, with no room left for invention and creation through the mind's owner him- or herself. This view is obviously not compatible with the constructivist flavor of Pico's idea of man as his own architect. From a scientific point of view, Pico's claim may even sound a bit paradoxical: How could it be possible that a thing like the mind creates itself? Doesn't such self-creation presuppose what it is meant to explain?

The ideas laid out in this book aim to make hard-nosed cognitive science more open to the constructivist spirit embodied in Pico's ideas. I am not going to offer a full-fledged theory of the mind, cutting across various domains of mental functioning. Rather, I will concentrate on an outline for a theory of human agency and subjectivity—certainly, as core features of human mentality, these are the hallmarks of the human mind. How do agency and subjectivity arise in human minds? How does a mental self emerge and what may it be good for? And how is conscious experience related to the sense of self?

Open Minds

These are the questions that I will address below. The answers I will offer follow a twofold commitment: to develop a *constructivist approach* within a *representational framework*.

As concerns constructivism, I follow the spirit of Pico's manifesto, though I deviate from its inspiration in one crucial respect. The spirit in which the manifesto is written suggests that the creation and invention of human selves is a matter of individual geniuses who design and fashion their lives and their minds as they choose. In that regard it follows the lead of the Renaissance understanding of architects, engineers, and artists, who were seen as the individual bearers of outstanding talents. By contrast,

2. Skinner (1972, p. 14).

the approach I am going to develop here holds that individuals can only create and invent themselves in and through interaction and communication with others. Accordingly, rather than working as closed, individual systems, their minds need to operate in ways that are fundamentally open to other minds. The "open minds" perspective holds that the role Pico attributed to individual geniuses is in fact played by collectives of individuals—by collectives of architects, engineers, and artists, who design and fashion their minds in and through mutual interaction.

As concerns representationalism, I start from a conventional framework as it is widely used in cognitive science. This framework sees the mind's proper function in representing and controlling selected features of the environment. The mechanisms subserving these functions can be studied in both behavioral performance and mental experience. According to this framework, nature has created minds for representing and controlling events in the environment. In terms of ultimate function, action is for control and representation is for action.

To fulfill these functions, animals require tools for representation and control. For most animals, how these tools work is not a target of representation and control itself. I will claim, however, that social animals like humans are an exception in this regard. They depend on not just representing and controlling their environment, but also representing and controlling the operation of the tools through which they represent and control their environment. In humans, I submit, such representation and control of tools for representation and control is first perceived and understood to be operating in others and only then becomes applied to one's self.

This is the path I shall follow in building a constructivist approach into a representational framework of the mind. As we will see, this path will lead us to two fundamental issues, both of which are addressed in the short passage from Pascal Mercier's *Night Train to Lisbon* that I have chosen as epigraph.[3] One pertains to the sources from which the construction of agency and subjectivity actually emerges. How is it that people acquire beliefs about their minds? How is public communication related to private experience? *"The stories others tell about you and the stories you tell about yourself: which come closer to the truth?"* What roles are, in other words, being played by third-person and first-person accounts?

3. The epigraph is taken from Mercier (2008, p. 142, with slight changes of translation suggested and authorized by Pascal Mercier). In Mercier's novel that passage serves a quasi-epigraphic function, too. It is quoted from notes and reflections left behind by a Lusitan nobleman, physician, and philosopher who lived and died in the first half of the twentieth century.

The other issue pertains to the reality and efficacy of social constructions about the mind. How real are people's beliefs about the workings of
their minds? Are such beliefs fact or fiction? Do they provide true stories
of their workings, or must we consider them fictitious, perhaps even illusory cover stories that mask the true ones? *"Is the soul a place of facts? Or
are the alleged facts only the deceptive shadows of our stories?"* Finally, and
most importantly, can beliefs be efficacious in the sense that people's
beliefs about the workings of their minds have an impact on the way their
minds actually work?

This latter question is crucial to the enterprise of merging constructivism with representationalism. The answer I am going to propose is therefore key to the message I would like to convey. Our beliefs about minds, I
will argue, are in fact not just beliefs about how our minds work, but also
powerful tools for making them work as we believe. It is through our belief
that our minds work in a particular way that we actually make them work
that way.

This proposal may be seen to suggest a third answer to the epigraph's
second question. Couched in its metaphorical language, the third answer
claims that the stories people tell about others and themselves should be
regarded as neither fact nor fiction about their souls but as tools for making
and shaping them accordingly.

This claim suggests that beliefs may become real. A claim like this
sounds like magic, and magic is hard to sell in science. However, as will
become apparent below, that claim is nothing but an emergent property
of the constructivist extension of representationalism that I am going to
develop. As I will show, this notion may help to reconcile the bold claims
of Pico della Mirandola's manifesto with the working principles of cognitive science. In fact, I believe that wedding the two to each other will rescue
each of them. Constructivism can only survive if representationalism provides functional architectures that instantiate abstract theoretical principles in concrete processing mechanisms. Conversely, representationalism
can only survive if constructivism provides theoretical principles that
explain how mental representation can give rise to mental experience.

Overview

My argument comes in four parts. Part I is broad and introductory, offering
a discussion of major views on the human mind and major approaches to
its study. The chapters of this part aim at laying the ground for the open
minds approach to human volition and cognition as it is outlined in Parts

III and IV. Before we get there, Part II takes another preparatory step toward this goal. Here I examine mirror systems and mirror games, that is, particular kinds of representational mechanisms and associated behavioral games and social practices. Mirror systems and games, I propose, provide tools for aligning individual minds and molding one's own after other minds. In this way they offer unique and unprecedented tools for building open minds.

Parts III and IV then address the social construction of architectures for volition and cognition. Part III traces the formation of an architecture for volition, addressing issues of agency and intention-based top-down control. Agency and intention, I contend, are initially perceived and understood to be operating in others, and it is only through practices of social mirroring that individuals come to apply these notions to themselves and to implement related control mechanisms for their own actions. Part IV sketches how the same basic ideas can be applied to an architecture for cognition, addressing issues of subjectivity and intentionality. My main focus here is on how social mirroring can help with building architectures for mental experience from preexisting architectures for behavioral performance. A side focus is on the contributions of language use to social knowledge dissemination and control.

Minds are thus open in two senses: One is that they are made and molded in and through the mirror of others, thus designing themselves after others. The other is that they are open and highly susceptible to any knowledge they may attain concerning others' acting, thinking, and knowing.

Can open minds be autonomous? I return to this question in the epilogue, this time going back to the Bible's tale of the Garden of Eden.

I Minds

How does the mind work, and how can its workings be properly studied? In this part, I take up two major lines of discussion on these issues that have been with us for centuries. Yet, my intention is not to provide a dispassionate historical record of these discussions. It is rather to build on them for making a case for a novel theoretical framework of human subjectivity. The hallmark of this framework is that it gives social facts a much stronger role for the constitution of human mentality than do traditional frameworks.[1]

The first line of discussion that I take up in chapter 1 concerns what we may call the two faces of mental functioning. The study of how the mind works can be approached from two sides: outside and inside. From the outside view, the focus is on *performance*, that is, on how people manage to cope with their actual environment.[2] From the inside view, the focus is on *experience*, that is, on how people perceive and understand their environment. In a way, then, the outside view studies what the mind does for organisms struggling for survival and reproduction. Conversely, the inside view studies what the mind does for experiencing subjects trying to understand the world and acting on it.

How are these two faces of the mind related to each other? Can we study performance through experience—or vice versa? Does performance

1. The claim that social and cultural facts play a strong role in the construction of mind is not new altogether. Ideas along these lines may appear to be strange and unfamiliar in the context of cognitive psychology and the cognitive sciences, but they are widespread in domains like cultural psychology, social anthropology, social philosophy, and the social history of science (cf., e.g., Barnes, 2000; Berger & Luckmann, 1966; Bogdan, 1997, 2009, 2010; Bruner, 1990; Cole, 1996; Danziger, 1990; Foucault, 1988; Gergen & Davis, 1985; Kusch, 1997, 1999, 2005; Markus, Kitayama & Heiman, 1996; Mead, 1934; Rose, 1990, 1996; Sharpe, 1990; Stigler, Shweder & Herdt, 1990; Taylor, 1989). The only classical exception in the domain of cognitive psychology comes from the Russian school of activity psychology, which draws on the notion that higher mental functions are reflections of social interaction (Vygotsky, 1979; Wertsch, 1985; see also Cole, 1996, for a more recent follow-up on this line of thought). For overviews of recent cognitive approaches see Baltes, Reuter-Lorenz, and Rösler (2006), Baltes, Rösler, and Reuter-Lorenz (2006), Hauf and Försterling (2007), and Prinz, Försterling, and Hauf (2007).

2. "Coping with one's environment" depends on two basic conditions: appropriate information and efficient control (on the afferent and efferent side, respectively). Information is appropriate when the system has access to information about relevant (i.e., to-be-controlled) features of the environment. Control is efficient when the system is capable of manipulating these features in accordance with its demands. See chapter 7 for a more detailed discussion of issues of control.

build on experience—or vice versa? To what extent can one be dissociated from the other? Of course, questions like these touch on deep philosophical issues concerning the nature of subjectivity and personhood. Yet, as far as I can, I will stay away from "big" philosophical issues. Rather, I will discuss major psychological views on the relation between performance and experience. As a result, I will reject the widespread claim that personal experience arises as an emergent product of subpersonal computations subserving performance. Instead, I will endorse the claim that mental experience arises from representations of outcomes of subpersonal computations in terms of personal categories.

Chapter 2 then addresses issues related to choosing a scientifically sound approach to the study of subjectivity. The standard approach that is widely used in both philosophy and various branches of the cognitive sciences relies on naturalism and individualism. According to this approach, subjectivity is a natural fact, emerging from *closed minds* operating in individuals. I will discuss this approach and confront it with its counterpart, which relies on constructivism and collectivism. According to that approach, subjectivity is a sociocultural fact, arising from interactions and communications among *open minds* in social collectives. I will end up by pleading for an *open minds approach* to human subjectivity.

Finally, in chapter 3 I will tie the two strings together and consider the outcome. If it is true that mental experience relies on personal interpretations of outcomes of subpersonal operations, and if it is also true that the categories that are used for those interpretations are matters of sociocultural construction, then the question arises: what *kinds of things* are we dealing with? Are we talking about artifacts, fictions, or perhaps illusions? My answer will be that sociocultural facts are artifacts but not illusions. They are as real and efficacious as natural facts.

1 The Mind's Two Faces

The Enigma of Subjectivity

Let us start with a really big question, hoping to find ways to break it down into smaller, more treatable ones later on: How does subjectivity enter the world, and what is it good for in an otherwise subjectless universe? Over centuries this question has been at the heart of ontological and epistemological debates in philosophy, and it has been at the heart of major theoretical systems in psychology as well. Obviously, it not only addresses philosophical and scientific concerns but also touches on the roots of our self-understanding as human beings. Still it seems that we do not yet have a satisfactory answer. And this is why we cannot abstain from posing this question over and over again.

In what way is subjectivity an enigma? What distinguishes the subjective from the objective? When we talk about stars, stones, and rivers, when we are dealing with viruses, algae, and fungi, or even ferns, grasses, and trees, we believe that everything that can be said about them can be said using the terms of physics, chemistry, and biology. This may also still hold for jellyfish, worms, and sponges, but then things start to become difficult—if not with insects, then perhaps with vertebrates, and certainly with mammals, particularly the primates, and inevitably, of course, with *Homo sapiens*. When considering these animals, we believe that we cannot say everything that can be said about them through the means of these sciences. What these sciences can take care of is the animals' *outer life*, that is, their life as far as it can be observed by external observers. But we also attribute them with an *inner life* to which external observers have no access. This is the life of their mental experience, and here we enter the realm of subjectivity.

How can we know about things that we cannot observe? Two answers have been proposed to this question, one relying on observation and the other on theory. The first answer stresses one obvious exception to the rule that inner life is unobservable. The exception applies to what philosophers have come to call the first person's perspective on human mentality. For each of us—and, hence, for each and every human observer—it seems to be the case that we can take the role of internal observers of our own mental life, furnished with direct observational access to our mental experiences.[1] Accordingly, we have a direct way of knowing what having an inner life amounts to. On that basis we may then come to attribute to others what we have observed in ourselves in the first place. The scope, richness, and degree of detail of those attributions may depend on factors like familiarity and similarity between others and the self: To our beloved ones (even our pets), we attribute a much richer inner life than strangers whom we don't know; we tend to attribute to humans more of an inner life than our fellow primates or other mammals, and mammals will again lead over other vertebrates like fish, frogs, or snakes.

The second answer relies entirely on theory. Here the argument goes like this: Inner life cannot be observed at all. The only thing that can be observed is humans' and animals' outer life, that is, the way they behave and act under given circumstances. Still we need to attribute to them an inner life if we wish to understand and explain what they are doing and—perhaps even more importantly—anticipate what they are going to do next. According to this view, mental experience is not a matter of observation (first observed in one's self and then perhaps transferred to others) but a matter of theoretical explanation (equally applicable to both self and others). Hence, the terms in which we account for inner life are theoretical constructs—unobservable in themselves but constructed for the sake of explaining what we can observe: the way in which people act under given circumstances. And since we can apply the same explanatory scheme to

---

1. It is sometimes even claimed that direct access to one's own mental states is not really observational (in the sense that we may draw a distinction between things being observed and an observer observing them) but nonobservational (in the sense that the observed and the observer coincide; cf., e.g., Russell, 1996). See below for critical comments on this view.

our own acting as well, there is, on that view, no principled difference between our own and other individuals' mental life. Still, the same grading according to familiarity and similarity may apply—this time based not on the ease of transfer from self to others but on the richness and degree of detail with which we observe people's and animals' conduct.

A similar approach to people's (and animals') inner life is entailed by the commonsense psychology that underlies our intuitive understanding of what people do and why they do it the way they do. Folk psychology provides a simple explanatory scheme for behavior. Normally we trace actions back to mental states that precede behavior. For instance, we may explain the observation that John washes his car by his belief that his doing so will impress his rich aunt. Of course, mental states that are considered reasons for and/or causes of subsequent action do not specify the details of how the action proceeds. But they do explain why the action is performed at all and what it is good for. In this way, subjectivity is ubiquitous in our folk psychology account of human conduct. Here, it does not appear to be enigmatic at all. It is just the case that in order to understand and explain people's outer life one needs first to understand their inner life. People do what they do as a consequence of their beliefs, desires, and intentions.[2]

As a result, we are faced with an uncomfortable dilemma. On the one hand, when we approach human subjectivity from a scientific point of view, it appears to be quite elusive and enigmatic. We do not understand how it fits into our otherwise subjectless picture of the universe. On the other hand, when we approach it from the point of view of our common-sense understanding of human conduct, we encounter inner life all over the place. Here inner life is just as natural and real as outer life, and outer (physical) life cannot be explained without reference to inner (mental) life. Hence, the challenge that the enigma of subjectivity poses for science has two sides. One is to account for its existence—that is, to account for how subjectivity is possible at all. The other is to account for its causal role—that is, to explain how inner life can bring forth outer life.

Performance and Experience

So far, I have been talking about outer and inner life (or, performance and experience, respectively) as if it were clear and obvious what I am talking

2. This is no more than a sketch of the logic of (certain kinds of) action explanation in (certain kinds of) folk psychology. For a broader picture, see, e.g., Greenwood (1991), Hutto (2008), Malle (2004), Malle, Moses, and Baldwin (2001).

about. But before I go ahead with exploring in greater detail how the two sides of mental life may be related to each other, I need to be more explicit about each of them. As a first step, we need to abandon the metaphor of inner/outer life. This metaphor may serve as useful shorthand for introducing approaches to subjectivity. But it is likely to be misleading when it comes to taking a closer look at what the two aspects of human mentality may refer to and how they can be approached. This is because inside/outside talk suggests (or even implies) the notion that there exists one identical thing that is viewed and approached from two different sides or perspectives. This may be a widespread notion. But, as we will see shortly, it does not provide the most convincing answer to the question of how performance and experience are related to each other.

Performance

Let us start with a naïve question and a perhaps somewhat trivial answer to it: Why do animals have minds at all?

Most animals—particularly those from the higher ranks in the animal kingdom—live in environments that undergo more or less unpredictable changes from time to time. The same applies to their bodily states and conditions. Here then is the trivial answer to the naïve question: Animals have minds in order to cope with these changes in their external and internal environments. Minds help them to adapt both bodies to environmental conditions and environments to bodily conditions. They provide them with the ability to evaluate the behaviorally relevant implications of each current stimulus situation and transform these evaluations into appropriate behavior, which then, in turn, alters the current stimulus situation.[3]

As a result, animals live in never-ending sequences of perception–action cycles in which minds play the role of controllers. These controllers match information about the current situation against information about animals' current needs and then transform the outcome of these matches into decisions about whether and how to act.[4] This is the way minds subserve

3. This idea can be traced back to Herbert Spencer, one of the early founding fathers of evolutionary psychology. According to Spencer's system of life sciences, the mission of psychology is to study organisms insofar as they adapt, from instant to instant, through reacting and responding to conditions that undergo permanent changes (as opposed to biology, whose mission is to study how organisms adapt to more constant conditions). See Spencer (1899, p. 138).

4. For the application of control theory to perception and action, see Hershberger (1989), Miller, Galanter, and Pribram (1960), Powers (1973, 1978, 1989).

animals' performance in their struggle for survival and reproduction, and this is the proper function for which evolution has engineered and optimized them.

Body, Brain, and Mind

Minds are implemented in brains, and brains form parts of bodies. Accordingly, one obvious way of studying how the mind works is to begin with the brains and the bodies in which they are embodied. Such studies can be set up in two different languages—a "wet" one and a "dry" one.

The "wet" language is the language of functional anatomy and physiology as it pertains to sensory systems, motor systems, and the brain systems in between. On closer inspection, the wet language turns out to comprise quite a large family of languages, each of which addresses a particular level of analysis. For instance, there is one language for the description of the molecular basis of synaptic transmission, another one for analyzing patterns of coordinated activation in assemblies of adjacent neurons, and still another one devoted to capturing spatiotemporal patterns of activation that are distributed across large brain areas. Different as these languages may be (and disjunct as the pertinent research communities may be as well), they still belong to the same family of languages and can be translated into each other. In other words, they are different, but not incommensurate.

The wet family is complemented by the "dry" family—the family of languages for abstract functional description and/or computational modeling of brain processes. The members of that family differ from each other not only with respect to the level of detail and resolution at which they try to capture the computational logic of putative operations in the brain, but also with respect to their underlying structural and functional ontologies. These ontologies specify kinds of representational states and kinds of computational operations that can occur in the brain. As far as modeling pertains to mechanisms that are (more or less) understood on the wet side, these ontologies will be (more or less) neurobiologically informed and, hence, constrained. However, in many cases, when dry modeling goes beyond the reach of knowledge on the wet side, these ontologies may be quite unconstrained, leaving room for different and incommensurate styles of modeling. As a result, languages from the dry family will often not only be different from but also incommensurate with each other.

At first glance, it may be tempting to assign the wet languages to the workings of the brain and the dry ones to the workings of the mind. But an assignment like this would not really be justified. As long as the languages on the dry side just aim at modeling what is going on on the wet side, that modeling may capture the workings of the brain, but certainly not of the mind. To get the mind into the picture, we need to broaden the scope of study and examine how people (or animals) use their bodies and brains to interact with their environments.

Perception, Action, and Mind

Consider, as an example of such study, the experimental analysis of human performance. Typically, in such experiments, participants are instructed to perform a particular task as efficiently as they can—for example, as fast as they can, or as accurately and precisely as they can. In a sense, the instructions require participants to invest their full mental resources into completing the task. Performance is then assessed in terms of, for example, reaction times, error rates, or measures reflecting the spatial and temporal accuracy of their movements. Remarkably, these measures reflect both a factual and a normative account of their behavior. The factual account captures what they do (or selective aspects thereof). The normative account captures how well they perform with respect to the prescriptions contained in the instruction: fast responses and/or low error scores reflect good performance, whereas slow responses and/or high error rates stand for poor performance.

In a way, then, performance experiments study how well people cope with their environment under artificially created task demands. Typically, performance is studied under a number of conditions that vary with respect to either the experimental setting under which the task is performed, or the task demands specified in the instructions, or both. The ultimate goal is to study how performance is affected by these manipulations of task conditions. The research logic is built on the assumption that understanding the way in which task conditions (i.e., the independent variables) modulate performance scores (i.e., the dependent variables) can help to elucidate the functional architecture of the computational machinery on which task performance is grounded.

At first glance this seems to imply that some hidden function is derived from observed performance. However, the picture is still incomplete. I started discussing the experiment itself—without mentioning what precedes it and what motivates it in the first place. The true beginnings of experiments lie in functional reasoning and theory. It is functional theory that dictates the choices of tasks, conditions, and performance scores. Thus, experiments start with function, move on to performance, and then come back to function again. Understanding the logic of an experiment therefore requires two switches: first from hidden functions to observable performance, and then back from performance to function.

Again, we are dealing with two (families of) languages here. One is the language for *performance*. This language describes what people do under given circumstances and how well they do. It comes close to the ordinary, everyday language that we use for exactly the same purpose. In any case, we need to resort to ordinary language when it comes to instructing participants in the experiment. In these instructions we talk about the details of the task to be performed, specify the task demands, and inform participants about the various environmental conditions under which the task will be administered. The language in which the scientific literature describes performance may sometimes be a bit more technical, but in principle it can be derived from everyday language.

This does not apply to the family of languages for *function*. These languages are designed to describe hidden mechanisms on which observable performance is grounded. The history of psychology has seen a number of such languages, each of which went along with a particular style of theorizing about the nature of these hidden mechanisms.[5] Over the past decades, most cognitive theorists concerned with human performance have homed in on dialects of one particular family of languages: the language family for information processing and computational modeling.

Thus, it seems that the same language family and the same style of theorizing that goes along with it are today used on either side—the brain side and the behavior side of cognitive research. This may be taken to provide a promising perspective for developing unified theories of brain functions and behavior. Still, we must not forget that on the brain side the modeling pertains to brain processes proper, whereas on the behavior side it pertains to mechanisms underlying task performance. For the time being these are two different projects. Still, the fact that we may use the same language for both nourishes some hope that we may, at some point in the future, be in a position to combine the two projects and eventually integrate them into a single united one.

5. Classical examples are Wundt's theory of association and apperception (e.g., Wundt, 1902/1903), Köhler's theory of gestalt-like processes in mind and brain (Köhler, 1924, 1947), Hull's theory of habit hierarchies (Hull, 1943) or Anderson's theory of production systems (Anderson, 1983). Different as these theories may be, their authors share the goal of developing a theoretical language that is neutral in the sense that its terms can, at least in principle, be linked to each of the three basic kinds of observable entities psychology has to struggle with: experience, performance, and brain processes. More recently, the notion of an intermediate, functional level of description between the level of neural implementation and the level of conscious perceptions and intentional actions has been advocated by Hurley (2005, 2008).

Experience

Mental experience poses two hard problems. First: What is it like—and how can we characterize it in analytic terms? Second: What is it good for—and what would be missing if it did not exist?

The second problem is particularly hard for theories claiming that the mind's proper function is to provide mechanisms for performance control—mechanisms that do their work perfectly without relying on any kind of mental experience. In fact, we demand of such functional theories that they account for performance in terms of subpersonal control mechanisms, with no functional role whatsoever for mental experience at the personal level. So why do we still have it, and what is it good for? Basically, there are three ways out: (i) reject the what-for question as unscientific, (ii) declare yourself for epiphenomenalism, or (iii) identify a hidden function. Below—and in fact in the rest of the book—I will make a case for the third option. In a nutshell, I will elaborate on the idea that mental experience offers a medium that opens up individual performance to social impact and, hence, mediates between private and public.

Before I get there let me return to the first hard problem. What is the hallmark of mental experience? How can we characterize it? For instance, how could we possibly explain to an alien from a distant galaxy what it is like to see a flower, to remember a poem, or to drive a car? As long as we talk to other humans, we need not really explain such experiences. Rather, we arrange for a situation in which the other is likely to have them herself. However, when talking to an intelligent alien who, on the one hand, does understand our language, but, on the other hand, lacks our type of experience altogether, we need an analytic vocabulary to give her at least a raw conceptual account of what having such experiences amounts to.

Though there is an enormous and still exploding literature on the nature of mental experience and conscious awareness,[6] I will leave most of it aside and concentrate on Franz Brentano, one of the major classical sources of the modern debate about intentionality and consciousness. For Brentano, conscious mental experience is organized in mental acts, such as seeing a flower or hearing a tone. Brentano poses the question of what actually happens when we hear a tone. What exactly is responsible for the

6. For major positions in philosophy, psychology, and cognitive neurosciences, see Block, Flanagan, and Güzeldere (1997), Cleeremans (2003), Cohen and Schooler (1997), Edelman (1989), Gray (2004), Hurley (1998), Kriegel and Williford (2006), Marcel and Bisiach (1988), Metzinger (2003), Pockett, Banks, and Gallagher (2006), Rowlands (2006), Shear (1995).

conscious nature of this event? According to Brentano, we must distinguish between two mental contents that are interwoven in the act: the
tone that we hear and the fact that we hear it. These two mental contents
are not represented in the same way. The tone is the primary object of the
act of hearing; we can observe it directly in that act. The hearing is the
secondary object of the act. Brentano believed that the secondary object
cannot be directly observed. Instead it attains awareness in a more indirect
form: "We can observe the tones that we hear but we cannot observe the
hearing of the tones. This is because it is only in the hearing of the tones
that the hearing itself is also assessed."[7]

This is as far as Brentano goes. However, if we want an exhaustive characterization of the structure of mental acts, we have to go one step further:
If it is true that the hearing of the tone entails not only the tone itself but
also, implicitly, its hearing, then the hearer who hears must also be entailed
in the act in still another encapsulation. This is because, just as a tone is
hardly conceivable without an act of hearing directed toward it, the hearing
of that tone is hardly conceivable without a mental self, or subject, who
hears. Hence, conscious mental acts seem to be characterized by, and, in
fact, require the implicit presence of a mental self in the act.[8]

Of course, we cannot be sure how much the alien could possibly make
of an account like this. Yet, if we take it as a valid description of the chief
ingredients involved in the formation of conscious mental experience, we
have in our hands a clue that may help us to proceed from description to
explanation. If conscious mental experience depends on the implicit presence of the self in mental acts, then, to understand the conscious nature of
mental experience, we need to understand the functional role of the mental
self and/or its implicit representation in those acts. An understanding of
this role would help us to understand both *when* consciousness arises and
how the conscious nature of mental contents arises. Because the quality of
conscious awareness does not just arise when the condition of the implicit
presence of the self is fulfilled but also consists precisely in this condition
being met, it becomes possible for us to understand not only under which

7. Brentano (1874/1924, p. 180).
8. A view like this is sometimes called an egolocial view of consciousness (as
opposed to nonegolocial views; cf. Gurwitsch, 1941; Zahavi, 2005, ch. 5; for overview, see Kriegel & Williford, 2006). The roots of egolocial or self-representational
theory go back to Kant's claim that the unity of apperception is grounded in the
fact that all mental acts that an individual performs are linked to the mental self.
The involvement of the self in all of these acts guarantees unity within the diversity
of mental life (Kant, 1996, §16).

conditions conscious mental contents emerge but also why they assume precisely this quality under these conditions and not any other.[9]

Having followed Brentano's lead on the first question, we are now in a position to rephrase the second one. If it is true that conscious mental experience arises from, and in fact consists in, some kind of implicit corepresentation of the self in mental acts, the explanatory burden shifts from conscious experience to the mental self. The question is no longer what mental experience is good for but rather what the mental self is good for (and what would be missing if it did not exist). This question will keep us busy over the pages to follow.

Bridging the Gap

Now we have two stories about the mind: a functional one that speaks of performance and underlying computational mechanisms, and a phenomenal one that speaks of experience, intentionality, and self. How are the two related to each other, and how can we bridge the gap between them?

In raising this question we must not forget that our two stories may not really be equivalent in terms of scope and weight. In fact there are some asymmetries here. One is that we have good reasons to believe that the functional story is about the mind's proper function—that is, the function for which evolution has optimized it—whereas the phenomenal story deals with kinds of things whose function is less obvious. Further, the functional story has a theoretical language of its own—the language of representation and computation—whereas the theoretical fundament of phenomenal experience is still unclear. Finally, and related to this, in the functional story the observational language (which speaks of performance) is, at least in principle, commensurate with the theoretical language (which speaks of computational and/or brain mechanisms), whereas these two languages appear to be incommensurate in the phenomenal story.

These asymmetries suggest that we should perhaps consider the functional story primary and fundamental and the phenomenal one secondary and derived. If so, how can phenomenal states build on functional mechanisms?

Correspondence

The default answer to this question invokes correspondence between the two stories. It relies on a simple and straightforward assumption: Functional processing is always paralleled by phenomenal experience, such that tokens

9. See below in this chapter where I discuss the distinction between correlational and foundational theories of consciousness and subjectivity.

of phenomenal experience correspond to tokens of functional processing. Basically, this was the idea on which scientific psychology was initially built in the nineteenth century. It led researchers to believe that, at least in principle, functional mechanisms that subserve performance can also be accessed through introspection, that is, through thorough analysis of conscious experience. For instance, Wilhelm Wundt, one of the founding fathers of experimental psychology, did extensive studies on performance in reaction tasks. He believed that performance on such tasks relies on a complex interplay of two fundamental mechanisms, association and assimilation. To study how these mechanisms work he ran experiments in which he recorded participants' performance (i.e., reaction times, error rates) and, at the same time, had them report in detail what they experienced. This procedure was based on the assumption that introspection can provide direct access to the functional machinery on which performance is grounded.

In retrospect, it is fair to say that this research program failed. It turned out that naïve participants could not report anything about these putative mechanisms. As a consequence, experimental research in Wundt's lab concentrated on a small set of handpicked participants who were thoroughly trained and preinformed about the underlying functional theory. Most of them were Wundt's students and colleagues. In fact, these preinformed observers then delivered in their introspective reports what they had been trained to expect. But such reports were not of great scientific value.

The failure of Wundt's programs suggests a general and a specific conclusion. The general conclusion is that the scope of phenomenal experience seems to be considerably smaller than the scope of functional processing. In other words, phenomenal experience is selective and reflects only a small portion of the ongoing functional processing. The specific conclusion is that that selectivity often takes a specific form: phenomenal experience mainly delivers mental states, or contents—things like thoughts, emotions, memories, percepts—but has not much to say about the mental acts, or processes generating them (e.g., thinking, feeling, remembering, perceiving).[10] Mental experience seems to be made of states, not processes,

10. The distinction between focus on contents vs. acts has a long tradition in theoretical accounts of introspective psychology (see, e.g., Boring, 1957). Historically, content-oriented approaches have always dominated over act-oriented approaches, but from time to time theorists stood up to emphasize the importance of acts (e.g., Brentano, 1874/1924; Stumpf, 1906). Still, in retrospect it is fair to say that act-oriented approaches were notoriously unsuccessful, perhaps owing to the trivial but obvious fact that introspection delivers (static) mental contents, but not (dynamic) mental acts.

whereas theories of functional mechanisms always require both states and processes. If so, the domain of mental experience can at best provide a highly selective, one-sided access to the domain of mental functioning.

Emergence

Perhaps the notion of emergence can help to provide a more realistic picture of the relationship between the two stories. According to this notion, phenomenal states are considered emergent properties, or qualities, arising from the operation of certain types of functional mechanisms. An approach like this has the potential to capture, at least in principle, two essential aspects of phenomenal experience and its relation to functional mechanisms that the notion of correspondence does not deal with very well: disparity and selectivity.

Phenomenal states and functional mechanisms appear to be entirely disparate kinds of things. Whereas one forms part of the mental world, the other forms part of the physical world, and there is no obvious way of bridging the categorical gap. This is where the intuition of emergent properties comes in: It considers phenomenal experience an example of a larger class of natural phenomena that exhibit emergent properties. Natural systems may, under certain conditions, exhibit entirely novel properties that, though they build on complex interactions of their constituents, cannot be derived from, and are in fact incommensurate with, any of the properties of these constituents.[11] Being alive, for instance, is often considered an emergent property of organisms. On the one hand, that property relies entirely on chemical interactions between certain classes of complex molecules. But on the other hand, it exhibits several properties (e.g., metabolism, growth, reproduction) that cannot be observed in those molecules, nor can they be derived from their interaction. Thus, being alive appears to be a novel property of systems that, while it relies on particular interactions between its constituents, cannot be reduced to them. In this sense emergent properties are disparate from the properties of the constituents from whose interaction they emerge.

Furthermore, the notion of emergence leaves room for selectivity. Emergent properties may be selective in the sense that they arise in systems only under certain conditions. For instance, it is often claimed that they can only arise when and if the pattern of interaction of constituents exceeds a particular degree of complexity. This notion is sometimes taken up in theories addressing the neural (or computational) basis of phenomenal experience. Likewise, it is often claimed that conscious awareness arises as an

11. See, e.g., Beckermann (1992), Broad (1925), Stephan (1992).

emergent property of global computational operations that take care of coordinating local computations (performed by specialized modules) and combine their results in some integrated representational structure (e.g., maintained in a globally available workspace).[12] On this view, phenomenal experience may arise from global computations, but not from local ones.

If we believe that the notion of emergence can help us understand how phenomenal experience enters the world, the question again naturally arises of what phenomenal experience might be good for. Once more, two options arise. On the first option, phenomenal experience has a functional role to play, implying that certain complex computations require, and in fact depend on, the emergence of conscious awareness. For instance, one could raise the claim that conscious awareness not only emerges from the workings of the machinery for integrating information in the global workspace, but at the same time also acts to boost the efficiency of that machinery. On the second option, phenomenal experience has no functional role to play and is good for nothing. It is just a by-product of the workings of a system that was built and optimized for a different purpose.

Self-representation

Though the notion of emergence is certainly much more appropriate for our purposes than the notion of correspondence, it is still somewhat unsatisfactory. True, it accounts for the fact that conscious mental experience delivers entirely novel properties that cannot be derived from the putative brain processes and computational mechanisms that generate them. Still, it gives us no clue whatsoever why these novel properties exhibit the particular qualities that make up the hallmark of conscious experience—intentionality and subjectivity—based on the implicit presence of the mental self. Emergentist accounts are correlational: They tell us which functional structures and processes subserve or even produce conscious mental experience and/or which neural mechanisms are correlated with consciousness. But they are not foundational. They tell us neither why these particular neural and/or computational processes bring forth precisely this particular quality, nor why this particular quality requires precisely this particular functional machinery. Hardly any of the currently proposed theories on the relation between functional mechanisms and conscious experience can offer answers to such questions. They can offer

12. This view is widespread among cognitive scientists; see, e.g., Baars (1988, 1997, 2002), Bayne and Chalmers (2003), Cleeremans (2003). To address this view, Morsella has even coined the term "integration consensus" (Morsella, 2005, Morsella, Krieger & Bargh, 2009).

formal, correlational relations that we may acknowledge, but not substantial, foundational relations that we can understand.

How can we develop a foundational account of mental experience? The proposal I wish to outline starts from the notion of representation and expands it into the notion of self-representation.[13] I certainly do not mean to claim that this notion provides a full account of what conscious experience amounts to. I do claim, however, that it captures essential aspects of the foundations of subjectivity that emergentist accounts have no way to deal with.[14]

As argued above, the notion of control offers a convenient framework for issues of representation. Animals can be viewed as systems that control certain features of their environment. To exercise this control, they make use of sensors, effectors, and controllers in between. Biologically speaking, sensors and effectors are implemented in their sensory and motor systems, whereas controllers reside in their brains. What control systems do is—speaking loosely—regulate their environment so that it meets various of their desires and requirements. To achieve this goal they need to be capable of perceiving and acting. Through their sensors, they take up information about (some selected aspects of) the current state of their environment. Through their effectors, they may alter this state if it does not please them.

Controllers are computational devices for linking perception to action. Roughly speaking, their operation proceeds in three major steps on each cycle. First, they receive, on the input side, information about the current state of some environmental variables. Second, they match this information against stored normative information (reflecting good or bad environmental states, given the current state of their needs). Third, depending on the outcome of the match, they generate, on the output side, information for modulating current states of environmental variables through appropriate action. Control systems are thus engineered for modulating their environment such that it matches normative standards implemented in them.

To achieve this aim, controllers need to exhibit an important functional feature: They need to be capable of decomposing the total pattern of infor-

13. In later chapters, I will elaborate on the proposal in greater detail (particularly in chs. 7, 10, 12). Self-representational frameworks for cognition and consciousness have also been advanced by, e.g., Barresi and Moore (1996) and Metzinger (2003). Whereas their approaches focus on perception and representation, the present approach emphasizes a strong role for action and volition.

14. The present proposal is meant to account for issues of intentionality; it does not speak to issues of qualia. Addressing qualia may or may not require one to resort to notions like emergence or supervenience.

mation that flows from input to output into two streams, one that reflects states of the environment and another one that reflects states of its own.[15] The functional roles of these two streams are entirely different. Since control systems are engineered for modulating environmental states, they need to form explicit representations of these states and keep them clear of any contamination through the system's own states. The system's own states must be known to the controller, too—not for the sake of explicit representation, but for the sake of taking them into account for determining environmental states. Control systems need to know their environments, but not themselves. They need to entertain explicit representations of pertinent environmental variables, but not of their own states. Metaphorically speaking, they need to represent the tone, but not its hearing or the hearer behind it. Thus, there seems to be no obvious way of grounding the intentionality entailed in mental acts in the representational architecture of controllers.

To get closer to such grounding we need to move from representation to self-representation. Here, I introduce this notion in two steps. First, I consider a hypothetical scenario in which a device for self-representation is already in place and examine what it entails. Second, I raise the claim that self-representation evolves from social interaction.

Let us assume, for the sake of a thought experiment, that in a given control system, a secondary controller C* evolves atop C, the basic, primary controller. For the time being, let us also assume that C* falls from heaven. Suppose that C* is built for representing and acting upon both the environment E and the basic controller C. There are two scenarios to consider, as shown in figure 1.1. In the first scenario, controller C represents and controls events in its environment E. In the second scenario, in which C* is in place, the compound of controller C and environment E is for C* what environment E is for C in the first scenario. Let us see what C* can then know about the environment E, the basic controller C, and the way the two are related to each other.

First, C* has the same direct access to the environment E that C has. Second, C* also has access to the primary controller C and its representational states. Third, C* has access to the way in which states of affairs in the environment (E) and states of affairs in the controller (C) depend on and modulate each other. As a consequence, C* can come to represent things in the environment E not only as such but also as things that are related to controller C—that is, as things that are represented and

---

15. See Epstein (1973) for the notion of "taking-into-account" in perception. Below (ch. 7) I come back to the separation of these two streams when I discuss the distinction between targets and tools of control.

Scenario 1   Scenario 2

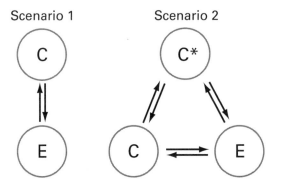

Figure 1.1
Two basic control scenarios. In Scenario 1 the domain of events to which controller
C has access is restricted to happenings in its environment E. In Scenario 2 the
control domain to which the secondary controller C* has access comprises both
environment E and the primary controller C.

modulated by C. Representations formed by controller C* have, in other
words, the potential of including representations of representational relationships between C and E. Furthermore—and related to this—C* will
represent C in a particularly prominent role: in the role of a constant
component that is involved in each and every representational act. In this
respect C is fundamentally different from things in the environment E that
come and go. Accordingly, C* will come to assign C the role of a permanent
center of perception and action.

As a metaphorical illustration of this kind of scenario, we may think of
a painter as he is painting a scene. Let the scene stand for environment E
and the painter for controller C. In this scenario, there is nothing more
than a painter watching the scene (on the sensory side) and then painting
a picture afterward (on the motor side)—as in Scenario 1 in figure 1.1. But
painters may occasionally choose to move on from representation to self-
representation. They may do so by including, in their painting of a scene,
the painter in the act of painting that scene.[16] In that case the artist may

16. The idea of painting the painter in the act of painting is fairly widespread in
Western art traditions. Famous examples are provided by Velázquez and Magritte.
For instance, in *Las Meninas*, which counts as one of Diego Velázquez's masterpieces,
we see the artist amid a family scene at the Spanish royal court, standing in front
of his easel in the act of painting that scene. Likewise, René Magritte has left behind
a number of paintings showing the artist in the act of painting, for example, an
egg, a bird, or a nude.

be seen to adopt the role of C*, representing in the picture both the scene E and the painter C as he paints it.

How can our thought experiment help us to understand the foundations of subjectivity? We need to assume that the two controllers represent two interacting subsystems within a single, unitary control system—a primary one that takes care of the environment E (representation) and a secondary one that takes care of the way in which the primary one interacts with the environment (self-representation). Each of these two subsystems is by itself capable of representing and modulating environmental events in its control domain, but not itself. Still, since the first system forms part of the second system's domain of control, that system may acquire the potential of representing and modulating the first system's activities. In other words, the second system will begin to represent and modulate the first one as it represents and modulates its own environment.

Obviously, a nested architecture like this can explain how one subsystem can come to represent and modulate the other as well as its environment as represented and modulated by that subsystem. Accordingly, the system as a whole may be said to represent and modulate both events in its environment and the ways in which it represents and controls these events. We may therefore claim that the notion of self-representation mirrors in functional terms what the notion of intentionality implies in phenomenal terms. If it is true that the hallmark of conscious experience lies in the intentional relationship between content, act, and subject (e.g., the tone, its hearing and he or she who hears), then architectures for self-representation offer themselves as building blocks for foundational accounts of mental experience. The structure of mental experience may thus be grounded in, and hence reflect, the structure of such architectures.

But so far we have no more than a thought experiment, built on something that falls from heaven. Let me now turn to the question how and why a secondary control system should evolve and what it could be good for. Does it evolve for the sake of improving the performance of the primary system? Or should we believe that having a secondary system that represents and modulates the primary system's interactions with its environment may under certain conditions become advantageous in and of itself? This is indeed what I am suggesting here. In what follows I will elaborate on the claim that the secondary system has its roots in the social domain, that is, in the domain of interaction and communication among individuals. Here, I maintain, lies the origin of mental experience, and only here can its proper function be assessed.

Self and Others

An important methodological gap between performance and experience pertains to the ways in which they can be accessed. Performance and experience require two different paradigms of study. Access to mental experience is based on observing ourselves (first persons) whereas access to behavioral performance is mediated through observing others (third persons).

As mentioned above, philosophers have sometimes claimed that the way we know our own mental experience is epistemologically privileged over other ways of knowing the world.[17] The privileged status of that knowledge is believed to be grounded in the fact that in this case the epistemological subject (he or she who observes) coincides with the epistemological object (he or she who is being observed). Related to this, knowledge about one's own mental states is often considered infallible—unlike all other kinds of knowledge, to which such subject–object coincidence does not apply. On this view we may entertain false beliefs about physical states of the world and mental states of other people, but not about our own mental states.

Of course, we can study mental experience in other people as well—but only in a much more indirect way. Our access to their minds is mediated through our observational access to their behavioral performance, including verbal communications about their mental states. From both performance and communication we may then infer and reconstruct their underlying mental states and processes. Accordingly, our access to these states or processes is, strictly speaking, a matter of theoretical inference, not of empirical observation. By contrast, when it comes to our own mental experiences, we seem to have direct, unmediated access that does not require any theoretical reconstruction.

Hence, we seem to be faced with a fundamental difference between two approaches to mental experience: direct/observational and indirect/inferential from the first- vs. third-person perspectives, respectively. When we adopt an epistemological perspective, that difference appears to be deep and categorical, with no obvious way to combine the two

17. The notion of privileged access to one's own mental states may be traced back to Descartes's claim that experiences of one's own mental states are both direct and infallible (i.e., undoubtedly true) whereas experiences of the external world are indirect and fallible (Descartes, 1641/1990). In more recent times, related claims have been discussed in the context of phenomenological and analytic traditions of philosophy (see, e.g., Russell, 1996; Shoemaker, 1996; Zahavi, 2005).

approaches. However, when we look at it from a psychological rather than an epistemological perspective, it appears to be much less deep and not categorical at all. This is so for two reasons. One is that the notion of privileged access to one's own mental experience is, from this point of view, highly questionable. The other is that psychological evidence provides us with good reasons to believe that our access to the mental states of others is much less inferential than epistemological theory might suggest.

Consider first *one's own mental experience*. How does knowledge about one's own mental events differ from knowledge about other kinds of events that we perceive, for example, physical events? As concerns physical events, psychological theories of perception tell us that perception is both realist and constructivist. It is realist inasmuch as it relies on the notion that the contents of perception refer to genuinely existing circumstances in the real world. But at the same time it is constructivist because it assumes that the contents of perception result from constructive procedures in which perceptual systems process incoming information according to certain categories, thereby using their own means of representation. Among other elements, these constructive processes include:

Selective representation   Only a small fraction of the incoming information actually gets processed, and only a small amount of what gets processed enters the conscious representation.

Focus on content   Perceptual representations include content only. Their underlying constructive processes are not represented themselves.

Semantic categorization   Perceptual contents reflect an interaction between currently incoming information and stored knowledge; hence, they carry meaning.

There are also other significant elements, but for our purposes these three suffice to illustrate that what we perceive is (of course) not reality as it is in and of itself, but is rather the result of construal: The content of human perception is highly selective, significantly transformed, and semantically categorized.

With this in mind, let us now turn to mental experience, that is, the perception of mental events. Is the way we perceive what goes on in our own mind really that much different from the way we perceive events in the world? Is introspection really privileged access? We have little evidence for it. On the contrary, the evidence we do have suggests that our perception of mental events is equally construed, transformed, and selectively focused as our perception of physical events.

A couple of examples may help to illustrate this point. For instance, studies on insightful thought indicate that when people think, they are unable to note, and report about, the actual nature of their thought processes. At best, they can report their individual thoughts; occasionally they can also reconstruct the direction their thoughts took leading up to a certain insight. But they know nothing about the thought-producing process itself. Here we must rely on theory to identify what they experienced (and what they can report) as a selective output produced by submental mechanisms to which experience has no access. Trying to recall a name one has forgotten is also a good example. When we try to remember a certain name, we often experience a disquieting mental state of being altogether unable to retrieve it, or of faintly fathoming only some fraction of it. And then, suddenly, the entire name emerges, seemingly from nowhere, and that is all a person can report when asked about what just took place. But theory tells us that more was involved: Once again, theory says that the phenomena accessible at the subjective level are the product of events at the subpersonal level, namely, mechanisms executing a search procedure. The same holds for comprehending written text: Try to observe yourself while reading and you will only notice whether or not you understand the text. The person who reads and understands never knows how understanding a text works; what we really need in order to understand how understanding works is a theory about the underlying subpersonal mechanisms.

In sum, then, the perception of our own mental experience provides only an inconsistent, incomplete picture of the underlying processes that work. It provides us with a highly selective, content-focused representation of the outcomes of the workings of mechanisms that are themselves unperceivable. Of the mental processes themselves we are actually not aware. What we are aware of are individual mental states that may perhaps reveal something about the underlying processes that caused them. Thus, mental experience is always a product of selective representation, focus on content, and semantic categorization. There is no privileged access at all. We rather perceive our own mental states basically in the same way as we perceive other kinds of things in the world.[18]

At the same time, we may cast doubt on the notion that access to *other people's mental experience* can only be based on inferential processes. On the one hand, this is certainly true in the sense that our knowledge about

18. As will be discussed in ch. 10, this view on mental experience and introspection has important implications for folk-psychology notions like free will.

mental states of others is always based on, and derived from, direct perceptual access to something else, such as their movements or utterances. However, on the other hand, we must not forget that perception is a constructive activity that always goes beyond the information contained in the pattern of stimulation from which it arises, reflecting the outcome of interactions between the current stimulus information and the perceiver's knowledge about the world. Another way to put this is to say that perception is itself, to some extent, based on inbuilt inferential mechanisms, and that the outcomes of these mechanisms reflect not only information derived from the stimulus, but also information derived from the perceiver's knowledge.[19]

The inferential nature of perception plays a particularly important role in the perception of dynamic events. For instance, when we see a billiard ball hitting another one, we cannot help but see not only the spatiotemporal kinematics of the rolling balls, but the underlying dynamics as well: the forces driving those motions and the causal impact entailed in the transition of force from one ball to the other. In the same vein, when we see a frog hopping, a bird flying, or a baby crawling, we cannot help but see, beyond the kinematics of visible movement patterns, the underlying dynamics of self-propelled motion and the animacy entailed in those dynamics. Finally, when we witness a scene in which a child is crying and an adult is trying to comfort it, we cannot help but perceive, beyond kinematics, dynamics, and animacy, a complex pattern of mental states behind and in fact underlying those patterns of observable behavior (in both the baby and the adult). Importantly, one of the characteristics of implicit perceptual inference is that the information that goes beyond the current stimulation will always be mandatorily contained in the

---

19. Back in the nineteenth century, Hermann von Helmholtz was among the first to stress the inferential nature of perception in the domain of space perception (Helmholtz, 1866, 1924/1925). It then took another century for a broader and more comprehensive approach to perception as a knowledge-based activity to emerge (see, e.g., Bruner, 1957; Garner, 1966; Neisser, 1967; Prinz, 1983). The claim that perception is inferential has often been criticized. Here, I take it in a descriptive sense (referring to perceptual content), not in a theoretical sense (referring to putative underlying operations). Accordingly, the claim is not meant to imply that the machinery subserving perceptual inference is of the same kind as the machinery subserving conceptual inference. For instance, unlike conceptual inference, perceptual inference is implicit (or unconscious, as Helmholtz would have said) in the sense that the inferential operations are unperceivable and the inferred properties therefore intrinsic to the perceived events, rather than being extrinsically attributed to them.

content of perception and that there is no way to detach or dissociate it from that content.[20]

In summary, we may conclude that the gap between what we know about conscious experience from the first- vs. the third-person perspective is not as deep and less principled as has often been claimed—at least when one views it from a psychological rather than an epistemological point of view. Neither can we grant introspection the special and privileged status that has often been claimed for it; nor can we defend the view that access to third-person mental experience is always strictly inferential. It seems, therefore, that we should not worry too much over the methodological gap between the two kinds of access to mental experience.

20. For relationships between movement kinematics and dynamics, see Runeson and Frykholm (1981); for perception and attribution of causality, see Michotte (1962); for attribution of animacy and agency to patterns of physical motions, see Heider and Simmel (1944). Wittgenstein's philosophy of psychology (Wittgenstein, 1980) has also served as a source of inspiration for psychological theories concerning the perception of one's own and others' mental states.

2   Approaching Subjectivity

Folk Psychology
Scientific Approaches
  Closed Minds
  Open Minds
  A Case for Open Minds

What does a scientific account of human subjectivity require? What exactly do we need to explain in order to be able to say that we understand what subjectivity amounts to? So far, we have identified three major issues that need to be addressed: the nature and the role of subjectivity, the relationship between phenomenal experience and the functional machinery subserving performance, and the difference in the access that we have to our own versus others' mental experiences.

Yet, before we go ahead with examining scientific approaches to these issues, we need to add one more item to our list, which we have only briefly touched on so far: folk-psychology beliefs and intuitions about subjectivity. We not only experience and perceive mental states in themselves and others; we also entertain what one may call a theory—a collection of certain beliefs concerning the nature of these states and their functional role for the explanation of action. Philosophers and psychologists keep telling us that these intuitions form a theory—a folk theory of (the workings of) the mind. Of course, in everyday life we do not really consider these intuitions to be a theory. We understand them not as explicit beliefs about (and separated from) our mental experience but rather as implicit beliefs inherent in (and integrated with) that experience. Therefore, they need to be added to our list of issues to be addressed: How can we understand the nature and the role of folk intuitions about the workings of the mind—and how are these intuitions related to the actual workings of the mind?

Folk Psychology

Over recent decades, the theory of mind (ToM) that ordinary people entertain has become a hot topic of debate in both philosophy and psychology. Philosophers study its implied ontology, its conceptual underpinnings, and its power to explain what people think and do—that is, what they experience and how they behave.[1] Psychologists study how ToM emerges in infancy and what role it plays in the individual's planning, understanding, and evaluating his or her own and others' actions, as well as in the communicative exchange of such understanding and evaluation.[2] Without going into the details I will concentrate on just a few essential features that are relevant to ToM's implied understanding of subjectivity.[3]

First, on the theory of mind that we share, physical action follows from mental activity: People act the way they do after and because they have experienced certain mental states giving rise to those actions. Typically, such states are beliefs, desires, thoughts, memories, emotions, and the like: Why did the chicken cross the street? Because it *wanted* to get to the other side. Why did Peter call Mary? Because he *believed* that she could help him with his homework. This is why ToM is called a theory from a scientific point of view: It explains observable actions through unobservable mental states. According to ToM, these mental states are causally relevant for physical action.[4]

Second, ToM applies equally to self and others. ToM explains other people's doings by resorting to their (implied) antecedent mental states. These may either be explicitly known through communication or implicitly inferred from the context in which the action is observed. At the same

1. See, e.g., Frankish (2004), Goldman (1993, 2006), Gordon (2001), Hutto (2008). For further details, see ch.4, note 10.
2. See, e.g., Baron-Cohen, Tager-Flusberg and Cohen (1993), Meltzoff and Moore (1995a,b), Perner (1991).
3. It is far from clear how universal folk-psychology notions are and how deep cultural and historical differences may go. Most theorists seem to imply that its basic logic is more or less universal, whereas some claim that it may be subject to substantial cultural and historical variation (e.g., Kusch, 1997; Wilkes, 1991). Here I concentrate on modern Western folk psychology, leaving it an open question to what extent it reflects a universal theory of mind.
4. Although a causal role of mental states for physical action appears to be obvious and natural according to our folk-psychological intuitions, philosophers have always struggled with such a role, trying to elucidate in what ways and under what conditions a causal link between the mental and the physical could possibly be accepted (see, e.g., Aguilar & Buckareff, 2010).

time, ToM explains one's own actions through antecedent mental states. Again, these may either be explicitly known from one's own mental experience or implicitly inferred from the context in which the action occurs (in which case we may speak of post hoc rationalization, or justification). Hence, ToM makes no principled difference between explaining one's own and other people's actions, and unlike philosophy and science it does not worry at all about the difference in access that people have to mental states when they adopt a first- versus third-person perspective.[5]

Third, in no way are mental states enigmatic for ToM. They are no less natural and less obvious than physical states. Unlike science, which finds subjectivity enigmatic since it views it against the background of a (putatively) subjectless universe, ToM's scope is from the outset restricted to the conduct of living things—humans in any case, but often also animals or even plants.[6] Within that scope, mentalistic explanations of individual conduct are, for ToM, perfectly natural. In many cultures, mentalistic explanations are even extended far beyond the scope of natural individuals, attributing observable natural events to the operation of hidden, intentional agents (e.g., in cultures that make gods, ghosts, or forbears' souls responsible for rain showers, thunderstorms, computer crashes, or diseases). Whatever ToM's scope may be, people's daily lives are crowded with interactions with living things to whom they attribute mentality and subjectivity. Since they encounter subjectivity nearly everywhere, they consider mental facts equally natural as physical facts.

In the bottom line, these three features of ToM lead us to the surprising conclusion that ToM itself does not find problematic the first three items on our list of explananda for a scientific theory of subjectivity. Subjectivity poses no enigma for ToM. Instead, it explains why people act the way they do, and it applies equally to self and others. Likewise, ToM sees no deep-rooted difference and no explanatory gap between performance and

5. Still, one may raise the question of how ToM emerges both logically and psychologically: Is ToM first applied to others and then transferred to one's self, or is it first applied to one's self and then transferred to others? Do we know ourselves after and because we know others, or do we know others after and because we know ourselves? Below I will come back to this issue in some detail.

6. It is not always possible to draw a clear distinction between animacy and mentality. Animacy is a feature that we attribute to living things that exhibit spontaneous activity and self-propelled motion. Animate things are thus furnished with the capacity to self-generate physical body movement. To the higher ranks of those animals we may also attribute mentality, i.e., the capacity to self-generate mental states, some of which may cause their bodily movements. In ch. 7 I will come back to a related distinction in the domain of volition (animacy vs. agency).

experience: One simply follows the other. In sum, the folk theory of subjectivity has no problems whatsoever with issues that pose major challenges for scientific theories. This very fact poses a fourth major challenge for the scientific approaches: We expect them to come up with an overarching theory that accounts for both the functional foundations of subjectivity and the foundations of people's beliefs about subjectivity—as well as the relationship between the two.

Scientific Approaches

Folk psychology does not really explain subjectivity, but rather takes it for granted—as a kind of basic fact of nature inherent in humans and, perhaps, some other living beings as well. What folk psychology does explain instead are humans' and living beings' actions. Action is the *explanandum*, and subjectivity serves as *explanans*.

Let us now turn to the cognitive sciences and see what they can contribute to the understanding of subjectivity. In our discussion thus far of how to bridge the gap between performance and experience, we have already touched on one of the core issues that scientific approaches to subjectivity need to address. In the following, I will place that discussion in a broader theoretical context. This context is provided by two major theoretical paradigms that science has to offer for the study of minds and brains.

Closed Minds

The classical paradigm believes in closed minds. This paradigm views minds as closed systems that develop autochthonously in individuals, forming part of their natural endowment. Accordingly, on this view, the proper way to study the mind is to study individuals as they interact with their environments. I call this the classical paradigm because it has been dominating the study of the mind for centuries. With only rare exceptions (to which I return below), philosophical and psychological approaches to the mind have taken (methodological) individualism and (ontological) naturalism for granted. Basically, the same holds true for more recent cognitive science and neuroscience approaches.

Individualism—Psychology is sometimes considered the science of the individual,[7] and rightly so, I believe. Historically speaking, the emergence

7. For the history and the role of individualism in philosophy, psychology, and related disciplines, see Barnes (2000), Danziger (1990), Honneth (1996), Kusch (1999, 2005), Porter (1997), Rose (1996).

of psychology as a scientific discipline was closely intertwined with the emergence of political individualism. It seems that the career of the political notion of the autonomous individual, which is at the heart of the theoretical underpinnings of the organization of modern societies, was an important driving force behind the career of scientific individualism as well. Systematically speaking, scientific psychology is the science of performance and experience in individuals (as well as the limits of individuals). Importantly, psychological individualism touches on both method and theory. With regard to method, individualism determines the level of inquiry and the units of study. With regard to theory, it specifies the locus and the nature of possible explanatory mechanisms. Thus, the science of the individual studies tokens of individuals' performance and experience and explains them in terms of functional mechanisms in individual minds.

Individualism does not only apply to psychology; theoretical and methodological individualism seems to be a key feature of major philosophical approaches to the mind as well. Philosophers, too, study the workings of the mind by reflecting on individual minds (preferably their own) and explaining their workings in terms of mechanisms that are rooted and grounded in those individuals. The same logic of study applies to the various branches of cognitive neuroscience. Neuroscientists, too, study and model behavioral performance and its underlying brain mechanisms in individual animals—within the limits of individual minds and brains.

Naturalism—Individualism goes hand in hand with naturalism—at least partially. By naturalism, I refer to the belief that the basic makeup of our minds forms part of our natural endowment. Naturalism posits that minds and brains emerge and develop in individuals just like lungs and livers: as organs whose basic makeup is determined by nature.

In psychology, the scope of naturalism is not as large and unrestricted as the scope of individualism is. Whereas individualism can be considered a universal feature of psychological inquiry, naturalism is more limited. Much of psychological theorizing is built on an implicit distinction between two fundamental aspects of mental processing: *universal form* and *specific content*. Given that distinction, most theories posit that universal form is built on internal, natural sources, whereas specific contents are acquired through interaction with external sources—sources that arise from individuals' physical, social, and cultural environments.[8] As concerns *universal form*, or structure, the history of psychology has seen a rich variety

8. See Prinz, Försterling, and Hauf (2007) for the distinction between universal form and specific content.

of classifications, models, and metaphors. For instance, medieval Christian philosophy believed in three faculties of the mind—reason, desire, and volition. Nineteenth-century phrenological systems posited more than thirty such faculties. Others systems, like that theorized by Wilhelm Wundt, replaced mental faculties with mental elements like sensations and feelings. In recent textbooks we no longer encounter such coherent systems of the mind's basic makeup. Still, we do encounter various building blocks for such systems. Some are general-purpose devices for storage and processing (e.g., episodic, semantic, and working memory, attention, executive control); others are dedicated devices for more specific representational purposes (e.g., for emotions, actions, faces, self, and other).

Though there is no consensus across textbooks about how universal functions and devices should be individuated and classified, there is consensus that such universals exist. They are considered natural building blocks of the structure of the human mind, as it unfolds in each and every individual. Universal structure is typically thought to arise from our biological nature, rooted in our genes and expressed in the functional architecture of our brains.

As concerns *specific contents*, psychological theories do not resort to genes, but rather focus on the individual's learning history. Since the early days of psychological research, learning mechanisms have attracted a vast amount of attention. This is certainly not surprising, as it is through these mechanisms that individual minds become shaped not only by their physical environments but also by the social and cultural environments in which they live. It is through social communication and interaction that universal form gets filled in with specific sociocultural content, be it culture-specific, group-specific, or family-specific. Individual minds become social minds by learning to share their mental contents with others—their beliefs, attitudes, norms, and behaviors.

Closed subjectivity—As concerns the mind's universal form, the classical paradigm thus relies on individuals and their natural endowment. As a consequence, it holds that the universals of mental structure and function need to be empirically studied and theoretically understood within frameworks that consider closed and isolated individual minds.

It is fairly obvious what the classical paradigm implies for the nature of mental experience and subjectivity. In this paradigm, subjectivity is considered an emergent property arising from the operation of certain constituents of the mind's natural makeup. If it is true that the sense of subjectivity is built on the implicit presence of the mental self, and if it is also true that the mental self is an essential (if not *the* essential) constituent of the mind's universal form, then the sense of subjectivity must be an emergent property arising in each and every closed and isolated mind.

Since subjectivity is, on this view, a naturally given fact, it follows that the intuitions that people have about their own subjectivity and the workings of their own minds must be regarded as direct reflections of natural facts rather than as theories about such facts. It is only when intuitions are used in order to explain other individuals' (observable) actions through their (unobservable) mental experiences that they acquire the status of theoretical explanations. In the closed-minds paradigm, understanding other minds is therefore regarded as derivative from knowing one's own mind: First, we know and understand our own minds, and only then and thereby do we come to understand other minds as well.

Open Minds

This paradigm views minds as open systems whose basic makeup is determined through social interaction and communication. The open-minds view holds that the social making of minds goes far beyond the shaping of specific mental contents and applies to universal mental form as well. Accordingly, the proper way to study the mind is to investigate how it is shaped—and in fact constituted—through collective practice and discourse.

Theoretical claims along these lines may be commonplace and widespread in the social sciences—particularly in sociology and in cultural and historical anthropology. Still, from a philosophical and cognitive science point of view, they appear to be quite strange and alien. Since these disciplines are built on individualism and naturalism, they cannot easily accommodate the claim that basic mental facts are made through social practices. To convince them of the feasibility of an open-minds approach we need to address two interrelated questions, a general and a specific one. The general question asks what implications the theoretical claims of collectivism and constructivism have for cognitive science and its research agenda for the study of the mind. The specific question raises the issue of how we can build collectivist and constructivist principles into the representational framework on which cognitive theorizing is founded and reconcile the notion of open minds with the methodology and theory of cognitive science. For the remaining pages of this chapter I turn to the first question. The second question will keep us busy for the rest of the book.

Collectivism—What does it mean to call for a scientific approach to the foundations of subjectivity that is grounded in collectivism? Let me first say what it does not mean. It does not mean giving up the study of performance and experience at the individual level altogether and replace it with the study of collective phenomena. Collectivism does not alter the ultimate goal of studying the workings of the mind: to understand how individuals act and what they experience under given circumstances. The difference between mental individualism and collectivism is not in the *explananda*, but rather in the *explanantia*: Collectivist approaches hold that the mind's universal form emerges from interaction and communication with other minds.

This is the basic claim of radical mental collectivism. I call it radical because it goes beyond the widespread claim that interaction and communication with other minds provides important constraints on the *shaping* of individual minds, accounting for the specific habits, beliefs, values, and so on that they adopt—that is, for the diversity of mental contents. By contrast, the radical claim posits that interaction and communication are key prerequisites for the *making* of minds, accounting for the universal structure that they adopt, that is, the uniformity of mental form.[9]

Accordingly, to be able to understand the workings of individual minds we need to study the mechanisms of their making and shaping through social context. Obviously, an approach like this requires us to broaden the scope of our studies. If the basic claim of radical mental collectivism holds, we cannot understand the workings of the mind and the formation of subjectivity just by studying how performance and experience arise in individual minds. We need to study minds in interaction and communication with other minds.

Constructivism—Mental collectivism goes hand in hand with mental constructivism. Roughly speaking, constructivism posits that what we know about the world is much more a matter of social construction than a reflection of natural facts (presumed to exist independently of our constructions). Mental constructivism applies this idea to the workings of the mind and the foundations of subjectivity, claiming that the mind's universal form is much more a cultural than a natural fact, arising from social construction rather than from an unfolding of natural dispositions.

Like collectivist notions, constructivist ideas are widespread in the social sciences. In that domain we encounter a variety of manifestos of collectivist constructivism—as well as a prevailing theoretical climate that is characterized by deep-rooted constructivist skepticism vis-à-vis all kinds of

9. It is quite possible, of course, that the mind's putative universal form will turn out to be much less universal than individualist naturalism would initially suggest.

naturalist intuitions. Accordingly, the majority of social scientists will be inclined to believe that minds are cultural artifacts that are not only shaped by but in fact made by social and cultural context. However, a serious problem arises here: The link between principles and mechanisms is missing. Collectivist constructivism may provide us with manifestos and principles at the macrolevel, but it provides us with no mechanisms at the microlevel that spell out how the alleged social construction of the makeup of minds can actually happen. This is what we need in order to reconcile the social science with the cognitive science perspective.

In fact, we may ask how such construction can work at all. How can it be possible that the makeup of a thing depends on the way we talk about it or interact with it? Of such things like tigers, trees, or tulips, for instance, we would certainly not believe that the way we deal with them, or talk about them—or even talk to them—makes any contribution to their makeup. To such natural kinds the constructivist credo that reality is created through social practice cannot be applied—at least not in any obvious or straightforward way. It can be applied, however, to social kinds like human minds, that is, kinds that are themselves sensitive to communication and interaction directed at them. Human minds can take two roles at the same time: the active role of talking about, talking to, or interacting with somebody else, and the passive role of perceiving communications and interactions directed at themselves. Not only do they communicate and interact with others in a particular way; they also perceive others of the same kind communicating and interacting with them in a particular way.

In fact, there are two claims here. One is that people may be able to perceive and understand, through communication and interaction, how they are perceived and understood by others. The second is that their perception of being perceived in a particular way may be constitutive of their becoming that way—thereby adopting or appropriating the mental organization others impute to them.

Open subjectivity—The open-minds paradigm relies on collectivism and constructivism. It requires that the foundations of subjectivity and the workings of the mind cannot be appropriately studied and understood unless we consider individuals as they interact and communicate with their social and cultural environment. According to this paradigm, the mental self on which the sense of subjectivity relies is not built from natural resources—and would not even exist in closed and isolated minds. Instead, it relies on social and cultural resources on which and from which it is built.

On this perspective, the theory of mind that people entertain is no longer considered a reflection of natural facts. We must rather consider it a social institution—a socially shared theory about how people's minds work and how experience accounts for performance. However, this institution, while it guides our intuitions about other minds, also plays a crucial role for making and shaping our own minds. Understanding one's self as a mental agent is thus regarded as derivative from understanding others as mental agents: First we understand other minds, and only then and thereby do we come to design our own minds accordingly.[10]

A Case for Open Minds

What do we need in order to build an open-mind approach to human subjectivity and defend it against closed-mind approaches as they dominate the current theoretical landscape? One thing is that we need to struggle against two basic asymmetries that seem to favor closed over open minds. First, there is an asymmetry in terms of *prima facie* validity or plausibility. As I pointed out above, closed-mind theories share major intuitions with our folk-psychology understanding of subjectivity, and they may in fact be regarded as scientific offspring arising from those prescientific intuitions. Therefore, we tend to consider closed-mind approaches the obvious and natural way of approaching subjectivity—not only in our commonsense understanding but in scientific approaches as well. It goes without saying that, in a situation like this, the burden of proof is on the open-mind side.

Second, and perhaps even worse, there is another asymmetry in terms of explanatory demands. Closed-mind approaches require us to understand how the workings of individual minds and the foundations of subjectivity emerge from the interplay between the basic makeup with which the mind is endowed by nature and the accidental environmental conditions under which it unfolds. Open-mind approaches require more. Since they do not believe that the basic makeup of the mind is really provided by nature they require us to also understand the mechanisms through which social interaction and communication contribute to the making of mind and subjectivity. These mechanisms need to be studied from two

10. The notion of folk psychology as a social institution has been extensively elaborated by Kusch (1999, 2005). Kusch's institutional view is closely related to Foucault's views on governance and self-technologies (Foucault, 1988; Rose, 1990). In a similar vein, Bogdan has coined the notion of folk psychology as a mind designer (Bogdan, 2000, 2009, 2010).

sides, sender and receiver. On the sender's side we need to understand how interactions and communications must be organized in order to subserve the making of subjectivity in receivers. Conversely, on the receiver's side we need to understand the mechanisms through which interaction and communication contribute to the basic makeup of their minds. Thus, to make a convincing case for open minds, we need to specify these mechanisms. Programmatic manifestos and theoretical principles are not enough. We need to fill in the details.

Finally, making a case for open minds does not imply that we should ignore, or even reject, the notion of closed minds altogether. Rather, since that notion forms an integral part of our folk psychology intuitions, we need to understand how intuitions about closed minds can arise in open minds: How can the notion of closed minds and the understanding of subjectivity that goes along with it emerge from interaction and discourse among open minds? In pursuing this question, we may eventually create still another asymmetry between the two approaches, this time in terms of epistemological status. We demand of the open-minds approach that it provide an explanatory framework that helps us to understand the ubiquitous emergence and the prevalence of closed-mind intuitions in our folk psychology theories of the mind.

Making a case for open minds, therefore, has two sides. One is to make a convincing case for the foundation of subjectivity through collectivist construal. The other is to explain the individualist and naturalist intuitions that folk psychology entertains about human subjectivity. We should be in a position to explain not only the foundations of subjectivity, but also folks' intuitions about these foundations.

3 The Quest for Reality

Kinds of Kinds
The Cognitive Reality of Artifacts
  Representational Reality
  Functional Reality
  Real Selves

As mentioned earlier, the proposition that subjectivity is a matter of social construction is not well received among philosophers and scientists. One of the reasons why they raise their eyebrows is certainly related to the wide gap between abstract principles and concrete mechanisms, as discussed in the previous chapter. But there is another concern that also nourishes their skepticism. This concern pertains to what we may call the quest for reality. If subjectivity were indeed a matter of social construction, would it then still be a "real" thing? Wouldn't we then rather have to conclude that the experience of subjectivity is an illusion—a kind of cover story that doesn't have much to do with the underlying facts? This raises the question of what kind of reality we can attribute to mental experience and subjectivity when we consider them to be social rather than natural facts.

Kinds of Kinds

Questioning the reality of subjectivity has two sides. First, we may ask in what sense it exists at all and how the way it exists compares to the way other kinds of things exist. Second, we may inquire in what sense it is causally relevant to other kinds of things and how that causal role compares with causal roles of other kinds of things. Importantly, the quest for reality is not an all-or-nothing affair. On both of the two sides, the question is not *whether or not* social constructs are real but rather *in what sense* they are real.

To address this question we need a minimal ontology—a coarse classi-fication of kinds of things that we encounter in the world and of the kinds of such kinds. Again, this is one of the big questions that have occupied philosophers for more than two millennia, and I will not go into these discussions at all. I will rather take a pragmatic stance and follow a simple scheme that I find useful for our present purposes. It relies on two basic distinctions: between natural and artificial kinds and—within artificial kinds—between physical and social artifacts.[1]

Natural kinds are kinds of things that exist and function independently of human activity and intervention. For instance, stars and stones, lions and livers, and also the basic makeup of the human body count as natural kinds. Of course, we may go ahead and subdivide natural kinds into sub-kinds, such as living and nonliving things, or viruses, fungi, animals, and plants, and so on. But for the present purposes I will not follow such divides any further. By contrast, artificial kinds are kinds of things that would not exist and function in the proper way without human activity and intervention. Spears and hammers, cars and airplanes are obvious examples, but such diverse things like farms, laws, traffic rules, and teach-ers fall into this category as well. Their existence is due entirely to human activity, and without humans using them or interacting with them they would no longer fulfill their proper function—the particular function for which they were designed and created in the first place. In a sense, they would then cease to exist as artifacts.

Rough and simple-minded as it may be, an ontology like this has impor-tant implications for addressing the quest for reality. It is generally under-stood that natural kinds are real in the sense that they exist, play their causal roles, and, as far as applicable, fulfill their proper functions out of the reach of and entirely independent from human observation and inter-vention. Hence, the reality of natural kinds is unlimited and uncondi-tional: They are equally real for anyone who approaches and studies them.[2] Conversely, artificial kinds are understood to be real in a different sense. They are real in the sense of existing, playing their causal roles, and fulfill-ing their proper functions only within the reach of (and, in fact, through) certain kinds of human observation and intervention. Therefore, the reality of artificial kinds is limited and conditional to the understanding

1. See Kusch (1997) for a discussion of these and related distinctions.
2. This is in fact what closed-mind approaches claim with respect to human sub-jectivity. They consider subjectivity a natural fact that emerges from other natural facts, fulfilling its proper function by itself.

of their proper function: Only for their creators and users are they are real and functional in the full sense.[3]

The Cognitive Reality of Artifacts

Yet, when we move from ontology to epistemology and cognition, the distinction between unconditional and conditional becomes blurred. This is because when we look at artifacts from the perspective of their creators and users, it turns out that both social and physical artifacts are for them no less real than natural facts. They all play the same functional role in constraining their doings. Natural kinds like gravity, trees, clouds, or the day–night cycle play for them exactly the same roles as artificial kinds like scissors, houses, and cars, or traffic rules, judges, and mothers-in-law: They know them, they think about them, and they take them into account when planning and constraining future action.

Representational Reality

Still, there are differences in the way people represent these constraints. We know that gravity and clouds are kinds of things that are naturally given and cannot be altered by human intervention. This is different for things like scissors and traffic rules: We know that these kinds can be altered—at least in principle. However, the difference is often not very deep. Many artifacts remain relatively constant over our lifetimes or undergo only very gradual changes—to the effect that they take on the appearance of natural facts. In other words, though these kinds of things may differ deeply in ontological terms they are equally real and effective in representational terms. For those who know what scissors and traffic rules are, the artificially constructed features of these things play the same roles in guiding and constraining their thoughts and actions as the naturally given features of trees and clouds do.

As concerns subjectivity we may therefore conclude that the deep-rooted ontological disparity between the closed- and open-minds approaches has no deep consequences in terms of representational reality. In

3. A radical version of this idea goes back to the Italian philosopher Giambattista Vico. Vico claimed that humans are capable of understanding artifacts, but not natural facts. They can understand artifacts because they have created and engineered them themselves. Yet, they have no way of understanding natural facts because it was God who created them. Accordingly, God is the only being capable of understand natural facts (Vico, 1710/1988).

either case the experience of subjectivity (in self and others) will be a real representational fact. Neither will closed-minds naturalism strengthen nor open-minds constructivism weaken its reality and effectiveness. This, then, is the first answer we can offer to the quest for reality: At the level of mental representation there is no reason to believe that social artifacts are less real and efficacious than natural facts. In terms of representational reality, social kinds are entirely equal to natural kinds.

Functional Reality

But this is not the whole story. We still need to elaborate on a second answer—one that addresses functional mechanisms rather than representational contents. At this level we may expect to see functional disparities that mirror the ontological divide between natural and artificial kinds. Consider, for instance, what difference it makes whether we regard the experience of subjectivity as a natural fact or an artifact. Closed-minds approaches hold that subjective experience emerges from (and, hence, reflects) certain features of the functional architecture of the underlying subpersonal machinery. According to this view, subjectivity is grounded in the natural architecture of the mind. Conversely, open-minds approaches hold that subjective experience is based on representational structures that are acquired through communication and interaction. According to that view, subjectivity is grounded in social learning about the mind.

This contrast seems to suggest a fundamental disparity in terms of the putative functional basis of subjectivity and the sense in which it must be considered to be real. The naturalist account implies a natural and, hence, unalterable fundament of subjectivity that forms part of each individual's natural endowment. The constructivist account implies a social and, hence, alterable fundament that individuals may acquire under certain social and cultural conditions. Since common opinion holds that natural endowment can create stronger functional constraints than social learning can, it seems to follow that the functional fundament of subjectivity is for the naturalist account real in a stronger sense than for the constructivist account. In fact, this intuition may be one of the reasons for repudiating psychological constructivism: Constructivist accounts fail to match the hard-core realism that is implicitly entailed by the naturalist intuitions that people entertain about their own and others' subjectivity.

Still, before we can draw final conclusions, we need to go one step further and address one more issue. So far I have discussed the mind's natural architecture and its learning history as if they were two disjunct and unrelated candidates for the foundations of subjectivity. As we saw above, this is well in line with the standard view of the mind that nature provides basic form and culture fills in specific content. Yet, as we also saw, this picture may be incomplete and perhaps misleading. Could it be that acquired cultural content has an effect on natural form? More specifically, could it be possible that the history of peoples' learning about their minds can contribute the formation of their minds?

This brings us to the core issue we are dealing with: How is it possible that the beliefs about the workings of the mind that people acquire through learning can affect its actual workings? How can beliefs about subjectivity become real in the sense that individuals actually become the kind of mental things that they believe themselves to be?

As said above, this appears to be an absurd idea at first glance. For instance, we do not believe that the beliefs we entertain about the temperature on the moon do anything to the moon and its temperature. The same applies to beliefs that we entertain about less remote things, like the height of the Eiffel Tower, the chemical structure of hemoglobin, or the color of the T-shirt my friend was wearing yesterday. The reason why this idea appears to be so absurd is simple enough: What we know and believe about the world is based on representations formed in our minds and brains. Though some of these representations may be causally dependent on things in the world (and hence represent certain features of those things), the reverse does not hold: Things in the world are not causally dependent on representations in the mind. Things in the mind may have the potential to reflect things in the world, but not to alter them.[4]

As I argued earlier, the mind's proper function is to help people to understand and act on the world. On that view, the mind is a tool directed at the world, fulfilling its function by forming and updating beliefs about selected states of the environment. When we apply this general perspective to the specific case of the mind's beliefs about its own workings, we address quite a peculiar scenario. In this case, we study the mind's beliefs about the way it works when it forms and maintains beliefs about things in the world—beliefs about beliefs, as it were. Here we may distinguish between first- and second-order beliefs. First-order beliefs are *about things in the world* whereas second-order beliefs are *about beliefs about things in the world.*

4. This is at least what most people believe, once they have left behind magical thinking. In that context it should not go unnoticed that there is one particular route through which representations in the mind can have an impact on events in the world (and in fact do so all day long): the route that goes through the will and the realization of intentions through bodily movements. Thus, though we no longer believe that our minds can affect the world directly, we still believe that they can affect our bodies, which then, in turn, can affect the world (at least with respect to selected to kinds of events). In Part III, I elaborate on these issues in greater detail.

Thus, second-order beliefs are beliefs about the mental structures, dispositions, and processes that subserve first-order beliefs. But the difference between the two goes beyond a mere difference in terms of hierarchical order. More importantly, they also differ in terms of causal efficacy. As we've already seen, first-order beliefs have no direct causal impact on the things to which they refer, that is, to happenings in the world. This does not hold for second-order beliefs, however. Since they are beliefs (in the mind) that refer to other beliefs (in the same mind), we are here dealing with two things that are made of the same stuff. They both coexist in the same individual mind and they both draw on one and the same functional architecture for processing and representation. Accordingly, it is quite possible that second-order beliefs and their underlying representations have a causal impact on representations subserving first-order beliefs. In principle, therefore, what people *believe about the workings of their minds* can come to *affect the actual workings of their minds.*[5]

Perhaps it is easier to capture the gist of this claim when we rephrase it in terms of the control framework for representation and self-representation as outlined in chapter 1. Talking about first- and second-order beliefs is in this framework tantamount to talking about primary and secondary controllers. First-order beliefs build on representations involved in controlling states of affairs in the world. Second-order beliefs build on representations involved in controlling the workings of that controller. To be efficient, that controller requires a body (furnished with sensors and effectors) that mediates between the controller and the to-be-controlled events in the world. The body solves the transmission problem between controller and controlled events. However, no such transmission problem exists for the relation between secondary and primary controllers since both reside in the same mind–brain machinery, interacting with each other in a direct fashion.

Accordingly, if we think of first- and second-order beliefs as operating in primary and secondary controllers, respectively, we begin to see how top-down directed causal efficacy becomes possible—provided that the transmission problem is either solved or does not exist. Beliefs and their

---

5. We may leave it open whether causal efficacy of second-order beliefs should be considered a special feature of mental systems or whether it also applies to other kinds of systems. Some theorists have claimed that it reflects a universal feature of self-organizing intentional systems: Whenever such systems start observing themselves, self-observation may have functional consequences for the workings of what is being observed (Luhmann, 1995).

underlying representations can then be used in two ways: to indicate states of affairs and to control them. Representations indicating certain states of affairs can thus be used for altering them.[6]

Real Selves

After all, how can we address the quest for reality in an open-minds framework that considers subjectivity a matter of social construction? At this point we are not yet ready for a full answer. But we can offer a partial answer that addresses the causal role of subjective experience. The constructivist stance adopted here by no means implies that we must consider the experience of subjectivity to be a causally irrelevant cover story that accompanies the real and hidden workings of the mind. True, it may be a story that people construct, but it is also a story that has the potential of making an impact on people's thoughts and actions and the underlying functional machinery.

This is the first part of the answer to the quest for reality. The second part will depend on how close the story about the mind comes to its actual workings. One option we can already exclude. If one posits that the story people entertain about their minds has an impact on the actual workings of their minds, then that story cannot be entirely wrong, misleading, or illusory. Individuals, populations, and cultures would soon die out if their mental activity were controlled by illusions and inappropriate beliefs about that activity. Hence, if we take the causal efficacy of those beliefs for granted, we may rule out illusionism—at least for those who haven't died out yet.

Still two more options remain, and for the full answer we will at some point have to decide between them. One is of course the naturalist option, according to which the story is real in the sense of providing an adequate framework for capturing the workings of the natural mind. The other is the constructivist option, according to which the story is real in the sense of providing a useful framework for creating and designing the mind. Naturalists believe that individuals detect their minds and selves as natural things that are independently there. Constructivists believe that they invent them as artificial things. Both, however, believe that they are dealing with real things that play a causal role for thought and action. Not only naturalism, but constructivism as well, is entirely compatible with realism.

6. Inspired by Dr. Dolittle's two-headed animal, Millikan speaks of "pushmi-pullyu representations" to address such dual use of representations for indication and control (Millikan, 1995).

II Mirrors

Mirrors are remarkable devices. In one sense, they are innocent physical things—smooth or polished surfaces reflecting light rays according to simple geometrical rules. Yet, in another sense, when we use them in their proper function, they may become powerful tools for exploring our surroundings and extending the reach of what we can see. For instance, mirrors can help us to look around corners or to see what happens behind our backs. Most notably, they help us to see our own face and our own bodies in exactly the same way as we see others all day and—by implication—as others see us all day.

Given that capacity, it is perhaps not surprising that mirrors have in many cultures been seen not only as practical instruments but also as symbolic devices in the context of self-recognition, self-reflection, and self-understanding. They function not only as technical tools for examining our outer (physical) appearance, but also as symbolic instruments for deeper ways of reflecting our inner (mental) self. Such symbolic use of mirrors is widespread in Western art and literature. For instance, mirrors play an indispensable technical role in acts of self-portraiture. In such an act the mirror is often thought to reflect aspects of the artist's inner self through his or her outer appearance. Occasionally, the mirror and the act of self-mirroring is even included in the self-portrait as a symbolic indication of the reflective intentions entailed in that act and in the painting that results from it.

Remarkably, the scope of the mirror concept is not restricted to physical mirrors proper. In the context of self-recognition and self-reflection, one also encounters a metaphorical use of that concept that applies to social rather than physical mirrors: Others serve as mirrors for the self. Individuals may come to understand themselves through mirroring themselves (and their actions) in other individuals (and their actions)—that is, by learning to understand how their conduct is perceived, understood, and appreciated by others. For instance, the notion that lovers perceive each other through the other, seeing themselves mirrored in the other's eyes, has been since medieval times a recurring theme in European literature.[1]

What such metaphorical use of mirrors suggests is that social mirrors may play for individuals a similar role to that played by physical mirrors:

1. For the cultural history of mirrors, mirror images, and the practical and symbolic use of mirrors, see Balensiefen (1990), Grabes (1973), Gregory (1996), Harbison (1995), Melchior-Bonnet (2002), Pendergrast (2003). For relationships between the role of mirrors in Buddhist reflections and Western phenomenology, see Laycock (1994). For lovers as mirrors of each other, see, e.g., Grabes (1973, pp. 90–92).

Both help them to perceive how others perceive them. Of course, there is an important difference as well. Unlike physical mirrors, which just reflect light rays, social mirrors are living beings who act and communicate.

In what follows I take a look at social mirrors from a more scientific point of view. Is there anything serious behind their widespread symbolic and metaphorical use in the context of self-recognition and self-reflection? In the following chapters I will examine what mirror devices can possibly contribute to the formation of self-related cognition. What does it mean for individuals that mirrors help them to perceive themselves in ways they can't otherwise perceive themselves, and what can they make of it? I will argue that mirrors can indeed play an important role for the formation of selves—provided that external mirrors are met by internal mirrors. By external mirrors I mean mirrors, both social and physical, that individuals encounter in their environments: mirrors outside (ch. 4). By internal mirrors I mean mirror-like representational devices that operate inside individuals' minds: mirrors inside (ch. 5). These two kinds of mirrors, I submit, interact with each other in ways that give rise to the building up of self-related cognition and the formation of mental selves (ch. 6).[2]

2. For discussions of historical, conceptual, and functional aspects of social mirror-ing and the reciprocal relationship between mirrors in the world and in the mind, see, e.g., Hurley (2008), Rochat and Passos-Ferreira (2009), Whitehead (2001). For a broad perspective on social mirroring in the context of mirror neurons and systems in the brain, see Iacoboni (2008).

4 Mirrors Outside

One may wonder what lies behind the widespread use of mirrors, mirror-related symbols, and mirror-based metaphors for both reflecting one's self and reflecting upon one's self. Given that we *are* ourselves all day long, what could mirrors possibly add to what we already know about ourselves? Don't we have direct access to our mental selves from within, that is, from the privileged first-person perspective? What then could any knowledge that we gain from external mirrors add to the internal knowledge we already have?

In this chapter, I propose a strong role of mirror devices for the formation of both bodily and mental selves. The claim is that mirrors are indispensable tools for the making and shaping of human minds. Human minds cannot be and become what they are without being reflected through mirrors in their environment. From now on, when talking about mirrors in the environment, I will only occasionally talk about physical mirrors proper. For the most part, I will be talking of mental or social mirrors, that is, human agents mirroring other agents.

Physical Mirrors

Let's first take a brief look at physical mirrors. What can individuals actually gain from looking at their specular images? In what ways could mirrors be instrumental for the formation of self-related knowledge?

In raising this question we should keep in mind that mirrors are technical artifacts that have only recently become ubiquitous in modern civiliza-
tions. Hence, though there may be some less widespread precursors (e.g.,
metal plates) and more widespread but less efficient natural substitutes
(e.g., the still surface of a natural body of water) we must certainly exclude
the possibility that physical mirrors have played an important role in the
history—or even evolution—of the human mind. The more surprising is
the widespread use of mirror-based metaphors for self-recognition and
self-understanding. Their prevalance seems to suggest that the novel technical practice of looking at oneself in a mirror is understood to capture
what the much older social practice of looking at oneself through others
is understood to entail.

Mirror Self-Recognition

How can we study self-recognition through physical mirrors and assess the
kind of knowledge individuals may gain from looking into them? A famous
example is the study of the emergence of mirror self-recognition in infants
and young chimpanzees. What does it mean that, at certain ages, infants
and chimps (but not monkeys) start "recognizing themselves" in the mirror?
In these experiments, self-recognition is probed by the so-called mark test.
In this test, an invisible color mark is placed on the infant's or animal's face.
Mirror self-recognition is established when appropriate responses are
directed toward the body, rather than the mirror (i.e., touching the mark or
trying to remove it from the face, rather than reaching for it in the mirror).[1]

1. Research on the mark test was pioneered by Gallup (1968, 1970) and has since
stimulated a large number of studies; for an overview, see Tomasello and Call (1997).
One of Gallup's remarkable early observations was that, unlike socially raised
chimpanzees who pass the test, chimpanzees raised in isolation tend to fail on it
(Tomasello & Call, 1997, p. 457; Gallup, McClure, Hill, & Bundy, 1971). Historically,
psychoanalyst Jacques Lacan was one of the first to draw attention to the potential
theoretical significance of mirror self-recognition. He claimed that on the first occurrence of mirror self-recognition the infant spontaneously (and jubilantly) identifies
the mirror image with herself, implying that a sense of self is already in place when
this happens (Lacan, 1949/1977). Lacan's interpretation of mirror self-recognition
stands in remarkable contrast with what is reported in the legend of Narcissus (on
which psychoanalysis draws as well). According to Ovid's testimony, Narcissus' self-
recognition is neither spontaneous nor jubilant. Initially he mistakes the mirror
image for an image of someone else and falls in love with the other. After a while
he begins to discover that the mirror shows himself. From the moment of that
discovery onward he falls into deep despair and is eventually even bound to die
(Ovid, 2005; see also Macho, 2004).

When this happens, it may be intuitively appealing to believe that the chimp or the infant recognizes herself in the mirror. But what does this actually mean? Does she really recognize herself in the mirror—or even her *self*? Does she, in other words, identify the third-person agent in the mirror with the first-person agent whom she knows as herself? Or should we perhaps resort to the more cautious interpretation that self-recognition in the mirror is restricted to bodily appearance, with no implication whatsoever for the mental self?

Let us briefly examine what kinds of information we can gain from looking at ourselves in the mirror. How do mirrors help us to see things that we otherwise do not see? And how can we characterize this surplus of information—that which goes beyond the information that would already be available in a mirrorless environment?

First, mirrors provide us with information about the outer appearance of our own face—information to which we have no other access (if we disregard the possibility of using active touch). This is the kind of information exploited in the mark test: The mark would be unperceivable if no mirrors were around. Second, and still related to the face, mirrors provide us with information about facial gestures. This is information to which we have access through facial proprioception as well. The mirror thus helps us to see what the grimaces that we make and feel actually look like. Marking in front of a mirror can teach us both what the things we feel look like and what the things we see feel like.

Third, we can see our whole body (including the face) from a perspective that would be impossible to take in a mirrorless world: that of an external observer who looks at himself from a remote position—just as he or she looks at other people and other people look at her or him. The difference is, of course, that when we observe others, what we see them doing is independent from what we feel ourselves doing, whereas when we watch ourselves in the mirror what we see in the specular image is perfectly correlated with what we feel ourselves doing. Again, mirror images can help us to learn both how actions that we feel from within look from the outside and how actions that we see from the outside feel from within.

Mirrors can thus help bridge the gap between the first- and the third-person perspective. They do so in a specific and limited way, however. One of their specific features is that the bridge closes a gap not between different individuals but rather between different perspectives on one and the same individual. One of their limitations is that they can reflect what bodies do but not what minds do. If there were a ghost in the machine the mirror could not reflect it. Therefore, we need to be cautious with our interpretation of the mark test. To individuals who pass the test, we may certainly attribute mirror recognition of their bodily selves. But from the test itself, we cannot infer any deeper recognition of the mental selves. The fact that they mirror-recognize their bodies does not imply that they recognize their minds as well.[2]

This is as far as chimps and babies go. Still, as concerns human adults, we entertain a strong intuition that looking at ourselves in the mirror can give us a deeper way of seeing ourselves (or our selves) than just scratching the surface of outer appearance. Our naïve impression is that the mirror also reflects the mind in our body. How can we understand that intuition? How can the impression of seeing the mental through the physical emerge?

Action Perception

To address this question let us first turn from the special case of watching oneself in the mirror to consider in more general terms how action and person perception works. Whenever we watch people acting we cannot help but see, in, through, and beyond their bodily activity, at least some traces of the mental activity that goes along with it. Whatever we see people do, we parse their doing in meaningful units, each of which entails and implies, more or less explicitly, some specific mental states like reasons, desires, beliefs, or intentions.[3] These mental states underlie and thereby

2. The point of the argument is that the infant can only recognize in the mirror what she already knows about herself (or her self) before she encounters the mirror. Thus, if one posits that the baby already knows herself as a mental agent, then recognizing herself in the mirror may pertain to both the bodily and the mental self. Conversely, if one posits that she doesn't know her mental self yet, then recognizing herself in the mirror can only pertain to the bodily self, not to the not-yet existing mental self. In that case, the infant may mirror-recognize her body but not her mind.

3. In the introduction to a book on issues of action identification, Vallacher and Wegner put this as follows:

There are two conspicuous sources of evidence about what a person is doing. First, there is the stream of activity that is observable in the person's bodily movements. From finger snaps and eyeblinks to dance routines and orations, there exists a seemingly continuous flow of activity in the course of the person's life (cf. Barker, 1963). Now, within this stream of action, there is a remarkable second stream—remarkable, because it appears to be a verbal commentary on the first. This is the stream of action identification. Along with the continuous activity of the body, we find the person continuously capable of offering a report on what he or she is doing. Of course, people do not volunteer this information at every point in the stream of action, nor do they need to, for we as observers are typically schooled enough in human actions to supply our own identifications much of the time. (Vallacher & Wegner, 1985, p. 4; see also Wegner & Vallacher, 1986)

explain the ongoing action. Moreover, we often see these action units organized in hierarchies, with implied mental states operating at several levels simultaneously.

Consider, for instance, what we perceive when we watch a person hanging a picture. In the performance of such an action, a hierarchy of nested action components arises. Components such as getting a hammer or gauging the optimal position of the nail appear to be nested in the overall action, and these components may again be composed of further subcomponents. Importantly, however, the units and subunits in the hierarchy are perceived as full-fledged goal-directed actions. We perceive them as intrinsically meaningful units, realizing both local goals and global functions. This, then, is what we perceive: actions, rather than just movements.

Everything we perceive in a situation like this is obviously grounded on (and entirely realized through) information about the physical surface of the ongoing action. We have access to this information through our eyes and ears (i.e., we have access to body movements, hammer noises, etc.). Still, we cannot help but perceive meaningful mental activity going on in the individual whose actions we are watching.

The claim that perceivers have access to hidden meaning behind the surface of visible structure may at first glance sound a bit mysterious. Yet, when we examine it from the broader point of view of a general theory of the workings of perceptual systems, this claim appears not to be mysterious at all. One of the basic tenets of perceptual theory is that perceptual systems are engineered not just for recoding and representing the information that is available to their pertinent sensory systems but rather for using that information as a basis for the computation of information that is relevant to the perceiver/actor. In other words, perceptual systems are made for going beyond the information inherent in the stimulus. They are made for providing perceivers/actors with useful knowledge about their environment.

When taken as a general principle, a statement like this may come close to triviality. Yet, when applied to the domain of action perception, it can be given a less abstract and less trivial interpretation. Consider what kind of information is potentially useful for an observer who watches somebody

Whereas the action identification approach addresses the way in which acting individuals perceive and understand their own actions, the present discussion addresses how their actions are perceived by external observers. For further discussion see ch. 7 below.

else's ongoing behavior. One thing that the observer might wish to recognize and understand is the other's past and present actions. However, it may be even more important that she be able to anticipate his upcoming actions. It goes without saying that for social animals like humans, knowledge about others' upcoming actions can be extremely useful. It helps them to plan and prepare their own complementary actions and interactions.

Therefore, a mechanism for efficient action perception needs to deliver information that is derived from past and present actions and, at the same time, allows for valid prediction of future actions. Our machinery for action perception has solved this problem by using the physical kinematics of past and present actions as a basis for computing the underlying mental dynamics. As a result, we perceive not only the (visible) physical action itself but also the (invisible) mental states and forces driving it. These mental states fulfill two basic functions. One is to explain past and present behavior. The other is to predict future behavior. One may even speculate that the power to predict upcoming behavior is the proper function for which the computation of mental dynamics has been built into the machinery for action perception. If mental states are believed to be causal antecedents of subsequent actions, then observers who are capable of perceiving these dynamic antecedents will also be capable of predicting their kinematic and dynamic consequences.[4]

A Latent Message

If this is true of the way in which we perceive other people, and if it is also true of mirrors that they help us to see ourselves like others, then it must also be true that what we get from our specular image is more than just information about our outer appearance. Mirrors help us to see, through and beyond the physical kinematics of our movements, the mental dynamics from which they originate.

Still, why should we need mirrors for this? Aren't we authors of our actions in the first place? And shouldn't we therefore be familiar with each

4. As mentioned above, the scope of these mechanisms goes beyond the perception of human action (see ch. 1, n. 20). It seems to apply to all kinds of events for which attribution of animacy or mentality may support the prediction of upcoming actions or events. Although the scope of such kinds of events may in part be culturally determined, animal behavior and animal-like behavior of physical events seem to be universally included (as is suggested by spontaneous attributions of animacy and mentality to things like chasing lions, roaring thunderstorms, or crashing computers).

and every detail of those dynamics from the act of planning and producing them?

Obviously, if the intuition of knowing ourselves from the inside were true, mirrors would provide useless and redundant information: They would just repeat and replicate knowledge that is already there. In that case it would be hard to understand how mirrors can have had such a fantastic career as cultural symbols for seeing one's mind through one's body. We may therefore conclude that that fantastic career suggests that the intuition of knowing everything about ourselves from the inside is mistaken. Accordingly, perceiving ourselves from the outside may in fact provide us with knowledge that goes beyond what we know from the inside. The outside perspective may even deliver a richer and more valid picture of our feelings and doings than the inside perspective can. Hence, one of the latent messages conveyed in the abundant use of mirrors as symbols for portraying and understanding the self is that people don't really know and understand themselves from the inside. To understand our feelings and doings we need to perceive ourselves from the outside.

Implied in this notion is a deep-rooted distrust of the validity of introspection (the first-person perspective) as compared to external observation (the third-person perspective). Such distrust stands in stark contrast to the classical Cartesian intuition that knowing one's self from the inside is the sole safe fundament for knowledge of anything. Moreover, at least for a fictitious world without mirrors, it suggests the remarkable conclusion that individuals know others (whom they perceive from the outside) better than they know themselves (whom they know only from the inside).

Social Mirrors

Yet, we have reason to believe that humans have never lived in a world without mirrors. Although physical mirrors are artifacts that have only appeared late in human evolution and history, social mirrors have been around from the outset. Ever since humans have existed, they have been acting as social mirrors, using their own bodies and minds to mirror others.

Social mirroring has two sides to it: that of the target individual T whose actions are being mirrored and that of the mirror individual M who is mirroring T's action. Though a full account of social mirroring will require an explanation of both the target and the mirror individual's performance, I will first focus on the target individual's perspective. For this individual, T, the mirror individual, M, provides a living mirror that exists in her environment in the same way as physical mirrors do.

In what sense and in what ways can T find her own action mirrored through M's action? In addressing this question, it may be useful to draw two distinctions. One refers to two basic modes of mirroring (reciprocal vs. complementary). The other refers to two basic modes of communicating what is being mirrored (embodied vs. symbolic). In suggesting these distinctions I do not mean to imply that we must distinguish between 2×2 basic kinds of social mirroring. In natural settings, we will always encounter combinations of these kinds. Still, since they differ in terms of their functional requirements and implications, it may be useful to distinguish them conceptually.

Two Modes of Mirroring

Perhaps the most fundamental form of social mirroring arises from settings in which T sees her own action imitated or replicated by M (*reciprocal mirroring*). In a setting like this, the other (M) acts as a mirror for self (T) in a more or less literal sense. Still, social mirrors are fundamentally different from physical mirrors. Even if M attempts to provide as-perfect-as-possible copies of T's acting, those copies will always be delayed in time and their kinematics will never be as perfectly correlated with T's acting as specular images are. Obviously, the mirror-like appearance of M's action will degrade even further if M does not even try to provide a perfect copy of T's action (or perhaps even a systematically distorted one).

Reciprocal mirroring can only work if these distortions are limited. We can only speak of reciprocal mirroring as long as T is in a position to recognize and understand M's action as a delayed copy of her own preceding action. As long as this condition is fulfilled, we may leave it open what the grain size of appropriate action units and the magnitude of appropriate delays may be. The constitutive feature of reciprocal mirroring is T's perception and understanding of (certain aspects of) M's action as a copy of (certain aspects of) T's own preceding action.

A slightly different form of social mirroring arises from settings in which T sees her own action continued and carried on rather than replicated by M (*complementary mirroring*). In a setting like this, the other (M) acts as a mirror not in the strict sense of reflecting the self's preceding action but only in the loose sense of continuing that action in a meaningful way. This is, of course, entirely different from what physical mirrors do, suggesting that we may perhaps be overextending the mirror metaphor a bit. Still, complementary mirroring has in common with reciprocal mirroring (1) that M's action is strongly contingent on T's own preceding action and (2) that that contingency must be perceived and understood by T. Once more, the reach of complementary mirroring goes as far as T is in a position to assess M's action as a meaningful continuation of her own action.

Hence, what is common to both modes of mirroring is that T perceives (certain aspects of) M's action as equivalent to (certain aspects of) T's own action. The difference is that in the reciprocal setting, M's action mirrors what T has actually done before, whereas in the complementary setting, M's action mirrors what T is potentially doing now. Yet, in spite of this difference we may still regard both settings as instances of social mirroring.[5]

Two Modes of Communication

Both of these settings require some kind of communication between the target individual T and the mirror individual M in their common environment. Such communication can take two basic forms: embodied or symbolic mirroring.[6]

The settings considered so far draw on mirroring through embodied communication: First T acts in a particular way; then M, on perceiving T's acting, starts replicating or continuing that action; and finally that replication/continuation is perceived and "understood" by T. Communication is here embodied in the sense that it relies entirely on T's and M's competence

---

5. We should perhaps think of the two modes of mirroring as two ends of a continuum rather than mutually exclusive categories. For instance, as has been shown by Clark (2007) and Chouinard and Clark (2003), verbal interactions between children and caretakers may often adopt the character of mirror games, with mixed contributions from reciprocation and complementation. In these interactions caretakers may repeat/reformulate the infants' utterances, and infants may then repeat/ reformulate these corrections. Such mirror correction games seem to exhibit gradual transitions between repetition, reformulation, and continuation of others' preceding utterances.

6. Here I use the term of communication in a broad (performance-related) sense, not in a narrow (intention-related) sense. In the performance-related sense, communication may be going on between individuals, without any of them entertaining an intention to communicate anything to anybody. Communication is thus seen from the third-person, not the first-person perspective. Importantly, the term of mirroring refers to a special class of communicative acts in which two persons share the same action (or representations thereof). This feature distinguishes them from numerous other kinds of communicative acts that rely not on sharing the same actions but on generating complementary actions (one individual performing action Y in response to another individual performing action X, etc.; see Graf, Bosbach & Prinz, 2010).

for both production of their own action and perception of foreign action (*embodied mirroring*). Embodied mirroring does not require a language system in which the two communicate—nor does it require explicit intentions to communicate something to someone on either side. The sole requirement is that competent perceivers/actors meet and interact.

By saying this, however, I do not mean to suggest that embodied mirroring is a simple procedure that relies on primitive representational resources. Though it does not presuppose language, it does require quite sophisticated machinery for action production and action perception—as well as for coordinating perception and production.[7]

Not surprisingly, routines for embodied mirroring are particularly prominent in interactions between preverbal infants and their caretakers. Babies and their mothers will often find themselves involved in what has been called protoconversational interaction, imitating or continuing each other's behavior and, from time to time, taking turns in their mutual roles in this amusing game. These interactions have been extensively studied, particularly with regard to the development of imitation and its underlying mechanisms.[8] In the majority of these studies, the focus is on the baby's competence for producing her own imitative action but not on her competence for perceiving foreign imitative action. In other words, most

7. It is sometimes claimed that this machinery operates in a preconceptual or even nonconceptual mode (Dokic & Proust, 2002; Gallese, 2005b; Gordon, 1995b, 1996; Proust, 2002). This claim may be meaningful if one holds that conceptual structures require language and cannot do without—as many philosophers do. It is not meaningful, however, if one believes that conceptual structures may also exist and operate independent of language—as most psychologists do. According to their view, both action production and perception are dependent on underlying conceptual structures—even if these structures are not language-based or language-coded (Gallese & Goldman, 1998; Goldman, 2002, 2006). In chs. 5 and 7, I discuss in greater detail the role that action concepts and ontologies play for action perception and production.

8. The term "protoconversation" is borrowed from Trevarthen's seminal work on the foundations of infant intersubjectivity in early interaction and communication (for overviews see, e.g., Trevarthen, 1998; Trevarthen, Kokkinaki & Fiamenghi, 1999). The role of imitation in early infancy and its underlying mechanisms have been extensively studied over recent decades. Much of this work was stimulated by Meltzoff's studies on neonate imitation (Meltzoff & Moore, 1977). For more recent overviews see Bråten (1998), Hurley and Chater (2005), Meltzoff and Prinz (2002), Nadel and Butterworth (1999), Raphael-Leff (2003), and Rochat (1999); see also Dautenhahn and Nehaniv (2002).

studies see the baby in the role of the mirror individual M (who mirrors the caretaker's actions) and not in the role of the target individual T (who perceives herself being mirrored by the caretaker). This, however, is exactly the perspective that we need to adopt when we want to understand how social mirroring can contribute to the formation of the self.[9]

More familiar to adults will be procedures for action mirroring through symbolic communication: T acts in a particular way, and M, upon perceiving T's acting, starts talking about T's acting, and that verbal account is finally perceived and "understood" by T (*symbolic mirroring*). In a setting like this, M's verbal account of T's acting can vary not only along the dimension of replication/continuation but on dimensions like description/ explanation and interpretation/evaluation as well. In any case, mirroring is here symbolic in the sense that it is entirely dependent on the two individuals' competences for the production and perception of spoken language. M communicates to T a verbal message concerning T's ongoing/ upcoming action, and that message needs to be decoded and understood by T.

Yet, on a closer look it becomes evident that competences for speech production and perception are not enough. Rather, what the two individuals need to share is a conceptual framework for the description and explanation of action, as far as it is coded in their language systems. For instance, in order to be in a position to understand M's account of T's action, T needs to form a commensurate conceptual representation of her own action in the first place—commensurate in the sense that T's representation needs to be coded in the same format as M's account. In a way, then, the two individuals, rather than sharing the same action, need to form

9. A noteworthy example is again Trevarthen's work, which has, from the outset, focused on ways in which protoconversational communication contributes to the making and the shaping of the infant's mental dispositions (e.g., Trevarthen, 1993, 1998; see also Feldman, 2007, Mundy & Newell, 2007, Reznick, 1999, Sommerville & Decety, 2006, Striano & Reid, 2006). More specifically, the importance of caretakers' mirroring and imitative action for the development of infants' cognitive and communicative skills has been stressed in work on imitation, imitation recognition, and imitation provocation (e.g., Agnetta & Rochat, 2004; Hauf & Prinz, 2005; Meltzoff, 1990; Nadel, 2002; Nadel et al., 1999; Nagy, 2006; Nagy & Molnar, 2004; Rochat, 2009; Rochat & Passos-Ferreira, 2009 and Trevarthen, 2005). The mirror role of others for the emergence of infants' selves also plays a crucial role in psychodynamic theories of early development (cf., e.g., Brazelton, 1976; Brazelton & Cramer, 1991; Fonagy et al., 2004; Grossmann & Grossmann, 2005; Winnicott, 1971; Wright, 2003).

commensurate representations of the same action. To be in a position to do so they need to draw on an action ontology that entails a shared understanding of what actions are, how they can be parsed and individuated, and how physical action can be explained through preceding mental action. This is, of course, precisely what folk psychology delivers: a commonsense framework for the description and explanation of action to which they resort for reflecting and communicating about what people are doing and why they do what they do. As ensuing chapters will show (chs. 5, 7, 10, 13), this framework not only subserves description and explanation but construction and formation as well: Folk psychology acts as a mind designer.[10]

Therapeutic discourse is one of the prototypical settings in which symbolic mirroring is common. Often it is even systematically cultivated. Here the client takes the role of the target individual and the therapist serves as

10. The term of mind designer is due to Bogdan (2009, 2010). Recent decades have witnessed a broad debate about the nature of folk psychology and the understanding of the workings of the mind that it entails. This debate stretches from philosophy to cognitive, social, developmental, and clinical psychology. One of its strands is concerned with the status and the role of action explanation. Here we may discern two major camps, a theory camp and a nontheory camp. The theory camp (advocated, e.g., by Churchland, 1970, 1991; Gopnik & Wellmann, 1994; Sellars, 1956; Stich, 1983) holds that folk psychology must be considered an empirical theory of the mind in a literal sense, building on observable and nonobservable states and causal relations between them. According to this view, folk psychology explanations of human action are in principle continuous with scientific theories. Such continuity is denied by the nontheory camp (advocated, e.g., by Dennett, 1991; Kusch, 1997, 1999; Wilkes, 1984, 1991). Unlike the theory camp, which focuses on the explanatory power of folk psychology, the nontheory camp emphasizes its practical role for communication and interaction. For instance, Dennett speaks of folk psychology as craft (rather than science). Others consider folk psychology an embodied practice (Gallagher, 2001; Hutto, 2004) or a social institution (Kusch, 1997, 1999, 2005). A further strand of the debate is less concerned with status and roles of action explanation and more with underlying mechanisms. Here we again encounter two camps (not unrelated to the first two). One camp, which believes in laws and theories as the core of folk psychology, posits that action explanation is a matter of nomological reasoning—just like scientific explanation. The other assumes that action explanation emerges from preconceptual practices like empathy, imitation, and simulation—with no laws and theories involved (e.g., Goldman, 1995, 2006; Gordon, 1995a,b, 1996, 2001; Harris, 1991). For overviews see, e.g., Bogdan (1991), Greenwood (1991), Kusch (1999), Malle, Moses, and Baldwin (2001). Malle (2004) has proposed an integrated approach, emphasizing both folk psychology's cognitive and normative functions for action explanation and action regulation, respectively.

a mirror, sometimes in a neutral, sometimes in an empathic attitude, either providing more descriptive or more explanatory responses and commentaries, depending on personal style and theoretical background. In any case, the basic rationale behind the therapeutic procedure is simple and straightforward: The "talking cure" in which the therapist mirrors selected aspects of the client's thoughts, needs, emotions and actions is expected to contribute to the building up and consolidation of the client's self.[11]

What Mirrors Afford

Let us summarize what physical and social mirrors have to offer to individuals exposed to them. First and foremost, mirrors afford perceptual access to things that are otherwise inaccessible. Through physical mirroring individuals can see what they are doing as others can. Here the correlation between doing and seeing is perfect. What they see in the mirror is largely under their own control. More importantly, through social mirroring individuals can see and understand how others see and understand what they are doing. Here the correlation is far from perfect. What they see in the mirror is partly under their own control but partly under the control of others.

Why is it that humans have fallen in love with both physical and social reflections?[12] Why are we so greedy to see ourselves in mirrors? This is the radical answer I would like to propose: We need mirrors for the sake of better knowing, understanding, and appraising what we are doing. This is not to say that without mirrors we could not act in a meaningful way. We could act as closed minds, uninformed by any knowledge, understanding, or appraisal of what our acting means for others. Mirrors—especially social mirrors—help us to open our minds. It is through the mirrors of others that we come to see and understand ourselves as agents like others.

This is in a nutshell what mirrors afford: that self can emerge from others. As always, there is good news and bad news. The good news is that a mental self is born. The bad news is that it is created from interactions with others rather than originating in the individual mind. We will see below, though, that the bad news turns out to have its good side, as well.

11. The notion of therapeutic mirroring is ubiquitous in psychotherapy. It started with Freud's idea that the therapist should act like a mirror (see Schmidt, 2001) and was later taken up as a key concept in client-centered therapy (Rogers, 1951, 1959) and self-psychology (Kohut, 1971, 1985).
12. This wording is borrowed from the subtitle of Pendergrast's book: *Mirror mirror: A history of the human love affair with reflection* (Pendergrast, 2003).

5 Mirrors Inside

How are individuals able to exploit what mirrors offer? What kinds of representational structures and processing mechanisms does target individual T require to be in a position to capitalize on M's mirroring for building a representation of self? Evidently, the mere fact of being mirrored from the outside will not do the job by itself. Pet-owners, for instance, often entertain mirror conversations with their cats and dogs—without any obvious consequences for their pets' mental architectures. Human babies seem to be different in that respect. They use social mirrors for shaping and, in fact, making their minds. What, then, do humans have that cats and dogs do not?

I submit that humans have *mirrors inside*. By mirrors inside I mean mirror-like representational devices that help them to understand and utilize what outside mirrors afford. Just like many other processing modules in the human mind, these mirror modules serve to couple perception and action, but they do so in a specific way.

Creating couplings between perception and action must be considered one of the most crucial and fundamental achievements of mental architectures, perhaps even the proper function for which they are optimized. In a way, we may thus regard minds as gigantic machines for mapping perception to action and action to perception. Mind machines compute what animals do under given circumstances (*control*: map action to perception) as well as what circumstances will follow from given action (*prediction*: map perception to action). Basically, the workings of this machinery build on associations or association-like couplings between states and processes on either side. Parts of these couplings may be hardwired and inherited, whereas other parts need to be acquired through ontogenetic learning. Yet, irrespective of how they are established, these couplings always link disparate and incommensurate entities: sensory input that builds on afferent information and motor output that builds on efferent information.

Given this sketch of the basic workings of the mind machine, what makes mirror modules special? What features distinguish these particular modules from all others concerned with the coupling between perception and action? I submit that mirror modules are special because they allow for the operation of similarity in the interplay between perception and action. They are engineered to overcome the incommensurability of disparate coding inherent in associative coupling.[1]

Design Principles

How do mirror modules work and how do they interact with mirrors outside? Let me start by illustrating the functional problem to be solved. Consider again our target individual T, watching what M is doing. Suppose that

1. The concept of similarity has always played an ambiguous role in philosophical and psychological theorizing on cognition. In some theoretical approaches it has served as a central explanatory concept (e.g., in Gestalt psychology). However, other approaches have eschewed it altogether and have regarded similarity relationships as by-products of associative mechanisms (e.g., in structuralist and connectionist approaches); see, e.g., Keil et al. (1998); Sloman (1996); Sloman and Rips (1998); Tversky (1977). The approach I am advocating here is based on a hybrid view that invokes the existence of both contiguity- and similarity-based links between perception and action in juxtaposition (Brass & Heyes, 2005; Heyes, 2001; Prinz, 1992, in press). According to this approach, the claim that mirror modules are engineered to overcome the incommensurability entailed in associative couplings is not meant to suggest that mirror modules push associative modules away and take their place. Mirror coupling rather must be seen as coexisting with associative coupling and even depending and building on it. Coexistence implies that mirror and associative coupling operate in parallel. Dependence implies that mirror coupling requires an underlying machinery for associative coupling on whose operation it builds. Similarity-based processing in one domain is thus made possible through contiguity-based processing in another domain.

M occasionally mirrors T, but that for most of the time M is doing something else. Here, then, is the functional problem: How can T tell mirroring from nonmirroring in the sequence of M's actions that she observes? As long as this problem is unsolved, T will have no way of capitalizing on what the social mirror in front of her affords. This is because T will not be in a position to detect M's mirroring and identify those actions as mirroring her own.

Common Coding

Common coding is the opposite of disparate or incommensurate coding inherent in associative coupling. Common coding requires a shared representational domain for perception and action—a shared space of representation that uses the same set of representational dimensions for coding one's own action and foreign perception. A shared domain such as this allows for commensurate coding of action-related and perception-related representations, which, in turn, allows for computing their overlap, within that space and, hence, their similarity. This is because any given token of one's own action will get its entry in that space on exactly the same dimensions as any given token of foreign perception. For the sake of convenience, we may call action-related entries *action codes* and perception-related entries *event codes*.

The notion of common coding of actions and events has a number of important implications. First, it matches perfectly with our commonsense intuition about the relationship between our (own) actions and all sorts of (foreign) events in our environment. According to these intuitions, we do not perceive our own actions as something fundamentally different from foreign events. Rather, we experience them in the same way as any foreign actions and events. For instance, what I see myself doing in preparing a pot of tea is not different in any principled way from what I see others doing in the same situation.

Second, common coding helps to explain a large variety of induction and interference effects between perception and action that have been studied extensively over the past decades. All of these effects are grounded on representational overlap, or similarity between one's own action and foreign perception. Depending on similarity, foreign perception can either induce a corresponding action or interfere with a noncorresponding action of one's own. Conversely, one's own action, depending on representational overlap, can either facilitate or impede the perception of corresponding or noncorresponding foreign events, respectively.[2]

2. For overviews, see Hommel et al. (2001); Neumann and Prinz (1990); Prinz (1990, 1992, 1997, 2002, 2005 in press; Prinz, Aschersleben, and Koch (2009). See also Hommel and Prinz (1997); Prinz and Hommel (2002); Proctor and Reeve (1990).

Third, and closely related to this, common coding makes it possible both to perceive and produce similarity, or equivalence between own action and foreign action. This has important implications for either of our two model individuals, M, the producer, and T, the perceiver of similarity. As concerns production, M's mirroring of T's actions will rely on induction of M's own action through the perception of the corresponding foreign action. Conversely, as concerns perception, T's understanding of the mirror nature of M's action will rely on matching the perceived foreign action to T's own previously produced action. Accordingly, common coding is a prerequisite for the mirror game between the two to work. Common coding makes it possible to reciprocate the others' actions and, at the same time, to understand the others' reciprocation of one's own actions (seen from M's and T's perspective, respectively).

Common coding may thus be a powerful design principle. But how is it instantiated? How can mirror modules that rely on common coding evolve from and coexist with associative modules that rely on disparate coding? One obvious solution to this problem is to implement a novel, supplementary representational domain for common coding that operates on top of, and in parallel with, the domain for disparate coding and associative coupling.

Yet, as already indicated in note 1 of this chapter, there is a price to pay for running a secondary system for commensurate coding on top of a primary one for disparate coding. Action and event codes can only be formed in the secondary system on the basis of sensory and motor codes in the primary system. The formation of these codes will therefore require another set of associative coupling algorithms that translate, as it were, the two disparate languages of sensory codes and motor codes into the single common language of event and action codes. Thus, the price we must pay for warranting commensurate coding in one domain is an increasing demand on disparate coding as it is required for translating information from the sensory and motor domains into the common coding domain.

Distal Reference

Common coding is just an abstract principle. How is it realized and instantiated? How can we characterize the representational content of action and event codes? A key feature by which these codes distinguish themselves from sensory and motor codes is entailed by the notion of distal reference.

Distal reference is fairly obvious on the perceptual side. The content of what we see and hear does not consist of patterns of sensory stimulation or patterns of brain activation. Instead, we perceive objects and events in the world—distal events rather than proximal stimuli or central activations. The flipside of distal reference is therefore proximal neglect: Perceptual content refers to distal events, but not to states and processes in the proximal machinery generating it.[3]

Distal reference has two remarkable implications for the functional efficiency of perception. One implication is what authorities like Brunswik and Gibson call *veridicality*. Perceptual content is, in virtue of distal reference, veridical in the sense of representing environmental events in a way that satisfies the requirements of successful interaction with them. This is because perceivers/actors need to interact with objects and events in their environment, not with activation patterns in their sensors, effectors, and brains. The other implication is what we might call *publicity*. Perceptual content is, in virtue of distal reference, public in the sense of representing events in a way that satisfies the requirements of successful communication about them. This is because distal events in the world can be collectively perceived and acted upon by all perceivers/actors who have access to them, whereas activations in their sensors, effectors, and brains are only available to each of them individually.

Distal reference is, at first glance, less obvious on the action side. Does this feature apply to action representation as well? If we trust introspection there can be no doubt that our willing and doing exhibit both proximal neglect and distal reference. For instance, when we plan to drive a nail into the wall, that planning does not refer to muscle contractions in our arm or to activations in our motor cortex. Instead, it refers to the planned action as an event in the environment (i.e., the kinematics and dynamics of the hammer as it is approaching and hitting the nail). The same applies to past action: We remember our actions as distal, public events in the environment (distal reference), not as proximal, private activities in our body (proximal neglect).

What about functional efficiency? Is there a functional role for distal reference in action? According to the ideomotor principle advocated by classical authorities like Lotze, Münsterberg, and James, distal reference is in fact a crucial prerequisite for the control of action through volition.

3. The notion of distal focusing in perception goes back to Brunswik's seminal work on perceptual constancies. Brunswik's conceptual framework was captured by the so-called lense model of the relationship between perception, cognition, and action (Brunswik, 1944, 1952, 1955).

These authors claimed that voluntary action is grounded in and preceded by representations of what is willed or intended.[4] Such intentions exhibit both distal reference and proximal neglect. They refer to public events interacting with other public events, not to private patterns of sensory, motor, or brain activations. Furthermore, these authorities suggested we distinguish different degrees of remoteness within distal action representations. For instance, as concerns the distinction between goals and actions, they agreed that representations of remote action goals are no less important for voluntary action control than are representations of the actions realizing these goals. Ideomotor theory claims that representations of goals make an indispensable contribution to the efficiency of the action codes involved in the steering of action through volition.[5]

Mirrors for Action

Let me briefly summarize the two design principles that support the buildup of mirrors inside. As we saw above, such mirrors are required for both the production and perception of action mirroring (in M and T, respectively). The two principles invoke a shared domain for the representation of one's own action and foreign action. Thus, for a given individual, any token of one's own or self-produced action gets represented in precisely the same format as any token of foreign or other-produced action that he or she perceives. Self-produced and foreign actions are both represented as environmental events that interact with all kinds of other objects in the environment.[6]

As a result of commensurate coding, a device like this allows for a functional role of similarity between perception and action, based on the

4. See, e.g., James (1890); Lotze (1852); Münsterberg (1888). For further implications of ideomotor theory see ch. 7, n. 18.

5. James argued that representations of remote effects may often be even more efficient for control than representations of the action itself. For instance, for the case of reaching for a target he concludes: "Keep your eye at the place aimed at [= the remote target], and your hand will fetch [it]; think of your hand [= the effector performing the action itself] and you will likely miss your aim" (James, 1890 II, p. 520). See Wulf and Prinz (2001) for experimental evidence in support of this claim.

6. It should be noted that a device like this in itself has no way to distinguish between self-produced and other-produced action. Telling one from the other acquires additional information from further sources, allowing the system to identify the agent at work (Decety & Chaminade, 2003; Decety & Sommerville, 2003; de Vignemont & Fourneret, 2004; Frith, Blakemore, & Wolpert, 2000; Jeannerod, 2005; Jeannerod & Pacherie, 2004; Synofzik, Vosgerau, & Newen, 2008).

computation of representational overlap between codes for self-produced and other-produced action. Similarity allows for mutual priming between perception and production: Perceived other-produced action primes the production of corresponding self-produced action, and self-produced action primes the perception of corresponding other-produced action. Therefore, a device like this can be used as a mirror. The mirror goes either way: producing one's own action resembling perceived foreign action and perceiving foreign action resembling one's own, self-produced action (M's production and T's perception of mirroring, respectively). Once a mirror device is established, individuals can adopt both of these roles and switch between them on demand. To mirror others and to perceive being mirrored by others then becomes part of their everyday social interactions.

Let us now see how these design principles are instantiated in the human mind. What kinds of mirror devices can we discern? This question will lead us back to the two basic modes of mirroring that we discussed above: embodied and symbolic. Devices for embodied mirroring operate on the basis of implicit procedural knowledge for the control of bodies, actions, and events. Conversely, devices for symbolic mirroring operate on the basis of explicit declarative knowledge about bodies, actions, and events.[7]

As concerns ontogenetic development, procedural embodied devices seem to start operating right after birth, whereas declarative symbolic devices come later. Given that order of appearance, symbolic mirroring

---

7. Embodied approaches to cognition have recently enjoyed increasing attention and acceptance among psychologists, neuroscientists, roboticists, and philosophers; see, e.g., Barsalou et al. (2003); Bermúdez, Marcel, and Eilan (1995); Daum, Sommerville, and Prinz (2009); Gallagher (2005); Kiefer et al. (2007, 2008); Klatzky, MacWhinney, and Behrmann (2008); Knoblich et al. (2006); Pfeifer and Bongard (2007); Pulvermüller (2001, 2007); Rowlands (2010); Wilson (2002, 2006). Their central claim is that symbolic cognition at the conceptual level is always grounded on embodied representations and operations at the sensory and motor level. Some even claim that cognition must be seen to extend beyond the body/mind, including happenings in the world that are causally linked to happenings at the sensory and the motor level in the body/mind. In a broader sense, embodied approaches to cognition are related to enactive approaches to intentionality and consciousness (Hurley, 1998; Hutto, 2008; Jeannerod, 2006; Noë, 2004; Rowlands, 2006, 2010). Whereas embodied approaches to cognition explain how sensorimotor processing may give rise to the emergence of cognitive processing, enactive approaches focus on embodied practices of action and social interaction as they may give rise to conscious awareness.

is likely to build on embodied mirroring—at least initially. Thereafter, however, the symbolic mode of mirroring seems to gain an enormous power of its own, taking over most of the business of interaction, communication, and social mirroring in which people engage in their everyday life. This enormous power is obviously due to the tight coupling between the resources for symbolic representation and those for language-based communication. Language thus acts as a booster for the efficiency of social mirroring.

Embodied Mirrors

Everything starts with embodied devices for the support of mirror-like interactions among individuals. In the first months of their lives, human infants depend entirely on them. These devices should therefore play a crucial and indispensable role in laying the initial foundations for the construction of selfhood and subjectivity. But also later in life, when language-based symbolic mechanisms are in place and have long taken over most of the mirroring, embodied devices will persist and continue to operate. Because of their implicit character, their operation may perhaps be less conspicuous than that of symbolic devices operating on explicit knowledge. Yet, we must be careful not to underestimate their contribution in later life as well. It may well be the case that, unbeknownst to us, the latent operation of ancient devices may often overrule the manifest operation of more recently developed ones.

In the following I will discuss two major kinds of embodied mirror devices: body schemes and action schemes.[8] By these terms I mean representational devices based on procedural knowledge for bodies and actions. I will argue that both are, contrary to widely accepted wisdom, from the outset shared between others and self—perhaps even first developed for others and then projected back onto self.

8. This is not meant to be an exhaustive list of such devices. A further obvious example of embodied mirror devices is what one could call emotion schemes, i.e., embodied devices for expressing and perceiving emotions. A rich body of evidence suggests that devices for affect mirroring play an important role in the perception and production of emotions and emotional expressions; see, e.g., Avenanti et al. (2005); Brazelton (1976); Calder et al. (2000); Decety and Jackson (2004, 2006); Fonagy et al. (2004); Gergely and Watson (1996); Grèzes and de Gelder (2005); Niedenthal et al. (2010); Singer et al. (2004); Sonnby-Borgström (2002); Trevarthen (1993); Winnicott (1971).

As we have already seen in previous chapters, this claim poses a challenge to the classical Cartesian notion that knowledge of self is the natural foundation from which other kinds of knowledge derive—particularly knowledge concerning other people. This is what we may call the *like-me perspective*: I know and understand you because you are like me. What the claim suggests instead is either a parallel emergence of understanding of self and others or even the reverse order: that knowledge of others is the natural foundation from which knowledge of self is derived. This is what we may call the *like-you perspective:* I know and understand myself because I am like you.[9]

Body Schemes

The notion of body scheme has both a confused and a confusing history. It was originally introduced to account for the tacit representational basis of posture and movement. On that approach, the body scheme was regarded as kind of an implicit, nonconscious internal model that actively monitors body posture and movement. Unfortunately, this procedural model of the body has often been conflated with more declarative kinds of body-related knowledge as they are sometimes addressed under the notion of body image. This conflation has been criticized, but in practice it is hard to avoid. It seems to reflect the fact that these two ingredients of body-related knowledge cannot be as neatly separated in empirical observation as they can be in theoretical conception.[10]

How does the body scheme emerge? What kinds of information does it contain and in what ways does it instantiate the design principles that determine mirrors inside? The most natural answer to the first question seems to be that the body scheme builds on, and is in fact created by, information provided by the various sense organs in the body, particularly those implanted in muscles, tendons, and joints. However, as the

9. For the *like-me perspective*, see, e.g., Gallese (2005a); Meltzoff (2005, 2007). For accounts discussing the possibility of a *like-you perspective*, see Barkley (2001); Bogdan (2009, 2010); Carruthers (2009); Cleeremans (2008); Cleeremans, Timmermans, and Pasquali (2007); Hauf and Prinz (2005); Prinz (2008).

10. The concept of body scheme was initially introduced by Head (1920) to account for posture and movement control. Later its scope became enormously broadened to cover and account for a large variety of neurological and psychiatric pathologies (Schilder, 1935). Unlike Head, Schilder did not distinguish between procedural schemes for and declarative images of the body. For critical accounts of the usage of "body scheme" versus "body image," see Gallagher (1995, 2005); Gallagher and Meltzoff (1996). For the social constitution of the body image, see Joas (1983).

widespread occurrence of phantom limb experiences in amputees suggests, this cannot be the whole story. Not only do amputees often feel their missing limbs as if they were still in place, they also sometimes try to use these limbs as if they were still functional—suggesting that the missing limb continues for a time to fulfill its proper function for action control even in the absence of proprioceptive input.[11]

Accordingly, we must think of the body scheme more in terms of a long-term model of the body that, once established, cannot be abruptly altered when sensory input from particular limbs is taken away. Furthermore, since phantoms are occasionally also observed in individuals with congenitally missing limbs, we may infer that even the initial buildup of the body scheme may not require proprioceptive input from the physical body at all. These observations suggest that the body scheme is an innate representational device that can be modulated through sensory experience but not entirely created through it.[12]

What kind of information does the body scheme contain? Does it just provide a proximal model of the body as a device controlled from the inside—or does it also provide a distal model of the body as a thing interacting with other things in a common environment? To what extent does it combine body-related information from the inside (proprioception) with body-related information from the outside (e.g., vision)?

In fact, theoretical arguments and clinical observations support such a combined view. As concerns theoretical arguments, we may recall our discussion of distal reference in perception. As shown above, distal representation is a prerequisite for perception to satisfy the needs of efficient action control. If we want the body to be spatially and temporarily attuned to the dynamics of the events in our environment, we need to represent both body and events in the format of distal events. Hence, to be in a position to control the body from the inside, the body scheme needs to "know" the body from the outside as well.

11. For overviews of the literature on phantom limbs, see, e.g., Gallagher (1986, 1995); Giummarra et al. (2008); Halligan (2002); Ramachandran and Blakeslee (1998); Ramachandran and Hirstein (1998).
12. See, e.g., Brugger et al. (2000); Melzack (1990, 1992); Vetter and Weinstein (1967); Weinstein and Sersen (1961); Weinstein, Sersen, and Vetter (1964). As Gallagher and Meltzoff (1996) have pointed out, individuals with aplastic phantoms (i.e., congenitally absent limbs) tend to perceive their phantoms but not to use them as if they were still in place. It is therefore an open question whether or not aplastic phantoms have both a declarative and a procedural basis.

This conclusion is supported by clinical observations of so-called auto-scopic phenomena. This term refers to a set of quite bizarre pathological symptoms that may form part of a variety of neurological and psychiatric disorders. The key feature of autoscopic phenomena is the illusory redu-plication of the body. People sometimes feel or see either their own body, or some body that comes very close to their own.[13] For instance, in auto-scopic hallucinations patients see their own face in front of them as in a mirror, or they see a person facing them and repeating their own actions in a mirror-like fashion. Conversely, in so-called Doppelgänger hallu-cinations, the double is not a mirror image but more an independent individual who acts (and sometimes feels) exactly like oneself. In out-of-body-hallucinations patients report seeing their own body from the outside, usually adopting a specific viewpoint in peripersonal space from which they look at themselves. Obviously, what makes these phenomena so spectacular is that the (distal) outside perspective on the body is dissociated from the (proximal) inside perspective. The pathological dissociation draws our attention to the fact that these two perspectives tend to be neatly associated and integrated under nonpathological conditions.

In autoscopic and Doppelgänger hallucinations the body scheme acts like a mirror. Patients see themselves like others, and they look at them-selves as others do. In these cases mirror-like properties are revealed through pathological functioning. However, they are certainly not limited to these pathologies. We may rather suspect that the creation of a functional equiv-alence between one's own and a foreign body is a genuine function that the body scheme has adopted beyond its primary role for the control of posture and movement. Such functional equivalence requires that the body scheme combines both proprioception and exteroception, thereby integrating the inside and the outside perspective.

In the pathological symptoms, one's own body appears like another one. Experimental evidence from nonpathological conditions suggests that the reverse may hold as well, that is, that foreign bodies or body parts may be experienced as equivalent to one's own. A striking demonstration of the tight coupling between the inside and the outside perspective on body parts is provided by the so-called rubber hand illusion. When observers watch a rubber hand in front of them while their own hand is hidden

13. For an overview, see Brugger (2002, 2006); Brugger, Regard, and Landis (1997). It should be noted that the same word of caution applies to autoscopic phenomena as to aplastic phantoms. They may reflect contributions from both procedural knowledge and declarative knowledge about the body.

behind an occluder they may come to perceive the rubber hand as their own. For instance, when the rubber hand is touched simultaneously with their own hand they tend to localize that touch in the rubber hand they are watching, not in their own hidden hand. In a way, they appropriate the rubber hand as their own.[14]

Perhaps even more striking are direct experimental demonstrations of the functional equivalence of perceiving what happens to others and to one's self. For instance, when people observe others as they are touched or pricked at certain locations on their body surface, this will activate in them as observers the same brain sites that become active when they are touched or pricked at these locations themselves. Obviously these brain structures act like mirrors. Not only do they respond to and represent what happens to one's own body, they likewise respond to and/or represent what happens to other bodies. In this sense body representations are social devices, linking self to others.[15]

We may conclude that the body scheme and its underlying brain structures are well suited to bridge the gap between the first- and third-person perspectives. Moreover, it seems that the mirror-like equivalence that the body scheme creates can be used both ways: for autoscopic alienation and empathic appropriation.[16]

14. See Armel and Ramachandran (2003); Botvinick and Cohen (1998); Longo et al. (2008); Makin, Holmes, and Ehrsson (2008); Schütz-Bosbach, Tausche, and Weiss (2009); Tsakiris and Haggard (2005).
15. For experimental studies demonstrating functional equivalence of touch applied to self versus others, see Keysers et al. (2004); Singer et al. (2004). For overviews, see, e.g., de Vignemont and Singer (2006); Frith and Singer (2008); Singer and Lamm (2009); Singer and Decety (in press). The notion that body representations may have social functions—or perhaps even be grounded in such functions—is not as new and surprising to social scientists as it may be to cognitive scientists. For instance, George Herbert Mead claimed that unity of body representation requires that body-related information acquired from the first-person perspective is complemented by information acquired from the third-person perspective, i.e., from an external observer's perspective. Likewise, information about other bodies may be complemented with, and interpreted in terms of, information arising from the observer's own body. Again there are, in principle, two ways of building a body scheme: inside-out (you are like me) and outside-in (I am like you); see Joas (1983), Mead (1938).
16. For the relationships between mirrors (both inside and outside) and empathy, see, e.g., Bischof-Köhler (1989); Decety and Chaminade (2005); Gallese (2005a); Iacoboni (2005); Keenan, Gallup, and Falk (2003); Smith (1759/1976); Whitehead (2001). For the role of empathy for intentional understanding, see Kögler and Stueber (2000); Stueber (2006).

Last but not least, there is another rich body of evidence suggesting that some parts of a mirror-like body scheme are already functional at birth. This evidence comes from studies of facial imitation in newborn babies.[17] When newborn babies, in the very first hours of their lives, watch a human face performing gestures like opening the mouth or protruding the tongue they tend to produce similar gestures themselves. Similarity here concerns both body parts and action patterns: Babies will respond to tongue protrusion with tongue protrusion, not lip protrusion, and they will respond to lip protrusion with lip protrusion, not lip opening. Again, to account for these observations one needs to invoke, as a minimum requirement, a mirror-like body scheme—some kind of basic representational device that matches the baby's own (invisible) tongue and lips to the other person's (visible) tongue and lips. At least as far as facial parts and gestures are concerned, babies at birth come with mirrors inside. They help them to relate others' faces that they see to their own face that they feel.

Action Schemes

Action schemes are representational devices for matching one's own action to foreign action and vice versa. Such devices have been extensively studied over the past two decades, often with explicit reference to the mirror metaphor (using terms like *mirror neurons*, *mirror systems*, etc.). However, since I am here using that metaphor in a broader sense, I need to introduce the more specific term of *action schemes* to refer to mirror-like representational devices for action proper.

Action schemes are closely linked to body schemes, and sometimes it may even be difficult to pry them apart. For instance, in neonate imitation the equivalence match concerns both the part of the face (body) and the structure of the movement (action). Likewise, in autoscopic hallucinations the double often does not only look like oneself (body) but also acts like oneself (action). Such close coupling may not be surprising since the equivalence of one's own and foreign action will, as a rule, go hand in hand with the use of equivalent body parts. Still, sometimes actions and body parts can be dissociated—for instance, when action equivalence

17. Work on facial imitation in neonates was pioneered by Meltzoff and his colleagues (Meltzoff & Moore, 1977, 1983, 1989). For recent overviews, see Meltzoff (2002, 2005). Though there is still an ongoing debate on the validity of methods and the scope of reliable observations (see, e.g., Anisfeld, 2005; Anisfeld et al., 2001; Jones, 1996), the occurrence of neonatal imitation seems to be an established fact, at least for selected facial gestures like tongue protrusion.

is specified in terms of action goals, and not in terms of body movements required to achieve them (the ends and the means, respectively).

How do action schemes work? What kind of information do they contain? And how do they instantiate the two design principles that determine mirrors inside? The notion of action scheme requires that representational resources that subserve the production of (one's own) action will also subserve the perception of (foreign) action. Over recent decades this notion has gained strong support from both behavioral and brain studies.

Let us first take a look at pertinent behavioral studies. Here the basic idea is simple and straightforward: If action production and action perception share a common representational basis, they should somehow interfere with each other when perception and production both draw on these resources at the same time. Perception of foreign action should then modulate production of one's own concurrent action, and likewise production of one's own action should modulate perception of foreign concurrent action. Further, the degree of mutual modulation should in both cases depend on the representational overlap between perceived and produced action within the representational domain that they share.

Let us first go from *perception to production*. In a sense, we all know that our perception of others' actions may sometimes modulate or even induce the production of related actions of our own. For instance, while watching a soccer match on TV, many individuals cannot help but move around in their armchairs, particularly in watching dramatic scenes when their home team is facing a serious threat. The same may apply to situations in which individuals are watching the outcomes of certain actions rather than the actions themselves. For instance, while sitting in the passenger seat of a car, many people cannot help but step on "phantom brakes," say, when the driver approaches a bend in the road at too high a speed.

More than a century ago William James offered a theoretical principle that can be read as a summary of such anecdotal evidence concerning the modulation of action production through action perception. The ideomotor principle claims that action representations are furnished with the power to evoke the actions that they represent.[18] The principle implies that

18. James (1890, II, p. 526); for more details see ch. 7. Ironically, the ideomotor principle was initially not meant to account for induction of action through perception of external events. James rather introduced it to account for action induction through internal representations such as thoughts and ideas. The principle was meant to explain how thinking of an act (or its remote effects) can prompt and instigate that act. It took another eighty years until Greenwald (1970, 1972) extended

action perception and production draw on common representational resources, to the effect that perception of (somebody else's) action will tend to induce production of similar action (of oneself).

One line of pertinent evidence comes from studies in which action perception interferes with concurrent action production. For instance, it has been shown that the initiation and selection of particular gestures may be modulated by the concurrent perception of related gestures.[19] Remarkably, the same interference effect may be obtained for the perception of static postures. Interference turns out to be particularly pronounced for target postures, that is, postures that reflect end states or goals of the gestures to be produced. This suggests that representations of end states or action goals seem to play a prominent role in the mechanisms that underlie gesture selection.

Studies on imitation also support a prominent role for action goals. Here it has been shown that movement errors (i.e., incorrect movements to correct goals) are much more frequent than goal errors (i.e., correct movements to incorrect goals), suggesting that goals dominate movements in the control of imitative action. As discussed above, we may therefore conclude that the representational resources giving rise to interference between action perception and production contain more information than just the kinematics of perceived and to-be-produced movements. They contain information about full-fledged, goal-directed

the principle to also account for prompting and guiding action through externally generated representations like percepts, thereby attributing to the perception of action the same action-inducing power that James had attributed to thought of action (see Prinz, 1987, 2005; Prinz, Aschersleben & Koch, 2009; Prinz, de Maeght & Knuf, 2005).

19. In these studies participants were required to initiate, as quickly as possible, a particular finger gesture while watching either the same or a different gesture being performed by a hand shown on a computer screen. Results showed that they initiated the required gesture faster when the gesture shown on the screen and the self-performed gesture were the same as compared to control trials in which they were different. A similar interference effect applies to the selection of the finger and hand gestures: The time it takes to select a particular gesture on command is shorter when the visual stimulus specifying that gesture is combined with a visually presented hand performing the same gesture (as compared to control trials in which the two gestures are different). See Brass, Bekkering, and Prinz (2001); Brass et al. (2000); Hamilton, Wolpert, and Frith (2004); Hamilton et al. (2006); Kilner, Hamilton, and Blakemore (2007); Prinz (2005); Stürmer, Aschersleben, and Prinz (2000).

actions, with goals (ends) even taking the functional lead over movements (means).[20]

Studies on action induction provide further support for a key role of goals in action schemes. Consider once more the soccer fan watching a match on TV. What actually happens to him as he moves around in his armchair? How is the pattern of induced body movements related to the pattern what's happening on the TV screen? Two answers to this question have been proposed: perceptual and intentional induction. Perceptual induction claims that people repeat, in their induced movements, what they see happening in the scene. Perceptual induction thus regards induced action as a special kind of imitative action—nonvoluntary imitation, as it were. Intentional induction claims that people realize, through their induced movements, what they would like to see happening in the scene. Intentional induction thus regards induced action as a special kind of goal-directed action—futile instrumental action, as it were. Experimental studies of action induction have shown that the two principles may both be effective at the same time. Action induction can thus pertain to both the observed action's physical surface (means) and its significance for the observer's goals (ends). Again we may conclude that the underlying action schemes address both means and ends.[21]

20. For instance, when the demonstration requires the subject to reach with the right arm for the left ear two types of errors can be made: movement errors (reaching with the wrong arm for the correct ear) and goal errors (reaching with the correct arm for the wrong ear). Experimental evidence shows that infants make a substantial number of movement errors, but virtually no goal errors: while they are more or less negligent about movements (i.e., the means for achieving intended ends), they are keen on getting goals right (i.e., the ends achieved through these means). See Bekkering and Prinz (2002); Bekkering and Wohlschläger (2002); Gattis, Bekkering, and Wohlschläger (2002); Gleissner, Meltzoff, and Bekkering (2000).

21. The relative contributions of the two principles depend on task conditions. When individuals watch the outcome of self-performed actions, different patterns of induced movements may emerge for instrumental and noninstrumental effectors. Whereas instrumental effectors show intentional induction but not perceptual induction, noninstrumental effectors show both intentional and perceptual induction. A different picture arises when individuals observe the outcome of actions performed by somebody else. In that situation perceptual induction is obtained throughout. Intentional induction is observed as well, dependent on what the observer (not the observee) wants to see happening in the scene. The pattern of intentional induction also depends on whether the observer and the observee compete or cooperate. See de Maeght and Prinz (2004); Häberle et al. (2008); Knuf, Aschersleben, and Prinz (2001); Prinz, de Maeght, and Knuf (2005).

Let us now take a brief look at the converse direction, from *production to perception*. How does action production modulate the perception of actions and events? One line of pertinent evidence comes from online interactions between production and perception. Numerous experiments have shown that features of ongoing action may modulate the concurrent perception of related features of objects, events, and actions. For instance, the perception of the direction of an arrow, the orientation of a line, or the rotation direction of an ambiguous apparent motion can be modulated through concurrent action.[22]

Remarkably, such modulation is often not only obtained while the action is actually being performed but also while it is being planned and prepared. Furthermore, it may take either form, facilitation or inhibition. For instance, the planning or execution of rotary hand movements has been shown to facilitate the visual perception of apparent rotary motions in the same direction. Conversely, the pressing of keys on the left-hand versus right-hand side has been shown to impede the perception of arrows pointing in the same direction. The conditions for facilitation and inhibition are thus far only poorly understood. Both seem to rely on code overlap in a shared representational domain.

More evidence concerning the modulation of perception through action is provided by studies showing that perceptual performance may depend on action-related skills and knowledge. For instance, when people see static traces of human action (e.g., handwritten letters, drawings, or body postures), they can often "see," beyond the stationary patterns to which they are exposed, the kinematics or even the dynamics of the underlying body movements. Moreover, they are often able to discriminate between traces of self- vs. other-produced movements, suggesting once more that the visual perception of actions and their traces draws on representational resources for the production of those actions.[23]

22. See, e.g., Craighero et al. (2002); Grosjean, Zwickel, and Prinz (2009); Jacobs and Shiffrar (2005); Koch and Prinz (2005); Müsseler and Hommel (1997a,b); Schubö, Aschersleben, and Prinz (2001); Schubö, Prinz, and Aschersleben (2004); Wohlschläger (2000); Zwickel, Grosjean, and Prinz (2007, 2008, 2010). For an overview, see Schütz-Bosbach and Prinz (2007a).

23. See Babcock and Freyd (1988); Freyd (1983, 1987); Kandel, Orliaguet, and Boë (1995, 2000); Kandel, Orliaguet, and Viviani (2000); Runeson and Frykholm (1981). On the perception of self-generated action, see Flach, Knoblich, and Prinz (2003); Knoblich and Flach (2001, 2003); Knoblich and Prinz (2001); Knoblich et al. (2002). For an overview, see Schütz-Bosbach and Prinz (2007a).

The same conclusion is supported by observations of apparent biological motion. These studies have shown that apparent motion that involves human bodies does not always follow the principle of the shortest path (as it always does for nonliving things). Instead the apparent motion that observers see takes longer paths and detours as if to avoid the perception of anatomically impossible movement patterns.[24] Similarly impressive is the impact of action-based knowledge on the perception of motion velocity. On the action side, it has long been known that the velocity of drawing movements is lawfully related to the radius of the curvature of the trajectory. More recent studies have shown that the same lawful relationship is effective in perception as well.[25]

Summarizing the behavioral evidence, we may thus conclude that action perception and action production in fact share common representational resources. Action schemes act like mirrors inside, providing embodied procedures for matching one's own actions to others' actions and vice versa.

The very same conclusion can be derived from an enormously large and still increasing literature that addresses the brain mechanisms that subserve action perception and production. Here the evidence comes from both electrophysiological studies of neurons in the monkey brain and imaging and interference studies in the human brain.

The monkey brain has at least three distinct neural systems that are involved in action perception. One of them is located in the temporal lobe.

24. Apparent motion is illusory motion perceived to occur between two intermittently flashing stationary objects. In most cases that motion follows the shortest path (i.e., a straight line between the two objects), and it does so even if a solid object is placed on that path. This principle is violated, however, when the solid object is a human body part. In this case, the perceived motion appears to go around the body part (rather than straight through it). See Heptulla-Chatterjee, Freyd, and Shiffrar (1996); Shiffrar (2001); Shiffrar and Freyd (1990, 1993); Shiffrar and Pinto (2002).

25. For instance, the perceived velocity of a moving dot is constant if (and only if) its physical velocity follows the laws that govern the production of that movement through the observer's motor system, i.e., if it lawfully accelerates and decelerates, depending on the local curvature of the trajectory. Conversely, if physical velocity is kept constant, perceived velocity is inversely related to the curvature of the trajectory. Together, these observations suggest the conclusion that movement perception relies on procedural knowledge for movement production. On the lawful relationship between radius of curvature and velocity in movement production, see Viviani and Terzuolo (1982). On the application of the law to movement perception, see Viviani, Baud-Bovy, and Redolfi (1997); Viviani and Stucchi (1989). For an overview, see Viviani (2002).

Neurons in this system respond selectively to stimuli involving bodies or body parts engaged in goal-directed action. For instance, a given neuron may fire when the monkey watches a hand reaching for an object and grasping it, but not when the same reaching movement does not end up grasping the object.[26] While the temporal system is only involved in action perception, the other two systems subserve both action perception and action production. One of them is located in the premotor area of the frontal cortex. This system has two types of neurons subserving action coding: canonical neurons and mirror neurons.[27] Concerning action production, both play similar roles: Both fire when the monkey performs goal-directed actions such as grasping an object of a specific size. Concerning action perception, their roles are different, however. Canonical neurons respond to the mere sight of those objects whose grasping is coded in action production. These neurons seem to code action-related affordances of objects. Conversely, mirror neurons respond to the sight of those goal-directed actions for which they code in production, say, grasping an object. They will not respond to the sight of the object alone, nor will they fire at the sight of the grasping movement in the absence of the target object. Mirror neurons thus seem to be engineered for matching production to perception, or one's own action to foreign action. The functional properties of the third system, which is located in parietal cortex, are quite similar to those of the frontal system. This system, too, codes for both production and perception.

The discovery of the amazing properties of these neurons and systems has in the meantime stimulated research into their anatomical interconnections and their functional cooperation. At the same time it has invited far-reaching speculations about their role and their adaptive value for behavior and cognition. While some authors see their primary role on the production side (e.g., as subserving action imitation), others see it more on the perception side (i.e., as subserving action understanding or action anticipation).[28]

26. See Jellema et al. (2000); Perrett and Emery (1994); Perrett et al. (1989, 1990). For overviews, see Jellema et al. (2002); Jellema and Perrett (2002).
27. Mirror neurons in the premotor cortex were first described by di Pellegrino et al. (1992); Gallese et al. (1996); Rizzolatti et al. (1996). For overviews, see Fogassi and Gallese (2002); Rizzolatti et al. (2002); Rizzolatti, Fogassi, and Gallese (2000, 2001); Rizzolatti and Sinigaglia (2008). On the parietal system, see Gallese et al. (2002).
28. On the functional architectures of mirror systems for action representation, see Gallese (2003, 2004, 2005a); Iacoboni (2005); Pineda (2009); Rizzolatti (2005);

Regarding the human brain, cortical structures subserving the perception and production of action have been established in both the frontal and the parietal lobe. Many of these studies show that brain sites that are known to take care of action production are also involved in action perception. Using modern technologies for brain imaging like MEG, EEG, PET, and fMRI as well as interference methods like TMS, numerous studies have demonstrated that activation in premotor, motor, and sometimes parietal areas of the cortex is not only obtained when participants perform certain movements or goal-directed actions themselves but also when they see those movements and actions being performed by others.[29]

Importantly, these activations depend on instructions. The observed pattern of brain activations depends, for example, on the particular purpose for which participants observe the other's actions, say, for later imagination, recall, recognition, or reproduction. Further, their activations depend on whether or not the actions they observe belong to their own motor repertoire. For instance, when they watch paths of apparent motion involving a human body, activations are different for biomechanically possible versus impossible paths. Motor and parietal structures get activated when possible movement paths are shown, but not when movement paths are impossible, suggesting that in this case the motor system has no way to resonate, as it were, with the observed movement pattern.[30]

On the one hand, brain structures for matching perception to production may be a nice thing to have. On the other hand, such structures may be seen to create a functional problem that we already touched upon: How can the brain know, in a given episode of activation, what the source of that activation is and how can it tell production of one's own action from perception of foreign action? Solving this problem obviously requires spe-

Rizzolatti et al. (2001); Rizzolatti and Sinigaglia (2008). These authors also address the possible roles of mirror systems for individual cognition, communication, and interaction (e.g., action understanding, imitation). For diverging views emphasizing prediction over perception/production, see Csibra (2007); Frith and Frith (2006); Hurley (2005); Iacoboni et al. (2005); Jacob and Jeannerod (2005); Prinz (2003, 2006b); Wilson (2006).

29. See, e.g., Blakemore (2006); Buccino et al. (2001); Decety and Grèzes (1999); Decety and Sommerville (2003); Rizzolatti, Craighero, and Fadiga (2002). For an overview, see Frith and Wolpert (2004).

30. See Candidi et al. (2008); Costantini et al. (2005); Romani et al. (2005); Stevens et al. (2000).

cific and unshared brain activations on top of shared activations. In fact, it has been shown that perception and production not only share common resources but that each of them also engages resources of its own. The same applies to imagining an action as being performed either by oneself or by another individual (first- vs. third-person perspective). In other words, the brain knows that one's own and foreign actions are both the same and different.[31]

If the brain resonates to observed actions by way of implicitly reenacting or simulating them, how far and how deep does such simulation go? Does it just refer to the physical mechanics of movement or does it capture aspects of the underlying mental semantics as well? This would require that, beyond premotor, motor, and parietal structures that are known to take care of the physical mechanics of action, action observation should also engage brain structures known to be involved in the underlying mental dynamics. Pertinent candidates are prefrontal brain structures known to support the mental dynamics of action, that is, its intentional antecedents such as planning, preparation, and initiation. In fact, it has been shown that prefrontal structures may become active in action observation, too—at least in tasks that allow for a clear separation between ends and means, that is, intended goal states at which actions are aiming and the patterns of movements through which those goal states are being achieved. The brain seems to have mirrors for both means and ends: Brain structures for generating one's own intentions are also involved in reading the intentions of others.[32]

Some theorists are pushing this point one step further, arguing that the scope of simulation goes far beyond understanding other people's intentional actions. They posit that simulation mechanisms are, in a general and principled sense, a prerequisite for understanding the mental states in others. According to this view, people understand what other people believe and desire by way of putting themselves in their shoes, thereby using their own minds to simulate what may be going on in others' minds—be it in a literal or a more metaphorical sense. In any case, the notion of mental simulation implies what we have called a like-me perspective: People understand others because others are like themselves. According to this view, self-understanding requires no further explanation. It is

31. See Decety and Chaminade (2003); Jeannerod (1997, 1999, 2003b); Ruby and Decety (2001, 2003, 2004); Vogeley and Fink (2003); Vogeley et al. (2004).
32. See Chaminade, Meltzoff, and Decety (2002); see also Decety and Grèzes (1999); Jeannerod (1999, 2001).

considered a natural and a priori given foundation from which understanding of others derives.[33]

Symbolic Mirrors

One way of looking at embodied mirrors is to regard them as prewired,
dedicated conceptual systems for bodies, actions, and minds. At first
glance, it may sound a bit strange to speak of conceptual systems here.
However, these systems are truly conceptual in the fundamental sense of
creating equivalence among nonequivalent things. It is through them that
objects and events that are, from the perceiver/actor's point of view, otherwise disparate and incommensurate become treated as equivalent things:
her own body and others' bodies; his own actions and others' actions.
Further, these systems are embodied in a twofold sense. One is that they
seem to rely on prewired structures and connections in the brain. The other
is that they are dedicated to subserve the perception and the control of
bodies and actions, respectively.

Concepts and Words

Yet, this is not the whole story about such conceptual structures. On top
of such prewired, dedicated structures, animals also create undedicated
conceptual structures that they acquire through learning. Here, too, the
acquisition of concepts is tantamount to the creation of equivalence classes
for kinds of objects and events. For instance, a concept like *furniture*
implies, and in fact creates, functional equivalence among such diverse

33. See, e.g., Goldman (2002, 2005, 2006). For overviews, cf. Dokic and Proust
(2002); Kögler and Stueber (2000). For a critical account, see Jacob (2002); Jacob
and Jeannerod (2005). See also ch. 4, n. 10. Regarding the foundations of mental
simulation and the like-me perspective entailed by it, it may be useful to distinguish between two different claims, one strong and one weak. Their common
assumption is that mental simulation serves to derive other-understanding from
self-understanding. The difference between them refers to the putative origin of
self-understanding. The strong claim posits that self-understanding is a priori given
and does not require any further explanation. Conversely, the weak claim posits
that mental self-understanding needs to be acquired in the first place before other-
understanding can then build on it. Below I will discard the strong claim while
supporting the weak claim. I will even argue that self-understanding initially derives
from other-understanding. On this view, the skill of simulating others through self
(mental simulation—the you-like-me-perspective) builds on an initial skill of modeling self after others (mental appropriation, me-like-you-perspective).

things like cupboards, sofas, and tables—things that do not offer themselves for equivalence in terms of similarity in obvious perceptual dimensions. However, unlike the formation of prewired concepts, the acquisition of concepts through learning is not limited to specific domains to which they are dedicated. Concept learning can rather pertain to everything—from flowers and rocks to kinds of rain and storms, to furniture and coins—and of course also to bodies and actions.

Therefore, we may assume that animals that are capable of acquiring conceptual structures through learning can, at least in principle, build up mirror-like conceptual structures for their own and foreign bodies and actions. Yet, learning is always opportunistic. Animals will not create such equivalence classes just for fun, but only if and when they are useful for them in terms of extending their potential for well-adapted action. For many species, it is not obvious how useful it would be for them to build representational structures supporting equivalence or similarity between their own and their conspecifics' bodies and actions. This may be different for primates, however, and particularly for humans—animals whose fitness is very much dependent on the flexible control of complex social interactions. Moreover, since these animals are also furnished with embodied mirrors, conceptual learning in the body and action domain may build on those prewired embodied structures rather than creating entirely novel structures from scratch. Disposing of dedicated, prewired concepts for bodies and actions may, in other words, be an ideal precondition for the formation of more elaborate undedicated conceptual structures in this domain.

What is more, humans have language. As is often argued, the acquisition of a language faculty must be considered a development of utmost importance in human cognitive evolution, perhaps the truly decisive change that makes the crucial difference to our species. In fact, as we will see in chapter 13, the language faculty creates in many respects entire novel options and opportunities for the functional organization of cognition, communication, and interaction.

One of the perhaps most crucial of these novel options is that the language faculty, by virtue of combining private concepts with public words, paves the way for the social control of private concepts. As soon as language is in place, individuals are no longer left to their own private resources for the formation of their concepts. The language craft makes their private concepts publicly negotiable. While using their own concepts for the perception and control of a given situation, individuals can at the same time observe what concepts other individuals use in that situation.

They cannot only observe what others are doing but can also talk to them about the conceptual foundations of what they are doing. As a consequence, they may choose either to modify their own concepts or convince others to modify theirs.

Accordingly, with language in place, concept acquisition through private learning becomes increasingly replaced by concept adoption through public interaction and communication. When this happens, the business of concept formation through learning shifts from individuals to collectives. On the one hand, collectives will acquire and maintain conceptual structures to be shared by their member individuals. On the other hand, these individuals will adopt those structures and use them for perception, action, and communication. By turning private concept formation into a public affair, the language craft not only boosts and extends humans' conceptual capacities but also lays the ground for the conceptual foundations of cultural knowledge transmission.

Action Talk

Beyond its general significance for cultural knowledge transmission, the notion of concept formation through public negotiation is of particular importance for the specific domain of action perception and understanding—that is, for the conceptual resources entailed by our folk psychology and our everyday action talk. We have already touched on these resources several times; here I once more address the vocabulary that goes along with them.

How does action talk work? A major part of our everyday mental life is filled up with thoughts we have about own or other individuals' actions. As a consequence, a major part of our everyday conversation consists of communicative exchanges about which persons have done what on which occasions, why they have done it, and what one thinks about what they have done. Yet, action talk does not only refer to actions in the past and, hence, to a retrospective analysis of human conduct. It equally applies to prospective planning of future actions as it occurs in our own as well as others' minds.

To explain actions that a person carries out under specific circumstances, folk psychology has a ready answer that we have already come across: We attribute most of the actions that people perform to mental states that precede the action. For example, we think that somebody attended a specific opera performance because she wanted to see or listen to a certain opera singer; or that somebody washes his car because he believes that doing so will impress somebody else. Naturally, the mental states that are viewed as causes of actions do not explain the course of actions in detail. But they do explain why the particular action came about. And common sense has no problem at all with the fact that this explanation views a mental event (the person believes, wants, or fears something) as the cause of a subsequent physical event (the action itself).

The mental states that can be viewed as causes of actions can be of different kinds and can bring different variants of action explanations into play. The simplest case is when we explain an action by assuming that it is based on an action intention that is directed toward the attainment of a specific goal. This is the prototypical case of a voluntary action in which we assume that the person has planned and carried out the action in order to achieve specific goals through it. If we were to ask the person why he had carried out the action, he would give us reasons.[34]

Hence, according to action talk, voluntary actions come into being because actors have certain goals that they want to attain and because they believe that these goals can be attained through certain actions. When these preconditions are fulfilled, the thought becomes the deed: Mental states evoke physical processes and reasons function as causes.

What is so special about action talk and its conceptual underpinnings? Action talk creates equivalence in two equally important respects. One is between one's own and others' actions, that is, between actions viewed from a first- versus a third-person perspective. The other is between planning/production and representation/perception, that is, between the perspective of generating future actions and the perspective of interpreting past and present actions. On either side of these two contrasts, action talk uses precisely the same conceptual scheme, thereby bridging the gap between one's own and others' actions as well as between the production of forthcoming and the perception of past and ongoing actions. It is in

34. Other kinds of action explanations use the logic of causes rather than reasons. For example, someone who throws her alarm clock at the wall because she is angry about having overslept does not, according to the commonsense interpretation, act for a reason. We take the mental state of anger as the cause for the destructive act but not as the reason for it. Furthermore, we also distinguish habitual actions from voluntary actions. If we were to ask somebody in the morning why he was brushing his teeth at that moment, he would, as a rule, not give a reason or a cause for that action. Still, we assume that in these cases the causal mental states used to be there when the individual developed the corresponding action habits and that they have since faded away as the habit has become established. Therefore, since they can be reactualized on demand, we regard habitual actions as a special form of voluntary actions.

virtue of these bridging capacities that the conceptual resources underlying action talk acquire the potential to act like mirrors inside, providing shared representational resources for the production and perception of one's own and others' action.

Consider first the equivalence between action production and action perception. For both one's own and foreign action, action talk uses exactly the same conceptual framework for deliberations and conversations concerning the planning of forthcoming action, the control of ongoing action, and the recollection of past action. For instance, one and the same set of beliefs, desires, reasons, and intentions may play a role in selecting and planning a particular action, in initiating and controlling its execution as well as in evaluating its outcome in retrospect. As with embodied mirrors, production and perception draw on the same representational resources— the same conceptual framework and the same way of talking about the pertinent actions.

On top of this, consider the equivalence of the accounts that action talk provides for one's own vs. others' action. These two perspectives are initially disparate in the sense that one and the same mental state, or action, takes on an entirely different appearance for each of them. However, this disparity will vanish to the extent the two individuals talk to each other. When they start talking to each other about their actions and their underlying mental states, each will have access to both her own view of herself and other and the other's view of other and himself, respectively. Thus for both of them their verbal exchange will play a pivotal role in the foundation of equivalence between self and other.

In talking about how they perceive themselves and others, individuals create mutual symbolic mirrors, both outside and inside. On the one hand, each of them, through talking to the other about the other, acts for the other as a mirror outside. That mirror is provided by the speaker to whose action talk the other is listening. At the same time, each of them, by listening to the other talking about himself, acts for herself as a mirror inside. That mirror is provided by the listener whose conceptual structures resonate with that action talk. As a result, symbolic mirrors help each of them to align their own production with others' perception, that is, to align the private production with the public perception of action. This, I claim, is precisely the proper function of action talk and its underlying conceptual resources: to lay the ground for public control of private action.

6   Mirror Games

Mirror Practices
Mirror Policies
From Others to Self

Our mirrors inside make a promise that cannot always be fulfilled. For instance, for individuals like Robinson Crusoe who live in isolation, schemes and concepts for bodies and actions cannot fulfill their mirror function. To make good on the promise, two basic conditions must be met. One is that other individuals need to be around. This is what Friday's presence affords: Mirrors inside need to be complemented by (social) mirrors outside. The other is that the two individuals need to interact in particular ways. This is what their reciprocal acting and talking affords: They need to engage in mirror games. Mirror games are, in other words, social practices through which individuals capitalize on the potential for the formation of mental structure inherent in the interplay between mirrors inside and mirrors outside.

The basic scheme for mirror games envisages a dyadic interaction between two individuals. There are always two roles in the game (for which individuals may take turns): the target individual T and the mirror individual M. The game has three major functional components that may overlap in time. First, the game begins with T acting or talking in a particular way. For instance, his acting may be some instrumental activity directed at certain objects or events in the environment, and his talking may refer to such events as well. Second, while T is acting or talking, his behavior is observed by the mirror individual M. This individual then herself starts acting or talking in a way that refers to T's acting or talking in a mirror-like fashion—for instance, by replicating it or commenting on it. Third, conversely, M's acting or talking is observed by T. Accordingly, T will recognize M's acting as referring to his own previous acting. In this way, T will come to perceive his own behavior through the mirror of the other individual.

For the game to work, two basic conditions must be fulfilled. One is that both individuals need mirrors inside for matching perception to production. M needs them to be in a position to mirror T's doing, but T needs them as well to be in a position to recognize his own previous acting and talking in the mirror of M's actual acting and talking. A further condition is that M's acting and talking needs to refer to T's acting and talking—and vice versa. This condition pertains to the social side of the game, as it requires that both M and T need to be sufficiently motivated to watch each other's actions and respond to them through their own action.

While the first condition refers to cognitive resources for matching perception and production, which we have already discussed at length, the second condition refers to social resources for regulating interaction and communication. These resources are provided by social practices that support interactive games and policies that are based on procedural and declarative mirroring.

Mirror Practices

Procedural games. Procedural games rely on the interplay between social mirrors outside and embodied mirrors inside. They emerge from situations in which procedural knowledge for action perception and action control gets activated on either side. Naturally, these games will play a large role in interaction and communication when language is not yet in place.

As we discussed in chapter 4, procedural games involving mutual action reciprocation and protoconversational communication may for preverbal infants be the only kinds of mirror games that work.[1] During infants' first year of life, these games are for them of crucial importance for tuning in with and becoming attached to others, as well as laying the ground for perceiving and understanding themselves like others. For these protoconversational interactions between babies and their caretakers, it is obvious that the critical condition that M (= the caretaker) is keen on both monitoring and mirroring T (= the baby) is fulfilled. In interacting with their babies, mothers and fathers tend to follow very closely what the baby is doing, and the practice of reciprocating or continuing these actions is common and widespread—perhaps even a human universal.

In these interactions, one often also encounters a somewhat different, more indirect form of action-based mirroring that comes close to a nonverbal form of commenting on the baby's behavior, rather than mirroring that behavior in a more direct way. For instance, caretakers will smile upon

---

1. See Daum, Sommerville, and Prinz (2009).

one kind of the baby's action and cease smiling upon another, thereby communicating to the baby how his behavior is received, rather than perceived. To be efficacious, such nonverbal commenting requires that the baby already has a way of knowing what he is actually doing: Understanding how his action is *received* requires it to be *perceived* in the first place. Accordingly, caretakers tend to expose their babies to action-based commenting somewhat later than more direct forms of mirroring like reciprocation or continuation. Still, what they have in common is that they all refer to the baby's previous actions, requiring that the baby is capable of recognizing that reference.

Action-based mirroring is by no means limited to interactions with preverbal infants, however. Various forms of such mirroring habits also apply to interactions among grown-ups. For instance, an individual may, in a conversation, shrug his arms in response to his conversation partner doing the same (reciprocation). Likewise, an individual may take up another individual's work (say, washing a car) when the other temporarily withdraws (continuation). In the same vein, individuals may accompany other individuals' behavior through pertinent facial and bodily gestures, thereby commenting on that behavior in a nonverbal format.

As these examples show, the scope of action-based mirroring goes beyond interactions with preverbal infants. There is a marked difference as well, however. In interactions among adults, action-based mirroring through motor mimicry is not really cultivated as a deliberate social practice. Instead, common practice considers such mirroring inappropriate and often requires suppressing it altogether. Accordingly, M-individuals have in most cases no explicit intention to communicate anything to T-individuals. In many situations, they are not even aware of what they are doing. Their mirroring seems to reflect automated habits that escape conscious awareness rather than controlled and deliberate practices.[2] Still, from the viewpoint of T-individuals these implicit habits lead to exactly the same consequences as explicit practices: They let people perceive and receive their own doing through the eyes of others.

Declarative games. Declarative games rely on the interplay between social mirrors outside and symbolic mirrors inside. These games emerge from situations in which declarative knowledge about actions gets

---

2. On the automatic and nonconscious character of motor mimicry, see Bargh (2005, 2006); Chartrand and Bargh (1999); Chartrand and Dalton (2009). On relationships between motor mimicry and language use and the role of motor mimicry in face-to-face communication, see Bavelas (2007); Bavelas and Chovil (2006); Bavelas and Gerwing (2007).

activated on either side. Unlike procedural games that build on mutual interlocking between production and perception *of action*, declarative games build on mutual interlocking between production and perception *of communications about action*. As soon as language is in place and action talk starts working, individuals will use it—among other things—for both mirroring others and perceiving being mirrored by others (as seen from M's and T's perspective, respectively).

Let us adopt T's perspective and see what he can gain from listening to what mirror individuals have to say about his conduct. How does the information that declarative mirrors offer differ from what procedural mirrors provide? Importantly, declarative mirroring provides target individuals with richer, more elaborate and more subtle information concerning their behavior than does procedural mirroring. This is fairly obvious in several respects.

First, since action talk comprises a rich vocabulary for mental states, declarative/symbolic mirror games can address in a direct and explicit way what procedural/embodied mirroring can only convey in indirectly and implicitly. While it is certainly true that perceiving someone's actions also provides perceivers, beyond the physical kinematics of their movements, with information concerning the underlying mental dynamics, it is also true that listening to talk about those actions will deliver them a much more direct and a much richer picture of those dynamics. Action talk allows us to address in explicit terms the beliefs, desires, and intentions that action perception can at best capture in implicit terms and at a much more coarsely grained level.

Second, the conceptual framework on which action talk relies pertains not only to transient mental states but also to more permanent mental traits. Commonsense action talk often sees transient states emerging from such traits and their interaction with current environmental circumstances. Declarative mirroring can therefore always go beyond actual episodes of mental and physical action to also capture information about the agent behind those actions, that is, his mental traits and dispositions as they give rise to his behavior. In contrast, since procedural mirroring always refers to concrete episodes of transient action, it in itself has no way to capture such abstract traits.[3]

3. This is not to say that procedural mirroring can provide no information about traits. Rather, to construct permanent traits from transient states, additional processing resources and operations are required for integrating state-related information over time and across episodes.

Third, compared with procedural mirroring, declarative mirroring relies much more on indirect modes of action mirroring (like interpretation, explanation, and evaluation) than on direct modes (like reciprocation or continuation). In other words, what M mirrors back to T are her declarative comments on his actions rather than procedural embodiments of his actions. Concerning traits, M will focus on T's individual profile of mental dispositions. Concerning states, she will focus on the interaction between that profile and the specific pattern of circumstances provided by the current situation. Conversely, what T gets out of being mirrored by M is declarative knowledge about his actions and the underlying pattern of mental traits and states. Again, this is different from procedural action knowledge, which has no way of addressing mental states and traits.

Mirror Policies

How do individuals become engaged in mirror practices? Should we think of mirror games as interactions that begin automatically when two people meet? Or should we think of them as interactions that individuals strategically control? Although we have no direct empirical evidence on this issue, it may be useful to think of mirror games as being embedded in what we may call mirror policies. By this term I mean traits, states, and strategies that may govern individuals' readiness to engage and become engaged in mirror games.

We may discern two basic dimensions on which mirror policies vary. One concerns the conditions under which an individual is prone to mirror others and/or perceive being mirrored by others. As recent evidence suggests, even newborns may, at times, be prepared not only to imitate certain gestures, but even to provoke imitative responses by their caretakers. Mirroring and becoming mirrored is thus for them already controlled by their proneness to become engaged in the game.[4]

The other dimension of mirror policies concerns selectivity. Individuals may in fact be quite selective in playing mirror games. For instance, they may mirror some kinds of behaviors but not others. They may engage in mirror games under some kinds of circumstances, but not others. And, most importantly, they may be selective with respect to the target individuals whom they grant their mirroring. They may be prone to mirror certain individuals, while refusing to mirror others. For instance, they may tend

4. See Trevarthen (2005). For details on imitation provocation, see Nagy (2006); Nagy and Molnar (2004); see also ch. 4, n. 9.

to mirror their children, their parents, and perhaps their peers, but perhaps not—or to a much lesser degree—strangers, disabled individuals, or much older people. We can thus think of each mirror individual entertaining an implicit list of target individuals with whom he or she is prone to engage in mirror games and of each target individual being included in some individuals' target lists, but excluded from some other individuals' lists.

In this way, mirror policies act to induce both social assimilation and dissimilation. Assimilation is based on the dialectics of mirroring and perceiving being mirrored. Likewise, dissimilation is based on the dialectics of refusing to mirror and perceiving being refused. Importantly, mirror policies always rely on both symbolic discourses and embodied practices. In any case, embodied practices will add to the various sorts of symbolic discourses through which social relations are established and maintained in the first place.

From Others to Self

To conclude, let us once more adopt T's perspective and examine what mirror games offer for the formation of self and what the two basic kinds of mirror games contribute. Obviously, their contributions are fundamentally different. What they have in common is that they both rely on M conveying T-related information to T. This is what mirror games afford in a general sense: They create access to self-related information through the other. However, the kind of information provided is specific and deeply different for the two kinds of games.

In the one case, the information is T-related in the sense that *M's acting reflects T's acting*. Therefore, T, upon detecting that reflection, will start to perceive his own actions in and through M's actions. By looking into the procedural mirror that M provides, T will take advantage of the primary capacity for perceiving and understanding others as mental agents for the formation of the secondary capacity to perceive and understand himself as a mental agent as well. Procedural mirroring thus lays the ground for the universal structure of the mental self as a dynamic source of action.

Conversely, in the other case, the information provided by M is T-related in the sense that *M's acting reflects on T's acting*. Therefore T, upon understanding that relation, will start perceiving his own actions through the eyes of M's communications. In this setting, M takes for T the role of an observer rather than an agent. Through the observer's communication of attributions concerning his actions, T will come to understand how his own acting is governed by specific states and traits. Here, too, by attending to the declarative mirror that M provides, T capitalizes on the primary capacity to apply action talk to others for the formation of the secondary capacity to apply this talk to his own behavior as well. Declarative mirroring thus elaborates on universal structure by filling in the specific details of states, traits, and their interaction.

On this account, procedural and declarative mirrors play different though complementary roles. Procedural mirroring creates universal form by laying the ground for the mental self as a dynamical source of action. This we may call the *procedural* (aspect of) mental self. Conversely, declarative mirroring fills in specific content by implementing the logic of action talk and applying it to specific configurations of states and traits. This we may call the *declarative* (aspect of) mental self. Since the declarative self presupposes the procedural self and builds on it, the procedural self needs to be in place before declarative mirroring can become functional. Still, what they have in common is that both emerge from using others as models for self. Others come first, self comes second, and mirror games help us to derive self from others.

III Volition

Humans are social and cultural animals. Wherever they live, they establish collective normative systems for regulating individual conduct. The functioning of their social systems requires that they have ways of controlling their individual actions according to these collective regulations, thus accommodating private action to public norms. To this end, the structure and function of individual minds needs to be tailored to the requirements of collective control.

How can private action be guided by public norms? This is where the will comes in. The term *will* is an old-fashioned one that is no longer used much—neither in commonsense talk nor in psychological theories about volition and action. Still, it reflects an important concept that we cannot dispense with. When we say that individuals act voluntarily we mean to say that they choose by themselves which ends or goals to pursue and which means or actions to take for accomplishing those goals. The will enables them to set goals, keep them active, ignore or suppress competing distractions and seductions, look for opportunities to realize goals, perform appropriate actions, evaluate their outcomes, and so on.[1] Accordingly, "will" denotes a set of mental functions that play a crucial role in our understanding of how the mind works in social contexts.

Understood in this broad sense, the will comprises more than just a cognitive system for making choices. The will has not only a "cool," cognitive side, but a "hot," dynamic side as well.[2] It is often the case that we need a considerable amount of will power, for instance, for sticking to a particular choice and resisting the temptations associated with other choices, or for maintaining a particular action goal for guiding our actions

1. Over recent decades the concept of will has experienced something of a comeback in the behavioral and cognitive sciences. Its first career took place over a century ago when authorities like Ach (1905, 1910), Münsterberg (1888), and James (1890) wrote influential chapters and monographs about the workings of the will. Their writings were based mainly on an analysis of conscious experience. A century later the will has reappeared in domains like motivation, volition, and decision (Ainslie, 2001; Gollwitzer, 1990b; Gollwitzer & Bargh, 2005; Goschke, 2003; Heckhausen & Heckhausen, 2008), executive control (Baddeley, 2007; Braver & Ruge, 2006; Monsell & Driver, 2000b), social cognition (Morsella, Bargh & Gollwitzer, 2009; Ross, Spurett, Kincaid & Stephens, 2007; Wegner, 2002; Wegner & Bargh, 1998), and several others (see, e.g., Maasen, Prinz & Roth, 2003; Sebanz & Prinz, 2006).

2. Although the hot and the cool side were still close together in the early literature on the will (e.g., Ach, 1905, 1910; James, 1890; Münsterberg, 1888) they tend to be more or less dissociated in recent approaches (for exceptions, see Gollwitzer, 1990a, 1999; Goschke, 2003).

over an extended period of time. In the same vein, we find individuals differing in their capacity to invest will power for pursuing their goals— often much more than in their capacity to make appropriate choices. The craft of willing is thus the craft of both making choices and putting them into action.

Unfortunately, there is no direct route that takes us from these commonsense notions about the will to scientific approaches to volition. As already noted, present-day cognitive science does not speak much about the will anymore. This reserve may be due to two major reasons. One may be that the commonsense notion of will is rooted mainly in private mental experience (i.e., mental acts like desiring certain things or intending to do certain things), whereas scientific enquiry is rooted mainly in public performance (i.e., observable movements, actions, or action outcomes). Therefore, science will (at best) talk about goal-directed action or rule-directed task performance, but it will tend to avoid talking about things like desires, intentions, or impulses of the will.[3] The other reason may be grounded in scientists' seemingly natural appreciation of causes and effects and their deep-rooted distrust of means and ends. Science likes causality, but it dislikes finality and any kind of teleological explanations. Accordingly, psychological theories of purposeful, goal-directed behaviors have a long tradition of drawing a sharp dividing line between description and explanation. While they may allow for means–ends talk at the level of description of ongoing action, they are careful to resort to exclusive use of cause–effect talk when they switch from description to explanation. Thus, to acknowledge goals and purposes at the descriptive level for these theories does not necessarily grant them a functional role at the explanatory level.[4]

In the following chapters I outline a theory of the will. Basically, the theory considers the emergence of volition to be a matter of social construction rather than an unfolding of natural endowment. This claim

3. The neurophysiologist Benjamin Libet was a late-twentieth-century pioneer in breaking this rule. He was one of the first who dared to talk about urges or impulses of the will in the context of experimental studies on the role of conscious will in voluntary action (Libet, 1985, 1993, 1996).
4. This holds for classical association-based approaches to goal-directed action as suggested by Ach (1905, 1910), Thorndike (1911), and Tolman (1932). These theories provide causal mechanisms (leading from given circumstances to ensuing actions) to account for goal-directed performance (leading from intended circumstances to actions suited to realize them), thereby instantiating the principle of bottom-up control (see ch. 7).

applies to both transient functions and permanent structures—states and traits of the will, as it were. At the level of transient functions I will discuss functional and social foundations of intentions, plans, and rules for voluntary action. At the level of permanent structures I will discuss the functional, social, and societal roots of free will, autonomy, and self.

In fact, as will become apparent below, the making of volition is intimately intertwined with the making of the self—perhaps even in the sense that the operation of the volitional machinery is the proper function for which selves have evolved and to which they have been tailored and optimized. In this sense, the theory of the will that I am outlining here is also a theory of the self. It can be understood to instantiate a self-representational approach to subjectivity as we touched on in chapter 1. Here we spell out in some detail what it takes and means to extend a representational system into a self-representational system.

In the following chapters I take four steps to examine the workings of the will. While the first three chapters address the making of the machinery for transient volitional functions, the last chapter of Part III addresses a social construction of more permanent volitional structures. In chapter 7, I place volition and voluntary action in the broader context of action control. Here I examine both intuitions and mechanisms of control. While intuitions serve to explain how a given action follows from inferred circumstances, mechanisms serve to explain how given circumstances can generate upcoming action. I will show that both intuitions and mechanisms make a basic distinction between two explanatory strategies to account for purposeful, goal-directed action. One is to understand goal-directed action as a result of operations that are themselves entirely ignorant of anything like goals, purposes, or intentions. The other strategy takes seriously the folk notion of will and voluntary action, assuming that purposeful, goal-directed behaviors are in fact guided by explicit representations of goals. While the first strategy relies on bottom-up control, the second relies on top-down control.

In chapter 8, I turn to the roots of the will. Here I examine how top-down control can develop from, and on top of, bottom-up control. To address this issue I outline a theoretical framework that derives mechanisms from intuitions, claiming a strong role for the needs of collective control in mediating that transition. More precisely, I maintain that top-down control is first construed in the perception of foreign action (based on intuitions for explaining other individuals' actions), before it can become functional in the production of one's own action (based on mechanisms for generating one's own actions). Further, I will argue that the transition from others to self is mediated through practices of social mirroring. Once established, top-down control complements and/or replaces bottom-up control. Thus, although top-down control initially emerges as a principle for understanding foreign action, it eventually ends up as a principle for controlling one's own action.

In chapter 9, I move to crafts of the will, focusing on representational resources and mechanisms that underlie goal-directed action. Here I discuss three major levels of goal pursuit: pursuit of intentions, pursuit of plans, and pursuit of rules. While intentions link and conditionalize action realization to conditions, plans likewise link intention formation to conditions, and rules link plan formation to conditions. These crafts cover the full range of control, starting with basic action control (choice of actions for given intentions) and ending up with executive control (choice of plans for guiding future action). Still, my discussion of these crafts will not really be comprehensive. It will be limited in the sense of focusing on their "cool" representational mechanics, while more or less ignoring their "hot" volitional dynamics.

Finally, after these three steps have been taken, the concluding chapter addresses permanent volitional structure and the disquieting puzzle of autonomy and free will. In chapter 10, I examine in what ways philosophical notions of free will can be regarded as meaningful scientific concepts. Here I will argue that intuitions of free will are intimately related to intuitions of self and that these intuitions, rather than reflecting universal and naturally given properties of the mind, reflect our socially construed and socially shared sense of freedom and personhood. Having free will, I will argue, is thus certainly not a natural fact like having a nose or a heart. Free will is rather a social artifact that humans fashion for themselves and integrate in their understanding of their individual and collective identity. Yet, as I will also argue (in line with what we already discussed in chapter 3) that such social artifacts must by no means be considered fictitious or even illusory. They are as real and efficacious as natural facts are.

7 Action Control

Action Interpretation: Intuitions
  Animacy
  Agency
Action Generation: Mechanisms
  Bottom-up Control
  Top-down Control
Intuitions and Mechanisms

What are brains and minds good for? Brains and minds seem to make special contributions to their owners' fitness and their chances of survival. They furnish them with the ability to behave properly and adaptively, that is, to do the right things at the right times. Brains and minds control what animals do. In fact, we may consider action control the proper function for which nature has engineered and optimized brains and minds.

A statement like this may be uncontroversial and perhaps even trivial—at least as long as it is applied to nonhuman animals. But does it apply to humans as well? Isn't the human mind in the first place engineered for understanding the world through conscious experience? I don't think so. I rather believe that human minds and brains, too, are engineered and optimized for behavior control. Still, I submit that they have invented a particular form of action control, which I will address under the term of top-down control. As I will try to show, the machinery for top-down control builds on representational resources that derive from certain kinds of interaction and communication with others—basically the same kind of resources that we touched on earlier when we discussed the representational foundations of mental experience (ch. 1).

Accordingly, I am not going to provide a comprehensive coverage of the variety of mechanisms that contribute to human action control. Instead I will focus on those mechanisms that are often qualified as "voluntary," "cognitive," or "conscious." Obviously, these terms belong to the domain of experience rather than performance. Taken together they characterize what is sometimes addressed as the *sense of agency*. This term reflects the notion that human action originates in the agent—in her conscious deliberations and voluntary decisions. This notion is widespread in our commonsense understanding of human action and conduct as well as in philosophical reflections and psychological analyses concerning such understanding.[1]

Why should we care about such a commonsense notion in the context of scientific explanation? Why should we believe that it reflects more than what its name suggests: just a category of mental experience that stands for the intuitions people entertain concerning the origin of their actions? It is far from clear how such intuitions relate to behavioral performance and functional mechanisms. Psychological science is crowded with theories about "true" mechanisms of action control that are entirely different from the ones that our commonsense intuitions suggest (and therefore hidden behind or underneath them). For instance, it has been proposed that human action results from such diverse things as dynamics of unconscious thoughts, hidden habits, latent automatisms, or fast-and-frugal heuristics.[2] These theories claim that the official picture we entertain about the way our actions come into being may be incomplete, perhaps misleading or even illusory. The official picture is, according to them, a phenomenal cover story with little or no bearing on functional reality. At best the intuitions of volition and agency may capture what happens at the tip of the iceberg, without reflecting the bulk of the underlying operations and mechanisms working in the deep body below the surface.

By contrast, I will here take the opposite stance. I am going to defend the claim that intuitions *about* action control may acquire an important role for shaping the mechanisms *for* action control. Thus, rather than telling misleading cover stories about mechanisms, control-related intuitions must be considered efficient resources for the formation and implementation of control mechanisms.[3]

---

1. See, e.g., Barnes (2000); Russell (1996); for clinical and psychoanalytic approaches, see Frie (2008).
2. These concepts go back to such diverse authors as Freud (1922), Gigerenzer (2004, 2008), Hull (1943), and Wegner (2002).
3. A similar view has been advocated by Bogdan (1997, 2009, 2010), who argues that the theories people entertain about the workings of their minds are not just tools for description but also tools for design: theories *about minds* act like designers *for minds*.

Action Interpretation: Intuitions

To start with, let us once more examine what kinds of intuitions people resort to when they watch others' behavior. What do they perceive and understand when they witness humans or animals acting and interacting, and on what kinds of representational resources is their interpretation grounded?[4] By raising the issue of interpretation we take ongoing action for granted, asking after the antecedent conditions and underlying circumstances that drive and shape them.

Systematically speaking, the domain of action perception forms part of the broader domain of event perception. Research in that domain was initially dominated by studies of interactions between nonliving things and objects. For instance, Albert Michotte, one of the pioneers in the field, investigated how the relationship between two objects is perceived when one of them moves toward the other and then stops upon touching it, while the other one is set in motion. What observers see in a scene like this is much more than the visual stimulus that configuration has to offer by itself. They cannot help but see "through" and "behind" the kinematics of the event configuration (i.e., the spatiotemporal relationship between the motion trajectories of the two objects), the underlying dynamics of one object impacting the other and the causal relationship entailed in that impact.[5]

One of the basic conclusions suggested by such observations is that perception goes beyond the information provided by the stimulus. The stimulus configuration by itself offers nothing but visual information concerning the kinematics of the two objects—their *when* and *where*. Still, observers perceive and capture both at the same time, the pattern of the movements and the pattern of the forces that bring them forth—their *why* and *what-for*, as it were. It seems that the information contained in the stimulus specifies other kinds of information that is not itself contained in the stimulus.[6]

---

4. The term *interpretation* may be somewhat unusual in psychological theories. I use it here to stress the fact that perception (of actions and events) always relies on interactions between current stimulus information and stored knowledge for processing and categorizing that information. "Interpretation" is thus meant to stress the fact that perception is a cognitive process that goes far beyond mere transformation and representation of the information provided by current stimulation.
5. See Michotte (1946, 1963); Shipley and Zacks (2008); Thines, Costall, and Butterworth (1991).
6. The notion of specification can be used in a descriptive or in a theoretical sense. In a descriptive sense, it is used to acknowledge the fact that the observers perceive

With this lesson from the domain of nonliving events in mind, let us turn to the action domain. What makes actions special for observers? What, for them, do actions have that movements of nonliving things do not have? One of the most crucial distinctive features is that animals, unlike nonliving things, exhibit self-propelled motion. Most of their movements are not perceived as resulting from external forces that impact their bodies but rather as originating from internal forces driving them from within. Here, too, observers see the dynamics of these forces, as it were, through and behind the kinematics of the movements to which they give rise. In other words, visible kinematics specify invisible dynamics; both are perceived alongside each other.[7]

Still, this is often not yet the end of the story. What individuals get from observing others' actions will in many cases go beyond even the kinematics and dynamics of movements and also capture what we may call the *semantics* of the actions instantiated in those movements. For each token of a given action they see and understand what the point of that action is: the *why* and *what-for* it is being performed and what it is meant to lead to.

What do observers require to be in a position to perceive and understand meaningful action "behind" physical movements? Obviously they require a knowledge base with two interwoven components: action ontologies and associated models for action control. Action ontologies specify what kinds of actions exist and how they can be identified. They provide knowledge about typical kinds of ways in which individuals interact with their environment. That knowledge helps observers to parse the stream of ongoing behavior and individuate meaningful units of such interaction.[8] While action ontologies provide structural information, control models

the dynamics underlying the event in the same direct and noninferential way as they perceive the event's kinematics. In a theoretical sense, it is used to address an explanation of that perceptual experience through processing mechanisms that allow for direct specification of dynamic through kinematic information (KSD principle; see Bingham & Wickelgren, 2008; Runeson & Frykholm, 1981; Wolff, 2008).
7. This distinction is highly correlated with a distinction referring to body structure. Bodies of externally driven (nonliving) things tend to be rigid and compact, whereas bodies of internally driven (living) things tend to be flexible and articulated. Recent literature indicates that the visual and the motor brain are furnished with special devices for the detection and analysis of biological motion. These modules are tuned to respond to self-propelled motion of flexible bodies (as opposed to externally imposed movements of rigid bodies; see Heberlein, 2008; Perrett et al., 1989; Rizzolatti & Sinigaglia, 2008).
8. As we have already seen in chapter 4 such parsing may work at various levels in parallel, laying the ground for perceiving local actions embedded in more global

provide functional information. Control models specify how actions are selected and initiated and how visible action is driven by invisible physical forces and the mental intentions behind them.[9]

Action ontologies and control models lay the ground for the semantics entailed by our intuitions about action and action control. Let us take a brief look at some of these intuitions. What kinds of intuitions do people entertain about action and action control—and how does the semantics entailed by these intuitions guide and constrain their perception and interpretation of that action?[10]

For a first rough answer, we may discern two basic kinds of such intuitions, revolving around the notions of animacy and agency. Animate control is the default mode that naïve observers grant all animals and most of their behaviors. Agentive control is a more advanced mode that observers grant only a happy few of them (and only some of their behaviors) while refusing it to the great majority.[11]

actions. For instance, the local act of raising an arm may be embedded in the global act of welcoming a friend, which may, in turn, be embedded in the still more global act of coming home from a long journey, etc.

9. It should be clear that the scientific study of behavior faces exactly the same problems. Like naïve observers, scientific observers of human behavior, too, depend on principles and algorithms for parsing the stream of ongoing behavior, individuating meaningful units, and inferring control modes (see Barker, 1963; Newtson, 1976; Stränger & Hommel, 1995).

10. Here I focus on semantic content of action knowledge, leaving aside issues of acquisition and processing. Concerning acquisition, I take for granted that action knowledge builds on both universal categories that may be innate and more specific categories that may be acquired through learning and cultural socialization (see, e.g., Carey & Spelke, 1994; Csibra & Gergely, 1998; Johnson, 2000; Meltzoff & Gopnik, 1993; Woodward, Sommerville & Guajardo, 2001). Concerning processing, I take for granted that action knowledge is deeply involved in each and every act of action perception and interpretation (Malle et al., 2001).While these two issues and related controversies touch on questions concerning *how* action perception works, I will here entirely concentrate on *what* people perceive when they watch humans and animals acting.

11. One way of conceiving this distinction is in terms of the scope of the observer's implicit theory. While attribution of agency builds on the mental dynamics entailed by a theory of mind (ToM), attribution of animacy builds on the physical dynamics entailed by what we may call a theory of body (ToB). Remarkably, scientific attention is not equally distributed between the two. Agentive control and ToM have always attracted more attention than animate control and ToB. Issues of agency and agentive control have in recent years become topics of extended debates that stretch from philosophy over social science to cognitive and neuroscience. For overviews,

Animacy

A convenient way of illustrating what it means to perceive animacy and attribute animate control is to realize how we understand the behavior of relatively simple animals like flies, fish, or frogs.[12] One of the first things that we note when we watch their behavior is that they are capable of generating self-propelled motion—motion that appears to be driven by forces originating from within their bodies. As we have seen, this motor capacity makes up the primary defining feature of animacy. Further, while we watch the animal moving around we soon notice that the pattern of its movements is far from random. Instead, we see that pattern temporarily and spatially attuned to things and events in its environment. For instance, it avoids collisions with rigid objects like rocks, it alters its path when some other animal approaches it, or it stops moving altogether when a light goes on or a noise becomes louder.

Hence, we understand that, besides motor capacities, the animal must be furnished with sensory capacities that provide information about happenings in the environment—as well as capacities for mapping one to the other, that is, for steering its movements in a way that takes happenings in the environment into account. For instance, we see and understand that the frog first detects the fly and then catches it, that is, that motor activity is driven by sensory activity. We see (and say) that action follows perception: The frog catches the fly upon seeing it.

Still, this is not yet the whole story about fish, frogs, and flies. When we watch them more closely (and over a more extended period of time and/or a number of the same or similar scenarios), we start to realize that their behavior is not only determined by current environmental circumstances but by other less obvious factors as well. For instance, the frog may catch flies at some particular time of the day, whereas it may be busy with other things at other times (e.g., mating, fighting, exploring its territory). In other words, we understand the frog's behavior to be contingent not only on external factors (reflecting states of affairs in its environment) but also on internal factors (reflecting states of affairs in the animal itself). Naturally, these inner states are for us as observers less obvious and less

see Barnes (2000); Frie (2008); Grammont, Legrand, and Livet (2010); Haggard (2006); Haggard and Tsakiris (2009); Jeannerod (2006); Roessler and Eilan (2003); Ross et al. (2007); Russell (1996).

12. It should be clear that simplicity is a folk concept, not a scientific concept. These animals are not "simple" in any reasonable scientific sense. We are talking here not about a scientific account of their behavior but about our pertinent folk intuitions.

accessible than the outer states in the environment, which we share with the animal. Still, we know (and say) that the way in which action follows from perception is modulated by inner states.

In sum, when it comes to animals like flies, fish, and frogs we believe that most of their behavior is guided by current states of affairs—both in the environment and the animal itself. Accordingly, we find these animals in a sense chained to the present: The control of their behavior appears to be driven by currently given inner and outer circumstances.[13] True, they may sometimes exhibit complex patterns of well-adapted behaviors that appear to be meaningful and goal related. Still, as long as we talk about flies, fish, and frogs, we tend to regard meaningfulness and goal-directedness as categories inherent in our observation, not in the observed behavior itself. We may occasionally talk about frogs as if they were sitting in their puddle all day long, thinking about flies and how to catch them. Yet, such "as-if" talk suggests that, though we may find it funny and entertaining to think of those behaviors in terms of agentive control, we still believe that it is more appropriate to think of them in terms of animate control.[14]

Agency

Let us now move on from frogs to humans, raising the issue of agency and agentive control.[15] To whom do we grant agency, and what does it mean for observers to perceive agency and attribute agentive control to someone else? Surprisingly, there is no clear and easy answer to the first question.

13. This includes certain episodic and semantic extensions to which we turn below.
14. This may be taken as a further example of allowing for finality at the level of description while maintaining causality at the level of explanation (see the introduction to Part III. While such a splitting between description and explanation may hold for educated adults who live in modern Western cultures, it may not likewise hold for, e.g., young infants, our forebears a couple of centuries ago, or humans living in non-Western cultures. The notion that animals act as/like human agents is widespread, if not universal across human cultures.
15. Agentive control is not thought to compete with, or replace, animate control. It is rather understood to develop and operate on top of agentive control. Accordingly, there is no way to grant agentive control without, by implication, granting animate control as well (see also this ch., n. 18). Moreover, the dividing line between animacy and agency is often less clear at the descriptive level than the categorical difference at the theoretical level seems to suggest. In empirical studies, animate control and agentive control are often considered to be two poles on a continuum rather than two discrete categories (see, e.g., Gao, McCarthy & Scholl, forthcoming; Gao, Newman, & Scholl, 2009).

As a default, we grant agency to human beings. But how far should we actually go with this? This issue is being addressed in ongoing debates that span from science to politics, law, and religion. Should we also grant agency to young infants (and from what age on)? Should we cease to grant agency to patients suffering from severe dementia (and from what stage of the disease on)? Should we grant agency to some of our close relatives in the animal kingdom, for example, to chimps, primates, monkeys, or all mammals? Should we grant it to our pets? As we will see, the reason that there is no easy and unequivocal answer to these questions is not due to the notion of agency as such but rather to practical problems arising in attempts to access its basic functional ingredients and assess their efficiency for action control.

This brings us to the second question. What does agency actually entail? One way of answering this question is to take a closer look at what we may call agency talk—the way we think and talk about peoples' actions. Thinking about the actions of others is not only an individual pastime, but also one of our favorite social hobbies: Everyday conversation consists in a large measure of communicative exchanges over who does what when, why people do what they do, and what they think about the whole business.

In many cases, we explain behavior by identifying an intention to attain a specific goal. Here we have the prototypical case for voluntary action and agentive control, which we already touched on in chapter 1: We assume that a person plans an action and then executes it in order to accomplish certain objectives. We say that John washes his car because he believes that doing so will impress his aunt. While the antecedent mental state does not indicate precisely how the action is carried out, it does indicate what the specific action is for. If we were to inquire why the person did what she did, she would give us reasons—reasons that would refer to the goal that she wanted to attain.[16]

---

16. Whereas explanations of voluntary action rely on reasons, other kinds of explanations for behavior rely on the logic of causes. If someone smashes a vase in rage, common opinion holds that he or she did not do so for a reason, but that nevertheless, the action was caused: A mental state of anger is understood as causative of destructive behavior, but not as a reason for it. Such acts are understood to have no goal that performing them may attain. Habitual behavior is different from voluntary action, too, but still somewhat closer to it. If we ask people during their morning grooming routine just why they are now brushing their teeth, the answer will normally not include any immediate reason or cause. Explanations for this type of behavior normally assume that the original mental states giving rise to it occurred long ago: At one time they were present, namely, when the person acquired the

Everyday talk about behavior usually revolves not only around the explanation of action but also around evaluation and justification; we want to know the reason for an action, how to evaluate it, and finally, whether or not it is justified. On one level we judge the actions themselves, and their consequences. But on another level we also judge the person responsible for that action. We hold people responsible for their behavior and we justify doing so by assuming that they are free in their decisions to act. Agency talk goes thus hand in hand with what we may call authorship talk—talk about agents as authors of their acting as well as the freedom and autonomy entailed in that authorship.

Planning is thus the key feature of agency and agentive control. We grant individuals agency if and when we understand their behavior to be guided by intentions. Metaphorically speaking, the attribution of intentions and plans implies that we understand their behavior as *attracted/ pulled* by future desired states of affairs rather than *driven/pushed* by formerly or currently given states of affairs.

Plan-based (agentive) control thus differs from state-based (animate) control in terms of both action ontology and control mode. As pertains to ontology, agency attribution relies on two conditions, one negative and one positive. On the negative side, it is required that the observer cannot give a full account of the observed behavior just in terms of current states and circumstances. Instead, that behavior appears to be guided by mental resources that go beyond the reach of what can be captured by state-based animate control. On the positive side it is required that he or she fills this attributional vacuum with ends and intentions. Intentions refer to things and events that are not given in the current situation. More specifically, they refer to desired or intended states of affairs—to goals to be attained and the actions suited to realize them. Thus, when we attribute to individuals intentions and plans for guiding their actions, we endow them, by implication, with the ability to act on the basis of self-generated mental resources.[17]

habit at issue, but they faded as the habit gradually took hold. The reasons have not entirely disappeared and can be recalled on demand: They know why they brush their teeth, but they don't state their reasons every time they do it.

17. Importantly, the notion of agentive control implies (and actually requires) that self-generated mental resources trigger self-generated physical forces that in turn lead to self-propelled motion. Thus, from the observer's perspective, plan-based (agentive) control does not replace state-based (animate) control. Rather, as indicated above, state-based control is understood to remain in the background while plan-based control comes to the fore.

Regarding control mode, agency attribution entails the attribution of agentive control—the ability to select appropriate action as a means to achieving given ends. In this respect, too, agency is fundamentally different from animacy, which entails the attribution of animate control—the ability to select an appropriate action in response to given states of affairs.[18] Thus, when we attribute agency and agentive control to individuals, we endow them, by implication, with the talent of going back from ends to means, that is, of planning and performing actions in the service of what is meant to follow from them.

In sum, it seems that human observers are furnished with a dualistic folk ontology for action interpretation that is deeply rooted in their perceptual and conceptual categories for action and event understanding.[19] According to the animate mode of operation, actions are understood to follow from antecedent and current states of affairs. According to the agentive mode of operation, actions are understood to realize intended states

18. If it is true that intuitions differ so deeply—why do we still find it difficult to draw a line that separates the large default realm of animate control from the (presumably) much smaller realm of animals and/or behaviors that exhibit agentive on top of animate control? One reason may be that, whereas animacy can be more or less directly perceived from the surface of ongoing behavior, agency and authorship need to be derived from behind that surface in a more indirect way. Thus, unlike animacy, which refers to overt bodily behavior, agency explains overt behavior through covert mental mechanisms and dispositions. As a result, inferences concerning demarcation lines for agentive control are intrinsically ambiguous. Further, according to our folk intuitions, the demarcation line between animacy and agency is often seen to be correlated with an involvement of conscious awareness in action control. As concerns planning and agentive control, we tend to believe that individuals are aware of the plans, intentions, and goals they are pursuing, whereas with respect to animate control, we tend to believe in automatically operating processing mechanisms that may escape conscious awareness altogether. Still, even if we accept that correlation, it does not help us to find a demarcation line. Just like agentive control itself, conscious awareness is hidden under the surface of observable behavior, and criteria for granting it or not are equally opaque.

19. Fritz Heider pioneered an integrated framework for event and action perception (Heider, 1944, 1958, 1967; Heider & Simmel, 1944). Heider and Simmel (1944) were the first to show that observers attribute features like animacy and agency not only to animals and humans but also to artifacts, as shown in animate cartoons. According to Heider's theoretical framework, perceptual attribution of such features to ongoing events was understood to rely on universal Gestalt laws of perceptual and cognitive organization.

of affairs. Let us now see how these intuitions for action interpretation of foreign action relate to mechanisms for action generation.

Action Generation: Mechanisms

The concept of adaptation provides a convenient starting point for understanding what it means for animals to control their actions. Animals can only survive and successfully reproduce under certain environmental conditions. We say that they need to be adapted to their respective environments. These adaptations can be studied at two levels, that of structural dispositions and functional interactions. At the structural level, we examine how a given species' long-term dispositions match the long-term conditions in its environment. Here we speak of the species as being adapted to the environment in which it lives. At the functional level, we take that global structural match for granted and consider local functional matches between fluctuating inner states and fluctuating outer conditions. Here we speak of animals' capacity to adapt, or adapt themselves, to changes in bodily states and/or environmental conditions.

When we talk about action control, we focus on a particular kind of these local adaptations—those that involve bodily movements as a means for altering environmental conditions or bodily states.[20] For instance, bodily movements may act to modulate environmental states (e.g., removing an obstacle) or bodily states (e.g., scratching one's itching arm)—or they may act to move the whole body to a novel environmental setting (e.g., through locomotion). The movements performed in the context of such local adaptations often exhibit an intriguing feature that has fascinated and puzzled scientists and philosophers ever since: They appear to be goal-directed. The adaptive value associated with them seems not to reside in the movements themselves but in the alterations of inner and outer states achieved through them. Any sensible description of the above examples will have to take into account that the movements are performed as a means for attaining certain ends: remove the obstacle, stop the itch, find shade, and so on. Accordingly, we think and talk about these movements in terms of the goals toward which they are directed.

To put it another way, we are talking here about actions rather than movements. Actions are, roughly speaking, segments of bodily activity that converge on some goal state. For instance, when a lion chases a zebra, that

20. See Morsella (2005); Morsella, Krieger, and Bargh (2009).

action terminates when the lion eventually catches it. Likewise, when someone hammers a nail into the wall, that action terminates when the nail is eventually fixed in the wall.[21] Accordingly, actions are often more flexible and variable in terms of their initial means than their ultimate ends. The chasing or the hammering may take various forms and trajectories, and it may entail a number of more or less successful repeated attempts. Yet, to qualify as acts of catching a zebra or hammering a nail in the wall, weakly specified initial means must converge on strongly specified final ends.

So far we are still closer to intuitions than to mechanisms, and we may still wonder what intuitions about control have to tell us about mechanisms for control. For instance, should we think of goal-directedness as an intrinsic feature of the machinery for action control operating in the chasing lion and the hammering human? Should we, in other words, think that goals and goal representations play a causal role in movement selection and control? Or should we just think of it as a category of action interpretation, arising in our eyes as beholders while we watch a lion chasing or a friend hammering? Of course, these two views may also be combined, assuming that one derives from the other. For instance, if one

---

21. Assuming that action identity is grounded in action goals, we may think of individuals performing several actions simultaneously. For instance, we may think of the lion chasing a zebra as part of a larger action context in which it feeds its offspring. Likewise, we may think of the act of hammering a nail into the wall as part of the larger action context of hanging up a picture. We may, in other words, cut as many actions out of the stream of ongoing behavior as we can discern goals at which segments in that stream are directed—ranging from fine-grained/short-term goals (e.g., using the impending hit of the hammer to correct the nail's position) to coarse-grained/long-term goals (e.g., decorating a new house to which one has recently moved). Each token of bodily activity may be seen as embedded in a nested hierarchy of actions of which it forms a part. Thus, though individuals may not be capable of generating more than one coordinated movement pattern at a time, they may be performing, through these movements, several actions simultaneously. This is why there is always more than one sensible answer to the question what individuals are actually doing—not only in terms of our folk intuitions (as already discussed), but also in terms of functional mechanisms. Different answers are mapped to different levels in the hierarchy of goals and goal-related activities to which current body movements contribute. This ambiguity applies to both the acting individuals' own account of their behavior (Vallacher & Wegner, 1985, 1989; Wegner & Vallacher, 1986) and scientific approaches to sensible ways of parsing the behavior stream and individuating actions (see Barker, 1963; Newtson, 1976; Stränger & Hommel, 1995).

believes that goal-directedness is intrinsic to the machinery for action production, it may be natural to posit that it will sooner or later also emerge as a category of action perception—assuming that perception delivers veridical representations of what actually happens. In that case, the claim would be that perception follows and reflects production. As indicated in earlier chapters, I will elaborate below on the certainly less intuitive claim that the relationship in fact is the other way round, that is, that production follows and reflects perception (see ch. 8).

Yet, at this point we may leave this issue undecided and turn to core issues to be solved by mechanisms for action control: How is goal-directed action possible? How are means and ends related to each other? Which is the chicken, which is the egg? Does control proceed from means to ends or from ends to means? And how are (representations of) means and ends related to (representations of) circumstances under which the action is performed? The answers that theories of action control have to offer to these questions can be divided into two major camps: bottom-up control and top-down control. Both camps agree that actions have the potential to achieve desirable outcomes in terms of the individual's current needs and interests, but they disagree on the machinery involved. Bottom-up control posits that ends follow from means, that is, that goals are attained as the outcomes of given actions. Conversely, top-down control posits that means follow from ends, that is, that actions get selected to achieve given goals.

Bottom-up Control

The notion of bottom-up control captures the idea that goal-directedness is an emergent property of the workings of control systems whose operation itself does not draw on goals or goal representations at all. Bottom-up control posits that goal-directed behavior can be explained as a consequence of currently given states of affairs (or representations thereof), with no role being played by future intended states of affairs (or anticipatory representations thereof). This control mode thus reflects many scientists' dream to explain goal-directedness in a nonteleological manner, that is, without resorting to goals and goal representations as theoretical constructs. As mentioned above, explanatory strategies along this line have been advanced by a number of classical approaches. They have devoted much effort to explaining purposeful behavior without purposes and goal-directed action without goals.

How can this happen? A useful conceptual framework is provided by the technical metaphor entailed by the concept of control. The basic idea is simple enough. Engineers furnish technical systems with controllers. Controllers are computational devices that determine, for each configuration of current circumstances, what action to take in order to establish or maintain certain states of affairs with respect to inner and outer circumstances. Likewise, we may think of animals as furnished with controllers. Controllers determine for them, under each configuration of current inner and outer circumstances, what actions to take in order to establish or maintain satisfactory or desired inner and outer circumstances.

We may characterize these devices in terms of the output they provide, the input they require, and the algorithms on which they rely. On the output side, controllers steer bodily movements suited to modulate inner or outer conditions.[22] These movements may, for instance, act to alter environmental conditions (e.g., the frog catches a fly) or to move the body relative to the environment (e.g., it navigates around an obstacle). To perform these computations properly, controllers need to be informed, on the input side, about the configuration of current outer and inner circumstances. For instance, they need to be informed about the position of the obstacle, or the concentration of oxygen in both the water and air surrounding them and their body. Third and finally, controllers need to dispose of algorithms for input interpretation and output generation. The operation of these algorithms depends on two kinds of knowledge: event knowledge and action knowledge. Event knowledge reflects what the controller "knows" about the to-be-controlled events. Conversely, action knowledge reflects what the controller "knows" about possible actions and interactions with these events. This, then, is what controllers do: Seen from the outside, they perform certain actions, given certain events. Seen from the inside, they select and generate certain actions, given certain interpretations of ongoing events.

Basic scheme. The knowledge resources on which event interpretation and action generation draw refer to occurrences in what we may call the controller's target domain.[23] These knowledge resources act to segment the

22. We are focusing here on a subset of controllers in the brain—those that address skeletal muscles on the output side. Since the skeletomotor system serves as output system for both bottom-up and top-down control, several controllers will, at any given instant, compete for access to that system (Morsella, 2005; Morsella, Krieger & Bargh, 2009; Neumann, 1990; Neumann & Prinz, 1987).

23. The scheme I am outlining here is far from providing a full picture of what control entails and requires. Here I focus on *target knowledge*, without giving full recognition to the role of *tool knowledge*. While controllers are built and optimized for dealing with happenings in the target domain, their access to these happenings

continuous stream of occurrences in the target domain into what we may call *events*. By this term we refer to meaningful units of these occurrences as they become individuated, and in fact created, through operations that take care of parsing that continuous stream according to preexisting categories of stored knowledge.

The concept of target domain refers to the domain of occurrences that a controller addresses on the input and the output side. Accordingly, we may think of living beings like frogs, flies, or humans as assemblies of controllers operating at different levels simultaneously, each addressing a different target domain. For instance, controllers may refer to target events in the environment (an obstacle in front of me), in the body (my itching arm), or both (someone touching my shoulder). The target domain is, in other words, a domain of occurrences that are, on the one side, situated outside the controlling device itself, but are, on the other side, still within reach of its interpretation/generation devices.

What do controllers need to know about the to-be-controlled events in their target domain? To fulfill their function properly, they need to know them from two basic perspectives: how they work by themselves and how their workings can be modulated through interventions in the controllers' reach. Accordingly, we may distinguish two basic knowledge resources on which their operation draws: event knowledge to subserve interpretation

is always mediated through sensory and motor tools (as indicated by the double arrows in fig. 1.1). On the sensory side, tool knowledge refers to the relationship between features of events in the target domain and features of the information about these events as it is available on the controller's input side. Conversely, on the motor side, tool knowledge refers to the relationship between intended modulations of events in the target domain and the information for effectuating those modulations as it is issued on the controller's output side. Tool knowledge is, in other words, knowledge about the distortions and transformations of information that are inherent in the use of the sensory and motor tools. To fulfill their function properly, controllers need to be in a position to disentangle targets from tools. The information they receive and generate will always entail a blend of target- and tool-related contributions. Incoming information reflects both ongoing events in the distal target domain and ongoing transformations in the proximal tool domain. Likewise, outgoing information needs to reflect both intended modulations of distal targets and required operations of proximal tools. Mechanisms for disentangling tools and targets on both the input and the output side have been extensively studied in the domain of visual-motor coordination and adaptation (e.g., Held, 1968; Held & Hein, 1963; von Helmholtz, 1867 and 1924/1925; von Holst & Mittelstädt, 1950; for overviews see Howard & Templeton, 1966; Redding & Wallace, 1997; Rock, 1966; Welch, 1978).

of ongoing events and action knowledge to subserve generation of actions suited to modulate those events. In more functional terms, we may think of these resources as being instantiated in two memory devices, one for events and another one for actions. The event memory comprises the repertoire of target events that the controller knows at a given time. Likewise, the action memory comprises the repertoire of actions that it is capable of generating at a given time. Further, as a third element, we may think of sets of mappings between the entries in the two repertoires. These mappings specify and determine the actions to be taken in response to given events, thus bridging the gap between event interpretation and action generation.

This is certainly no more than a sketch of the basic layout of a bottom-up controller, but it helps us to understand the minimum requirements for its workings. Event interpretation relies on matching current events against the stored repertoire of discriminable events. Likewise, action generation relies on mapping the outcome of event interpretation against the stored repertoire of discriminable actions.

At first glance, this scheme looks like a simple linear sequence that leads from event interpretation to action generation, and hence from stimuli to responses. To complete the picture we need to acknowledge that these sequences are embedded in cyclical interactions between controllers and

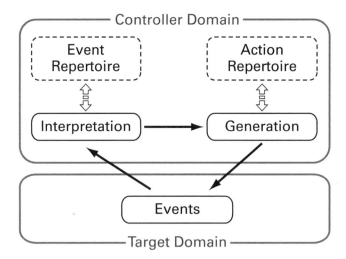

Figure 7.1
Basic scheme of the interaction between a controller and events/actions in the target domain.

target events (as indicated in figure 7.1). This is because actions alter events that in turn give rise to new cycles of interpretation and generation, and so forth. Still, within each given cycle, action generation will always depend on event interpretation and, hence, follow it.

The scheme sketched in figure 7.1 is of course far from complete.[24] It is meant to capture the abstract functional logic of bottom-up control, not the concrete anatomy of a device for instantiating that logic. In particular, I in no way mean to suggest that the controller outlined in the scheme is coextensional with a given individual's machinery for bottom-up control. The idea is not that that machinery acts as a single, coherent controller of this kind, but rather that it houses a large number of controllers whose operations follow the logic of that scheme. We may think of these controllers as individuated on the basis of kinds of target events that are subjected to control, and we may think of each of them as associated with knowledge resources for interpreting these events and for generating appropriate action.

Acquisition. Our sketch of the controller's makeup draws a sharp line between event interpretation and action generation. This may be useful for understanding how it works. However, the functional divide between the two sides is less obvious when it comes to understanding how the knowledge bases for its workings are acquired, that is, how animals learn what to do under given circumstances.

Different kinds of learning mechanisms have been proposed for answering this question—both on the ontogenetic and the phylogenetic scale. Divergent as mechanisms for individual and evolutionary learning may be, they still share the same basic functional logic—the logic of trial, error, and success. On the ontogenetic scale, learning applies to individual animals. On this scale one of the most powerful mechanisms for the acquisition of mappings between stimulus events and responding actions relies on the production of behavioral variation plus subsequent selection of those behaviors that prove to be successful. Eventually, the animal will home in on stimulus-response mappings that turn out to be successful in terms of its current needs under current conditions. On the phylogenetic scale, learning applies not to individuals but to populations and

24. For instance, for a more complete picture one needs to introduce a tool domain that houses operations mediating between the controller and the target domain (see this ch., n. 23). In the present sketch, these tools are hidden behind the oblique arrows between target events and controller operations (indicating sensory and motor tools, respectively).

their gene pools. On that scale, generations of populations may "learn," through production of genetic variation and selection, that some stimulus-response mappings are more advantageous than others and eventually come to incorporate those mappings into their genomes. Such phylogenetic learning may require hundreds or thousands of generations, but it is also based on variation, selection, and survival of the fittest mapping.[25]

Learning mechanisms thus serve to establish mappings that have proven to be successful in the past—in terms of the animals' needs or the species' fitness. At the same time they help in creating event and action knowledge. On both time scales, learning mechanisms take care of providing useful entries for the two respective knowledge repertoires. Entries are useful when they help to segment and individuate events and actions in ways that allow for successful mappings. For instance, there is no point in building a smarter (i.e., more differentiated) system for event interpretation than for action selection—or vice versa. Rather, to provide a useful basis for successful mappings, the two knowledge repertoires need to be built up in a closely coordinated manner. As a result, action generation will always put constraints on event interpretation: The depth of event interpretation will be limited by the needs of action selection.

In a nutshell, this is what bottom-up control can offer: It explains the occurrence of meaningful, goal-directed actions as a causal consequence of two kinds of factors, currently given circumstances and outcomes of previous learning (at both the ontogenetic and the phylogenetic level). The outcome of learning history is embodied in the controller's functional machinery for event interpretation and action generation. It generates actions that have previously proven to be successful under the same or similar conditions. Naturally, such actions are often meaningful and may, in many cases, look as if they were goal-directed in a literal sense, that is, guided by explicit representations of intended goal states.

Extensions. Up to now we have discussed the scheme depicted in figure 7.1 as a device for mapping entries from one repertoire to the other. Let

25. These brief remarks on ontogenetic and phylogenetic learning should be taken as mere placeholders for a far broader and deeper discussion that the topic requires. The point here is not to discuss *how* ontogenetic and phylogenetic learning work; the point is just to make clear *that* basic forms of learning can bring forth basic forms of goal-directed behaviors.

us now see what can we do to make it smarter and more flexible and, hence, more realistic. We may think of two basic measures that have been proposed by a number of psychological theories that are grounded in associationist frameworks. Both refer to the nature of the entries in the repertoires for events and actions. So far we have treated these entries as isolated and undifferentiated items. For a more realistic picture, we need to acknowledge that they are in fact richly interconnected and organized in complex episodic and semantic networks.[26]

One required extension pertains to *episodic breadth*. The picture outlined so far posits a passive controller that generates actions in response to given events. A picture like this may apply to nonvertebrates and perhaps to some lower vertebrates as well. But when it comes to higher vertebrates like mammals that depend on more flexible organization of interactions with their environment, the notion of control through passive response may no longer be sufficient. These animals require control devices for active prediction rather than mere passive response. To accomplish this, they need to be furnished with knowledge resources that go beyond the current state of affairs.

Actions and events are never isolated. They are embedded in sequences of other actions and events. To the extent that these sequences exhibit inbuilt regularities, associative learning mechanisms will capture those regularities and eventually incorporate them into the respective knowledge bases. Activation of entries in the event or action domain will therefore always go along with coactivation of a number of related entries that have either preceded it in the past or are likely to follow it in the future. Naturally, the future course of events and actions is of particular interest here. For instance, when I see a colleague approaching me in the office I may anticipate that she is going to stop and talk to me. Importantly, her stopping and talking is not contained in what I see while she is approaching me. Still, I have a way of "knowing" what is likely to happen without seeing it (and in fact before seeing it).

Thus, to the extent events and actions follow certain regularities (and the animal has learning mechanisms to capture them), event interpretation and action generation will rely on event and action episodes that look

26. The distinction between episodic and semantic knowledge is based on a widely accepted distinction between two memory systems, one dedicated to episodes of personal memories and the other to patterns of nonpersonal knowledge (see Schacter, Wagner & Buckner, 2000; Tulving, 1983).

ahead in time, rather than on isolated entries that are limited to reflecting current states of affairs.[27]

A further extension pertains to *semantic depth*. As we saw earlier, tokens of events and actions are embedded in semantic networks that place any given entry in a hierarchy of sub- and superordinate entries. For instance, my colleague may be approaching me to join me for dinner. In that case, the act of her approaching me forms part of the act of joining me for dinner. Likewise, that act may comprise a number of sub-acts, such as taking a few steps, navigating around an obstacle, and lifting one's arm to say hello. Again, we may assume that animals have learning mechanisms for capturing the relationships between various levels of grainedness for event and action representation and for building them into the structure of the pertinent knowledge bases.

As a result, any given token is now embedded not only in episodes of related tokens in the time domain but also in hierarchies of related tokens in the semantic domain. When we take both of these extensions into account, we are faced with an enriched device for bottom-up control whose operation is now based on mappings between activation patterns in episodically and semantically structured knowledge bases, not on isolated entries in unstructured repertoires. With these extensions, event interpretation relies on much broader and deeper representations of current events, providing information about a variety of episodically and semantically

27. Representations of such episodes are sometimes called *forward models*. This term is borrowed from the motor control literature where it is often used in a narrow sense, referring to the forward relationship between actions and their immediate outcomes (Jordan, 1996; Miall & Wolpert, 1996; Wolpert, Ghahramani & Jordan 1995). Taken in a broader sense, forward models may pertain to both events and actions. On the event side, they provide knowledge about possible upcoming events, given current events. On the action side, they provide knowledge about possible upcoming actions as well as possible events that may follow from ongoing action (Frith, 1992; Frith, Blakemore & Wolpert, 2000; Wolpert & Flanagan, 2001; Wolpert & Kawato, 1998). Forward models are probabilistic: As a rule, they specify not particular event trajectories but rather fanlike patterns of possible alternative trajectories. Further, they may operate on several time scales simultaneously, modeling event dynamics in the range of seconds, minutes, hours, days, etc. As a result, the controller has, at each instant, access to several forward models that specify, at various levels of grainedness, how the present state of affairs in the target domain is likely to be continued in the near and far future. In this sense, dynamic forward models provide prospective knowledge about events in the target domain (see Schütz-Bosbach & Prinz, 2007b).

related events, particularly about possible future happenings. Likewise, the knowledge base for action generation is extended in itself, providing enriched information about present and upcoming actions and their possible outcomes. As compared to the simple, unstructured repertoires with which we began, these enriched structures will allow for the operation of much more context-sensitive and flexible mapping algorithms. Accordingly, when furnished with these extensions and enrichments, bottom-up controllers may become quite powerful devices for the production of meaningful action.

Top-down Control
Bottom-up control is thus in essence a stimulus-guided affair. Bottom-up controllers select and generate actions on the basis of episodically and semantically enriched event interpretations. As a result, though everything is built from the bottom up, the outcome looks meaningful—just as if purpose and intention were residing in the acting individual and guiding its behavior. Still, we know that this impression is misleading: Purpose may perhaps reside in us as observers, but not in the individuals whose conduct we witness.

On the one hand, in the interest of explanatory parsimony, it may in fact be useful to push the limits of bottom-up control as far as possible. On the other hand, however, there is no principled reason to believe that bottom-up control is the only game in town. Top-down control may perhaps be a late arrival in the evolution of devices for action control, but in humans it is certainly in place and plays a strong if not dominant role. In fact, as I will argue below, top-down control has in humans developed on top of a preexisting smart and sophisticated machinery for bottom-up control and taken over much of its business.

Before we get there, let us first consider what the notion of top-down control entails. Top-down control posits that means follow from ends, that movements are selected and generated for the sake of goals. As we saw earlier, our commonsense intuitions of goal-directedness and voluntary action entail precisely the same claim: that goals come first and movements second, and that movements become selected as means for attaining given ends. According to these intuitions, individuals first set goals, and then and thereby come to perform movements which they know or believe to be suited to attain those goals. Since this is exactly what the technical notion of top-down control entails, we may conclude that that notion addresses in terms of mechanisms the very same functional logic that notions like agency and agentive control address in terms of intuitions.

Put somewhat paradoxically, top-down control requires that movements are selected on the basis of desired or intended circumstances—circumstances that can only be attained through (and hence after) performing those movements. Whether or not this sounds like magic depends on what we are considering: circumstances in the world (the target domain) or representations of those circumstances (in the controller). If we think in terms of states in the world, we are in fact invoking a teleological explanation according to which certain movements are performed at t_1 in order to achieve certain states of affairs at t_2. Yet, when we express the same relationship in terms of the agent's representations, the paradox goes away. At that level, certain movements are performed at t_2 in order to achieve certain states of affairs (perhaps at t_3) that are intended or desired at t_1. What we thus require at that level are representational states like intentions and desires that act as temporal and causal antecedents of the movements in question.

To build a top-down controller, we need to take two major steps that move us beyond the scheme for bottom-up control. First, we need to furnish our device with the ability to create action goals—that is, to form explicit representations of events that are independent from the configuration of currently given circumstances. Second, we need to furnish goal representations with the power to make an impact on action selection and generation. The first step concerns the implementation of dual representation, the second the implementation of the ideomotor control.

Dual representation. In a general sense, the notion of dual representation refers to the ability to maintain two parallel streams of event representations and keep them separate from each other—one for events that are currently present and another for events that are not present in the current situation. While the first stream is fed from external sources (stimulus information pertaining to the current situation), the second is mainly fed from internal sources (memory information pertaining to events beyond the current situation).

To illustrate: Consider an individual receiving a message that refers to circumstances that lie beyond his or her current perceptual horizon. To understand such a message, the individual must be capable of forming representations of circumstances that cannot be perceived at the present time. While forming these memory-based representations, he or she needs at the same time to be able to discriminate between perception- and memory-based representations and to keep them apart from each other. This is because he or she must ensure that representations from the second (memory-based) stream do not impede action control based on representations from the first (perception-based) stream. A device for dual representation thus has two major functional implications. On the one hand, it makes representational decoupling from the current situation possible, permitting "freedom from the present."[28] On the other hand, it guarantees that the stream of memory-based representations is never mixed up with the stream of perception-based representations: One is shielded from the other.

The requirement of simultaneous processing of memory-based representations alongside stimulus-based representations calls for a cognitive processing architecture that discriminates between foreground and background processing and makes it possible to process memory-based information in the foreground while simultaneously continuing to process current stimulus-based information in the background. The mode of representation coupled with this new architecture is what I label *dual representation.*[29] I understand this as the ability to maintain stimulus-based information and memory-based information in juxtaposition but separated functionally from each other.

Dual representation has two sides to it, cognitive and dynamic. The cognitive side refers to mental states like thoughts, memories, or fantasies, that is, to representations in the service of making abstract ideas and absent (or even nonexisting) things mentally present. The dynamic side, on which I focus here, refers to mental states like plans, intentions, and desires, that is, to representations in the service of effectuating desired states of affairs through action.[30]

When applied to action control, the implementation of dual representation provides the first step toward a device for top-down control. Top-down

28. Edelman (1989, p. 188). For further discussions of notions like dual representation and representational decoupling, see, e.g., Cosmides and Tooby (2000); Leslie (1987); Perner (1991); Stanovich (2004).

29. Issues pertaining to the origin of the new architecture will be repeatedly discussed in later chapters (chs. 8, 10–13). As I will also show below, dual representation is a prerequisite for symbolic communication to work, particularly with respect to message understanding. This may be taken to suggest either that language-based communication requires dual representation, or that dual representation comes for free with language-based communication (chs. 10, 13; Prinz, 2003; see also Edelman, 1989).

30. We should remind ourselves that talking about mental states does not necessarily imply talking about conscious awareness. Though notions like thoughts, fantasies, intentions, and desires certainly carry a strong mentalistic flavor, one can easily think of functionally equivalent kinds of mental states that lack conscious awareness.

controllers need to be capable of maintaining two independent streams of event episodes, one referring to given states of affairs and another referring to intended or desired states (perception- and intention-based episodes, respectively). While the first stream gets fed and updated from external resources and relies on the perception and interpretation of current events (including their episodic and semantic extensions), the second stream is entirely based on stored information resources and relies on internal construction of intentions. Thus, while perception-based episodes address ongoing and upcoming events (to which appropriate action may be responding in a bottom-up control mode), intention-based episodes address to-be-attained events (which appropriate action may make happen through top-down control).

These two streams require strict functional separation because the two kinds of episodes entail entirely different kinds of representations, one for facts and one for fiction.[31] Perceptual episodes refer to facts, that is, events that are actually happening or going to happen soon. By contrast, intention-based episodes refer to particular kinds of fictitious events, that is, events that the agent would like to make happen and would not happen without her appropriate action. Strict separation is required since mistaking fact for fiction is no less maladaptive than mistaking fiction for fact.[32]

Ideomotor control. The ideomotor principle provides the second step toward implementation of top-down control. That principle explains how goal representations contained in intentional episodes can become functional for action control.

Ideomotor theory views actions as creations of the will. The basic ideas underlying the theory were first spelled out by Rudolf Hermann Lotze and William James in the nineteenth century. According to Lotze, in order to carry out a voluntary action, two conditions must be fulfilled. First, there must be an idea or a mental image of what is being willed (*Vorstellung des Gewollten*). Second, any conflicting ideas or mental images must be removed

31. Separation between the two streams needs to be functional, but not necessarily structural. They may both share the same knowledge base, but when it comes to addressing information in that base, access to one kind of episode must occur independent from and be unconfounded with the other.
32. The first mistake is to misattribute an event that actually happens by itself to somebody's intention. The second is to misinterpret an event that is actually caused through somebody's actions as happening by itself. Both kinds of symptoms form part of various pathologies of cognition and volition (Frith, 1992).

(*Hinwegräumung aller Hemmungen*). When these two conditions are met, the mental image acquires the power to guide the movements required to realize the intention, thus converting representations in the mind into facts in the world.[33]

How should it be possible for representations of movements to awaken the actual movements to which they refer? Lotze and James both argue that these links arise from learning. Whenever a movement is performed it is accompanied by perceivable consequences, or action effects. Some are directly linked to carrying out the movement itself, such as the kinesthetic sensations that accompany each movement (so-called resident effects). Others are linked to the movement in a more indirect way since they occur in the agent's environment at a spatial and/or temporal distance from the actual movement (so-called remote effects). For example, when one's fingers operate a light switch, the light does not appear at the location of the switch but comes on at a distance. Likewise, when one throws a basketball it takes a little while before it lands in the basket—at quite a distance from the time and the location at which the throw is performed.

Ideomotor theory posits that the regularities between actual movements and their resident and remote effects are captured in associations. Representations referring to perceivable bodily and environmental movement outcomes will thus become associated with representations of those movements themselves. Once established, such associations become functional in two ways. One is that they allow individuals to anticipate certain outcomes, given certain movements or motor commands—that is, to predict perceivable consequences from given movements. This is the case of forward-directed computation in the service of bottom-up control. Second, and more importantly, they also allow for backward-directed computation in the service of top-down control—that is, to select and generate movements required to achieve given intentions. Such backward computations guarantee that events that have been learned to go along with or follow from a particular action will hereafter exhibit the power to call that action forth. Importantly, that power of representations to drive action applies to

33. James summarized these ideas in what he called the *Ideomotor Principle* of voluntary action: "*Every representation of a movement awakens in some degree the actual movement which is its object; and awakens it in a maximum degree whenever it is not kept from doing so by an antagonistic representation present simultaneously in the mind*" (James, 1890, vol. II, p. 526).

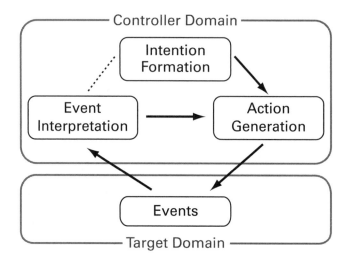

Figure 7.2
A combined scheme for sensorimotor, bottom-up control (inner loop) and ideomotor, top-down control (outer loop). Note that the inner loop is equivalent to the scheme depicted in figure 7.1.

both representations of resident, body-related action effects and representations of more remote effects in the environment.[34]

Ideomotor theory thus relies on two major principles, one for learning and another for performance. The learning principle claims that the system is capable of establishing associations between actions and their outcomes (both resident and remote). The performance principle claims that, once established, these associations can also be used in the reverse direction, that is, from outcomes to actions effectuating them.[35]

Combined scheme. The scheme depicted in figure 7.2 helps to summarize some of the ideas discussed so far. The inner loop of the scheme instanti-

34. As discussed in chapter 5, ideomotor theory claims that the perception of certain events and actions will prompt the production of similar events. Ideomotor theory thus invokes a common representational domain for perception and action, with shared resources for event perception and action planning (Hommel et al., 2001; MacKay, 1987; Prinz, 1984, 1990, 1997, in press).
35. For evidence in support of this claim, see Elsner (2000); Elsner and Hommel (2001, 2004); Koch, Keller, and Prinz (2004); Kunde (2001, 2003); Kunde, Koch, and Hoffmann (2004); Stock and Hoffmann (2002). Related evidence is provided by studies on action-outcome learning in animals and infants (de Wit et al., 2007; Dickinson, 1985, 1989; Klossek, Russell & Dickinson, 2008).

ates the functional logic of bottom-up control (as in figure 7.1). This loop starts from events in the target domain and then proceeds through event interpretation and action generation back to actions modulating those events. Likewise, the outer loop reflects the functional logic of top-down control. This loop starts in the controller domain, proceeding from intention formation through action generation to events in the target domain.

We may discern two basic readings of the scheme, depending on how we understand the thin dotted line that connects intention formation with event interpretation. One possible reading is that intention formation is grounded in event interpretation, that is, that representations of intended events derive from representations of given events. On this reading the outer loop would be closed in itself. According to the other reading, intention formation draws on sources and resources not shown in the scheme. On that reading the outer loop would not really be closed. Rather, intention formation would be attached to the inner loop as a loose end. With both readings, though, the role of intentions for control relies on their power to influence action generation. Just like event interpretation, intention formation generates input for the action-generation device.

Below we come back to the relative merits of the two readings in some detail, discussing the sources from which intentions derive and the resources on which they build (chs. 8 and 9). In any case, whatever the reading may be, the two loops share the same central machinery for action production, either for the sake of modulating given events or the sake of realizing intended events. In a sense, both loops have loose ends: Both rely on input generated from sources and resources outside the controller itself. Just as top-down control takes intentions for granted and determines actions suited to realize them, bottom-up control takes events in the target domain for granted and determines actions suited to modulate them.

What do these loose ends mean? We should certainly not see them as reflecting principled limitations of scientific enquiry. Rather they should be seen to reflect limitations of the approach we have been following so far, namely, control theory and its associated conceptual framework. Yet, although the origin of events in the world is beyond the reach of cognitive science altogether, the origin of intentions in the mind is not. On the one hand, since intentions refer to events in the world, intention formation is likely to draw on the same representational resources on which event interpretation draws as well (ch. 8). On the other hand, since intentions are grounded in needs and desires, intention formation will also draw on representational resources pertaining to motives derived from such needs and desires. Although the "hot" (i.e., motivational) side of the will goes beyond the scope of the "cool" (i.e., cognitive) approach we are taking here, we will briefly touch on these issues in chapter 8, too.

To conclude, let us see how the combined control scheme in figure 7.2 relates to the control scenarios depicted in figure 1.1. At first glance, the two sketches appear to be fairly incommensurate. Still, taking a second glance we may translate one into the other. The functional logic entailed by the first control scenario from figure 1.1 is basically captured in the bottom-up control loop of figure 7.2: controller C interacts with environment E through event interpretation and action generation (on the afferent and efferent side, respectively). Likewise, the logic entailed by the second control scenario is (at least partially) captured in the top-down loop. Since C* interacts with both E and C, it can take two routes for modulating E, direct and indirect. The direct route connects C* with E in precisely the same way as C is already connected with E. It is therefore redundant by duplicating what C is doing anyway. By contrast, the indirect route opens novel options for control. Since it connects C* with E through C, it offers the possibility to modulate C for the purpose of modulating E. That relationship between C* and C (as depicted in figure 1.1) is now captured in the relationship between ideomotor and sensorimotor control (as depicted in figure 7.2): Whereas ideomotor control modulates the operation of sensorimotor control, sensorimotor control has no way of modulating ideomotor control. As I will argue in chapter 8, the hierarchy of the two control modes may reflect the history of their making, that is, the fact that devices for top-down control have been erected on top of devices for bottom-up control.

Intuitions and Mechanisms

Much of what has been said in this chapter so far appears to be fairly redundant. The two kinds of intuitions that we have identified above seem to capture the functional logic of the two kinds of mechanisms that we have discerned, and conversely, the mechanisms seem to instantiate what the intuitions entail. As we have discussed, the most obvious interpretation of this near-to-perfect correspondence is that intuitions just reflect the operation of mechanisms in a more or less veridical way. According to this view, intuitions about control mirror mechanisms for control.

But this conclusion may be premature. When we examine more closely how intuitions and mechanisms are related to each other, we begin to see structural differences that challenge the notion of near-to-perfect correspondence. For instance, since intuitions about control must be grounded

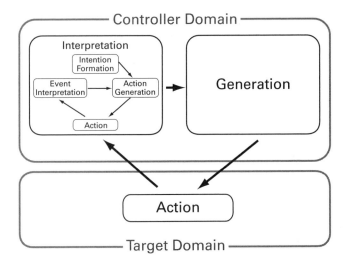

Figure 7.3
Operation of a bottom-up controller with foreign actions as target events. While the
controller itself instantiates bottom-up control (as in figure 7.1), it houses in its
interpretation device a combined scheme (as in figure 7.2) that provides action
interpretations in terms of both animate/bottom-up and agentive/top-down control.
Note that action interpretation pertains to foreign action in the controller's target
domain, whereas action generation pertains to the controller's own action (performed to modulate foreign action).

in the bottom-up directed machinery for event interpretation, it is by no
means obvious how they could reflect the workings of the top-down-
directed machinery for intention realization. The machinery for event
interpretation is tailored to the needs of understanding events in the target
domain, not to reflecting operations in the controller domain. Interpretations of ongoing events must therefore be entirely detached and independent from the way in which the controller works.

   To illustrate what this independence may imply, consider a bottom-up
controller addressing foreign actions in the target domain. Suppose that
the controller interprets these actions in terms of both bottom-up and
top-down control (as illustrated in figure 7.3), and suppose furthermore
that it generates (its own) actions suited to modulate ongoing (foreign)
actions. Since foreign actions can be interpreted in terms of both bottom-
up and top-down control, suitable modulations will not only address
environmental circumstances pushing the actions but also goals and
intentions pulling them, as it were. Accordingly, while the controller is a

bottom-up controller by itself, it may still deliver interpretations of foreign action in terms of agentive, top-down directed intuitions. Bottom-up controllers can thus deliver top-down interpretations without being capable of operating in the top-down mode by themselves.[36]

Accordingly, as figure 7.3 illustrates, the interpretation of foreign action is, in functional terms, entirely detached from the generation of one's own action. In particular, intuitions about foreign action may be richer than mechanisms for generating one's own action. This opens an interesting possibility: that mechanisms may learn from intuitions and even build on them.[37] Pursuing this possibility will now take us to the roots of the will.

36. This scenario seems to entail a strange and somewhat tricky asymmetry: If the controlling individual generates actions aiming at modulating the controlled individual's behavior through modulating his or her goals and intentions, such modulation can only be efficacious if it encounters appropriate devices for top-down control in that individual. Thus, even if the controlling individual's action relies exclusively on bottom-up control, that action can only be effective if the controlled individual operates under top-down control. I come back to this asymmetry in ch. 8.
37. A similar difference may apply to interpretations of foreign and one's own action. Unlike foreign actions, which are perceived as events in the target domain, one's own action is perceived as a tool for control of these events. As we saw earlier, tools are not treated as targets of interpretation. This asymmetry in functional status may explain why controllers (and individuals housing them) may often have richer information about foreign actions that they perceive/interpret than about their own actions that they produce/generate.

8   Roots of the Will

Let us now narrow down our focus from issues of control to issues of will. This chapter addresses the machinery of the will—its basic workings and its putative origin. By "will" I refer to the representational machinery that carries and realizes goal-directed action through intentional goal pursuit. In terms of our foregoing discussion we may think of that machinery as underlying both the sense of agency and the workings of top-down control. As we have seen in the previous chapter, these two notions are two sides of one coin: The notion of agency seems to capture, in terms of intuitions, what the notion of top-down control entails in terms of mechanisms. In this chapter I come back to the chicken-and-egg problem that I touched on above: How do the two derive from each other? Which is chicken and which is egg?[1]

Why should we bother about this question? Isn't it obvious that intuitions follow from and, hence, reflect functional mechanisms? Isn't it

1. In raising this question, I am assuming that the notions on either side are equally well grounded. In other words, I am not following the above-mentioned strategy of regarding folk intuitions about the workings of the mind as a misleading or perhaps illusory coverup story. That strategy would be in place if one believed (on some a priori grounds) that forward control is the only game in town and that top-down control does not exist.

obvious that the sense of agency reflects the operation of an inbuilt machinery for top-down control? The obvious answer may in fact apply to individuals who are already furnished with full-fledged and efficiently operating devices for top-down control. Yet, the merits of that answer are less clear when we envisage individuals whose machinery for top-down control is still in the making, such as young infants or our evolutionary ancestors 1,000, 10,000, or 100,000 generations before. When posed for early stages of ontogenetic and phylogenetic development, the hen-and-egg question may invite a different kind of answer. At those stages it is quite possible that first a sense of agency emerges as a category of action interpretation on the perception side, and only then a mechanism for top-down control starts working and taking care of action control on the production side. If so, an obvious assumption is that the building up of that production machinery makes use of representational resources that are derived from the machinery for action interpretation.

In the following I will explore this idea in more detail. My claim is that individuals indeed develop and implement top-down control from outside to inside, going from interpretation of foreign action (perception) to selection of their own action (production). First they attribute agency and agentive control to others whom they see acting, and then, upon seeing others mirroring their own actions, they appropriate agency for themselves, attributing agentive control to their own actions. Eventually, these intuitions of agency lay the foundations for mechanisms of agentive (top-down) control of their own action, thus turning perception of agency into production of goal-directed action. According to this claim, individuals become willing agents by appropriating for themselves what they have first attributed to others. The claim is that they model their own will after that of others (*me-like-you*), rather than modeling others' will after their own (as held by the mainstream view: *you-like-me*).

If this view holds, top-down control develops in individuals as a private outcome of public interaction and communication, relying on the dialectic interplay between attribution and appropriation. In one sense the claim that control in the mental domain derives from control in the social domain is far from new. As we saw in chapter 1, similar claims have occasionally been raised in philosophical, sociological, and psychological theories. However, in most of these theories such claims apply to contents, not to mechanisms of volition. For instance, they apply to ways in which individuals acquire values and norms from the public domain and appropriate them for their private mental domain. By contrast, the claim I am raising here adopts a cognitive science perspective. It pertains to the fabric of the will and the way in which each individual's private machinery of volition may emerge from his or her public interaction and communication.[2]

Collective Control

Before I elaborate on this claim in greater detail I will look at varieties of collective control. By this term I mean scenarios in which control is distributed over individuals, either in the sense that they share information that is relevant for control or in the sense that they split up control in a division of labor. Examining these scenarios will shed some light on the roots of the will in collective control. It will help us to understand the intimate relationship between the requirements of collective control and the emergence of the will as an individual device to serve them.

Sharing Control

Social animals depend on collective control. This term refers to ways in which they may modulate each other's actions. To get a grasp of what collective control may entail and what it may require in terms of individual control, let us consider a dyadic scenario in which an observer watches a target individual and tries to modulate his behavior. Let us call the observer S (*Self*) and the target individual O (*Other*). Basically, we may divide up this

2. Related claims have occasionally been raised in practical and political philosophy. Smith (1759/1976) and Hegel (1802/1967) were pioneers in discussing the possibility of a collectivist origin of the fabrics of volition, based on mutual mirroring of action and appreciation (Smith), or mutual recognition of personhood and autonomy (Hegel). Some of their ideas were later taken up by sociologists and anthropologists like Mead (1934, 1980) and Taylor (1989). While the collectivist heritage of these authorities is still alive in modern philosophical and sociological debates (Elias, 1939/2000; Foucault, 1988; Honneth, 1996; Maasen, Prinz & Roth, 2003; Maasen & Sutter, 2007; Ricoeur, 2005; Rose, 1990; Sellars, 1956), it is widely ignored by cognitive science approaches to the will. There are some exceptions, though. A few authors have discussed the notion that the functional machinery for (private) mental control may derive from mechanisms for (public) social control (e.g., Barkley, 2001; Bogdan, 2000, 2007, 2009; Carruthers, 2009; Cleeremans, 2008; Cleeremans et al., 2007; Jaynes, 1976; Olson & Kamawar, 1999; Wegner & Erber, 1993). Still, it is fair to say that these voices have so far been more or less ignored by the cognitive science community—perhaps because they have failed to provide conceptual and functional frameworks spelling out the details of the putative transition from public interaction to private control.

endeavor into two steps: interpretation and modulation. So far we have focused on individual S's representational resources for interpretation, that is, action ontologies and implied control modes—implied to be operating in individual O whose actions she is observing and interpreting. In a second step, we may now move on from interpretation to modulation, addressing the representational resources that S requires in order to control O's actions. By taking this step, we shift focus from action interpretation to action selection and execution. Importantly, we are now talking about actions that S selects and performs in order to modulate O's acting—that is, about S's control of (her own) action in the service of modulating O's (foreign) action.[3]

To illustrate what it means for individuals to share control we may think of two controllers as illustrated in figure 7.2, assuming that they operate in two individuals acting and interacting in a shared environmental setting. In a scenario like this, perhaps the most obvious way in which each individual can modulate (or perhaps manipulate) what the other is likely to do is by providing him or her with information that may be suited to modulate his or her ongoing action control. When this happens, control is shared among them in the sense that control of their own actions becomes partially dependent on information supplied by others. In such a scenario, control is no longer encapsulated in the acting individual, since it relies on information resources that are (at least partially) shared with others. By sharing that information, individuals rely on public resources for action control that may go beyond the reach of their private resources.

3. This scenario instantiates perhaps the most basic scheme for social modulation of action control. To modulate O's acting, S's controller needs to generate actions that are suited to modulate the working conditions of O's controller. The business of control is thus divided up among two individuals: O, who controls his own action (through his own controller), and S, who controls foreign action (through her own controller modulating the working conditions of the foreign controller). It should not go unnoticed that the structure of the dyadic scenario is reminiscent of the structure of the self-representational scheme outlined in figure 1.1. This scheme, too, has two controllers, one controlling environmental events (C) and another one representing and controlling C's interaction with these events (C*). In that scheme, however, the two controllers are meant to interact within, not between, individuals. The equivalence between the social scenario and the individual scheme may be taken to indicate that key features of individual volition and cognition may be related to key features of social scenarios and interaction games. This chapter elaborates on this idea for building a will; chapter 12 will return to this idea for building a self.

Shared environments. In what ways can individuals provide shared resources for modulating foreign action? One obvious option is to rely on shared environmental conditions and to modulate these conditions through instrumental action. For this option to work, the modulating individual (S) needs to know how the target individual's (O's) acting depends on current circumstances. To the extent S finds that these circumstances are also in the reach of her own actions, she will then try to alter them accordingly. Thus, in this setting S performs her actions in order to modulate the environmental conditions under which O then performs his actions. As a result, they are, at least partially, sharing environmental conditions for action control.

Shared representations. The other obvious option is to modulate action control through relying on shared representations rather than shared conditions.[4] Shared representations build on communication of pertinent information. The way in which S's communication may influence the control of O's action will be constrained by two basic factors: mode of control and mode of communication. Regarding control modes, we need to distinguish between implied animate and agentive control. Sharing animate control among individuals requires communicative exchange about current circumstances (suited to modulate action in a bottom-up manner). Conversely, sharing agentive control requires exchange about plans and intentions (suited to modulate action in a top-down manner). Regarding communication modes, we need to distinguish between embodied communication (based on production and perception of action and emotion) and symbolic communication (based on production and perception of linguistic utterances). Whereas the scope of embodied communication is more or less limited to exchange about currently given circumstances, the scope of symbolic communication is virtually unlimited and covers both given and intended circumstances.

One important way in which individuals may share control through communication is by *sharing attention.* We speak of joint or shared attention when one individual's attention gets directed to a particular target object in her environment if this happens by virtue of the fact that she

4. See, e.g., Barresi and Moore (1996); Hurley (2008); Tomasello and Herrmann (2010); Whitehead (2001). The scope of theories that address representational sharing goes far beyond the domain of control sharing. Notions such as shared reality, common ground, or shared intentionality play a key role in recent theories of social cognition. We will come back to this broader notion of representational sharing below (ch. 12).

perceives another individual's attention as directed at that object. For instance, we look at certain targets when we see others looking or pointing at them. We approach objects that we see others approaching, and likewise we stay away from things that we see others avoiding. Sharing attention and the implied sharing of interest for certain kinds of target objects is widespread among socially living mammals, particularly among social primates. Likewise, joint attention games are ubiquitous in infant–caregiver interaction, emerging at early stages in infant development.[5] From this, we may conclude that the social guidance of others' attention plays an important role in aligning individuals with respect to their current environment.

What does attention sharing do to action control? Basically, we may think of attention sharing as a means of altering the saliency profiles in the individual's representations of current environmental circumstances. These profiles will act to modulate the relative weights of current events for bottom-up control. Importantly, they will do so in a way that ensures that the follower's current profile gets aligned with the leader's profile. Still, this alignment notwithstanding, we must consider attention sharing a relatively weak form of control sharing, as it does not provide entirely new information but just restructures saliency profiles of information that is already available.

A more powerful way in which individuals may share control is through *sharing knowledge*. Unlike attention sharing, which relies on embodied communication, knowledge sharing builds on symbolic communication through language. We speak of knowledge sharing when individuals use symbolic communication in order to broaden their knowledge of currently given circumstances through aligning their own knowledge with that of others. Knowledge sharing may be particularly powerful in scenarios in which individuals complement each other's knowledge about the current situation, taking advantage of the fact that each of them has a different perspective on that situation. Consider, for instance, a scenario in which people talk about objects in a spatial layout under conditions where one of them can see certain objects that the other can't see—and vice versa. In the same vein, consider scenarios where people talk about internal circumstances like needs, moods, or emotions—about circumstances to which the others have only limited and indirect perceptual access.

5. See Call and Tomasello (2005, 2007); Mundy and Acra (2006); Mundy and Newell (2007); Sommerville and Decety (2006); Striano and Reid (2006); Tomasello (2008).

A further way of sharing control with others is to engage in *sharing interpretations.* Interpretation sharing may even apply to scenarios in which all individuals have access to the same information. Consider, for example, two individuals who consult each other on how to understand and interpret a given event in their shared environment—for example, what a third person did and why. Such an exchange may for each of them add new elements to their understanding of their current situation and, hence, to their knowledge base for control.

Knowledge and interpretation sharing thus both serve to extend the knowledge base for individual action control: They broaden the scope of what individuals know about the current situation. Communication allows each of them to combine their own with foreign knowledge and interpretations. The implications for action control are fairly obvious: Knowledge and interpretation sharing serve to enrich the database for bottom-up control and extend it beyond the reach of what each of them can perceive him- or herself. At the same time, these modes of sharing ensure that private knowledge gets aligned with public knowledge and, hence, is shared with others.

Finally, probably the most efficient way of control relies on *sharing intentions.* Intention sharing requires both agentive interpretations of foreign action and efficient top-down control of one's own action. If these two conditions are met, language-based communication about intentions and goals may serve to modulate current and future action intentions of those who perceive these communications, aligning them with goals and intentions of those who produce them.[6]

In terms of its inherent potential for modulating the actions of others, intention sharing differs substantially from knowledge and interpretation sharing, let alone attention sharing. These modes of sharing extend and align others' knowledge about current circumstances, while leaving their goals and intentions unaffected. Intention sharing, by contrast, can give rise to much deeper-going and longer-lasting modulations of the conditions of control. This is because it has the potential to alter the internal standards that drive individuals' top-down control. Intention sharing addresses their will, not their knowledge.

6. It should be clear that communicative sharing of intentions must be seen as a necessary but not a sufficient condition for aligning one's own with foreign intentions. Naturally, a vast number of other factors contribute to determine to what extent the communication of intentions will actually lead to sharing them.

Intention sharing can therefore operate in ways that are entirely detached and decoupled from current conditions. For intention sharing to work, it is not required that the involved individuals share a common scenario to which their communications refer. Intention sharing can work over large spatial and temporal distances, provided that appropriate means of communication are available. This is why communication in the interest of intention sharing is at the heart of political discourses for negotiating goals and intentions. They aim at aligning private intentions with public goals and vice versa.

Splitting Control

Sharing contents for control may often be combined with splitting functions of control in a division-of-labor mode. Again we may think of two controllers, operating in two individuals who act and interact in a shared environmental setting. While control sharing addresses scenarios in which they modulate each other's doings, splitting of control addresses scenarios in which they jointly engage in shared control loops. For instance, individuals may split up the business of bottom-up control into perception and production, one taking care of interpretation of current circumstances and the other of selection of appropriate action. Likewise, they may split up top-down control, one taking care of generating intentions and plans and the other of taking action to realize them. In a similar vein, one may think of control functions divided up among groups or even institutions rather than individuals.

Control splitting has two sides, functional and political. The functional side refers to the communication requirements entailed by function splitting: To get the business of control done, individual and institutional actors need to engage in communicative sharing of interpretations and intentions, respectively. The political side refers to the implications that splitting of control has for the formation of social roles and distribution of power at the individual and institutional levels. In regard to roles, actors need to know their respective parts in the control game and they need to commit themselves to adopting them. In regard to power, control functions are not symmetrical in the way they constrain each other. In a given control loop, interpretation and intention constrain performance, but performance does not constrain intentions and interpretations in the same way.[7] Thus, as

7. This is only true within each given control loop. In the long run—over a sequence of repeated loops—performance will of course modulate events and, hence, their related interpretations.

long as the involved actors do not take turns at these functions, splitting of control will often entail an asymmetrical splitting of power.

This is particularly obvious in the case of splitting between intention and action, both at the individual and the institutional level. This kind of splitting creates leaders and followers—those who specify intentions and plans and those who realize them. For instance, when leaders communicate action goals, their followers are expected to adopt them and eventually realize them through suitable actions. In a slightly different scenario, leaders may even specify full action plans (i.e., ends and means) and leave their execution to the followers. Thus, by splitting top-down control, actors give away part of the functional autonomy that is associated with the full business. While some of them will be more involved than others in planning and others more in performance, all of them need to accept that the game is organized in a top-down fashion. Accordingly, the loss of functional autonomy is greater for those involved in performance than for those involved in planning. Efficient control splitting may therefore not always be compatible with egalitarian forms of social interaction and organization.[8]

The Power of Intentions

It is perhaps a truism that a good deal of the evolutionary success of humans can be traced back to their extraordinary social skills. Much more so than other social animals, humans are capable of coordinating their actions through division of labor and altering that coordination on demand. They are, in other words, experts in the collective control of individual action and the communicative skills entailed in sharing and splitting control.

Sharing intentions is certainly the most important and the most powerful of these skills—particularly when sharing intentions is combined with splitting control. Sharing leads individuals to align their intentions and plans with those of others. Splitting leaves them to their own resources when it comes to realizing these intentions and plans according to given circumstances. The power of intentions thus lies in allowing individuals to combine sharing with splitting, that is, collective top-down control with individual bottom-up control.

8. Perhaps it is more telling to look at this relationship the other way around: Splitting up top-down control is a particularly efficient means for creating leaders and followers—wherever such a hierarchical kind of interaction and organization may be required or desired. In a way, then, the social distribution of power follows the social distribution of control.

Yet, to exploit this potential, individuals require devices for top-down control—devices that allow them to realize given intentions through appropriate actions. This brings us back to the roots of the will. What we have discussed up to now concerns the roots of the will in terms of ultimate explanation: *why* and *what for* the will has emerged and what adaptive function it serves. In the following section, I address the roots of the will in terms of proximate explanation: *how* it has emerged and how it serves the function of realizing intention through action.

Building a Will

A convenient way of understanding what it means for individuals to model their own will after that of others is to run through a thought experiment that aims at engineering a device for top-down control. This section will engage in such an engineering exercise for building a will. Once we have accomplished this exercise, the final section will then compare artificial will with real will.

How could we build a will? What would we require to implement top-down control in systems that initially lack that control mode? More specifically, how could we endow them with top-down control in an outside-in mode, that is, by capitalizing on their (presumably already extant) capacity to perceive and understand agentive control in foreign action for building top-down control for their own action? How, in other words, can individuals or systems proceed from the attribution of agentive control to others to the appropriation of top-down control for themselves?

I submit that there is indeed a way to align control between perception and production, adopting top-down control from perception and using it for production. Yet, such alignment cannot occur within individual systems but requires communicative interaction across two or more systems. To accomplish the alignment of production with perception, our thought experiment will require them to engage in a peculiar kind of interaction game that is fundamentally different from the collective control games considered above. These games are conservative in the sense that they take the workings of controllers for granted, combining two or more of them in scenarios of information sharing and control splitting. What is needed here instead is a novel kind of game that aims at deeper modulations that pertain to the workings of controllers themselves. The new game needs to enable individual systems to align control modes and associated architectures, not just transient representations and functions in ongoing control loops.

To design such a game, consider once more a dyadic scenario with two individuals who act, interact, and communicate. Again, the scenario begins with one individual performing actions and the other watching those actions. For the sake of convenience we may again call them S and O—Self and Other. Regarding action production, we must keep in mind that we think of the two individuals as exclusively driven by bottom-up control, lacking top-down control altogether. Yet, as we saw above, this in no way implies that action perception is likewise confined to the categories of animate control. Rather, bottom-up control in production will often generate smart and well-adapted actions in one individual that appear to exhibit agency and agentive control in another individual's perception.

Assuming that both individuals are furnished with this kind of asymmetrical architecture, they will perceive and interpret each other's doings in terms of both animate and agentive control. Importantly, this applies not only to their instrumental interactions with external events but also to communicative interactions among the two. For instance, when O points at a particular object in the environment, S will not only direct her gaze toward that object (based on bottom-up control in production) but at the same time will understand O's pointing as a goal-directed communication (based on agentive interpretation in perception). Thus, as long as we consider scenarios in which production and perception refer to different individuals and actions at a time (S and O, respectively), bottom-up control in production and agentive control in perception can coexist without conflict.[9]

9. To understand the functional foundations of that coexistence, we may return to the sketch of bottom-up control (see figure 7.1). In this scheme, the resources and mechanisms subserving bottom-up control are implemented in the production module (which takes care of action generation), while the corresponding resources for agentive control are implemented in the perception module (which takes care of action interpretation). Though both modules deal with actions, they differ fundamentally with respect to the functional roles that actions take. While the perception module deals with foreign actions as targets of interpretation, the production module generates the system's own actions as tools for control. Given that division of labor, there is no reason why top-down, agentive interpretations of target actions should be incompatible with bottom-up selection of tool actions. One's own tool action does not show up as an event in the target domain and is therefore never subject to interpretation in the same way as a foreign target action is. While the controller has explicit (declarative) knowledge of foreign action as a target, it relies on implicit (procedural) knowledge for his or her own action as a tool.

Alignment: From Other to Self

To start our engineering exercise, we need to design a novel alignment game for this dyadic scenario. The distinctive feature of the new game pertains to the content of mutual communication and perception. Crucially, in the new game, O's communications will always refer to S's actions—to the effect that S perceives and understands O's communications as communications pertaining to her own actions. The alignment game that we are engineering here is, in other words, a game of social mirroring, which we have encountered and discussed in previous chapters. At first glance, this game seems to support social functions like interindividual alignment, not individual functions like action control. Yet, with a closer look it will become apparent that interindividual alignment lays the foundations for a novel architecture for individual control.[10]

To get a clearer picture of what this game may entail in terms of action control, let us briefly consider how it works, what it requires, and what it may lead to. How can O communicate his perception of S's acting, and how can S perceive and understand that communication? Following the ideas laid out in chapter 4, we may think of their communicative interaction taking two basic forms, embodied and symbolic. For embodied communication to work, we need to endow individual O with the ability to reproduce foreign action, that is, to produce his own action that reproduces the perceived foreign action. For symbolic communication to work, we need to endow him with the ability to redescribe foreign action, that is, to produce a verbal account that redescribes foreign action. Further, in both cases we need to endow individual S with the ability to perceive and understand these communications. Importantly, this must include the ability to relate them to his own produced action, that is, to understand O's productions and descriptions as reproductions and redescriptions of his own action.

Figure 8.1 sketches the major functional ingredients of the alignment game, relying on interaction between two bottom-up controllers, S and O. While S interacts with events in the environment, O watches and interprets that interaction, aligning his own with foreign action. As a result, these aligned actions will then show up as a particular stream of events in the two controllers' shared target domain (S/O-action).

10. I am deliberately mixing languages here. While the thought experiment is meant to be an exercise in engineering, I am switching back and forth between the construction of interacting controllers and a description of the interacting individuals. Notably, talk about individuals in this section is understood to refer to functional systems, not intentional agents.

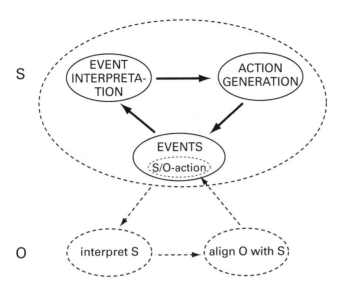

Figure 8.1
Alignment of control, with two bottom-up controllers engaging in an alignment game (S: solid lines/upper case; O: dotted lines/lower case). While S is engaged in controlling events in its target domain, O engages in interpreting S's actions and aligning his own action with S's action (*interpret S* and *align O with S*, respectively). As a result, O's aligned actions show up in the joint target domain shared by both controllers (S/O-action).

If that interaction makes up the heart of the alignment game between the two, what does it earn them? It serves to align, for each of them, their own action with foreign interpretation. Consider, for example, individual S. This individual will now, based on her perception of O's aligned action, begin to perceive her own acting in and through the other individual, that is, she begins to perceive and interpret her own action like foreign action. Thus, through the detour of her perception of O's aligned actions and communications (reflecting his interpretations of her acting), her own action becomes for S as explicitly represented as foreign action is: as a special kind of event in her target domain.[11] The alignment game turns

11. The scheme can actually be read in terms of both horizontal and vertical alignment. Horizontal alignment refers to the operation of perception and production modules within controllers. For controller O, action generation is explicitly aligned with its interpretation of controller S's action. For controller S, the alignment goes the other way: While perceiving O's aligned actions, it constructs interpretations that refer to, and are hence aligned with, its own previously generated action.

tools into targets: S's actions, which were initially generated as tools for control, may now themselves become targets of interpretation and control. The game makes it possible for her to subject her own action (or O's derivative thereof) to exactly the same action ontology and the same control models that her controllers have already acquired for interpretation of foreign action. As a result, individual S may now begin to self-attribute agency, that is, to attribute agentive control to her own doings. The alignment game lays the ground for her to understand herself as an agent, authoring own intentions and plans.

In a way, then, we have here from each individual's perspective a sequence of three major steps:[12] (i) One individual acts in a particular way; (ii) the other watches those actions and generates aligned action; and (iii) the other's aligned action is perceived and interpreted by the first individual. As a result, the game supplies individuals with interpretations of their own actions that are derived from, and hence aligned with, those provided by the other individual. It delivers them what we may consider a declarative redescription of their own action. That redescription builds declarative knowledge *about* their own action into their perception modules—on top of the already existing procedural knowledge *for* control of their own action in their production modules.[13] Importantly, such repre-

Conversely, vertical alignment refers to interpretation and generation modules across controllers. The logic of the game leads to S following O with respect to interpretation (of actions performed by S), while it leads to O following S with respect to the generation of those actions.

12. In the dyadic episodes considered so far, the two individuals take different roles in the game, adopting different perspectives on target events and actions. This asymmetry applies to single alignment episodes, but not to chains of such episodes in long-term interaction. Since individuals take turns in the two roles, they will, in the long run, both become socialized in playing the game from either perspective, S or O.

13. The notion of representational redescription goes back to Karmiloff-Smith (1992, 1994). The claim that representational redescription of procedural knowledge for action through declarative knowledge about action is based on social mirroring is not meant to imply that episodes of social mirroring are always necessary for representational redescription to occur. For initial stages, it may be true that such episodes will only lead to transient, short-lived declarative representations of tokens of one's own action. However, at later stages, after numerous such episodes have been experienced, the algorithms for event interpretation are likely to build more permanent types on top of transient tokens. When this happens, individuals will move on from perceiving states of agentive control inherent in some of their actions to perceiving traits like agency and authorship as residing in their minds. When this

sentational redescription cannot be accomplished within the confines of single closed systems but requires a detour via alignment games among two (or more) open systems.

We should not be surprised that, as a result of implementing our mirror-like alignment game, we are now facing an outcome worthy of being depicted in a cartoon: While both individuals rely themselves on bottom-up control in production, they both perceive and understand each other's production to rely (at least partially) on top-down control. Further, since they communicate that understanding to each other, they both will eventually find their bottom-up controlled actions accompanied by communications reflecting the other's interpretations of these actions in terms of top-down control. Each of them is, in other words, exposed to a running account of agentive interpretations of his or her own action.[14] Importantly, for each of them these agentive interpretations build on the other's knowledge base for interpretation of foreign action. Accordingly, when they begin to self-attribute these interpretations, they begin to align their knowledge base for self-interpretation with the other's knowledge base for other-interpretation.

Takeover: From Perception to Production

Let us now take the next step in our engineering exercise and see how such self-interpretation can help with the control of one's own action. How can we get from self-attribution of agentive control in perception/interpretation to top-down control in production/generation? Is there a way to model one after the other and use perception as a blueprint for production, empowering representational resources originating from the perception domain to take over control in the production domain?[15]

transition from states to traits occurs, representational redescription of one's own action becomes decoupled from the episodes of social mirroring on which it initially builds. See chapters 10 and 12 for further discussions of the emergence of permanent traits from transient states.

14. Since these running accounts emerge from mirror-based alignment games, they must be restricted to episodes in which such games are actually being played—at least initially. After a while, however, when individuals have appropriated the rules of those games, they may start playing similar games themselves. This may enable them to fill in the gaps between alignment episodes with episodes of self-monitoring and self-interpretation.

15. In principle, one could think of two ways of reconciling perception and production. The first option is to accommodate perception to action, that is, to model perception after production. That option would eventually end up in impoverishing

As we saw in chapter 7, building an architecture of the will requires two basic design features: dual representation and ideomotor control. Dual representation lays the ground for the capacity to generate intentions that are detached from current events. Ideomotor control reflects the capacity to realize intentions through actions. Let us see how we can derive these two constitutive features of top-down control from the representational resources for self-attribution of agentive control.

Dual representation. As we saw earlier, dual representation implies that representations of absent events (such as thoughts, beliefs, desires) can be processed independently from representations of present events (as currently perceived/interpreted). Dual representation is an indispensable design feature of any architecture of the will since top-down control can only work if intentions (referring to absent, desired states of affairs) can be strictly separated from interpretations (referring to given states of affairs). The will requires dual representation.[16]

How can we derive this feature from self-attribution of agentive control and its associated representational resources? Not much needs to be done here, since dual representation is already implicitly entailed by these resources. As attribution of agency to one's own action is assumed to rely on aligning interpretations across individuals and adopting foreign interpretations as one's own, that attribution will already imply the notion that one's own action is always driven by two sources: interpretations referring to given events and intentions pertaining to desired events.

We may therefore conclude that dual representation must already be entailed by agentive interpretation of foreign action and, by implication, by agentive interpretations of one's own action derived from them. It is

perception, because it would deprive the perception module of interpretations in terms of agentive control and have it rely exclusively on animate control. The other option is to accommodate production to perception, that is, to model production after perception. This will end up in enriching production since it endows production with top-down control. For our engineering exercise, the second option is more favorable than the first since it opens a way to transfer top-down control from perception to production.

16. Confounding the two sources of control will confuse both bottom-up and top-down control. Taking intentions for interpretations will mislead bottom-up control because intended circumstances will in that case take the role of given circumstances. Conversely, taking interpretations for intentions will mislead top-down control because in that case given circumstances will take the role of intended circumstances. To avoid such source confusions, strict functional separation between interpretations and intentions is required.

impossible for individuals to attribute agency to themselves without implying that they entertain representations of absent, intended events and keep
them separate from representations of present events. Therefore, the notion
of agentive control implies the notion of dual representation. Self-attribution of dual representation comes for free with self-attribution of agentive
control.

Ideomotor control. Finally, in order to implement ideomotor control, we
need to find a way that takes us from attribution to appropriation. We
need to enable individuals/systems to move from action interpretation to
action generation, that is, to make use of their beliefs and attributions
about the workings of their will for building a machinery that instantiates
their will.

As we have seen above, we may regard the knowledge base for agentive
control as a repertoire of action knowledge—action ontologies and associated control models for action explanation in terms of goals and implied
intentions. The device for event interpretation addresses this knowledge
base to derive intentions from actions that are currently available in the
target domain. Thus, what the knowledge base for agentive control could
in principle contribute to our endeavor of building a top-down controller
is a body of stored knowledge of mappings between given actions and their
implied goals. The only problem we need to solve is to find is a way to
make that knowledge available for action production, that is, to enable the
production machinery to exploit it for top-down control of one's own
action. Crucially, whereas agentive interpretation uses these mappings
to derive intentions from given actions, top-down control depends on
using them the other way round, that is, to derive actions from given
intentions.

To get there we need to find a way to exploit the intelligence entailed
by action perception and interpretation for the machinery of action production and generation. For that endeavor, we need to take two major
steps. The first one takes us *from interpretation to prediction* of self-generated
action. More specifically, we need to proceed from interpretation of current
action to prediction of forthcoming action. For this to work, we need to
endow our system with the capacity to acquire knowledge concerning two
kinds of sequential dependencies: current and forthcoming actions, and—
more importantly—intentions implied in current and forthcoming actions.

Both kinds of sequential dependencies are easy to acquire, since the
information on which they rely is automatically provided and comes for
free. As soon as one's own actions show up in the target domain, knowledge concerning their sequential dependencies between ongoing actions

will be automatically provided by the stream of perceptual interpretations that the device for event interpretation delivers for these actions. In principle the same applies to intentions. As soon as the individual's action stream becomes accompanied by a correlated stream of self-attributed agentive interpretations, information concerning intentions implied in given actions is as automatically provided as information concerning the actions themselves. As a result of such automatic monitoring of actions and implied intentions, we may think of the system entertaining a running account of its doings at both levels, actions and underlying intentions. Crucially that account will allow the individual to acquire sequential dependencies not only within the two streams but across the streams as well. In particular, it will allow the individual to derive forthcoming action from current intention, that is, to predict actions from intentions.

Naturally, such dependencies can only be acquired to the extent that given intentions are indeed correlated with upcoming actions. Yet, this condition will in most cases be fulfilled. Even in cases of actions resulting from pure bottom-up control, implied intentions will not only explain and postdict current (and perhaps past) action but also anticipate and predict future action. We may therefore assume that our individual is from now on endowed with the capacity to predict upcoming action from current intention.[17]

The second step takes us *from prediction to production* of self-generated action. This step is both easy and difficult. On the one hand, it is easy because the functional requirements for production coincide with those for prediction: Both require the individual to derive forthcoming action from given intention.[18] On the other hand, it is far from easy because prediction and production operate at different levels of control. Whereas action production addresses operations at the level of the controller (per-

17. The step from interpretation to prediction instantiates for our engineering exercise what we have discussed above with respect to natural controllers as extensions of episodic breadth of event interpretation.

18. Although this step may be small in terms of functional requirements, it is large and decisive in terms of conceptual implications. It takes us from description (of currents and future states of affairs) to prescription and execution (of actions to be performed in order to achieve intended states of affairs), and thus from indicative to imperative functions of representations (see Millikan, 1993, 1995). Such transitions may be commonplace in magic practices and religious beliefs that view supernatural minds endowed with the power to make thoughts real, i.e., to create things through thinking them. Functional theory, however, needs to find a way to fill the gap between description and prescription, rather than just claiming that the transition miraculously happens.

formed by the controller as a whole), action prediction addresses interpretations of these operations (represented in one of its functional components). How, then, can we enable representations of operations to generate the operations they represent?

An answer to this question can be derived from the scheme depicted in figure 7.3. In chapter 7 we introduced that scheme to illustrate a controller's ongoing interpretation of foreign action. Now, when we apply it to an alignment scenario in which the controller's own action functions as a target of control, we encounter quite a remarkable situation in which a top-down controller watches its own doings and generates both animate and agentive interpretations of its operation. In a scenario like this, the device for action interpretation mirrors what the controller is doing as a whole. The interpretation device represents and redescribes in a declarative mode what the functional architecture of the controller instantiates in a procedural mode. As far as that redescription represents and duplicates what is already instantiated in the controller's machinery, it will be redundant and of no functional use. This will be different, however, for any surplus components of the declarative redescription—that is, components representing information that has no procedural counterpart in the controller's operation mode. This applies to intentions and agentive interpretations of ongoing action. Accordingly, the stream of intentions entailed by one's own actions will offer itself as an additional, nonredundant source of information for action generation at the level of control. Intentions may thus come to switch roles: from action prediction (at the level of interpretation) to action production (at the level of control).

To close our engineering exercise, we may now approach this final and decisive step in which control is taken over by intentions. We may design this step as a gradual transition rather than a punctual event, starting from a system whose stream of actions is accompanied by a stream of interpretations and predictions. The stream of actions is controlled entirely bottom-up (at least initially), but it is accompanied by a stream of interpretations and predictions in terms of implied underlying intentions. The critical transition begins to unfold when intentions acquire the power of generating forthcoming actions, rather than just predicting them. As a first and still preliminary stage of that transition we may envisage intentions joining forces with ongoing bottom-up control, supporting the generation of actions that the production machinery is generating anyway. At a later stage we may think of intentions taking over control altogether, initiating and generating actions entirely by themselves.

When this happens the will is born. It relies on a mechanism for ideomotor control, capable of generating actions from intentions. To get there, our engineering exercise needed to go through three major steps. Going backward, we had (iii) to endow the system with intention-based production building on intention-based prediction), (ii) to derive intention-based prediction from intention-based interpretation, and (i) to ground intention-based interpretation of the system's own action in agentive interpretation of aligned foreign action as it arises from mirror-like alignment games.

Real Will

We may now close our thought experiment and abandon the engineering exercise it entails. Turning from artificial to real will, we may raise the issue of how nature and/or culture may have engineered it and to what extent its architecture builds on learning on the phylogenetic versus the ontogenetic scale. In principle we may think of the human animal going through most of these steps on the ontogenetic scale—provided, of course, that suitable conditions for learning from and through others are met. Yet, whatever the share between the two time scales may eventually turn out to be, in both cases the will can only emerge in open, interacting minds, not in closed individual minds. Through their will, individuals appropriate for themselves what others need to attribute to them in the first place.

As a matter of fact, the scenario for the social alignment of the will through which our thought experiment has taken us is, at least in some respects, less artificial and hypothetical than I have introduced it here. Naturally, that scenario was from the outset inspired by the notion of social mirroring and associated representational mechanisms and social practices—that is, mirror devices and mirror games, respectively.

When we discussed these games and devices at some length in previous chapters, we saw that their functional potential may pertain not only to reflection of transient mental states but also to construction of more permanent mental traits (see also n. 13). Scenarios in which individuals mirror their actions and/or perceive being mirrored by others may not only help them to understand their own current actions through others (reflection), but at the same time prepare them for modeling their machinery for action production after others (construction). Thus, while reflection helps them to understand themselves as agents, mirroring-based construction helps them to actually become agents.

Regarding the will, we may relate the distinction between reflection and construction to the distinction between alignment and takeover. Alignment is reflective in that it changes the way in which individuals perceive their doings. Takeover is constructive in that it leads them to model production after perception. Mirror devices and mirror games can therefore be seen to instantiate reflective alignment, but not constructive takeover. By instantiating alignment, mirroring lays the ground for takeover. However, in order to instantiate takeover we require additional mechanisms that explain how construction builds on reflection.

The roots of the will are thus grounded in mirrors and mirror games. It is tempting to reverse the argument, speculating that the evolutionary and historical roots of mirrors and mirror games are grounded in their inherent potential for the collective control of individual action. Though we have no way of testing the validity of such speculations, it is certainly fair to say that the interplay between attribution, self-attribution, and appropriation that social mirroring invites looks like a highly efficient instrument for endowing individuals with a private mechanism for action control that builds on publicly negotiated interpretations of action and action control. It is hard to think of a more powerful instrument for modeling the privacy of individual minds after public interests of collective minds.

One way of looking at the hypothetical scenario that we have passed through is as a scenario for modeling an inner agent after outer agents. Are we here invoking a homunculus? Are we explaining the will through a little man in the head to whom we attribute intentions and plans? While this is true in the sense that we posit that our own individual wills build on the will of others with whom we interact, it is not true in terms of the explanatory role that theories of cognition, volition, and action sometimes attribute to the homunculus. Invoking a homunculus is for them tantamount to waiving further explanation: The homunculus is meant to explain an individual's actions, without its own actions being explained in turn. This is why it has fallen in disrepute and why science has tried to banish it: It shifts the burden of explanation from outer man to inner man, without explaining how the inner man works.[19] Yet, such a critique does not apply to the will as our theory has construed it. Rather than taking the will for granted, it seeks to explain how it is formed and shaped through interaction and communication with others. Instead of deriving outer man from inner man, it undertakes to derive inner wo/man from outer wo/men—that is, self from others.

19. On banishing the homunculus, see Monsell and Driver (2000a). The term "inner man" and the discussion of the role of the homunculus for action explanation is borrowed from Skinner's sarcastic remarks on notions like autonomy and free will that we have already touched on in the prologue (Skinner, 1972). (Female counterparts to *homunculus* or *inner man* are not offered in the literature.)

9 Crafts of the Will

Once the will is in place, individuals become capable of generating actions suited to realize given intentions. To begin to understand the adaptive potential of that mechanism, we need to examine how it works in more natural scenarios and on what kinds of representational resources it draws.[1]

One issue we need to address concerns the origin of intentions. Our scenario for the roots of the will has so far focused on intentions that are conservative in the sense of initially building on interpretations of actions that are already happening. It first construes intentions as indicative accounts of ongoing action before it then converts them into imperative instructions for forthcoming action. Now, to understand the workings of the will in more natural settings, we need to consider to scenarios in which action control starts with intentions that are entirely unrelated to actions that are being performed and observed. How can independent intentions be formed? Where do they come from and how do they get implemented?

A further issue concerns the realization of intention through action. It is fairly obvious that action needs to be appropriate not only in terms of realizing the intention driving it but also in terms of matching the actual circumstances under which it is being performed. Thus, in order to be successful in terms of generating appropriate action, top-down control needs

---

1. This chapter will again focus on the "cool," cognitive underpinnings of volition, and only marginally touch on its "hot," dynamic sources.

to combine forces with bottom-up control. Successful action needs to satisfy both what intentions of desired circumstances require and what interpretations of current circumstances suggest.

Here I examine these issues at several different levels of control. First I turn to the most basic level, considering the fundamental craft of controlling actions through given intentions. Then I turn to higher-level crafts of control like controlling intentions through plans and controlling plans through rules. As will become apparent, these crafts and their underlying representational resources, though they need to be instantiated in individual minds, are always deeply embedded in social practices and discourses. Individuals share these crafts with others and adopt them from others, thus aligning their own intentions and actions with those of others.

Pursuing Intentions

To illustrate what it means to pursue an intention, we may consider performance in a simple reaction time task that Frans Cornelius Donders, one of the major nineteenth-century pioneers of mental chronometry, called an *a-type* response task.[2] This task requires the participant to perform a certain predefined action (e.g., operating a light switch) in response to a certain predefined stimulus (e.g., a tone). Obviously, a task like this is easy to perform. It requires no more than detecting the occurrence of the stimulus and triggering the predefined action. Unlike other kinds of tasks, to which we turn below, the a-type task involves no more than one particular stimulus and one particular response. Performing it does not therefore require the individual to identify the stimulus (i.e., as a particular one out of several possible ones) but just to detect its occurrence. Likewise it does not require the individual to select a response (i.e., a particular one out of several possible ones) but just to trigger it.

Simple as it may be, the a-type task illustrates what it means to pursue an intention. Consider the participant while she is waiting for the next occurrence of the stimulus. At that time she is in the functional situation of maintaining the intention of switching on the light (intended event) upon occurrence of the stimulus (occasion). At the moment the stimulus is presented, she realizes that intention through operating the switch (appropriate action). Thus, to understand how this can happen, we must assume that the intention contains representations of three elements: the intended event, the appropriate action, and the occasion for triggering the action.

2. See Donders (1868/1969).

Whereas these things happen as the intention is actively maintained, other things must have happened when the intention was implemented in the first place. In psychological experiments, intention implementation occurs through listening to experimental instructions, understanding what they entail, and appropriating what they require. The social setting of participating in an experiment implies that the experimenter instructs the participant how to perform the task and that the participant tries to follow that instruction. Accordingly, the participant adopts the intentions that the experimenter shares with her through instructions. Thus, while the participant appropriates foreign intentions, the experimenter (or whoever has designed the experiment) has created those intentions in the first place.

Implementation

Where do intentions come from and how do they get implemented? Let us first see what it takes to create intentions by oneself before we then turn to social games for intention sharing and intention induction across individuals.

Creating one's own intentions. Top-down controllers are devices for generating actions that realize given intentions. They take intentions for granted, without explaining how they emerge. What do individuals require to create their own intentions, that is, representations of intended or desired states of affairs? To answer this question, we need to take a closer look at the relationship between intention formation and event interpretation. So far we have stressed their functional difference and the need for distinguishing them: Whereas interpretations refer to given events and lead to actions that alter them, intentions refer to desired events and lead to actions that realize them. Still, what they have in common is that they both refer to events in the target domains of their respective controllers. Accordingly, despite their functional separation they need to draw on common representational resources. If it is true that top-down control has evolved after and on top of bottom-up control, the formation of intentions is likely to draw on representational resources that are provided by the machinery for event interpretation. Based on these resources, intention may be created in two basic modes: by externally driven anticipation and internally driven construction.

As we saw, the machinery for event interpretation not only provides perception-based interpretations of current circumstances but also delivers certain extensions of these circumstances into the future—*anticipations* of possible future events that serve to increase the breadth of the episodes that enter interpretation. Suppose that the system is sophisticated enough to create, for each current situation, not only a single forward-directed event trajectory, but a fan of alternative trajectories that may arise from the current situation. However, these alternative trajectories will be of limited use, as far as bottom-up control is concerned. In that context we may perhaps see their function in preparing the controller for upcoming action, but not in contributing to action selection in response to the current situation. This is because responses to current circumstances must always rely on unequivocal interpretations of ongoing events, ignoring possible future extensions altogether.

Still, such fans of alternative trajectories can play a major role for top-down control, offering themselves as representational resources for creating intentions. They qualify for that function for two reasons. One is that events on these trajectories stand for possible future events, given the current configuration of events. They are, in other words, possible and realistic extrapolations from the current situation. The other is that, because of their origin in event interpretation, they will automatically become evaluated in terms of current needs, desires, and so on. Still, in the context of bottom-up control, they can only be used as more or less realistic anticipations of more or less desirable events in the near or far future—events that help the controller to prepare for possible future actions in response to these events. In no way does that machinery enable them to generate action to realize them. To make this possible they need to be accessed by the machinery for top-down control. Here they adopt a new functional status, switching from anticipations to intentions, that is, from representations of future possible events to representations of future intended events. Their new status empowers them to realize these events through appropriate action.

As discussed above, the scope of intentions that can be created this way is limited by the scope of the fans of event trajectories from which they are derived. Limitations will concern both content and distance. Content is limited in that these fans always depart from the event configuration that is currently given; thus all events on their trajectories will be related to, and derive from, current events. At the same time, distance will be limited since, given the combinatorial explosion of alternative trajectories, efficient prediction will become increasingly poorer as distance increases. Yet, these limitations notwithstanding, individuals will learn to generate such fans of event trajectories, exploiting them as a representational resource for creating intentions.

Intention formation through internally driven *construction* is not limited in this way. Whereas the anticipatory mode of intention creation starts from possible future events that it evaluates in terms of needs and desires, the constructive mode takes the reverse course, starting from needs and desires and constructing event trajectories suited to match them. Although this mode of intention formation is entirely detached from current circumstances and future extensions, it also has to determine events and event trajectories in the target domain and is therefore dependent on the controller's representational resources for event interpretation. The crucial difference, though, is that intention formation in this case starts not from the domain of external events but from the domain of internal needs and desires. This brings us again in touch with the hot side of the will—the side that we are leaving out of detailed consideration here.[3]

Adopting foreign intentions. Adopting intentions from others may often be a simpler and less demanding way of implementing intentions than creating them by oneself. As we have already discussed, much of the adaptive value of intentions for action control derives from the ease with which they can be shared with and hence adopted from others.

Intentions can be shared in explicit and in implicit modes. The explicit mode is illustrated by instruction scenarios. In these scenarios individuals communicate to make sure that one adopts certain intentions from the other, to the effect of adopting and implementing foreign intention for the control of their own action. As noted above, they share the explicit understanding that both their current communication and the social setting in which it is embedded aim at ensuring that the instructee appropriates the intentions that the instructor is attributing to her.[4] Implicit modes of sharing intentions and adopting them from others are perhaps an even more important means for intention induction across individuals. Implicit intention sharing applies to scenarios in which individuals

3. For overviews of classical theories of motivation and the history of the field, see, e.g., Aarts and Elliot (2011); Atkinson (1964); Gollwitzer and Bargh (1996); Gollwitzer and Moskowitz (1996); Heckhausen (2008); Heckhausen and Heckhausen (2008); Kruglanski et al. (2002). According to textbook systematics, the formation and evaluation of goals and intentions is often considered a matter of *motivation* whereas the realization of intentions through actions is considered a matter of *volition* (see, e.g., Achtziger & Gollwitzer, 2008; Heckhausen & Gollwitzer, 1987).

4. Importantly, this applies not only to symbolic communication but to embodied communication as well; see, e.g., Csibra and Gergely (2006); Gergely and Csibra (2005); Hassin et al. (2009).

adopt intentions from others (or modulate their own according to foreign intentions), without being aware of this at all. For instance, they may come to implement or modulate their own intentions just through watching what others are doing, listening to how they explain their actions, and so on.

Over recent decades, the enormous power of implicit intention induction has become apparent in a growing literature on so-called priming effects of social stimuli. Studies from this literature have repeatedly demonstrated that people tend to adopt intentions from others or accommodate their own to implied foreign intentions without being aware of it. Such priming effects have been shown to occur in a broad variety of social settings and in response to a broad variety of social stimuli or communications pertaining to such stimuli.[5] We may take these observations to suggest that our minds are open to other minds to a much larger degree than our folk intuitions would suggest. Although we continue to believe that we create our intentions in controlled and explicit acts of individual deliberation, we need to acknowledge that intention formation is in fact highly susceptible to automatic and implicit ways of social induction.

Realization

To get an idea of what it means to realize an intention, we may return to our simple reaction task of operating a switch to turn on a light. Here the intention is realized through operating the switch (as quickly as possible) whenever the stimulus tone comes up. What does it take to realize an intention like this? Consider first the intention itself. What does it entail? On the one hand, it must, of course, refer to the intended event (*a light going on*). On the other hand, the intention needs to be associated with two other pieces of knowledge, one referring to actions suited to realize it (*operating the switch*), the other referring to occasions for performing it (*an upcoming tone*).

This is as far as the information contained in the intention goes. But what does it take to actually operate a light switch? When we take a closer look at the action itself, it becomes apparent that it requires a full-fledged interpretation of certain kinds of currently given events and circumstances. The notion of operating a light switch is in itself an abstract action concept that cannot be realized as such. To be realized, it needs to be instantiated

---

5. For overviews, see Aarts, Gollwitzer, and Hassin (2004); Aarts and Hassin (2005); Bargh (1989, 1990, 2005, 2006); Dijksterhuis and Nordgren (2006); Hassin et al. (2009); Shah (2005).

through concrete movements whose spatial and temporal configuration needs to be attuned to the concrete circumstances in each current situation. To perform the action properly, the controller needs to "know" where the switch is, where the operating hand is relative to the switch, what the current positions of the relevant fingers are, what forces are required to move the switch, and so on. Thus, to be successful in terms of realization, top-down control needs to engage a mechanism for bottom-up control. In this particular example, top-down control determines *what* to do, while bottom-up control determines *how* to realize that action in the current circumstances.

The need for such interaction becomes even more obvious when we consider more complex scenarios. For instance, what does it take to pursue and realize the intention of visiting a friend? That abstract intention as such will not be in a position to effectuate appropriate action. What it may generate instead is a set of options for realization (e.g., taking a walk, driving by car, taking a bus). One obvious way of narrowing these options down is by matching them against the current situation and selecting the one for realization that is particularly easy to perform in the given circumstances.

We may think of these operations as working simultaneously at several levels of action control. At each level, intentions generate options for realization, and interpretations select among these options according to given circumstances. Accordingly, intentions and interpretations jointly select, at each given level, what concrete actions to take in order to realize more abstract intentions. Abstract intentions thus become instantiated through increasingly concrete actions. Eventually, this stepwise instantiation reaches the bottom of the hierarchy, where the action becomes realized through concrete body movements—those movements that are suited to realize the hierarchy of given intentions under the conditions of the given circumstances.

According to this view, realization of intentions requires a complex mechanism for multiple constraint satisfaction that operates simultaneously at various levels of action representation.[6] The action chosen must, at each level, satisfy the needs of both the intention driving it and the configuration of current events constraining it. On the one hand, the mechanism guarantees that abstract initial intentions are translated into increasingly concrete intentions and their associated actions. On the other hand, it guarantees that the choice of intentions and actions takes into

6. See, e.g., Goschke (2003); O'Reilley, Braver, and Cohen (1999).

account currently given circumstances. Production of top-down controlled action is thus always constrained by both intentions, referring to desired events, and interpretations, referring to given events.

Pursuing Plans and Rules

Let us now take a look at more sophisticated crafts of the will—crafts that go beyond the reach of mere intentions. Our discussion so far has mainly focused on local intentions, without taking into consideration the more global contexts in which they may be embedded. When we do so, we begin to see that the craft of pursuing intentions is embedded in the higher-order craft of pursuing plans—which may in turn be embedded in the still higher-order craft of pursuing rules.

Thus, to get a full picture of the crafts of the will, we need to move on from local control structures like goals and intentions to global structures like plans and rules. At the basic level, intentions serve as control structures for action realization. At higher levels, plans serve as control structures for intention formation—and rules as control structures for plan formation.[7] As will become apparent below, these higher-order crafts of volition serve two major functions. At the individual level, they provide routines for delegating much of the control of intention formation to public environmental circumstances, thus relieving the agent from the burden of creating intentions from his or her private resources. At the collective level, they provide routines for communicating and coordinating representational resources for intention formation across individuals, thereby laying the ground for aligning individual and private willings with collective and public interests.

Plans for Intentions

Though concepts of plans and planning are common and widespread in theories of movement and action control, it is not clear what the common

7. On the one hand, the terminology chosen here may appear to be somewhat arbitrary and idiosyncratic, particularly since there is no principled reason to posit just two higher levels of control, and not more. Still, on the other hand, the distinction between plans and rules captures the gist of related distinctions in the literature. For instance, it may be seen to be equivalent to the distinction between voluntary and cognitive/executive control of action, or between first-order control (of intentions through plans) and higher-order control (of plans through rules). Similar proposals are also entailed by metarepresentational approaches to executive control (see, e.g., Fernandez-Duque, Baird & Posner, 2000; Norman & Shallice, 1980, 1986).

denominator of their various uses may be.[8] Plans, as I use the term here, are representational structures subserving the control of intention formation. Plans specify, in other words, what intentions to form under what conditions. In the same way as intentions serve to conditionalize the realization of ongoing actions to current circumstances, plans serve to conditionalize the formation of ongoing intentions to current conditions.

According to this notion, pursuing a plan is tantamount to delegating the control of intention formation to external events. Plans thus link intention formation to event interpretation. Relying on these prespecified links relieves the individual from the requirement of creating or adopting local intentions by herself. Plans tell her what to do and when to do it.

Plans may be characterized from two perspectives, cross-sectional and longitudinal. The cross-sectional perspective considers how plans subserve event-related intention formation. To illustrate what it means to pursue a plan we may consider performance in the Donders *b-type* task. This task requires the participant to perform certain predefined actions (e.g., pressing different response keys) in response to certain predefined stimuli (e.g., tones of different pitch). Obviously, a task like this is more complex than the a-type task discussed above. Since more than one stimulus and one response are involved, the task requires the participant (i) to identify this stimulus (as a particular one out of several possible ones) and (ii) to select the appropriate response (a particular one out of several possible ones). Performing the task presupposes, of course, that the mapping of responses to stimuli is prespecified in the instruction (if *pitch=1*, then *press key a*; if *pitch=2*, then *press key b* . . .). Once the set of these mappings has been acquired by the participant, it acts as a plan: It specifies which action intention to form (i.e., which key to press) under current environmental conditions (i.e., the tone of a given pitch). The plan thus specifies what to do, and it ensures that the appropriate intention is formed in an event-related way. It delegates the formation of the action intention to the stimulus event.

The longitudinal perspective captures more directly our commonsense intuitions of plans and planning. It considers how plans contribute to event-related formation of intentions over time. On this perspective, sequential dependencies become apparent, that is, that outcomes of earlier actions may constrain and determine the conditions for the formation

---

8. Though the term "plan" is widely used in a descriptive sense, it is seldom used in a well-defined theoretical sense (see, e.g., Gollwitzer, 1990b; Hayes-Roth & Hayes-Roth, 1988; Logan, 2009; Miller, Galanter & Pribram, 1960).

of intentions for later actions. Such sequential dependencies do not require any further explanatory principles. They just follow from the basic assumption that plans serve to conditionalize intention formation to current circumstances. If this assumption holds, sequential dependencies of subsequent actions will arise to the extent that current circumstances depend on foregoing actions and underlying intentions. The "intelligence" that plans exhibit when viewed from the longitudinal perspective is thus a natural consequence of their basic makeup as we see it from the cross-sectional perspective: Plans tell individuals what kinds of intentions and actions may be appropriate when certain kinds of events happen.

To understand how plans are implemented, we need not go far beyond what we have already discussed with respect to intention formation. Intentions are formed when representations of expected events turn into representations of desired events, furnished with the power to realize those events through appropriate action. There are two problems here: intention formation and plan formation. Intention formation addresses the issue of *how* intentions are created and what kind of functional machinery their creation requires. Plan formation addresses the issue of *what* information gets selected for that conversion and on what representational basis that selection is performed. Thus, while intention formation is concerned with mechanisms, plan formation is concerned with contents.

Like intentions, plans can be acquired by the agent herself, or adopted from others. Without going into any detail we may discern three major kinds of mechanisms for plan formation: learning, observation, and communication.

Learning. Perhaps the most basic form of plan acquisition is through instrumental learning. According to the classical interpretation of instrumental learning paradigms, organisms learn to conditionalize their responses to stimuli. They come to establish links between stimuli and responses, dependent on the extent to which these links have proven to be beneficial in their learning history (in the sense of leading to desirable consequences, or reinforcements).

As has often been shown, the classical reading can be replaced by post-classical, more cognitive readings. One particularly attractive alternative framework is to conceptualize instrumental learning in terms of event representations.[9] As indicated above, we may assume that individuals create, for each current situation, a fan of alternative trajectories that may arise from that situation. This step takes us from interpretation of current

9. See, e.g., Pearce (1997); Rescorla (1998); Rescorla and Wagner (1972).

events to prediction of possible future events. If we further assume that events on these alternative trajectories are automatically evaluated in terms of the individuals' needs and desires, we may think of that machinery as a device for providing plans. That step takes us from prediction of possible events to planning of desired events that are based on previously acquired knowledge about event trajectories and their evaluations.

A device like this provides, for each current event, a profile of evaluated predictions of possible future events. This profile then serves as a basis for both plan formation (i.e., selection of the preferred option) and intention formation (i.e., conversion of prediction into intention). Accordingly, what the classical framework considers a response to a given stimulus is now considered an action, aiming at accomplishing certain goal states under given conditions.

Observation. Plans may be acquired not only through instrumental learning but also through observation and reenactment of other individuals' behavior. At first glance, this may appear to be a natural and seemingly simple means of plan acquisition. Still it requires a sophisticated machinery for action perception and production. Critically, it requires two basic capacities: the ability to derive hidden plans from observable actions (in others) and the ability to adopt and reenact these plans (in and for oneself).

Deriving hidden plans from observed action in turn requires two elementary skills. First, the observer needs to be in a position to individuate meaningful action segments in the observee's stream of activity—segments that are individuated and specified in terms of their implied goals and underlying intentions. Second, he or she needs to be in a position to understand how these intentions depend on the circumstances under which the observee is currently acting.

When these two skills are combined they put the observer in a position to be able to derive hidden plans from observed actions. He or she then understands both the intention underlying the action and the circumstances giving rise to the formation of the intention. Complex as this combined skill may be, it still does not necessarily require a high-level mechanism for abstract thought and inferential reasoning. As we have seen in previous chapters, it may rather emerge from the workings of a dedicated mechanism for action interpretation that seems to form part of the natural endowment with which humans (and perhaps some other primates, too) are furnished from birth onward.

The same applies to the capacity for reenactment, that is, of adopting foreign action plans for the formation of one's own intentions and actions. If it is true that the roots of the will are grounded in action perception and understanding, it is natural to believe that representational resources are shared between interpretation and control. Hence, no explanatory gap is left between understanding plans as operating in others and using plans for oneself.

We may therefore conclude that humans—and perhaps some other primates—from very early stages in their lives onward, are furnished with a dedicated machinery that allows them to adopt action plans from others through observing their actions. Obviously, a skill like this opens individual minds to collective cultural experience. Junior and/or less competent individuals may learn from senior and/or more competent individuals what is appropriate to do in certain circumstances. As has been pointed out in various scenarios for human cultural evolution, intergenerational transfer of cultural knowledge and experience may largely be grounded in such mimetic practices. Such practices seem to play an important role not only in transfer of technical and instrumental knowledge but in social and normative knowledge as well (know-how and know-what, respectively).[10]

Communication. Let us move on from embodied practice to symbolic discourse. Besides observing others, people talk and listen to others. In doing so, they make ample use of verbal communication for sharing their interpretations, intentions, and plans. As we have already seen in chapter 2, such communication requires not only a system of shared expressions in the linguistic domain, but also a system of shared representations in the conceptual domain. It requires, in other words, shared concepts for actions, intentions, and plans. Taking these requirements for granted and assuming that language-based communication is in place, we may examine in what ways verbal communication can contribute to plan formation and plan acquisition in individuals.[11]

The first contribution comes from the conceptual framework itself. Verbal discourse about actions, intentions, and plans does not only *require* shared conceptual resources for that domain but at the same time *provides* those resources to individuals, helping to shape them and align

10. This is not only true for intergenerational transfer on the time scale of human evolution (Donald, 2001), but may also apply to pedagogical interactions on the time scale of ontogenetic development (Csibra & Gergely, 2006).
11. For the present scenario, I take language for granted and examine what it does to the will. This should not be taken to be the last word on the relationship between language and volition. Below I will outline a broader scenario, invoking the claim that language-based communication has emerged as a tool in the service of collective control of individual action (rather than simply having fallen from heaven and then helped with building the will). I will return to these issues in chapter 13.

them with those of others. As a result, each individual who participates in that discourse will eventually make use of a socially shared framework of concepts for the description, evaluation, and interpretation of actions, intentions, and plans. Once established, that framework is likely to subserve any mode of plan formation, be it through learning, observation, or communication.[12]

Further, more specific contributions come from the use of that framework in concrete episodes of communication. Here we may distinguish between descriptive and prescriptive uses and episodes. While descriptive episodes aim at sharing action interpretation, prescriptive episodes aim at sharing control.

Descriptive communication typically revolves around interpretation of past and present action as well as prediction of forthcoming actions. From a given individual's point of view we may discern various kinds of scenarios. For instance, individual A may talk to B about A's actions, B's actions, or C's (somebody else's) actions. Likewise, A may listen to B talking about A's, B's, or C's actions. Different as these scenarios may be in terms of their functional demands, they have one crucial feature in common: They allow both individuals to match observable actions against verbal accounts of those actions—and vice versa. By comparing and aligning their interpretations and evaluations, individuals share private (= hidden) plans for public (= observable) actions, thus making plans available to public discourse.

Once established, this discourse provides participants with a wealth of socially shared resources for individual plan formation. These resources tell them what actions are reasonable in given circumstances—reasonable in terms of both instrumental success and social norms. While they may sometimes offer a rich choice of options for planning, they may at other times put heavy instrumental and social constraints on those options and the degrees of freedom associated with them. In any case, individuals will have a hard time ignoring the suggestive guidance of public discourse for action planning.

---

12. It is sometimes claimed that learning and observation may rely on more primitive representational resources than does symbolic communication (i.e., on noninferential operations that draw on pre- or subconceptual resources; see, e.g., Goldman, 2002; Proust, 2002). This claim seems to imply that true concepts require language. As we saw above, a claim like this may be appealing to philosophers but not to behavioral and cognitive scientists. Still, even if one is willing to accept the claim it certainly does not preclude the possibility that language-based concepts may help in shaping learning and observation.

While descriptive communication serves to offer intention- and plan-related deliberations that others may choose to use for their own plans, prescriptive communication seeks to impose some individuals' action plans on other individuals—from leaders on followers, respectively. Prescriptive communication occurs in asymmetrical social settings, allowing for division of labor in the sense that some individuals take care of plan formation and others of plan realization through intention formation and action execution. These are settings for splitting control, as discussed in chapter 8.

Scenarios for asymmetrical, prescriptive communication cover a wide range of such settings. For instance, in formalized military settings, officers take the role of leaders, issuing orders to privates to obey them. Likewise, in semiformalized settings like sports, coaches provide instructions to athletes who are supposed to follow them. In even more informal settings like psychological experiments, experimenters and participants take the role of temporary leaders and followers, respectively. Here participants volunteer for a social game in which they agree to follow experimenters' instructions.

As these examples illustrate, prescriptive communication is—by definition—concerned with shared planning of forthcoming action rather than interpretation of past and present action. Shared planning through prescriptive communication requires that both leaders and followers agree on the asymmetry of the social setting, the prescriptive character of communication, and the division of labor between plan formation and plan realization entailed by that setting.[13]

To conclude, we may consider language-based, symbolic communication an extremely powerful tool for plan formation and plan acquisition in social contexts. Since descriptive and prescriptive uses of that tool will

13. Although prescriptive communication builds on the same linguistic and conceptual resources as descriptive communication, their implications for plan formation are still quite different. Unlike descriptive communication, which provides public information for individual plan formation, prescriptive communication serves to communicate plans among individuals. Accordingly, followers are understood to adopt ready-made plans from leaders, rather than forming their own plans from resources shared with others. This does not necessarily imply, though, that there is nothing left for followers to do. How much is left will depend on the nature of commands and instructions they are following. Although not much may in fact be left to do when commands and intentions specify plans in terms of concrete intentions and concrete conditions for realization, substantial room may be left for followers' own contributions when plans are specified at more abstract levels.

in many real-life situations be mixed together and hard to disentangle, we should certainly not draw a definite dividing line between them. Instead, we should see plan formation through communication as a powerful instrument for collective control of individual action. An instrument like this has two sides to it. One is that it helps to build individual plans on collective norms and experiences. The other is that it may at the same time constrain individual plans to collective norms and experiences as expressed in prescriptive communication. As always, loss of autonomy is the price to be paid for social support.

Rules for Plans
In the same way as plans serve to conditionalize and, hence, automatize intention formation, rules are routines that help conditionalize and automatize plan formation. Like the term "plan," the term "rule" has multiple uses and meanings in a variety of theoretical contexts.[14] As I use the term here, rules are representational routines for the control of plan formation, specifying what plan to form under given circumstances. By helping to retrieve suitable plans for given conditions, they relieve individuals from the burden of creating novel plans for each given configuration of conditions.

At a higher level, rules do for plans what plans do at a lower level for intentions. We can therefore be brief about rule formation and rule pursuit, emphasizing differences rather than commonalities between rules and plans. To get an idea of what rule pursuit means in the context of experimental task settings, we need to go one step beyond reaction time tasks of the Donders style and envisage task environments in which mapping rules (= plans) are conditionalized to ongoing events (= instruction cues eliciting them). A classic example of a task environment like this is provided by the so-called task-switching paradigm. In these experiments, participants are required to switch between two alternative tasks that both involve the same sets of stimuli and responses. For instance, in the classic version of the task, the stimulus set comprises the numbers 1–4 and 6–9, and the response set is made up of two response keys, left and right. One of the two tasks requires the participant to map numbers to keys according to

---

14. Again there is no canonical use of this term as a theoretical construct. Still, it is broadly used in the literature with two essential readings: descriptive and prescriptive. In the descriptive sense, rules are (representations of) regularities inherent in happenings in the environment. In the prescriptive sense, (in which I use the term here) rules are abstract normative regulations for ongoing and forthcoming action.

magnitude (e.g., press left key for numbers below 5, right key for numbers above 5), whereas the other task requires mappings according to parity (e.g., press left and right key for odd and even numbers, respectively). Running the task then requires two independent specifications that are usually provided by two different stimuli on each trial. One stimulus—the instruction cue—specifies the task to be performed on a given trial, while the other one—the imperative stimulus—specifies the stimulus on which that task has to be performed.[15]

This paradigm illustrates how plans can be conditionalized by rules. We may think of each of the two tasks in terms of a plan that gets implemented as soon as the task has been specified for a given trial. For instance, the parity task would link the intentions referring to left and right responses to stimulus sets 1/3/7/9 and 2/4/6/8, respectively. Thus, as soon as one of these stimulus events comes up, the appropriate intention can immediately be realized through appropriate action. This is as far as plan realization goes. Yet, before plans can be realized, they need to be formed and implemented. This is where rules come in. According to the logic of the experimental paradigm, rules link task sets (magnitude vs. parity) to instructions cues. According to the logic of our functional account, they conditionalize plan formation to given circumstances.

Thus, while plans create intentions to be pursued, rules create plans to be pursued under given conditions. As a result, each token of action becomes selected in a routine of twofold, nested conditionalization. While one serves to tailor plans to certain conditions (= instruction cues) the other serves to tailor intentions to certain other conditions (= imperative stimuli). In view of the complexity of rule-based routines, we may wonder whether they can be acquired in the same ways as plan-based routines. In the experimental setting, rules are acquired like in many natural real-life situations: through explicit verbal communication. Though the task is quite complex, adult participants can easily learn to perform it, provided that instructions are carefully worded. One of the major advantages of verbal communication seems to be that it allows us to explicitly address

15. There is a vast variety of task switching paradigms (see Monsell, 2003; Pashler, 2000). For instance, in a slightly different version of the task, the imperative stimulus may be presented first and the instruction cue second. In still another version, instruction and imperative information may be carried by one and the same stimulus. Further, the instruction cue may be replaced by a (descriptive) rule that specifies a particular sequence of tasks to be performed over a sequence of consecutive trials, etc.

the functional distinction between task selection (rule-based/cue-triggered) and action selection (plan-based/stimulus-triggered)—as well as the nested hierarchical relationship between them.[16]

Less obvious is how complex rule-based routines can be acquired through learning and observation. On the one hand, there is certainly no principled reason why it should not be possible to acquire rules through learning and observation, that is, through procedures that do not rely on conceptual resources associated with verbal communication. On the other hand, given the functional complexity of rules, the roles that learning and observation can play for rule acquisition are likely to be much weaker than for plan acquisition.[17] This leaves us with a strong, if not dominant, role for language-based communication (both descriptive and prescriptive) in rule acquisition and plan formation. The higher we go in the hierarchy of crafts of the will, the more the crafts of individual willing will rely and depend on the use of language and the collective resources for normative and instrumental planning that language entails.

16. The functional hierarchy need not necessarily entail a temporal sequence: Task performance is not much impaired when imperative target stimuli come first and instruction cues second. These and related observations have given rise to an interpretation of task-switching performance in terms of responding to integrated compounds made up of cues and target stimuli (Logan & Bundesen, 2003, 2004; Logan, Schneider & Bundesen, 2007).

17. Pure forms of nonverbally mediated forms of rule acquisition have been studied in animals. On rule acquisition through observation and teaching, see Caro and Hauser (1992); Fischer, Dreisbach, and Goschke (2008). On rule acquisition through learning, see Stoet and Snyder (2007, 2009).

10   Free Will

The notion of free will is deeply entrenched in our commonsense intuitions about willing and doing. Remarkably, the scope of that notion seems to go beyond the practical needs of action explanation. For instance, everyday talk about our willing and doing revolves not only around psychological explanation of action but also around moral evaluation. We want to know the reason for an action, how to evaluate it, and finally, whether or not it is justified. Further, two different levels of explanation and evaluation seem to be at work in these intuitions: On one level we judge the actions themselves and their consequences. But on another level we also judge the agent responsible for that action. We hold people responsible for their actions and we justify doing so by assuming that they are free in their decisions to act.

These underlying convictions permeate our everyday phrases for describing the freedom of will. They are so familiar that they hardly need explanation. We simply assume that, in almost all walks of life, we could act other than we actually do—if only we wanted to. We understand our actual acting to be an outcome of free, voluntary decision. While our decisions are also invariably shaped by a number of circumstances, of which we are more or less aware, we believe that ultimate responsibility for the final decision rests with each person individually. We are ourselves the authors of our decisions and actions. We all experience this authorship and freedom and attribute it to each other. This is at the core of what we may call our intuition of free will.

Thus, talk of free will has two sides. On the one hand, we use it to describe psychological facts, that is, to describe the personal experience of our intuitions of free will that seem so blindingly self-evident. On the other hand, it serves an essentially moral (or even legal) purpose, namely, that of ascribing action outcomes to individual persons. What should we think of this shorthand? Chicken or egg—which came first? Is free will a basic fact of human mental constitution that issues welcome social by-products? Or should we regard it as a social device serving to collectively regulate individual conduct? Do psychological facts precede social institutions—or do social functions produce psychological facts?

To discuss these issues we need to change perspectives—at least partially. As mentioned in the introductory remarks to Part III, this chapter will move from actions to agents. Whereas previous chapters have focused on transient actions and their underlying transient states and operations, this chapter will also envisage the permanent sources of those actions: agents and their underlying functional traits and structures. This chapter looks, in other words, at volition from the perspective of the agent, not from the perspective of the action.

Free will has long fascinated philosophers, theologians, and lawyers. At the same time it has troubled scientists of various brands ranging from physics over biology to modern brain and behavioral sciences. Yet, I believe that some of these seemingly unsolvable problems go away when one considers free will a matter of social construction, that is, a social fact rather than a fact of nature. This is the basic idea on which I will elaborate in this chapter, thus extending the claim of the will's social roots to the claim of free will's societal roots. In the first step I confront our commonsense intuitions of free will with maxims of scientific psychology, concluding that it is not easy to reconcile a strong concept of free will with scientific principles. Having discussed these conceptual concerns I then turn to the empirical side, examining how the intuition of free will may be grounded in the intuition of the mental self and the associated notion of action authorship. Then, in the third step, I look at free will as a normative social construct. On this perspective, free will is seen as a societal institution—a social fact rather than a natural fact. Yet, as we have already seen in chapter

3, social facts are no less real and efficacious than natural facts. I will therefore conclude that free will is not an illusion but a real thing: Those who have appropriated it actually have it.[1]

Trouble

Let us first see why free will and intuitions related to this notion may trouble science. When we raise this issue we need to distinguish between the empirical fact of experiencing free will and the theoretical construct of free will. The empirical fact is a phenomenon like any other that can be explored and explained using the tools of psychology. I return to this issue below. Trouble arises when we switch from viewing free will as an empirical phenomenon to thinking of it as a theoretical construct, maintaining that we *feel free* (in an empirical sense) because we *are free* (in a theoretical sense). Of course, this is exactly what our commonsense intuitions of free will entail. These intuitions allow for no distinction between feeling free and being free. However, we run into trouble when we confront this intuition with principles of scientific explanation. Using a strong notion of free will we find ourselves running up against two standards of science: first, that we must distinguish between perception and reality in psychological explanation; and second, that we must posit causal closure and thoroughgoing determinism in scientific explanation in general.

Perception and Reality
Psychology has a long history of confusing observational facts with theoretical constructs. Cognition, attention, will, feelings—in the past all of these phenomena have mistakenly been promoted up from the ranks of mere observational facts to be seen as explanatory constructs. This has happened—and in some areas of research still occurs today—because of a deep and stubborn misconception about the status of introspection.[2]

   A widespread but false construal says that the way we perceive mental events in our minds is fundamentally different from the way we perceive physical events in the world. As concerns the perception of physical events, more than a century of experimental research has opened our eyes to the fact that human perception involves what we may call *realistic constructivism*—a somewhat paradoxical term meant to characterize the

1. For related ideas, see Prinz (2003, 2006a).
2. Here I return to the discussion in the final section of chapter 1, applying it to the notion of free will.

supposed relationship between perception and reality. The working model underlying research in perception is, on the one hand, realistic inasmuch as it relies on the notion that contents of perception refer to genuinely existing circumstances in the real world. But at the same time it is, on the other hand, constructivist because it assumes that contents of perception result from constructive procedures in which perceptual systems process input data according to certain categories, using their own means of representation. Major principles of perceptual construction pertain, for example, to *selective representation* (perceptual representation is selective in the sense that only a small fraction of stimulus information is taken up and fully processed), *content focus* (perception delivers representational contents, not processes), and *categorical transformation* (perceptual content is the outcome of interactions between current input and stored knowledge). These three principles may suffice to illustrate that what we perceive is not reality as it is in and of itself, but the result of construal: Human perception is highly selective, significantly transformed, and shaped to suit given categories.

So much for the perception of physical events in the world. In contrast, widespread opinion holds that our perception of mental events in our minds is not a normal perceptual process at all, but a mental activity *sui generis*, in which a subject is aware of its own mental goings-on. On this understanding, the perception of mental events is not a process of representation, transformation, and categorization for which it may make sense to question how perceived contents relate to genuine facts. Instead, the perception of mental events is considered an immediate and infallible awareness of the genuine mental facts themselves, with no room for error and misrepresentation. Percepts and reality are one and the same, and this makes it seem legitimate to view mental phenomena, as they present themselves to us, as theoretical constructs. Accordingly, it seems natural to conclude that we *are free* because we *feel free*. The empirical fact of feeling free implies the theoretical fact of being free.

This intuition may be appealing and intuitively plausible, but it is false and misleading when it is spelled out in functional terms. For reasons that we touched on in chapter 1, we must distinguish between reality and our perception of reality for both physical events in the world and mental events in our minds. Like perception of physical events, perception of mental events, too, provides only an inconsistent and incomplete picture of the underlying processes at work. It is a highly selective, content-focused representation of products created by mechanisms that are themselves unperceivable. We are not actually aware of mental processes themselves.

We are aware of individual mental states that may perhaps be taken to reveal something about the underlying processes that caused them.

It is therefore not only perfectly respectable but also necessary that we inquire how our perception of mental events relates to the reality of the underlying functional machinery. Whatever introspection about the nature of mental events may tell us, it is itself a product of selective representation, content focus, and categorical transformation. So the fact that we feel free in our decisions to act says nothing whatsoever about the freedom entailed by the workings of the underlying volitional machinery.

Waiving Explanation

A remarkable implication of claiming that we have free will is that raising the claim tends to go hand in hand with waiving further explanation. For instance, when a court judge asks a defendant why he did a certain thing, the accused often details causes and reasons apparently beyond his own control. In other words: A defendant will say that under the circumstances he had no choice but to do as he did, thus turning over the causal responsibility for the actions in question to the circumstances that prevailed. To the extent that the judge accepts such explanatory causes and reasons, she forgoes the option of attributing both action and consequences to that person. As a result, personal responsibility will evaporate into thin air. In order to attribute personal responsibility, a judge must cut off the causal chain at some point and dispense with further explanation.

Unlike judges, scientists will never give up on explanation. Waiving explanation is therefore fundamentally incompatible with the ethos of scientific research since it compels us to accept local gaps of explanation. What is more, a strong notion of free will even suggests that gaps of action explanation may reflect corresponding gaps of action determination. It thus demands that we accept local pockets of indeterminism in an otherwise deterministic worldview. Yet, while we may be prepared to incorporate in this worldview various sorts of domain-specific indeterminism in areas such as quantum physics or chaos theory, we need to realize that the challenge of free will goes further than this.[3] A strong notion of free will makes more radical claims than merely invoking breaks in causal chains. Instead, it invokes—to put it paradoxically—a determination that is itself

3. For a more sophisticated discussion of these examples, one would need to draw a distinction between (ontological) indeterminism and (epistemological) lack of determinability/predictability. But this distinction has no bearing on a strong notion of free will that invokes an unmoved mover's autonomous self-determination.

undetermined, an authorship that is meant to determine ensuing action but at the same time thought to be free from determination by antecedent events. Such authorship is attributed to an autonomous subject deciding on her own—an unmoved mover, furnished with the godlike capacity of creating action *ex nihilo*, as it were.

Accordingly, any attempt to derive freedom of the will from the operation of chaotic systems or quantum processes in the brain is doomed to failure, because the claim made about free will is not simply the claim of absence of causal determination or predictability. The concept of free will is more sophisticated: It demands that we view subjects as the autonomous authors of their actions, equipped with a will and in a position to decide freely.[4]

From a scientific point of view, waiving explanation is unfathomable; it is incompatible with an enlightened and critical scientific stance. Accepting the tenets of indeterminism would require that we surrender our practice of explanation. In lieu of that, there is only one possible conclusion, namely, that science has no room for a theoretical construct of free will—at least not in the strong sense of an unmoved mover. Unlike judges, scientists must be intellectually committed to deny a notion such as this if their work is to be deemed scientifically sound.

Intuitions

Let's now take a step back from heavy theoretical constructs and turn to empirical facts. Where do our intuitions of free will come from? Why do individuals feel free, although, in fact, they may not be—at least not in a strong sense? To answer these questions we need a theory that distinguishes the phenomenal awareness of personal choices from the functional reality of subpersonal volitional mechanisms. We must make a distinction if we want to have it both ways: a perception of free will and a deterministic machinery of volition.

Typically, intuitions of free will emerge in situations that involve decisions to act in some way. It seems that these intuitions are, by their very nature, linked to decisions to act. Yet, while decisions to act constitute the occasions on which intuitions of free will are articulated, we attribute the

---

4. Here we again encounter autonomous man with whom we began in the prologue—celebrated by Pico della Mirandola but reduced to ridicule by Burrhus F. Skinner: "We say that [man] is autonomous—and so far as a science of behavior is concerned, that means miraculous" (Skinner, 1972, p. 14).

underlying freedom not to the actions but to the acting agent. A decision is not free in and of itself; the self, we say, is free to make a decision. It is *us* who experience that freedom—*we* make decisions, *we* are free to make those decisions, and *we* believe that we could decide and do otherwise. Surely we may be confronted with an interplay of motives, interests, and preferences that may influence our choice. Yet, in the end, *we ourselves*, being more or less aware of all these forces acting on us, seem to decide *on our own* what to do.

If this is true, we may also see it the other way around. If the ability to make decisions on one's own is a constitutive feature of the self, then explaining the intuition of free will is, to a large extent, tantamount to explaining the role of the self. In fact, there are two problems here. One is to explain, at a subpersonal level, how mechanisms for making decisions work. The other is to explain, at the personal level, how the sense of self and authorship and the associated intuition of free will emerge.

Regarding the first problem, we may consult psychological theories of decision making. Most of them agree that decision making requires at least three basic kinds of ingredients that we may call preferences, action knowledge, and situation evaluation. The first ingredient is systems of ordered preferences (drives, needs, motives, interests, and so on). These systems represent hierarchies of objectives, and they do so on various time scales, from very long-term preferential dispositions (at most: lifelong) to short-term and current sets of needs. Current needs are embedded in long-term dispositions, but not entirely determined by them. The second ingredient concerns action knowledge—knowledge about how action is related to the effects it brings about. This knowledge is organized in a way that makes it accessible and allows it to be used in two ways: from actions to effects and from effects to actions. Both uses are elements of action planning. Forward-directed models provide information about possible effects of certain actions. The other way around, inverse models provide information about possible actions appropriate for achieving certain goals (intended effects). Action knowledge is, as are preferences, organized along various time scales, corresponding to the periods that action-effect-relationships may last. Third, action-decisions require situation evaluation, that is, procedures and algorithms that provide running interpretations of prevailing circumstances in terms of current goals and behavioral options. These procedures guarantee that the current situation, in which an agent is involved, is represented in a format that is commensurable with his or her representational systems for preferences and action knowledge.

Different theories combine these ingredients in various ways.[5] But no matter how the process itself may be conceptualized in detail, the decisive fact is that decisions to act are a combined product of preferences, knowledge about action, and evaluations of circumstances. Accordingly, there is no agent actually making the decision. When we examine these theories we learn that most of them provide a rich variety of ideas about subpersonal mechanisms and algorithms for decision, but not much, if anything at all, about a role of a personal self in decision. In these theories, in other words, no room is left for a personal agent who makes the decision: Decisions happen on their own.

Construals of Self

So what should we think of the constitutive role of the self in our intuitions of free will? What is real about our perception of being/having a self? Does our sense of self and our intuitions of action authorship and free will refer to something real—or should we consider them nice illusions, produced by vain self-deceit? Our answer depends on how we understand what we call the self. Here we return to the two basic construals of self and subjectivity that we already discussed in chapter 1—the naturalist and the constructivist view.

The classical, naturalist view includes concepts of subjectivity and claims that the self is a natural organ of the mind. This organ is the bearer of subjectivity, personality, and individuality. Like an organ of the body, it is a naturally given component of the mind that develops prior to and independent of experience. We may call this construal *self-naturalism*: The self is the naturally given, central organ of the mind, coordinating and controlling the activity of other mental functions. This intuition is deeply rooted in our folk psychology. So it is not surprising to find this type of self-naturalistic intuition—in various guises—playing prominent parts in philosophical and psychological theories, as well.[6]

In contrast, constructivist construals of subjectivity hold that the self is not a natural organ of the mind, but rather an acquired knowledge structure. The idea here is that the self is a particular kind of mental

5. For overviews, see, e.g., Hastie and Dawes (2001); Koehler and Harvey (2004).

6. Prominent examples are Descartes's intuition that awareness of one's own mental states provides the foundation of all other kinds of epistemic acts and Kant's intuition that self-consciousness lays the foundations for the unity of the mind through providing a common reference for the vast variety of mental contents (Descartes, 1641/1990; Kant, 1996).

content. Representational structures supporting it develop parallel to and in interaction with representational structures supporting other kinds of mental contents and operations. In particular, the self will evolve along with representational structures supporting decisions to act. We may call this construal *self-constructivism*: The self is based on knowledge organized in a special way, but its relationship to other representational structures is not predetermined. It is made and shaped in the individual's history of learning and socialization that creates patterns of personal knowledge. According to this view, the role of the mental self for action authorship is not given from the outset, but generated secondarily. The history of self thus becomes an object of developmental, historical, and/or evolutionary reconstruction (or, perhaps, deconstruction, as some would claim).

Let us now return to the question of what is real about our intuition of being/having a self. Is the self real, or should we think of it as an illusion or perhaps a useful fiction? As I said, the answer depends on how we view the mental self. If we adhere to the naturalistic construal, we must conclude that the feeling of free will is an illusion. Trying to accommodate both notions—namely, that on the one hand, decisions can be entirely explained through the operation of subpersonal mechanisms, while on the other, the personal self is an independent, natural organ of the mind—entails that any ascription of decisions to the self must involve self-deception. We fool ourselves in thinking that we are autonomous authors of decisions to act. If, by contrast, we adhere to the constructivist construal, the notion of illusion becomes meaningless, because there is no independent, natural self appropriating things that do not belong to it. Instead, the diagnosis here is that patterns of knowledge that bear the self are arranged in such a way that the self develops to serve the function of an author of decisions to act. This authorship is then its proper function—the very function for which it is made.

Sources of Self

Since naturalism is the mainstream view, the burden of proof is on the constructivist side. If the mental self is not considered a natural organ of the mind—how then does it get produced and fabricated? We may raise this question at two levels and time scales, the evolution of human mentality and the development of individual minds. Regarding evolution, we may resort to hypothetical stone-age scenarios, explaining how the notion of self may have emerged from the interplay of symbolic communication, dual representation, and authorship attribution. Regarding ontogenetic development, we may once more resort to attribution discourses and mirror practices.

Evolution. How may selves have emerged in evolution, or human evolution, or, perhaps, even early human history? Let us take a brief look back to the stone age for a moment and try to imagine how the development of selves may have started.[7] We envisage an intelligent proto-human being with the capacity to evaluate behaviorally relevant implications of a given current situation and to convert that knowledge into appropriate action. Imagine that such evaluation depends on complex algorithms that developed over the course of lengthy learning processes, and that additional algorithms guarantee that the outcomes of those evaluations are compared to current priorities and transformed into decisions to act. As complex as these calculations may be, they are subject to one essential restriction: They evaluate only those options related to the prevailing situation. Processes related to remembering past or planning future events do not exist. Our being is, in other words, entirely chained to the present, relying on bottom-up control, but not top-down control.

How can our being escape this imprisonment and achieve "freedom from the present"?[8] As we discussed in chapters 7 and 8, dual representation has two important implications. One is that it allows representational decoupling from the current situation. The other is that it ensures that the normal perception of the current situation continues to function. As a result, representations of both the present and the absent coexist. Naturally, we have no way of knowing when, where, by what means, or how often evolution brought forth a mental architecture enabling dual representation. But we can be certain that the ability became advantageous to survival when animals started living in groups that rely on symbolic communication. Under such circumstances individuals will often be in the position of recipients of communications that are related to things beyond their currently perceived horizon. Accordingly, they can only understand such communications if they are capable of generating representations of these unperceivable things. However, they must be able to do so without losing contact with their present environment. Dual representation is thus a prerequisite for symbolic communication to function. Humans, whose

7. In recent years, pertinent psychohistorical scenarios have been outlined by, e.g., Dennett (1990, 1992); Donald (2001); Edelman (1989); Jaynes (1976); Metzinger (1993, 2003); Mithen (1996). The following scenario is constructed from combining some of their suggestions with some novel ideas.
8. See Edelman (1989, p. 118).

evolutionary career is entirely founded on symbolic communication, must therefore possess a highly efficient system of dual representation.[9]

Dual representation enhances the cognitive potential of our being in many ways. One of them is to develop a notion of self, based on attribution and appropriation of action authorship. As soon as a system of dual representation is in place, there is room not only for generating externally induced representations (based on receiving communications), but also for generating internally induced representations like memories, fantasies, and plans. For the sake of brevity I use the term "thoughts" for these kinds of internally induced representations.

Thoughts are comparable to communications: Both refer to things that are not present in the current situation. However, there is one important feature that distinguishes (internally induced) thoughts from (externally induced) representations. Externally induced representations are always accompanied by a perception of an act of communication, that is, by a perception of the person who is the author of the message, whereas, by contrast, when internally induced thoughts occur, we have no awareness of an immediate author at work. So how can our being link those thoughts to the current situation?

One natural solution is to adhere to the notion of personal authorship in these cases, too. Yet, in the case of thoughts, personal authorship can be construed in a number of different ways. For instance, one might think that thoughts can be traced back to hidden authors/authorities, like the voices of gods, priests, or kings who are believed to be invisibly present in the current situation. Another historically perhaps more modern construal is to locate the source of thoughts in one's own body and to trace them back to an independent, personal subject bound to the body of the agent: the mental self. In both cases, the author of the thoughts is not a component of those thoughts, but remains external, related to them by mental authorship—just as communicative messages are related to those who communicate them. When this idea is applied to thoughts concerning action, such as goals, intentions, and plans, it leads us to posit mental selves that not only act as cognitive authors, producing mental contents, but also as dynamic authors, making decisions to act and setting action into motion.[10]

9. Below we come back to the role of language crafts for dual representation (ch. 13).
10. The question of where goals and intentions come from is more than simply a problem regarding individual source attribution. It is also a political problem regarding the social distribution of power and control. Construals concerning the sources

In sum, this scenario says that the mental self is a device for solving an attribution problem: The self is construed as the author of internally induced representations.[11] These self-construals emerge from the same interplay of attribution and appropriation that previous chapters have claimed to lay the ground for top-down control of voluntary action. Like the scenario for voluntary action, the scenario for the self builds on two principles: dual representation and attribution/appropriation of personal authorship. Dual representation forms part of the natural history of human cognition and action, whereas personal attribution concerns their cultural history. The emergence of mental selves, then, requires both natural and cultural conditions to be met.

Development. Let us now see how mental selves may evolve in individual development. Here, too, we encounter a strong role for the dialectic interplay of attribution and appropriation. Attribution discourses provide culturally standardized schemes of interpretation of and communication about human conduct. In Western cultures these discourses attribute to individuals a mental configuration centered on the self. Such discourses

of goals, intentions, and plans are of considerable social and political importance since they specify and locate the causes that make people act as they do. According to Jaynes (1976), one kind of construal (the ancient one) locates authorship of intentions and acts in invisible personal authorities—external, obedience-demanding forces telling the agent what to do. The other kind of construal (the more modern one) locates authorship in a personal self—an internal source of autonomous action decisions. Notably, both kinds of construals are meant to reflect cultural artifacts, not natural facts.

11. If this is true, any misattributions of action authorship must be expected to be associated with disorders of self-organization. Such associations have indeed been discussed with respect to schizophrenia and multiple personality disorders (MPDs). For subpopulations of schizophrenic patients it has been argued that positive symptoms like hallucinations and delusions may be interpreted in terms of disorders of action monitoring and self-attribution of action (see, e.g., Blakemore, Frith & Wolpert, 2002; Daprati et al., 1997; Farrer, Franck, d'Amato & Jeannerod, 2004; Frith, 1992, 1994; Frith & Done, 1989; Frith, Blakemore & Wolpert, 2000; Jeannerod, 2003a, 2006; Jeannerod et al., 2003). Whereas schizophrenic patients may be lacking a stable mental self as a center of volition and cognition, MPD patients seem to be suffering from conflicts between two or more such centers (Confer & Ables, 1983; Greaves, 1993; Hilgard, 1977; Kluft, 1993; Spiegel, 1993). More transient dissociative phenomena have also been reported to occur in split-brain patients (Gazzaniga & Smylie, 1984; Zaidel, 1990) and under conditions of posthypnotic amnesia (Coe, 1989; Hilgard, 1965, 1977; Kihlstrom, 1985).

permeate our daily life at several levels, predominantly, for instance, when using psychological common sense for explaining people's actions. Folk psychology is based on the notion of individuals having/being explicit, lifelong identical selves at their core. Discourses about morals and rights are no less relevant. These discourses identify the self as an autonomous source of decisions to act, thereby ascribing action authorship to it.

Such discourses are often embedded in narrative discourses of various kinds. Fictional stories in books and movies are packed with talk about willing and acting. We tell stories to our children in order to explain to them just what it means to be a person. We thereby provide them with two tools. One is the explicit semantics of the culture in which they live—its customs and practices, values and standards, myths and legends. The other is the implicit syntax of its folk psychology, which specifies how human agents function, what they think and do, how their thinking is related to their actions, and how they are rewarded or punished for their actions—be it in heaven or on earth.

Now, when agents in social groups organize their mutual interaction and communication in such a way that each one expects all the other co-agents to also have a self, every one of the agents—new arrivals, too—is confronted with a situation that already provides a role for him or her—in the shape of a self. Awareness of foreign attributions to oneself induces self-attributions, and the agent becomes accustomed to the role of a self attributed to him by others. A person thinks of herself as others think of her. She appropriates for herself what others have attributed to her in the first place.

Whereas attribution discourses rely on declarative knowledge about action, mirror practices rely on procedural knowledge for perception and production of action. As we have seen, such embodied mirroring is of particular importance in early infancy. For caretakers, the practice of reciprocating or complementing the baby's behavior is fairly universal. For babies, these games seem to be of crucial importance for tuning in with and becoming attached to others, as well as laying the ground for perceiving and understanding themselves like others. Further, as we have also seen, mirroring habits may also apply to interactions among grown-ups. Yet, adults will often have no explicit intention to communicate anything to others and they may not even be aware of what they are doing. Their mirroring reflects automatic habits rather than controlled and cultivated practices. In any case, both explicit practices and implicit habits have the same consequences: They let people perceive their own behavior through the mirror of others.

Institutions

Attribution discourses and mirror practices offer answers to the question
of how people come to understand themselves as authors of cognition and
action, governed by intuitions of free will. Now we see that free will is a
social institution, made by people and for people.[12] Like most social institutions, it builds on compelling intuitions that are shared and communicated
among individuals. Intuitions of action authorship and free will emerge if
and when individuals learn, through social discourse and practice, to build
a mental self as a source of action decisions and actions. And since the
mental self is predominantly created for the purpose of establishing action
authorship, it makes little sense to question whether or not that authorship
is an illusion.

To conclude, we may ask what a social institution of autonomous selves
equipped with action authorship and free will is good for. What psychological effects does it offer individuals, and what social functions does it
serve for their collectives?

Individuals

The psychological effects that the ascription of self, action authorship, and
free will has for an individual depend on the role that we attribute to the
personal interpretation of the subpersonal mechanisms for decision
making. Thus far, I have described the subpersonal processes as being
something real and the personal processes of interpretation as providing a
perceptual representation of that reality. Yet, it would be misleading to
conclude from this that only the subpersonal is efficacious, while its personal perception is inefficacious and epiphenomenal. Like every other
social institution, autonomous selves are not fictions; they are real. As we
saw in chapter 3, social facts are no less real for individuals than natural
facts.

How can socially shared intuitions be as real as natural facts? Their
status derives from the fact that intuitions reflecting personal interpretations of subpersonal processes must, in turn, also be supported by subpersonal processes. Accordingly, there is no reason whatsoever to view them
as less real or less efficacious than the subpersonal decision-making machinery to whose operation they refer. Social discourses and practices ensure
that notions like self, agency, and free will are implemented in individual
knowledge structures in terms of both personal intuitions and subpersonal

12. See Kusch (1997, 1999, 2005).

mechanisms. As a result, individuals' intuitions of self, action authorship, and free will have precisely the same causal potential to influence their behavior as do their intuitions about the workings of other things and events in the world.

Still, what exactly are these intuitions good for? What consequences do they have and on what kinds of behaviors do they make an impact? I submit that these intuitions mainly induce procedural changes—alterations in the algorithms underlying our decisions that result in an elaboration of decision-making processes.

One of the major procedural effects of intuitions of self and free will is to slow down the subpersonal decision-making system, which is itself designed to be quick and efficient. Delaying decisions to act provides an opportunity for elaboration and deliberation, and thus increases the depth of processing in the representational systems relevant to a certain decision. It allows an expansion of the representational resources for making a decision, and this additional information may modify the eventual decision itself.

Moreover, language users are in a position to break down the solipsistic closure of their representational systems through communication. When individuals communicate about, and argue for the products of their (initially private) elaborations and deliberations, they establish reciprocal suggestions for modifying their decisions. The impact of such communicative exchange is twofold. First, communication allows another step of expansion of representational resources for making decisions. Second, it offers the opportunity to link private action decisions to public discourses on rules and laws for proper conduct.

Collectives

Intuitions of action authorship and free will not only influence the psychological dispositions of individuals, they also alter the shape of the collective to which those individuals see themselves as belonging. It is probably not off the mark to propose that this is their true achievement—perhaps even their genuine psycho-historical raison d'être.

For one thing, authorship and intuitions of free will have effects on the discourses and institutions that regulate behavior—namely, morals and rights. As we saw above, one central achievement of our talk of free will is that it allows us to attribute actions and their consequences to the people that perform them. We make people responsible for what they do, and we believe that they could have done otherwise. Responsibility is the price of freedom. The vernacular of free will, then, identifies a source that issues decisions to act. It identifies that source as being the same instance that gets sanctioned and rewarded: the person, the agent.

Finally, talk of free will reflects on discourses and institutions for the political development of will. To the extent that agents in social collectives mutually ascribe autonomy and responsibility for their private decisions to act, they will also come to apply these ascriptions to public decisions of the collective itself. As a consequence, they will replace authoritarian leadership with mechanisms of collective will development. In the case of modern Western democracies, these mechanisms are supported by the notion of a social contract between equal and autonomous individuals and embodied in democratic forms of will development at various levels of society. The idea of democracy is to a large extent founded on the notion of personal autonomy and free will. If we cherish one, we must praise the other.

Open Will

In the end, then, do we or don't we have free will? Not surprisingly, the answer depends on what we mean by having or not having free will. We don't have free will in the same sense as we have organs like a liver or a heart, or skills like seeing or grasping. We have these organs and skills by virtue of the fact that their blueprint is entailed by our genes, forming part and parcel of our natural endowment.

Although we don't have free will in the sense of a natural fact, we do have it in the sense of a social artifact. Free will is an artifact that we fashion for ourselves and integrate in our sense of our social and mental self. Such social facts and artifacts are by no means fictitious, or even illusory. For those who have appropriated them they are just as real as natural facts are. They govern and constrain our actions with precisely the same logic as natural facts do. In that sense, then, we certainly do have free will.

And what does it mean to have it? What it does not mean is to have (in a factual, descriptive sense) the power to free oneself from causal chains, to act like an unmoved mover. What it does mean, instead, is to commit oneself (in a normative, prescriptive sense) to act as a reason-sensitive agent, engaging in public discourses for action regulation and taking personal responsibility for one's private decisions and actions. Free will is open will: Intuitions and institutions of free will act to open and commit private minds to public discourse.

IV Cognition

In the initial chapters, we began with general considerations on minds and mirrors before we then focused in on the will, examining in detail how the idea of the collective construction of individual mentality may work in the domain of volition. For the final part of the book, I would like to turn from volition to cognition, focusing on issues pertaining to the foundations of knowledge, experience, and language crafts. In addressing these domains, I will examine how powerful the idea of collective construction of individual mental architectures may prove to be for solving issues of knowledge representation and language crafts.

My discussion will in the following three chapters be less detailed and elaborate than the foregoing discussion of volition. The idea here is not to offer comprehensive theoretical frameworks for knowledge and language processing but rather to provide selective discussions of ways in which crucial features of cognition and language may be embedded in the open architecture of the human mind. Regarding cognition, I will show how the key feature of intentionality may emerge in individual minds from interactions and communications with other open-minded individuals. Regarding language, I will examine both how open minds subserve the building up of the representational basis of language crafts and how language crafts subserve, and actually boost, the potential that open minds bear for collective control of individual actions.

Chapters 11 and 12 outline for cognition what previous chapters have elaborated at some length for volition. While chapter 11 outlines a representational architecture for intentionality, chapter 12 discusses how that architecture may have emerged. Here I will argue that in the same way as individuals become volitional agents by virtue of seeing others and being seen by others as such, they become experiential subjects through the interplay of attribution and appropriation. I will propose that the construction of individual cognition follows the same outside-in scheme as the construction of individual volition, proceeding from others to self. Crucially, as I will show, the open-minds approach to cognition offers a novel and surprising perspective on the nature and the emergence of intentionality, a key feature of mental experience and human mentality. Importing intentionality from others to ourselves is certainly less demanding than first construing it for ourselves and then exporting it to others. Import is less demanding for both the individuals under consideration and the theory that reconstructs the underlying cognitive operations.

Given the idea of common roots of cognition and volition, it appears to be natural to regard volitional functions as a subset of cognitive functions—the subset of those functions that are concerned with action representation and control. This view may, on the one hand, certainly be justified in systematical and conceptual terms: To be efficient, the representational basis of volition must exhibit precisely the same functional features that apply to cognition in general (e.g., representational reference, distal reference). In this sense, volition may be seen as part and parcel of cognition. Yet, on the other hand, in more functional and evolutionary terms, a different view may be justified as well. Adopting this perspective, we may speculate that the crucial driving force for building and shaping an architecture that enables the interplay between attribution and appropriation may be rooted in volition—in the needs of individual/private action control and its collective/public modulation. In that sense, the narrow domain of volition may have taken the lead over the broad domain of cognition, acting as the driver for shaping the system accordingly.[1]

Finally, in the concluding chapter I address both the role of open minds for the emergence of language crafts and the role of language crafts for shaping open minds. Unlike previous chapters, this chapter will focus much more on ultimate functions than proximate mechanisms. Basically, I will argue that the proper function for which language crafts have evolved pertains to requirements of social control, that is, to social modulation of others' actions. I elaborate the argument in two ways. One goes from language to control, examining how language crafts may act to boost the efficiency of social control. The other takes the reverse perspective, going from control to language and examining some quite speculative ideas on how the requirements of social control may have given rise to the emergence of language crafts.

1. This is why I have decided to examine volition first (and in quite some detail) and turn to cognition second (in less detail). Accordingly, Part IV will reiterate much of what has been said in Part III, but from a different and somewhat broader perspective.

11   Subjects and Systems

Whereas the study of volition looks at the mind in terms of its capacity to generate forthcoming intentional action, the study of cognition considers its capacity to provide the individual with knowledge concerning his or her current surroundings, the broader environment, and eventually the world in which he or she lives.[1] Of course, as we saw earlier, the two are closely intertwined, since in order to be efficient, action always needs to be grounded in knowledge about current states of affairs in the individual's body and environment. Yet, though it may be true that cognitive functions have mainly evolved to subserve action control and volition, it is also true that cognitive capacities have, at least in humans, developed in ways that go far beyond the needs of individual control of forthcoming action. In our species, the business of knowing the world has become quite detached from the business of acting and deciding what to do. Obviously such detachment applies not only to our individual lives but to our social and institutional lives as well. For instance, while some engage in science for the sake of understanding the world, some others engage in politics for the sake of deciding what to do. Such division of labor seems to imply that the two systems may obey different kinds of rules and operate fairly independently.

1. Importantly, that knowledge includes the individual's body, as well as the way in which the body is related to the environment that surrounds it (see below).

Human cognition has over recent decades become the target of a new and widely differentiated multidisciplinary science. Cognitive science is flourishing, and it has boosted our knowledge and understanding of the operation of cognitive systems enormously.[2] Given this background, the fact that I am devoting no more than two brief chapters to this topic should be taken to indicate that I am far from trying to give it a comprehensive treatment. Instead, I will concentrate on one particular issue that is often considered key to understanding the workings of human cognition: the issue of intentionality, or representational reference. Remarkably, this issue has mainly been discussed in the philosophical literature (where it is often considered deeply enigmatic), whereas it has been more or less neglected or not even mentioned at all in psychological and neuroscientific accounts of cognition.[3] The difference in scientific attention may be due to the fact that philosophical traditions often focus on subjective experience whereas empirical sciences tend to emphasize objective performance. Accordingly, since intentionality is mainly a matter of experience, it has attracted the attention of philosophers and at the same time escaped the notice of empirical scientists.

This chapter addresses both subjective experience and representational systems that may account for experience and performance. Starting from a discussion of the nature of percepts and thoughts, I will in the first section address the feature of intentionality, or representational reference. This feature must be considered a hallmark of cognitive experience and, hence, a key explanandum for cognitive theories. In the second section I move from description to explanation. Here I discuss what kinds of representational resources and systems are required to account for performance and experience. I will suggest a distinction between two basic modes of representation, implicit and explicit. Whereas performance may entirely

2. Cognitive science builds on long-standing scientific traditions in philosophy, psychology, and physiology and has more recently become enriched by intellectual input from such diverse fields as linguistics, computer science, robotics, and a number of neuroscientific disciplines. For systematic and historical overviews of cognitive science and cognitive neuroscience, see, e.g., Albright, Kandel, and Posner (2000); Baars (1986); Dupuy (2009); Nadel (2003); Nadel and Piatelli-Palmarini (2003); Posner (1989); Wilson and Keil (1999).

3. Much of the philosophical discussion on intentionality can be traced back to Brentano's distinction between physical and mental things (Brentano & Kraus, 1924). For more recent contributions, see, e.g., Aquila (1977); Chisholm (1967); Dennett (1978, 1987); Fodor (1975, 1992); Lycan (1999); Perry (1994); Searle (1983, 1994); Smith (1999).

rely on implicit representation, experience requires an architecture for explicit representation.

Kinds of Intentionality

What do people experience when they perceive objects and events in their surroundings or when they imagine and think about things beyond the scope of current perception? By raising this question I do not mean to call for a systematic ontology of kinds of percepts and thoughts.[4] Rather, what I am aiming at is a more general and abstract characterization of the kinds of things that percepts and thoughts are. What makes them special? What makes mental things like percepts and thoughts different from physical things like stars and stones, from living things like flies and frogs, or from cultural artifacts like tools and toys or popes and presidents?

As a starting point for addressing these questions, we may go back to our introductory discussion in chapter 1 concerning the nature of mental experience, in particular to Franz Brentano's seminal account of mental acts. Based on his analysis, it is largely agreed that the crucial distinctive feature of such acts is entailed by a feature that he called *intentionality* and that I will here refer to under the notion of *representational reference*.[5] The fundamental distinction is this: The meaning of things like stones, frogs, toys, and presidents is defined through frameworks of ontologies for objects and events in the world. They are what they are in virtue of these ontologies, without referring to anything beyond themselves and beyond these frameworks. The meaning of mental things, however, appears to be embedded in two such frameworks: the framework of mental acts (i.e.,

4. In the following discussion I use the term *thoughts* in a somewhat unusual sense. Basically, I contrast percepts with thoughts. Whereas percepts are mental states that refer to things to which the perceiving individual currently has access, thoughts are mental states referring to things to which no such access is currently available. The term *thoughts* is thus used as a collective name for a broad variety of mental states and associated intentional relationships, e.g., memories, fantasies, plans, deliberations, or thoughts (in the more usual narrow sense). Importantly, thoughts (in the broad sense) require dual representation (see ch. 7), whereas percepts do not.

5. See Brentano (1924); Fodor (1992); Lycan (1999); Searle (1983, 1994). The concept of *intentionality* is often defined and explained by going back to the concept of *content*: Mental or intentional states are things that *have content*. However, as I argue here, *having content* is a characteristic of a specific form of intentionality, not intentionality per se. Therefore I here propose to define and explain the concept of intentionality through the notion of *representational reference*.

percepts and thoughts in the mind) and the framework of things to which they refer (i.e., objects and events in the world).

What does representational reference entail? How is it possible for a mental thing to refer to something beyond itself? Depending on the scenario we consider, representational reference may take two basic forms, one in percepts and another in thoughts. When we look around in the world, we experience ourselves being in direct contact with and having direct access to things and events that surround us. Yet, when we close our eyes and start thinking about things in the world, that direct access goes away. In that kind of scenario, we rather experience ourselves being in more indirect contact with things in the world and our thoughts bearing content that refers to them.

Thus, while percepts provide perceivers with *access* to things and events, thoughts provide thinkers with *content* that refers to things and events. Still, what the two modes of representational reference have in common is that they both carry the signature of subjectivity. Both entail a particular kind of referential relationship between an experiencing subject, on the one hand, and things and events being experienced by him or her on the other. Furthermore, both carry the intuition that the experiencing subject remains constant across the variety of ongoing mental acts, thus linking them together and creating unity within the diversity of percepts and thoughts.

Percepts

Percepts are tokens of mental experience that are generated through perceptual acts like seeing, hearing, or feeling events in the environment and, at the same time, are understood as the outcomes of such acts. Percepts inform perceivers about the here and now—the circumstances in which their immediate surroundings and their bodies currently are. Let me briefly consider the what and the how of percepts in turn.

What? In ordinary perceptual acts perceivers understand what they see and hear as reflecting what is actually out there. This refers to both qualities and structure of perceptual experience.

Concerning qualities, a long-standing philosophical and scientific tradition distinguishes between primary and secondary attributes of perception. Primary or first-order attributes are thought to directly reflect corresponding features of things in the world (e.g., the pitch and the loudness of a tone reflecting the frequency and amplitude of the physical stimulus giving rise to perceiving it), whereas higher-order attributes are thought to be more indirectly derived from things in the world (e.g., the identity of a person whose face one sees, or forces entailed in one billiard ball hitting the other).

A distinction along these lines may, on the one hand, be justified in epistemological and functional terms. This is because the extraction and/ or construction of higher-order attributes requires some kind of interaction between the information provided by the current stimulus with information stored in memory, whereas no such interaction is required for primary attributes that can, in a more direct fashion, be read out from the current stimulus information.[6] Yet, on the other hand, when one adopts a more descriptive and phenomenological perspective, examining the content of perceptual experience from the perceiver's own point of view, the difference between first- and higher-order attributes seems to go away. The meaning of things is perceived precisely in the same way as are their sensory attributes: Meaning resides in them, rather than being attached to them. Phenomenologically speaking, higher-order attributes are inherent in percepts, not adherent to them—just as are first-order attributes.

In other words, to perceive things is to know them.[7] Ordinary perception always goes beyond the information contained in the stimulus. Percepts provide perceivers not only with knowledge concerning sensory surface attributes reflecting physical properties of things and events but at the same time with rich semantic knowledge concerning various kinds of nonsensory, deeper attributes reflecting their meaning. Importantly, such meaningful knowledge comes for free: For perceivers there is no such thing as "deep" semantic perception on top of "shallow" physical sensation. Perception delivers meaningful knowledge—tacitly but mandatorily.[8]

6. Talking about *direct reading* entails a somewhat dangerous metaphor that may give rise to misunderstandings if it is taken to imply that no further processing is required. The term *direct reading* is not meant to entail the notion that primary attributes can be processed without any transformations and computations whatsoever. The crucial difference is that for higher-order features, these computations need to address sematic knowledge about things and events, whereas no such knowledge is required for primary features. Primary features build entirely on information delivered by the stimulus. In that sense, the underlying computations may be addressed as operations of *reading out* that information.

7. The wording of this conclusion is borrowed from Garner (1966).

8. The distinction between sensation and perception has a long and troublesome history in philosophy and psychology (see Boring, 1942). It was grounded in both description and explanation. In terms of introspective description, it refers to the difference between so-called *bare sensory content* and so-called *apprehended perceptual knowledge* (Boring, 1942, p. 3). As concerns theoretical explanation, it refers to a

With regard to structure, perceptual content tends to be individuated in terms of objects and events and organized in space and time. Thus, unlike content, which goes beyond the information given, structure mainly builds on patterns of sensory attributes reflecting physical features of the perceiver's current surroundings. Perceptual systems thus seem to rely on sensory attributes for creating structure (generating objects and events and specifying their layout in space and time) and on both sensory and semantic attributes for creating and/or enriching content.

How? What does it mean for a perceiver to see a tree in a meadow, to hear a doorbell ringing, or to feel the itch of a mosquito bite on her arm? Following the lead of authorities like Kant and Brentano, we need to combine three complementary answers to such questions, focusing on different kinds of relationships between the perceiver and the perceived. The first answer addresses objects and events as such: Seeing the tree, hearing the doorbell, or feeling the itch means for the perceiver that there is a tree in the meadow (not a house), that the doorbell is ringing (not the telephone bell), and that her arm is itching (not her hand). This kind of answer makes no explicit reference to the perceiver at all. Still, it will in most cases satisfy the informational needs of ordinary perception: Through perception, people get to know what is going on out there. The second answer goes beyond the first by also addressing the way in which such knowledge is acquired: through seeing, hearing, and feeling the tree, the doorbell, and the itch, respectively (rather than through other channels of knowledge acquisition). This kind of answer does not address objects and events as such, but speaks of them as targets being accessed in and through certain kinds of perceptual acts (the tree as being seen, the doorbell as being heard, the itch as being felt). Finally, the third answer also addresses the perceiver and the fact that things are being seen, heard, and felt by her (rather than by somebody else). This kind of answer entails an even weaker role for the perceived objects themselves, since it addresses them as being accessed through particular perceptual acts performed by particular individuals (e.g., the tree in the meadow as seen by her).

According to Kant and Brentano, we need to combine the three answers in order to provide a full account of what the act of perceiving

putative difference between raw information delivered by sensory processing and more elaborate information delivered by higher-order enrichment of that raw information. Over recent decades, the distinction has fallen out of use. If revived, modern cognitive theory would have to rephrase it in terms of outcomes of purely stimulus-based processing as opposed to stimulus- and memory-based processing.

means for the perceiver: While explicitly perceiving a particular event (*the doorbell ringing*) she is at the same time implicitly aware of the fact that that ringing *is being heard* and that it is being heard *by her*. The referential relationship entailed in an act like this (and actually established through it) relies on the intuition of mental *access*: The act of perceiving provides the perceiving subject with *access to* the perceived things out there.[9]

Although access-based intentionality may be appropriate for scenarios in which perceivers have direct perceptual access to objects and events in their environments, it becomes useless when one considers scenarios in which this access is blocked or interrupted. For instance, when the perceiver closes her eyes, she cannot see the tree in the meadow anymore. In this scenario, access to the tree becomes replaced by knowledge or *content about* the tree: Based on previous perceptual access, she may know that it is still there and what it looks like. Thus, while the notion of having content about something may be misleading for characterizing perceptual acts themselves, it is appropriate for characterizing the nature of the knowledge acquired in and through such acts. We may therefore conclude that access-based intentionality can only emerge as long as the perceiver is in direct perceptual contact with objects and events in the world. As soon as that contact gets disrupted, the awareness of being in contact with things turns into the awareness of having knowledge about things. It is through this operation that access-based (weak) intentionality turns into content-based (strong) intentionality.

Let us sum up what access intentionality entails. We may distinguish three fundamental features that are closely interrelated. First, access intentionality implies the existence (and/or entails the creation) of a mental subject (the perceiver: she who perceives). Second, access intentionality establishes particular kinds of relationships between the

9. According to this three-level scheme, the crucial distinctive feature of perceptual acts is seen in *having access to* things and events in the world, rather than *having content about* them: Even if the perceiver realizes that the ringing of the bell is being heard by her, her perceptual experience will still not contain two things of which one is the content of the other (i.e., the ringing of the bell itself and her hearing of the ringing of the bell) but only one thing (i.e., the ringing bell as heard by her). The fact that her perceptual access to that ringing is also contained in the percept does not by itself create a distinct and separate content-bearing mental entity. In ordinary perceptual acts, the perceiver perceives herself to be in direct perceptual contact with objects and events, with no kind of content-bearing entity in between.

perceiver and the perceived (seeing, hearing, etc.: being in particular kinds of perceptual contact with, or having particular kinds of perceptual access to, things in the world). Third, in these relationships, the perceiver is understood to be disjunct and separated from the perceived—to the effect that things and events are external to perceivers (perceived to be out there, as it were). Access intentionality implies, in other words, a world of things and events out there and a perceiving subject attached to a body moving around in that world. From the perceiver's perspective, her body and the world are both surrounding her, and at any time she may choose to access certain things and events through creating perceptual contact with them.

Thoughts

Let us now move on from percepts to thoughts—to tokens of mental experience pertaining to objects and events beyond the reach of perceptual access. Such tokens may, on the one hand, refer to things that are not happening here and now but rather happen, have happened, or will happen there and then—at other places and/or at other times. But they may also refer to attributes of things happening here and now that perception does not deliver for free and are therefore not contained in respective percepts. In the foregoing discussion we already took a first glimpse at "thoughts" when we touched on scenarios in which perceptual contact is blocked or interrupted, indicating that the structure of cognitive experience gets fundamentally altered when percepts turn into thoughts. While some of these changes concern the what, the major ones pertain to the how of cognitive experience.

What? Not surprisingly, the scope of thoughts is broader and richer than the scope of percepts can ever be. This applies to both qualities and structure. Regarding qualities, thoughts may assign highly arbitrary and abstract semantic attributes to objects and events—attributes that may go far beyond the reach of what perception can deliver. Thoughts may, for instance, classify objects in novel and unprecedented ways, thereby assigning to them attributes that are not (and cannot be) contained in their percepts. Regarding structure, the scope of thoughts is much larger than the scope of percepts because thoughts may, unlike percepts, extend into the past and the future and apply to happenings at large temporal and spatial distances. For instance, through their memories, plans, and fantasies, thinkers may address real or fictional scenarios and episodes that may be entirely detached from the scenarios in the reach of their current perception. In sum, thoughts extend the scope of percepts with respect to both attributes and structure. While attribute extension increases the semantic depth of mental experience, structural extension increases its episodic breadth.[10]

How? What changes when we move from perceiving to thinking, or from perceivers to thinkers? Basically, the relation of *having access to* things in the world is replaced by the relation of *having knowledge about* those things. To understand what this entails, we may consider the three basic features of access intentionality that we identified above.

One feature pertains to the who of mental acts, that is, the experiencing subject and his or her role in the mental act. Here we encounter a deep change. Thinkers differ from perceivers in that they play a more active role in building a relation between the subject who thinks or knows and the thoughts or knowledge he is aware of. Whereas perceptual objects and events are taken to be given from the outside, knowledge and thoughts are understood to arise from within—originating in the thinker's own mind—or even generated by her own mind. Accordingly, whereas subjects who perceive are only implicitly entailed by their perceptual acts, subjects who think are entailed by their thought acts in more explicit forms: Their thoughts are always theirs—be it in the sense that they harbor them, own them, or even author them.[11]

This takes us to the second feature that concerns the relationship between the who and the what of the act—the thinker and the thought. The structure of this relationship is also fundamentally different from its counterpart in perception. This is because it now involves three components (rather than two) and two different kinds of relations between them (rather than one). In a nutshell, we may say that *thinkers* entertain *thoughts* about *things* in the world. The first relation is that of the thinker having thoughts. Thoughts belong to the thinker; they are therefore not understood to be "out there," but "in here."[12] The second relation concerns the

10. In chapter 7 I introduced these terms to denote two kinds of information extension in the context of generating percepts. Here I extend their use to the context of generating thoughts.

11. It is certainly not by accident that we use possessive pronouns for thoughts but not for percepts. The tree I perceive out there is a thing in and by itself. It is *a* tree, but not *my* tree. By contrast, an idea or an intention that comes to mind will, as a rule, be experienced as being owned or authored by me and will hence be communicated as indexed by a possessive pronoun: *my* idea, *my* intention.

12. In one sense, the relation between thinkers and thoughts may be seen to resemble the relation between perceivers and things. Just as perceivers have direct access to things (out there), thinkers have direct access to thoughts (in here). The crucial difference pertains to the nature of what is being accessed: things (as such) or thoughts (about things).

content of thoughts: Thoughts are about things out there. The simple scheme of a perceiver who has direct access to things out there is thus replaced by the more complex scheme of a thinker who has thoughts about things out there.[13] Thus, while perceivers have direct access to things in the world, thinkers have more indirect knowledge about these things. Therefore, we may speak of *content intentionality* inherent in thinking, in contrast to *access intentionality* inherent in perceiving. Content intentionality makes explicit what is only implicitly entailed by access intentionality: that mental acts establish relationships between things in the world (what) and mental subjects experiencing them (who).

Accordingly, a more complex picture arises with respect to the third feature—"out-thereness." While this feature certainly applies to the relation between thoughts in the mind and things in the world, it does not apply to the relation between thinkers and thoughts: It is certainly true that thoughts will typically refer to things that are independent of the thinker (i.e., out there), but it is also true that thoughts as such belong to the thinker (i.e., in here).

Experiential Subjectivity

Having stressed the differences between perceiving and thinking in the first place, we may finally emphasize and summarize what they have in common. Since perceivers are also thinkers and thinkers are also perceivers, there must be a common denominator for both. That common denominator should deliver to us what we must consider the hallmark of cognitive experience and, hence, the benchmark for assessing the explanatory power of cognitive systems.

The common denominator is provided by a feature that we may address under the notion of *experiential subjectivity*. Tokens of cognitive experience exhibit this feature in the following sense: They not only address things in the world as such but rather address these things as being perceived by the perceiver (seen, heard, etc.) and/or being thought by the thinker (remembered, intended, etc.). Thus, three elements are intrinsic to them at a time: the things out there, the experiencing subject, and the particular way in which the two are related to each other. The character of this intentional relationship is fundamentally different for percepts and

---

13. A slightly different way of looking at thoughts is to see them combining access and content, rather than replacing one with the other. According to this view, thoughts provide access to things in the mind that, in turn, bear content about things in the world.

thoughts, though. Whereas perceivers have access to things in the world, thinkers have knowledge about them.

Thus, although intentional relationships may be variable across different kinds and tokens of mental experience, the feature of experiential subjectivity is common to all of them. This, then, is what we demand of cognitive theories: They need to explain how it is possible that experiencing subjects are aware not only of the things contained in their percepts and thoughts but also of their perceiving and thinking—as well as of themselves as experiencing subjects who perceive and think.[14]

Representational Resources

Let us now abandon our experiencing subject for a while and take the role of a cognitive scientist. Cognitive science tries to understand, in more general terms, what cognitive systems are, how they work, and what they do for the animals and robots in which they are implemented.[15] As soon as we broaden our perspective in this way, we begin to see that the topics we have discussed so far cover only a small segment of the issues that cognitive systems and theories of their workings need to address—a segment, though, that is often neglected or even ignored.

There are two obvious reasons for the marginal role of mental experience in cognitive science. First, as we have already seen in chapter 1, it is natural to assume that cognitive systems have mainly evolved for the sake of adaptive behavior and performance, not for the sake of experience. Accordingly, cognitive science has largely evolved as a science of behavioral performance and has only to a lesser degree taken care of issues of mental experience. Second, even if cognitive science does approach such issues, it tends to focus on the what rather than the how of mental experience—on issues of mental content rather than mental acts. Accordingly, we should

14. It goes without saying that cognitive theories have much more to explain than the feature of experiential subjectivity on which I focus here. Moreover, it is obvious that they can accomplish much of their explanatory mission without making reference to the notion of experiential subjectivity at all. Accordingly, the claim I am raising here is not that we cannot understand the workings of the cognitive machinery until we understand the underpinnings of experiential subjectivity. The claim is rather that we cannot understand the special way in which humans make use of that machinery until we focus on its capacity for grounding subjective experience.
15. Whereas cognitive science addresses both natural and artificial systems, the present discussion will concentrate on complex natural systems as they are instantiated in the brains and bodies of animals.

not expect that the project of understanding the workings of natural cognitive systems has much to offer for addressing how-issues pertaining to mental experience, such as having access to or knowledge about things in the world and the intrinsic subjectivity entailed by such states.[16]

In this section, I discuss representational resources that cognitive theories offer for explaining performance and experience. I start with discussing the broad idea of representation of which most major theoretical approaches make use in one or the other way, suggesting a fundamental distinction between implicit and explicit representation. Then I move on to examining how that idea can be used to account for performance and experience. As will become apparent, this project is well under way regarding the role of implicit representation for performance, but it is less developed regarding the role of explicit representation for experience. I will submit that understanding experience requires a theoretical framework for self-representation. The final section of this chapter spells out what self-representation entails and how it relates to explicit representation; the subsequent chapter will then elaborate on the roots of selfhood and subjectivity.

Kinds of Representation

The term *representation* has had the unfortunate fate of a shooting star in the heaven of cognitive theory—unfortunate because it has become used and misused for a number of diverse purposes. Not surprisingly, it has been suffering from lapse of meaning and loss of explanatory power. For instance, with respect to the issue of *what is being represented*, the use of the term may range from elementary physical features like color and orientation of visual stimuli to highly complex structures like symphonies, laws, or scientific theories. Likewise, with respect to the issue *what or who is representing*, the term is used for both subpersonal entities like neurons, cell assemblies or memory codes and personal entities like perceivers, thinkers, and volitional agents.

Given such variety of uses, it seems on the one hand obvious that there is more than a single and coherent concept underlying them.[17] On the other hand, it is no less obvious that there is still one central intuition that

16. This statement is meant to apply to the science, not to the philosophy, of mind. Pertinent philosophical discussions do in fact address issues of phenomenal experience and intentionality (e.g., Block, Flanagan & Güzeldere, 1997; Roy et al., 1999; Zahavi, 2005). However, these contributions have so far had no major impact on theories and methods of experimental approaches to the workings of cognition.

17. Philosophers have come up with various suggestions for parceling the field; see, e.g., Dretske (1981, 1995); Fodor (1981, 1987); Lycan (1996); Pylyshyn (1986).

they all share. We may call it the *placeholder intuition*. The placeholder intuition implies that a thing can be two things at a time: the thing itself and a placeholder for something else that it stands for. The firing of a neuron is, on the one hand, a physical event in the brain and, on the other hand, a placeholder for the orientation of a bar to which the neuron is tuned. Likewise, hearing a dog bark is on the one hand a given hearer's perceptual impression, but at the same time it stands for the fact that there is a dog out there that is barking. In a similar vein, knowing what Maxwell's equations entail is, on the one hand, a knowledge state in a thinker's mind that, on the other hand, stands for relationships and interactions between certain kinds of physical things in the world.

The placeholder intuition carries with it two major implications. One is that the domain in which the placeholder exists (i.e., individual brains and minds) is detached from the domain in which the things exist whose place they are holding (i.e., sensory stimulation, things in the world). The metaphor entails, in other words, a structural separation between two disjunct domains. The other implication is that there must be some causal links between the represented and the representing domain that are specific enough to allow for at least partial reconstruction of features of represented things from features of representing things. If these two conditions are fulfilled, placeholders can be said to carry information about the things whose place they are holding. In other words, they carry the potential to represent these things.[18]

What exactly do mental placeholders need to contain in order to exploit that potential and satisfy the needs of performance and experience? For addressing this question, it is useful to distinguish between two basic kinds of representation, implicit and explicit. They differ with respect to both structural complexity and functional power.

Implicit. Loosely speaking, implicit representations are representations in the mind that stand for things in the world without "knowing" it. We may call representations implicit if the fact that they are internal placeholders for external things is itself not contained in what they represent. Accordingly, they are placeholders from an external observer's perspective, not from the system's own perspective. From the outside view, they are internal states that represent external states of affairs, but from the inside view, they are nothing but internal states. Their representational character is, in other words, not intrinsically inherent in them but can only be extrinsically assigned to them.

18. For the relation between carrying information (about a thing) and representing (a thing), see Dretske (1981).

Still, irrespective of the fact that they are themselves blind to their potential for representation, they *are* in fact representations and *can be used* as such. The sole requirement for such use is that sufficiently reliable causal links can be established between features of external things and features of internal states. As long as this requirement is fulfilled, internal states can be used as representations of external things.

At first glance, implicit representation may appear to be a rather primitive and weak mode of representation, but in fact it is not. Rather, when one views it in terms of its power for performance control, one begins to see that implicit representation can in fact account for most of what we call animal intelligence. If it is true that animals' mental systems are optimized for efficient action control, the functional power of the involved representations will mainly depend on the validity and reliability with which they fulfill their placeholder function—but not on their representation of that function itself. Below I will elaborate on kinds of implicit representations that account for the behavioral performance of natural animate systems.

Explicit. The spontaneous intuition that implicit representation is regarded as a weak and primitive mode of representation may be due to the fact that we, as open-minded observers, rely very much on explicit modes of representation—to the effect that we find implicit modes a bit simple and narrow-minded. We speak of explicit representation when the fact that representations are internal placeholders for external things is also represented itself. Explicit representations are thus placeholders not only from an external observer's perspective but from the representing system's own perspective as well. Their representational character is, in other words, intrinsically inherent in them. They are represented as representations in and for the given system.

What does explicit representation require beyond implicit representation and how can we build one on the other? Basically, explicit representations are much more complex than implicit representations. Two major features are required for building one on the other, one general and one specific. First, in a general sense, explicit representation relies on linking two kinds of representations, one pertaining to represented things and another pertaining to the system representing them. It thus presupposes that the representing system represents itself, along with the things that it represents. Second, in a more specific sense, explicit representation relies on a variety of ways of linking these two kinds of representations to each other. Different kinds of links are, for instance, required for the representation of perceiving things, thinking thoughts, or planning actions. Together, these two features require an architecture for representation of representation—an architecture that builds explicit representation from creating links between different kinds of implicit representations.[19]

This leaves us with the issue of functional efficiency. If it is true that implicit representation already suffices for the basic needs of action control and efficient performance—what is gained by building a costly and demanding architecture for explicit representation on top of implicit representation? As I will show below, the answer to this question is once more entailed by the transition from closed to open minds and the potential for the social control of individual action associated with that transition. While closed minds rely on action control at the individual level, open minds are open to, and in fact dependent on, sharing control with others. Such sharing requires abandoning implicit representation and moving on to explicit representation. In order to be shared, knowledge needs to be explicit; sharing knowledge about X requires that individuals who know X also know which other individuals know X.

Explicit representation thus does for open minds what implicit representation does for closed minds. They both provide the information required for efficient action control in their respective systems—private and implicit in closed minds and public and explicit in open minds. Whereas closed minds deliver performance without experience, open minds deliver performance through experience.

Explaining Performance

Up to now we have concentrated on representations as basic, individuated units of cognition. On that view, representations are regarded as placeholders that exist within cognitive systems and carry information about things happening outside these systems. In the next step we need to extend our scope, considering the architecture of systems generating and maintaining such representations and exploiting their representational potential for action control and performance. What kind of architecture do natural animate systems need for grounding efficient action control on implicit representation?

19. Though it may be tempting to apply the elegant notion of metarepresentation here, it does not seem to be appropriate (Sperber, 2000). The claim here is not that given representations become re-represented (at higher levels of representation), but rather that representations of represented things and things representing them become linked to each other, to the effect that the representational relationship between them is represented as well. Thus, what explicit representation adds to implicit representation is the representation of their representational character.

Much of what needs to be said on this issue has already been addressed in chapter 7 as we examined the representational underpinnings of bottom-up control. Yet, where the focus in that chapter was on action control, the focus will now be on event interpretation and the transition between interpretation and control. What is required to enable cognitive systems to generate implicit information that subserve the functions of event interpretation and action generation? How can we understand the act of constructing representations, and what kinds of resources are required for that act?[20]

The basic scheme that I am suggesting for addressing these questions has two major components: transient construction and permanent resources. Since these two components apply equally to both event interpretation and action generation, they may be seen to provide building blocks for a simple framework for the workings of cognition in the service of action.[21]

Constructing representations. A convenient way of viewing the role of knowledge for representation and performance is to think of representations as outcomes of constructive processes that draw on two major information resources: information delivered by current stimulation and information available from memory. Accordingly, the process of building representations must be understood to draw on both transient construction and permanent resources.

To understand what the notion of *transient construction* entails, first consider the metaphor of construction itself. This metaphor pertains to the production of specific, structured things from less specific and less

20. As in previous chapters, I will mainly discuss this question with regard to declarative resources, taking procedural resources for granted. Whereas procedural resources refer to knowledge entailed in the computational algorithms for generating, maintaining, and manipulating representations (*know-how*), declarative resources address the content of the knowledge that gets generated, maintained and manipulated that way (*know-what*). The focus of the present discussion will thus be on kinds of declarative knowledge that enable cognitive systems to construct implicit representations to subserve event interpretation and action generation.

21. Since the framework is meant to rely exclusively on implicit representation, a word of caution is again in order with respect to terminology. The terminology I am using speaks of, e.g., understanding, knowledge, meaning, event interpretation, and action generation—i.e., terms whose use in everyday language carries a distinct and (unavoidable) mentalistic flavor. However, it should be clear that I am here using these terms as shorthand for functional/computational states and operations, without implying any reference to their mentalistic connotations.

structured material resources. As a result, the outcomes of construction will differ from the resources from which they are built. Typically, they will be more complex and they may exhibit novel properties that are not contained in those resources but rather emerge from the act of construction. The construction metaphor thus reflects what we may call the functional autonomy of representations: Although they are constructed from stimulus and memory information, their functional status is independent from these resources, and they contain information that goes beyond both of them.

Second, consider what the transient character of representational construction entails. It reflects the fact that constructional computations are going on all the time, based on information currently available on the stimulus and the memory side. Accordingly, representational constructions are short-lived things. Their coming and going and their relative strengths (in comparison with other concurrent constructions) are determined by computational algorithms operating to combine stimulus and memory information.

Consider as a third element the two kinds of resources. Depending on their relative contributions, the resulting representations may subserve percepts or thoughts. Whereas perceptual representations are structured by strong contributions from the stimulus side, such contributions may be entirely lacking in representations underlying thoughts. Thought-subserving representations must therefore be entirely structured by stimulus-independent algorithms that control their coming and going and determine their strength.

We may further consider constructional hierarchies—hierarchies of more finely and coarsely grained levels at which things and events in the world may be represented. Construction may yield, for example, representations at the level of attributes, of spatially extended objects, of temporally extended events, or even of larger scenes and scenarios comprising complex assemblies of objects and events. There are two options here. One is that construction needs to choose among these levels, constructing representations at one level at a time. The other is that it delivers nested hierarchies of representations, delivering not only attributes, objects, and events as such but also covering the hierarchical relationships in which they are embedded. In either case there must be ways of switching between levels of representation on demand.

Finally, and more importantly, we may consider constructional episodes—a step that takes us closer to issues of performance. Whereas hierarchies address the construction of several things at a time, episodes address the construction of coherent events over time. In a similar way as hierarchies subserve the function of reflecting structural relationships between things that happen simultaneously, episodes serve the function of reflecting sequential and temporal relationships between things that happen one after the other. This may be trivial for purely perceptual episodes whose construction is entirely determined by incoming stimulus information, but it is not trivial for episodes whose construction is not determined that way.

A crucial example is provided by representational episodes entailing transitions between event interpretation and action generation, as discussed in chapters 7 and 8. In their initial phase, as long as they subserve event interpretation, these episodes will mainly be structured by stimulus information. Later, however, as they move on from event interpretation to event prediction and action production, memory information will take the lead in structuring their course. Obviously, such mixed episodes are a prerequisite for action control. Action control requires that the system constructs episodes that are capable of linking memory-based representations (of still-to-be-performed actions) to stimulus-based representations (of already-happening events). Efficiency of control will then depend on the extent to which previous learning has enabled the system to distinguish between linkages that have proven to be more or less successful under given circumstances.

Let us now see what the notion of *permanent resources* entails. To fulfill its function properly, transient representational construction must draw on long-lived memory resources that serve as a knowledge base for constructing short-lived hierarchies and episodes of events and actions.[22]

We may discern two major kinds of such resources: frameworks for structure and ontologies for meaning. Whereas frameworks provide general organizational principles for structuring representational constructions, ontologies provide more specific knowledge resources concerning the meaning of currently constructed events for future events and actions.

---

22. Once more, it may be useful to remind ourselves of the dilemma of using an explicit representational language for characterizing the workings of an implicit-representational system (see this ch., n. 21). For instance, when we talk about knowledge resources, we characterize the system from an external rather than an internal perspective. Yet, when seen from an internal perspective, these resources do not provide any (explicit) knowledge about something out there. Instead they provide (implicit) representations that have in the past proven to be useful for operations like event interpretation and action generation. When seen from an external perspective, this information is useful because it carries information about body and world (and, hence, provides explicit representations).

Borrowing a distinction from the language domain, we may think of frameworks and ontologies as taking care of the syntax and the semantics of representational construction, respectively.[23]

Frameworks for structure need to reflect aspects of the structural organization of things in the world as far as they are relevant for performance and action control.[24] We may posit at least two such frameworks: one for space and time and another for world and body. Both provide principles of structural organization that are required for each instance of representational construction.

It is a truism that, in order to survive, animals need to do the right things at the right places and at the right times. While the things they do are taken care of by ontologies (to which we turn below), places and times are taken care of by frameworks for space and time. As witnessed by their behavioral performance, animals like flies and frogs "know" where things are and when they happen—not only under conditions of direct perceptual contact but also when such contact is interrupted or broken. We must therefore conclude that their representational constructions are organized in ways that mirror—and actually reconstruct—the spatial layout of objects and the temporal course of events in the world.[25] Cognitive theory must therefore posit such frameworks to account for spatially and temporarily adapted behavior.

23. Although the linguistic metaphor seems to suggest a categorical difference, I do not mean to ontologize the distinction here. It should rather be seen as a pragmatic distinction between two kinds of long-lived knowledge structures that are required for short-lived constructional operations. There may even be transitions between (universal) frameworks and (specific) ontologies (see this ch., nn. 21, 29).

24. This qualification is meant to emphasize the fact that knowledge is selective. An animal's knowledge will typically not pertain to happenings at the micro-level (say, the level of molecules or even atoms) nor to events at the macro-level (say, the level of stars and galaxies), but rather at the meso-level of happenings in the animal's environment—basically at the same level at which its responding and complementary action needs to be specified.

25. One can think of two basic ways of instantiating these structural resources: extrinsic and intrinsic. Whereas the extrinsic view holds that spatial and temporal dimensions are tools for structuring things on universal dimensions that are extrinsic to these things, the intrinsic view holds that spatial and temporal attributes may be intrinsic to these things themselves. These two views may be taken to illustrate the difference between frameworks and ontologies. Whereas the first considers spatial and temporal dimensions as universal tools for ordering things, the second regards spatial and temporal features as a basis of domain-specific ontologies.

A further structural problem that transient construction needs to solve concerns the representational divide between body and world. While this divide is indispensable for efficient action control, it is not inherent in the stimulus information that arises from sensory contact with body and world. It rather needs to be established through appropriate representational (re-)construction. From the representing system's perspective, the sources of information that arise from body and world are both equally external so that additional information is needed to structure them accordingly. That information must be provided by a framework that construes the body as part of the world.

This construal needs to address both commonalities and differences between body and world. Regarding commonalities, it implies that the body is a thing in the world in precisely the same sense as are, for instance, trees and cows or houses and cars. In other words, the spatial and temporal framework that applies to these (remote) things must apply to the (less remote) body as well. As concerns differences the construal must acknowledge that the body also has a special status that makes it unique. One aspect of this uniqueness is that access to the world is always mediated through the body. The body is, in other words, a tool that mediates access to the world. A further important aspect in which it is unique is that certain kinds of bodily events are under the system's control and can be generated and/or modulated by it. Owing to this feature, the body is for the system a tool for both navigating in and operating on the world—which obviously requires close cooperation between the frameworks for body-world and space-time.

There is a rich literature in philosophy and science on both the special role of space-time and the importance of the body-world divide for cognition and action.[26] Whereas the philosophical literature mainly addresses these issues from the perspective of contents of experience, the scientific literature stresses issues of mechanisms for performance. Still, there is one central theme that philosophy and science share. Both harbor never-

26. For theoretical treatments of these topics, see, e.g., Bermúdez, Marcel, and Eilan (1995); Eilan, Marcel, and Bermúdez (1995); Gibson (1986); von Helmholtz (1924–1925); Kant (1996); Mach (1897/1959); Merleau-Ponty (1945/2003); Schilder (1935). For overviews of experimental research, see Adolph (2008); Bertenthal and Longo (2008); Butterworth (1995); Epstein (1977); Graziano and Botvinick (2002); Howard (1986); Howard and Templeton (1966); Kinsbourne (1995); Loomis and Philbeck (2008); Maravita (2006); Proffitt (2008); Sedgwick (1986); Stiles-David, Kritchevsky, and Bellugi (1988); Warren and Wertheim (1990); Welch (1978, 1986).

ending debates on the origin of these frameworks. While some believe that they must be innate or given a priori, others believe that they are acquired through learning or a posteriori construction. Rather than entering into this discussion, I would like to emphasize what both sides still agree on: that the structural knowledge provided by these frameworks must, in functional and temporal terms, precede any act of representational construction. There can be no efficient transient representation without structural organization provided by these frameworks.

Frameworks for structure are complemented by ontologies for meaning. While frameworks lay the ground for structuring representations, ontologies help to fill them with meaningful content. Ontologies are systems of semantic knowledge. For the sake of convenience we may think of them as individuated in terms of the categories of things that need to be distinguished at each level in the underlying representational hierarchies. Accordingly, we may distinguish between ontologies for categories of things like attributes, objects, events, scenes, scenarios, and so on—and within each of them between subontologies for various subcategories of these things. Ontologies specify, for each given category, what kinds of things exist, how they differ from each other, and what functional knowledge is associated with them.

Ontologies thus reflect the semantic knowledge that the system has acquired through previous learning. By making that knowledge available to current representational construction, they serve the function of implementing meaning in representations. They help to individuate attributes, objects, and events, to identify and understand them, to predict what they are leading to, and to select actions suited to modulate them. The meaning of representations resides, in other words, in their potential for interpretation and prediction of events and generation of appropriate action.

To illustrate, consider ontologies for some basic categories of things. Ontologies for objects, for instance, need to provide lists of kinds of objects that are differentiated according to basic attributes relevant for dealing and interacting with them—such as dead things and living things (and again among living things, such things as plants, animals, agents, etc.). These kinds differ from each other in a number of attributes. Some of them specify shallow features of outer appearance (which can be directly matched with corresponding stimulus information), but most of them address deeper features pertaining to inner dispositions and action-related functionalities. For instance, at some place in the subontology for furniture, chairs are known to be as high as one's hips are, to be less broad than high, to be made of wood, to have a certain weight, and to afford actions like sitting on them or standing on them to extend one's reach in the upward direction.

Likewise, animals and humans are known to exhibit self-propelled motion, implying that the shallow kinematics of their seen movements is driven by the deep dynamics of unseen internal forces. Some kinds of animals may even be known to operate as agents—animals whose physical dynamics is understood to be driven by the even deeper dynamics of mental states and forces. As the examples illustrate, ontologies for objects depend on underlying ontologies for attributes that may be assigned to them. These ontologies, too, exhibit lists of kinds of attributes that are differentiated on the basis of their functional use for event interpretation and action generation.

Whereas objects are timeless things, episodes of events and actions are much richer entities since they also exhibit temporal patterns that may be associated with causal patterns specifying their inherent dynamics. There are two major reasons why ontologies for events and actions are of particular importance for performance. One is that dynamics paves the way for extrapolation and prediction. When it comes to scenarios like a stone rolling down a hill, a bear chasing a deer, or a hunter watching a bear, observers are in a position not only to understand these events as they have happened so far (past) and are happening now (present), but also to predict what is going to happen next (future). This is because their underlying ontologies "know" what rolling stones, running bears, and watching hunters are, what kinds of forces drive them, and, if applicable, what kinds of internal states and dispositions generate these forces.[27] These ontologies provide, in other words, multilayered models for events and actions— models that cover not only their (shallow) kinematics but also extend to their (deep) dynamics and the underlying causal machinery. Accordingly, they help observers to be prepared for what is going to happen next.

The other reason is that action control requires representational construction of episodes that proceed from interpretation of (foreign) events to generation of (one's own) action. It is reasonable to assume that the efficiency of such control episodes will—among other things—depend on the representational overlap between ontologies for events and actions.

27. What appears to be applicable or not is to some extent determined by cultural context. For instance, in Western cultures, hunters and, perhaps, bears are understood to be driven by internal forces, and perhaps mental states behind them, whereas stones are not. Other cultures may rely on other kinds of attributions, resulting in different kinds of attributes perceived to be operating.

Going back to figure 7.1, we may think of these ontologies as instantiated in the repertoires for events and actions. An obvious way of creating such overlap is to align the dimensional structures of the two ontologies, thus laying the ground for common coding in the transition between events and actions.[28] As we already saw in chapter 8, common coding is particularly obvious in the domain of action representation. This is because action ontologies adopt two functional roles at a time: interpretation of foreign action (running bears, watching hunters) and generation of one's own complementary and responding action (e.g., shooting the bear, warning the hunter).

Although there is a huge debate in the literature concerning the origin of structural frameworks, there is no such discussion with respect to the origin of ontologies.[29] It is generally believed that they are acquired and that their contents reflect the outcome of lifelong learning procedures through which the system has acquired its semantic knowledge about objects, events, and actions.

Representation and control. Representation is for control—at least in animate systems that rely entirely on forward control and implicit kinds of representation. As we discussed in chapter 7, we may capture the functional logic of control in terms of two basic operations: event interpretation and action generation. While using these terms we should once more remind ourselves that they are meant to characterize the workings of control from an external observer's perspective, not the system's own perspective. While external observers know that these operations involve

28. This applies to both bottom-up control (proceeding from given events to selection of responding actions) and top-down control (proceeding from intended events to selection of actions suited to realize them). It should not go unnoticed that our above discussion on the origin of intentions (ch. 9) has provided further arguments in support of representational overlap between ontologies for event interpretation and action generation.

29. An important exception is provided by the literature on the roots of cognition in early infancy. In this field the nature–nurture debate is still very much alive (see, e.g., Baillargeon, 2001; Carey, 2009; Carey & Spelke, 1994; Gopnik & Meltzoff, 1997; Piaget, 1954; Spelke & Newport, 1998). It is not always clear how theoretical proposals arising from that debate match up to the present distinction between frameworks and ontologies (e.g., Piaget's notion of sensory-motor schemata or Spelke and Carey's notion of core knowledge and core cognition). This may be taken to suggest that the framework–ontology distinction, though it is useful for understanding mature performance, may be inappropriate to account for the initial stock of a baby's representational primitives.

placeholders for events and actions outside the controller, the controller itself doesn't know. It just performs computational operations proceeding from input to output.

Given the architecture for transient representational construction just outlined, we may now take a novel look at the functional logic of control, which provides us with a slightly different view on event interpretation and action generation and the relationship between the two. These two components are now no longer considered two distinct operations but rather two phases in certain kinds of episodes of representational construction. We may call them *control episodes*. Control episodes range from initial steps of stimulus-structured interpretation over medial steps of event prediction (as structured by event knowledge) to final steps of action production (as structured by action knowledge).

In a sense, this view regards action generation as a particular kind of extension of the episodical breadth of representational construction. It posits a continuous transition between event interpretation and action generation: Action generation is a late extension to early event interpretation. For the workings of the system, there is no principled functional difference between attribution of meaning (as based on object and event ontologies) and generation of action (as based on action ontologies).[30] Actions that are selected in response to events contribute to their interpretation in exactly the same way as do semantic attributes assigned to them. The difference is not in the underlying operations but in the eye of the external beholder. We as beholders draw a conceptual distinction that is actually not entailed by the controller's intrinsic functionality.

If it is true that representation is for control, control episodes must be seen to instantiate the proper function for which transient representational construction has evolved.[31] Accordingly, there is a further sense in which the operations of event interpretation and action generation are not as independent as the conceptual distinction suggests. When we look at them in terms of their contributions to the animal's fitness it becomes apparent

30. A closely related idea is entailed by various brands of motor theories of perception, cognition, and consciousness (see, e.g., Galantucci, Fowler & Turvey, 2006; Hurley, 1998; Liberman et al., 1967; Noë, 2004; Viviani, 2002).

31. This should not be taken to imply that any kind and instance of transient representational construction must be considered a control episode. There may be instances of transient construction that do not contain action-related extensions at all, whether this is because no such extensions are available in the pertinent ontologies, or because the act of construction terminates before these "late" extensions are reached.

that the action-related contribution is direct, whereas the event-related contribution is indirect and can only become effective through the other. What counts in terms of fitness are overt actions, not covert representational states leading to them.

Explaining Experience

Let us now move on from performers to perceivers–thinkers and see what our architecture needs in order to accommodate the structure of cognitive experience. How can we get there? The first thing we should keep in mind is that perceivers–thinkers are performers as well. This may be taken to suggest that we should think of extending the architecture for performance, rather than altering or restructuring it altogether. The second thing is to remind ourselves what we need to explain. Here we may discern a distant goal and a near goal. The distant goal is to understand how experiential subjectivity becomes possible. The near goal, through which we may hope to reach the farther one, is to understand how explicit representation can emerge from and on top of implicit representation.

Accordingly, the first step I am going to take is concerned with extending permanent resources. This step addresses the formation of a framework for the mental self and the creation of an ontology for intentional relations. The second step then addresses the enrichment of transient representational constructions that these extensions make possible. Here I show how explicit representations can emerge and how they help to ground both the unity and the diversity of mental experience.

Extending resources. Let us once more adopt an engineering perspective, trying to build a system for experience from a system for performance. From what we have discussed so far, it is apparent that we need to extend the long-lived representational resources on which short-lived representational constructions rely. Here we need two major extensions, pertaining to frameworks and ontologies, respectively.

As concerns structural resources, we need to build an *extended framework—* a framework for a mental self. Here we may go back to ideas that we touched on in chapter 1 when we discussed transitions from representational to self-representational systems. We may now specify what this transition requires in terms of extensions of permanent resources. How can we extend a representational framework for body and world into a self-representational framework that also includes a mental self?

Since explicit representations require that things in the body and the world become represented in a way that also represents the system representing them (as well as the fact that that system is representing them), we need to construe a self-referential representation of the representing system. For the sake of simplicity, I call that representation a *mental self*.[32] Once established, this framework offers the opportunity to build a mental self into each and every act of representational construction. Representational construction will then contain three things at a time: the things being represented, the thing representing them, and the intentional relationship between the two things.

To make this possible, we need a structure for the mental self. The most obvious way to get there is to extend the already existing framework for body and world. As we have seen above, this framework structures representational constructions according to a topological scheme that locates the body in the world (so that the world is surrounding it), furnishing the body with particular capacities like navigating in the world, acting upon it, and providing perceptual access to it. To that scheme, which takes care of representing body and world, we need to add a further, novel component. The structure of that addition must meet two requirements. One is that the extended scheme must capture the fact that the representing system is attached to the body: It is always where the body is and its access to the world goes through the body. The other is that it is still not located within the body. It must rather be located at a separate level of mental things that represent physical things (both body and world). Figure 11.1 outlines a scheme that meets these two requirements.

The extended framework needs to be flanked by *extended ontologies*. These ontologies must capture both kinds of intentional relations between representing selves and represented things and kinds of beings to which intentional relations may apply. Whereas the first ontology addresses transient constructions, the second addresses permanent resources.

The first ontology lists kinds of ways in which a representing self can be related to represented things, and vice versa. It provides a catalog of

32. The term "mental self" must be seen in opposition to "bodily self." This distinction is meant to emphasize the functional autonomy of the mental self. In the literature the distinction between the mental and the bodily self is often not as clear as it needs to be. As discussed in chapter 4, a famous example is provided by the popular idea of taking mirror self-recognition as an indication of the emergence of a mental self (see, e.g., Amsterdam, 1972; Gallup, 1970; Lacan, 1949/1977). Mirror self-recognition may indeed reflect the discovery that the body in the mirror corresponds to one's own body in front of the mirror, but it does not speak at all to the discovery of a mental self in, behind, or attached to that body (see Prinz, 2009). For the building up of representational frameworks for mental selves, see, e.g., Metzinger (2003); Neisser (1993); Neisser and Jopling (1997); Zahavi (2005).

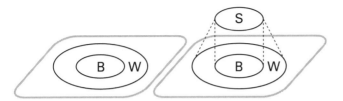

Figure 11.1
Frameworks for body, world, and mental self. The left-hand panel depicts the basic scheme for body (B) in the world (W). The right-hand panel illustrates how a mental self (S) can be added to the scheme. The self is both attached to the body and detached from both body and world. It is a mental thing entertaining intentional relationships with physical things in body and world. Whereas mental things may be attached to physical things (as S is attached to B), the spatiotemporal framework that applies to physical things (like B/W) does not likewise apply to mental things. Note that the difference between the two panels is equivalent to the difference between the two schemes in figure 1.1. In both cases a basic representational scheme develops into a self-representational scheme through the inclusion of a novel level of representation that represents and controls the workings of the basic representational scheme.

intentional relations from which ongoing representational construction may choose. For instance, one of the fundamental divides the catalog must offer is between kinds of relations exhibiting access versus content intentionality. Access intentionality is attributed to acts of perceiving, providing for the mental self the relatively weak and passive role of having access to currently ongoing things. Content intentionality, by contrast, is ascribed to acts of thinking, providing for the self the more active role of generating and entertaining mental representations about things beyond the reach of current perceptual access.

The second ontology lists kinds of living beings that are understood to maintain intentional relationships—kinds of mental beings, as it were. One way of building such an ontology is to extend already existing ontologies in a way that meets the requirements of representing intentionality. For instance, we may think of extending the ontology for animate things with new kinds of things that are mental in the sense of entertaining nonphysical, intentional relationships with other things (such as seeing, knowing, or intending them). There are also several ways of conceiving the gradual building up of the novel category of mental beings. One is to think of each individual's own self as the sole initial exemplar of that kind. Another is to extend its scope from the outset and think of both our own selves and some others' selves as belonging to it. A third way, to which I return below, is to have it the other way round, thinking of the novel category initially applied to and populated by foreign selves and only later becoming extended to also include our own selves. While these options address different ways of acquisition of the novel ontology of mental beings, they share the notion that each individual's own mental self is eventually included in that kind: Individuals come to understand themselves as mental things, furnished with the capacity to entertain various kinds of intentional relations with other things.

Enriching constructions. Coming back to the near goal, it is now fairly obvious how we can account for explicit representation. Representations of things in the body and the world are explicit if they corepresent the fact of being represented in and for a given representing system. The crucial ingredients that we need to account for constructing explicit representations are delivered by the extended framework and the extended ontology: a representing system that represents itself as such and a catalog of kinds of representational references or intentional relations. Together, they serve to enrich the structure of transient representational construction in a way that turns implicit representation for performance into explicit representation for experience.

This takes us to the distant goal of accounting for experiential subjectivity. The notion of intentionality—the hallmark of mental experience—must be seen as the experiential counterpart of the functional notion of explicit representation. Explaining explicit representation is therefore tantamount to explaining major foundations of mental experience—not only in terms of what-issues but also in terms of how-issues, such as having access to things or knowledge about things.[33]

Importantly, we may now account for both *diversity and unity* of mental experience. The diversity of mental acts is grounded in the diversity entailed by the ontologies involved in construing them. Mental things like percepts, thoughts, and intentions differ in the way in which the relation between represented things and the representing self is understood. Yet, at least as impressive as the variety is the unity of mental acts. One source of unity derives from a distinctive feature that they all share. They are biva-

33. The claim here is not that explicit representation provides a full account of mental experience. Explicit representation is meant to account for intentionality— one major feature of mental experience. As said above the notion of explicit representation does not speak to the issue of qualia, which concerns a further major feature pertaining to the qualities of mental experience.

lent in the sense of carrying two features at a time: objective (i.e., referring to things outside the experiencing subject) and subjective (i.e., being experienced as the subject's own percepts, thoughts, and intentions). A further source of unity derives from the role of the experiencing subject. Crucially, under normal, nonpathological conditions, it is one and the same subject who takes part in all kinds of mental acts. One and the same subject is involved in both acts that co-occur at the same time (e.g., thinking and perceiving while driving) and acts that follow each other in time (e.g., a sequence of thoughts while solving a problem). Thus whereas diversity goes back to the variety entailed by the ontologies for mental acts, unity goes back to the basic structure contained in the framework for a mental self.

12 Roots of Intentionality

Self from Others
   Construing Others
   Self Like Others
   Blessings of True Selves
Subjectivity Demystified

In this chapter I move from issues of structure to issues of acquisition. More specifically, I raise the question of how cognitive systems can move from implicit to explicit representation. How may that move have taken place, what conditions may have given rise to it, and what kinds of functional benefits may be associated with it?[1]

In the first section, I outline a novel perspective on intentionality. Here I show how a representational architecture for intentionality can emerge from the same kind of interplay between attribution and appropriation that we have already seen at work in the formation of one's own will after that of others' will. In the second section, I discuss ways in which the novel perspective helps to demystify issues of human subjectivity that are often regarded as deeply enigmatic.

Self from Others

As mentioned above, the proposal I am going to put forward is that the transition has proceeded from the outside in—that is, from others to self.

1. There are two readings of the ideas I am laying out here. The first regards the move from implicit to explicit representation as a psycho-historical event, that is, as a transition that nature and/or culture arranged at some point in the evolutionary history of our species. The second reading, which is likewise applicable, considers it a biographical event, assuming that the psycho-historical transition needs to be reinstantiated in corresponding transitions in individual biographies.

I am going to reiterate here in brief what I have discussed in some detail in chapter 8, thereby extending the claim of the social making of the mind from volition to cognition. The claim here is that the functional organization of human cognition is deeply structured through the interplay of appropriation and attribution: Individuals become perceivers–thinkers by appropriating what they attribute to others and what they perceive others attributing to them.

One of the obvious issues that this claim raises pertains to the kinds of others involved in that interplay. What kinds of others count for these social games—peers, conspecifics, pets, mammals, or even more remote kinds from the animal kingdom? In the following, I will proceed from broad to narrow. First, I consider others in a broad sense, including animals, examining once more major intuitions that we rely on in accounting for their behavior, both in everyday life and in science. Then, in a second step, I narrow down my focus to human others. Here I examine how mirror games for attribution and appropriation subserve the takeover of mental architecture from others to self. In a final step, I conclude by summarizing how that takeover helps to open closed individual minds through sharing common ground with others.

Construing Others

To begin, let us consider an observer watching others acting and interacting with things in their environment. Since the goal of our exercise is to trace a trajectory of transition from implicit representation for performance to explicit representation for experience, we need to conceive the initial architecture from which we depart as a pure system for performance, void of any extensions and enrichments that subserve explicit representation and experiential subjectivity. Such an observer may be a somewhat artificial character, but we may use her as a hypothetical model that helps us to understand what the tools of purely implicit representation afford when it comes to representing others' actions and interactions with things in the world.

In line with our discussion in chapter 7, we may come up with two prototypical kinds of such construals emerging from a system like this: behaviorist and mentalist.[2] We may say that behaviorist construals rely on

---

2. This distinction is closely correlated with the distinction between animate and agentive construals of action control (see ch. 7). Although the two construals can be easily combined in accounting for different actions of the same individual, they exclude each other with respect to one and the same action. Likewise, there is no gradual transition from one to the other.

reading others' bodily activity, whereas mentalist construals rely on reading their mental activity (body reading and mind reading, respectively). The two construals clearly differ from each other in terms of depth of representational construction, but they nevertheless resemble each other in terms of general structure: Both address both the variety of (physical and mental) acts that come and go and the unity of the acting individual who remains constant across these acts.

Behaviorist construals. Behaviorist construals of others and their actions provide what we may call a lean account of their behavior, pertaining mainly to their bodies interacting with things in the environment and the various kinds of physical acts that instantiate that interaction.

Regarding bodies, it draws on an ontology that views bodies as physical things that are furnished with special kinds of functional features. These features pertain, for example, to the capacity for generating self-propelled motion or the capacity to act as animate controllers. To instantiate these capacities, bodies must be furnished with two kinds of devices through which they interact with their environment: sensors and effectors. Through sensors, the environment acts on them; through effectors, they act on the environment.

Regarding acts, behaviorist construals must draw on two kinds of ontologies, one for movements and another for responses. Ontologies for movements construe bodily activity in terms of patterns of spatiotemporal trajectories of body parts and the underlying pattern of forces generated by the body (kinematics and dynamics, respectively). Whereas these ontologies see bodily activity in reference to the body, ontologies for responses see it in reference to both body and environment. Unlike movements that do not go beyond their inherent kinematic and dynamic features, responses also entail a strong semantic dimension: Responses are tokens of bodily activity through which the individual responds to and interacts with things and events in the environment. Responses can thus be seen to implement instances of control through which the individual acts on the environment.

The power of body reading and the behaviorist construals entailed by it are often underestimated. These construals are in fact less lean and less superficial than they may at first appear. This is because they construe both bodies and acts of behavioral activity not only in terms of shallow features that can be matched by current stimulus information but also in terms of deeper semantic features. Bodies may, for instance, be furnished with capacities and dispositions, movements may rely on forces, and responses may reflect meaningful interactions between body and environment. The potential for semantic depth is particularly obvious for responses. Since responses refer to both body and things in the environment, they draw on ontologies that reflect, among other things, normative knowledge that the observer has accrued concerning their appropriateness and efficiency—that is, what may be good and bad for the individual under given circumstances.

Mentalist construals. Mentalist construals go one decisive step further than behaviorist construals, providing richer and deeper accounts of others' actions. Basically they construe what others do as a result of what they know about the world and their current environment. Mentalist construals thus pertain to minds who know their environment and to mental acts that instantiate that knowledge.

Mentalist construals draw on an ontology that views minds as mental things—things that are furnished with the functional capacity of representing things. That representing may refer to both things happening in the representer's current surroundings and things that are far away in space and/or time, as well as abstract things that do not exist in space and time at all. To fulfill their function, other minds are at least partially dependent on their bodies. For instance, they use sensors to establish physical contact with the world. Likewise, they use effectors to act on the world. However, at the same time, minds may also operate independently from physical support by the body. Crucially, they are furnished with the capacity to generate knowledge by themselves and from within. For instance, they may entertain memories, plans, fantasies, beliefs, intentions, and so on. In sum, minds are understood to act as centers for creating knowledge from without and within. Minds know how the world is, how it will be, how it could be, and how it should be—and what measures to take to change it accordingly.

Regarding mental acts, mentalist construals rely on ontologies that specify what mental acts are (as opposed to physical acts) and what major kinds of such acts need to be distinguished. As we have already seen in the previous chapter, observers will, for instance, construe a basic distinction between perceptual and nonperceptual mental acts, yielding knowledge from without and within, respectively. Likewise, they may construe distinctions between kinds of nonperceptual knowledge ("thoughts") that refer to past and future things, for example, memories and anticipations/intentions, respectively. In any case, the attribution of mental acts will entail the attribution of private knowledge concerning public things. Knowledge is private in the sense that it is understood to exist in a given individual's mind and can only be accessed by that mind. On the other hand, the things to which such private knowledge refers are public in the sense that other minds can access them as well.

We are all quite familiar with such mentalist construals. We use them all the time when we try to understand what others do and why they do what they do. We are, in other words, all experts in mind reading and in the folk psychology that builds on that craft. Still, when one realizes how rich and complex these construals are and how deep they actually go beneath the surface of observable behaviors, one may doubt whether they can indeed be sufficiently explained as instances of deep semantic extensions of interpretations of observable behavior. Don't we need to resort to other kinds of representational sources and resources to explain their depth and their richness? Don't we, for instance, need to follow the claims of theorists who posit that the sole way to understand other minds is to project our own mentality onto them?[3]

I don't think so. First, we must not forget that minds are related to bodies. Other minds are for observers not free-floating things, but rather are attached to their bodies and steering them from within. Their ontology for minds must therefore match their ontology for bodies. Second, and relatedly, we must keep in mind that mind reading builds on body reading. Knowing is for doing, and others' knowing can only be derived from their doing. Accordingly, ontologies for kinds of knowing must be parasitic on ontologies for kinds of acting. Both arguments join in the conclusion that minds and mental acts may well have their origin in observers' construals of foreign action and that they emerge as semantic extensions of the interpretation of others' action.[4]

Blessings of mentalism. How can we assess and compare the merits of body reading and mind reading? While raising this question we need to keep in mind that we are not talking about behaviorism and mentalism as scientific theories. What we address instead are the implicit ontologies

3. This is in fact what mainstream theories claim. They account for mentalizing others as a (secondary) consequence of the (presumably primary) experience of mental states in the self. As will be discussed in the final section of this chapter, these theories believe in *projection* of mental states from self to others, whereas the present approach invokes *introjection* of mentality from others to self.

4. These preliminary arguments are not meant to provide a rebuttal of the mainstream view that we understand other minds through projecting our own mentality onto them. Instead they are meant to support the idea that it is possible to ground mentalist construals on nothing but deep semantic interpretations of others' action. The rest of the chapter will defend the stronger claim that this is not only possible but also true.

underlying naïve observers' construals of others and their behavior. Another thing that we need to keep in mind is that the structure of these construals is, at least in principle, entirely independent from the "true" architecture of the cognitive systems to which they refer. Though we may be accustomed to apply mentalist construals to our fellows and friends while leaving behaviorist construals to flatworms and honey bees, we could in principle do otherwise. At least as a thought experiment, we could come up with both mentalist stories about worms and bees and behaviorist stories about our fellows and friends.[5]

Still, when we now narrow down our focus to concentrate on human observers, mentalist construals are the default option and behaviorist construals the exception. So, what does mentalism have that behaviorism does not? Where do the blessings of mentalism come from?

The first and perhaps most obvious answer is that it may simply be true—true in the sense of providing an *adequate description* of others' machinery for cognition and volition. Given what we have discussed above concerning architectures for performance and experience, an answer along these lines seems to suggest itself. Mentalist construals instantiate fundamental functional features of architectures for experience: (i) their context is enriched, capturing deep semantic attributes extending beneath the surface of physical attributes of ongoing behavior; (ii) they go beyond body and world and posit a mind attached to the body; (iii) representation is explicit for them, addressing things within the mind that refer to things outside the mind. Mentalist construals thus attribute to others precisely the same functional features that make up an architecture for experience. In a way, we seem to be facing a paradox here—at least as long as we stick to the assumption that our observers' own architecture relies exclusively on implicit representation. In fact, we have already encountered a related paradox in chapter 7 when we talked about alignment games between controllers. The seeming paradox here is that when we consider a collective of mutual observers, each of them may come to construe the actions of the others in terms of explicit representation while their own architecture relies on implicit representation.

Before we come back to this paradox, let us consider a second answer to our question. Rather than providing adequate descriptions, mentalism may just provide a useful tool enabling *efficient performance*. This answer

5. While the first approach is adopted by fairytales and children's books, the second approach has been vigorously defended by Skinner (1953, 1972).

views the observer as a performer interacting with others rather than a mere interpreter of their behavior, thereby raising the question of what mind reading contributes to the observer's performance. An important feature of mentalist construals that may be crucial to the observer's own performance is entailed by the fact that they explain what the others are doing through causal factors at work in their mind—factors that derive from their percepts and thoughts. Behaviorist construals, by contrast, rely on explaining what others do through factors operating in their environments. Thus, while body reading relies on external explanation, mind reading entails explanation through internal factors.[6] This difference has important implications for the efficiency of prediction and control. This is because remote causal links (such as between actions and external factors causing them) must, on average, be more noisy and less reliable than closer links (such as between actions and internal factors causing them). Thus, when it comes to prediction (or foreign action) and production (of one's own action in response to ongoing or upcoming foreign action), mentalist construals will often be more reliable than behaviorist construals.[7] From this perspective, the paradox already begins to look somewhat less problematic. Observers who themselves rely on implicit representation may still use mentalist construals for others as tools for improving prediction and control of their behavior.

The two major blessings of mentalism thus pertain to adequate description and efficient performance. The natural interpretation of how they are related to each other is that mentalist construals are efficient because they are adequate. However, when we adopt an evolutionary and developmental perspective, we may also consider the converse, that is, that they become adequate because they prove to be efficient. This perspective requires us to understand how construals that have first proven to be useful and efficient for dealing with observed others and their actions can then become functional within observers' own mental architecture. We need, in other words, a mechanism for modeling observers' own selves after foreign selves observed in others. As soon as we adopt this perspective, the paradox evaporates.

6. Internal explanations may invoke both states and traits. Whereas construals of mental states pertain to ongoing mental acts, construals of mental traits pertain to perceivers–thinkers involved in those acts.
7. Provided, of course, that mentalist construals are valid, i.e., that observers are capable of assessing those internal factors in a veridical way.

Self Like Others

But let us consider the paradox once more. It derives from the fact that our hypothetical observer construes others as explicit representers while her own representational architecture (which actually generates those construals) relies on implicit representation. Thus, although we may see a paradox when we adopt an external point of view and compare the way she construes the workings of other minds with the workings of her own mind, no such paradox exists for her. Since she has no way of knowing herself (let alone her self) she has no way of comparing others with self and self with others. As long as she is lacking a representational framework for a mental self, there is no way to apply the rich resources for mentalist construals of others to the self.

In logical terms, we may perhaps discern two distinct steps that may be needed for such a move from others to self, one in which she begins to construe herself like others and another in which she actually becomes like others. Yet, in more functional terms, these two steps turn out to be two sides of the same coin. The problem that needs to be solved here concerns the formation of a representational framework for the mental self. As soon as such a framework is in place it will immediately allow her both to construe herself as a mental thing like others and to move on to explicit representation and experiential subjectivity. No further steps are needed, since the second ingredient that an extended architecture for experience requires is already in place: an ontology for intentionality and kinds of intentional relationships. As soon as a mental self is in place, this ontology can readily be applied to self as it has before been applied to others.

How, then, can mentalist construals about mental others be used to implement a framework for the mental self? This question is certainly pivotal to the present approach, but I will in this chapter provide only a brief sketch of an answer. I am here addressing the very same mechanisms and procedures to account for the putative transition from others to self on which I have already elaborated in some detail in chapters 6 and 8. Although that discussion was largely tailored to issues of control and volition, the key ideas can equally be applied to the domain of cognition. Here I briefly summarize them in two major steps. One takes us from understanding others to understanding self as an experiencing subject. This step is based on episodes of mirroring. The other takes us from construal to reality, that is, from understanding to becoming an experiencing subject. Taken together, they yield an architecture for explicit representation and experiential subjectivity.

Social mirroring provides our observer with opportunities to see her own behavior mirrored by and through other individuals. Whereas previous chapters focused on mirroring the action side of this behavior, we now focus on the cognitive side, that is, on the way in which they are related to and depend on environmental circumstances. At this point we should once more remind ourselves that our observer, since she does not know herself, initially has no way of perceiving and construing what she is actually doing. This is where mirroring comes in.

As we have seen in chapter 6, mirroring makes it possible for her to perceive her own actions through others and construe them like others' actions. She thus begins to understand herself as performing mental acts such as perceiving and thinking, entertaining intentional relationships with things out there. In other words, she begins to apply mentalist construals to her own actions. Crucially, such self-attribution of mental acts will not only pertain to the transient intentional relationships entailed by them (such as the coming and going of seeing, believing, thinking, desiring, etc.) but also to the mental self as subject of experience. Mirroring thus makes it possible for the individual to exploit the ontologies for mentalist construals of other minds for understanding herself.

Given that mirroring episodes help individuals to understand themselves as experiencing subjects, how is it then possible for them to actually become such subjects? In other words, how can they build a permanent mental self from transient constructions arising from occasional episodes of mirroring?[8] A natural way to get there is to assume that the mental self, once it has been established through mirroring, will from then on become involved in all kinds of representational constructions, taking the role of the representing and experiencing subject. The mental self will become corepresented in a large variety of mental acts, now taking the role of the representer, not the represented.[9] Accordingly, since the representer

8. In chapter 8, as we discussed the hypothetical sequence of steps in which the will emerges from the interplay of attribution and appropriation in social mirroring, we discerned still another step in the transition from construing others as volitional agents to becoming such an agent ourselves: the takeover of control. Whereas a step like this is in fact required in the domain of volition (where it is meant to account for the causal efficacy of goals and intentions), it has no counterpart in the domain of cognition (where causal efficacy for action is pointless).

9. Adopting Brentano's terminology, we may say that the first role refers to the mental self as the primary object of mental acts (e.g., in mirroring episodes), whereas the second role refers to the mental self as the tertiary object of acts—the role of the experiencing subject implicitly corepresented in them.

remains constant across acts, one and the same mental self will be corepresented and cocontained in a large variety of mental acts. As a result, it may gradually turn into a permanent framework for structuring transient representational constructions. Such a constant and coherent self will help to create unity and coherence among the variety of mental acts.

Taken together, these two steps instantiate an architecture for explicit representation and experiential subjectivity. Whereas the first step depends on interactions among individuals, the second does not. It is rather concerned with functional reorganizations of representational resources acquired through the first.

This touches on an issue pertaining to a final question that we still need to address: What are the blessings entailed by becoming and being a mental self? What are the benefits entailed by explicit representation and experiential subjectivity at both the individual and the collective level? We have already discussed the blessings of construing mental things, but it remains open what the blessings entailed by becoming and being a mental thing may be. Likewise, we have shown that it may be possible to derive self from others, but it remains open what the benefits of realizing this possibility may be.

Blessings of True Selves

Again, I submit that the potential of mental experience for social control is key to answering these questions. This claim may sound a bit strange, if not counterintuitive. Since mental experience is by definition a private first-person affair, it is not obvious how it could subserve social control—by definition a public affair pertaining to second and third persons. However, we must not forget that private experience builds on public interaction—on perceiving and understanding others' behavior and on perceiving one's own behavior mirrored through them. Thus, while experience may be private in a phenomenal sense, it is derived from interacting and communicating with others and therefore bears the potential of being shared with others and being modulated and controlled by them. In this section, I first move from private to public experience before I then elaborate on the causal role of shared experience for the social control of individual action.

Private and public experience. Consider once more an individual furnished with a mental self and mental experience. Since we assume that the underlying architecture has been made and shaped through attribution and appropriation of mentalist construals, we may use the logic of mentalism to provide an adequate description of its operation. Accordingly, we may say that the individual will "know" what is going on in the world and the body, be it through perceiving things or thinking about things (access and content intentionality, respectively). Acts of knowing pertain to both the what and the how of knowing. Furthermore, the knowing self is included as well, making up the who component entailed by such acts. In virtue of being constant and identical across a large variety of acts of knowing, the self becomes a center for integrating experience over time. Further, owing to the intentional opposition entailed by knowing the body and the world, the mental self is, on the one hand, an entity of its own kind, independent and functionally detached from the body. On the other hand, it is at the same time topologically attached to it: The mental self is always where the body is.

Still, as concerns blessings, it is not really obvious what an architecture for experience and explicit representation earns the individual beyond the underlying architecture for performance and implicit representation on top of which it has been built. As long as we have no reason to assume that the transition between the two architectures goes along with a substantial increase in computational power, there is also no reason to believe that implementing a framework for experience helps in improving individual performance. Yet, if it is not for performance—what else can explicit mental experience be good for?

When we move from individuals to collectives, we begin to see that explicit experience is not only private but to some extent also a public affair. In collectives, experience may be public in two different (though interrelated) senses: Each individual X knows (to some extent) what certain others know, and these others know (to some extent) what X knows. Such mutual knowing of others' knowing arises by itself when individuals come together, watch others acting and build mentalist construals of their actions. Importantly, since each of them is now furnished with an architecture for mental experience and a mental self, they will apply the same kinds of construals to all individuals, treating others like self and self like others. All individuals are for them separate mental beings (attached to separate bodies), but operating in a shared world. Now, when an observer watches an observee's actions and keeps track of his acting for a while, she will, through her mentalist construals, always to some extent know what the other knows. Accordingly, an observer has both her own knowledge about the world and knowledge about the observee's knowledge about the world. Both individuals thus come to construe themselves as individual knowers of certain things in a shared world. Furthermore, since each individual in the collective is both observer and observee, we end up with a scenario in which they all know the world (from their own perspective) and also how others know the world (from their respective perspectives).[10]

Mutual knowing and social control. Again, what are the benefits entailed by such mutual knowledge of others' knowledge? To address this question, we need to go beyond their knowledge itself and consider the potential entailed by knowing others' knowing for controlling their actions. When we adopt that perspective we begin to see that the architecture for mental self and experience opens up an entirely novel arena for social control of individual action.

To illustrate this claim, consider an extremely simplified scenario of mutual knowing. Suppose that a given knower (K) knows three items of knowledge (a, b, c) and three other knowers (X, Y, Z). Suppose furthermore that K knows that X knows items a, b, and c, that Y knows items a and b, and that Z knows item a. An instructive way of looking at this scenario is to examine how K's knowledge of these items is structured by the fact that he also knows by whom they are known. The fact that item a is known to all knowers (including K), while item b is shared by X, Y, and K and item c by X and K, thus becomes part and parcel of K's own knowledge concerning these items. Accordingly, such mutual knowing can be seen to impose a social superstructure on each knower's knowing: It structures his knowing of things in the world according to its being shared with others. As a result, knowledge items may range from entirely public (shared by any other human) over semipublic (shared by certain others) to entirely private (i.e., unshared).[11] Thus, under conditions of mutual knowing, knowledge items

10. The notion of shared reality or common ground (in the sense of experienced commonality with others' mental states referring to the world) has recently become a core concept in the domain of social cognition (see, e.g., Barresi & Moore, 1996; Echterhoff, 2010; Echterhoff, Higgins & Levine, 2009; Higgins, 2010; Higgins & Pittman, 2008; Semin & Cacioppo, 2008; Tomasello et al., 2005; Tomasello & Herrmann, 2010; Whitehead, 2001).

11. Percepts and thoughts differ in sharability. Percepts (which rely on access to objects and events in a shared surrounding) can be more easily shared than thoughts (which, by definition, do not build on such common ground). Sharing thoughts will therefore often require additional acts of communication, whereas sharing percepts will not. Yet, even in the case of objects and events in a shared environment, perceptual access may be different for two individuals. Bodies, for instance, have a special status on the public–private dimension. Bodies are public things, but access to a given body is quite different for the self (attached to the body) and others (detached from it).

may be seen to be tagged by social markers indicating by whom they are known.

The implications of such knowing for social control are fairly obvious. In the architectures we are considering here, experience is for performance and knowing is therefore for doing. This has two important implications concerning interpretation/prediction and intervention/control. The first is that knowing by whom given things are known and by whom they are not known helps the knower to understand and predict what these individuals are doing and are going to do. The second implication is perhaps even more important: Mutual knowing enables the knower to take measures for altering others' knowing for the sake of altering their actions. For instance, he may act to include other knowers in sharing a given knowledge item or he may act to alter the content of that knowledge item itself. Whatever the structure of such interventions may be, the crucial point here is that they address others' knowing (experience) as a means for altering their actions (performance).[12]

Since experience tends to precede performance in temporal and functional terms, the domain of experience thus offers itself as a novel arena for social control.[13] As far as others' behavior relies on their knowing, modulating what they know may often be an easy and efficient way of modulating what they do.

To conclude, let me add a remark on what modulation of knowing may entail and how it can be implemented. Since knowing is for doing,

---

12. The same conclusion follows from a different way of looking at the same scenario, focusing on knowers rather than knowledge items. What does knower K gain from knowing what other knowers know? A first answer takes us from knowing others' knowing to prediction of their upcoming actions and intervention through one's own complementary action. As we saw above, such construals may even be efficient in guiding the knower's doings if they provide inadequate descriptions of the workings of the systems to which they refer. Yet, when we concentrate on true mental selves, we may go one step further. A second answer takes us from prediction and intervention at the level of performance to prediction and intervention at the level of the experiential basis of performance. Since true mental selves generate performance through experience, any kind of social modulation of their doings may in principle address both performance and/or experience.

13. Here I use the concept of social control in a very limited and narrow sense, pertaining to small collectives of individuals interacting in face-to-face situations. Taken in a broader sense, the notion of social control of or through knowledge may of course be seen to be at the heart of research agendas for social sciences like sociology, history, political sciences, etc.

modulations of knowing must likewise be understood in the context of modulations of behavior. Accordingly, we may consult the scheme for action control (as developed in ch. 7). According to the scheme depicted in figure 7.2, action generation draws on two major representational resources: interpretations (referring to given events) and intentions (referring to intended events). Further, as we discussed in chapter 8, interpretations and intentions qualify as potential targets of external interventions that are directed at modulating actions through knowing.

Accordingly, we may discern two basic routes for such intervention: a direct route via intentions and an indirect route via interpretation, addressing top-down and bottom-up control, respectively. Interpretations of things and events can be modulated in various ways: through altering environmental circumstances, through directing attention to certain things and events at the expense of others, and through sharing thoughts concerning perceptually inaccessible events and their interpretation. Some of these interventions aim at modulating others' knowledge through providing them with perceptual access to certain things in the world. These interventions rely on instrumental action (like altering environmental circumstances) or on procedural kinds of communication (like directing attention to things). By contrast, other interventions aim at modulating thoughts rather than percepts. These interventions will, of course, typically depend on some kinds of communication between modulators and modulatees.

This is the point at which language-based communication enters the scene. Whenever it comes to modulating others' thoughts—that is, their knowledge of things beyond their current perceptual reach—language and language-based communication become indispensable tools for such modulation and the potential for social control entailed by them. We may take this to indicate that, just like mental experience, language, too, is engineered and optimized to serve the needs of collective control of individual action. I come back to these issues in chapter 13.

Subjectivity Demystified

To conclude, let me turn from blessings for the individuals under study to advantages for the cognitive scientists studying them. What benefits does cognitive theory convey from adopting a self-from-others framework of human subjectivity? What can we say about the explanatory potential associated with that framework?

I believe that a framework like this in fact has an enormous potential for helping to demystify human subjectivity. I certainly do not mean to claim that it solves the puzzle of subjectivity altogether.[14] It does, however, help us to account for key features of subjectivity that are otherwise difficult to understand and often considered deeply enigmatic. At the beginning of this chapter, we identified three key features that are inherent in tokens of mental experience: things out there, a subject experiencing them, and ways in which things and experiencing subjects are related to each other. How can we account for these features? How can an architecture subserving mental experience evolve from, or be constructed on top of, an architecture subserving behavioral performance?

Traditional cognitive theories, which rely on theoretical and methodological individualism, have a hard time answering these questions. Since they must explain the emergence of the novel architecture within the confined territories of individual minds, they need to make it plausible that adding experience to performance provides substantial fitness advantages to the individual—a task for which there are no obvious and convincing solutions.[15] By contrast, for the collectivist approach I am advocating here, the task is quite easy, with obvious solutions suggesting themselves. As soon as one adopts this approach, it is as if major key features of subjectivity come for free and can be explained without resort to any further explanatory principles. Here I address three such features: distal reference, dual representation, and shared reality.

14. For instance, as noted in previous chapters, the self-from-others framework is silent on issues pertaining to qualitative aspects of mental experience ("qualia").

15. A frequent answer to the question of what an architecture for consciousness and experience may add to an architecture for performance addresses the putative power of consciousness for integration and coordination of cognitive operations and function (see, e.g., Baars, 1988, 2002; Mandler, 1998; Merker, 2007)—a view that has been addressed as *integration consensus* concerning the primary function of conscious awareness (Bargh & Morsella, 2008; Morsella, 2005; Morsella, Bargh & Gollwitzer, 2009; Morsella, Krieger & Bargh, 2009). An obvious shortcoming of this consensus is the correlative character of the explanation entailed by it. It posits (in a correlational manner) that conscious states are more integrated and coordinated than nonconscious states, but it has no way of explaining (in a foundational manner) why functional integration should go along with (or even require) experiential subjectivity, or why experiential subjectivity should instantiate functional integration and coordination. (See ch. 2 for a discussion of correlational and foundational explanations of consciousness and subjectivity.)

Distal reference. Tokens of mental experience address two kinds of things at a time: events in the world or body and a subject experiencing them (i.e., perceiving, remembering, imagining, expecting them, etc.). In a more functional language we may speak here of representational reference: Mental experience builds on representations (in the mind) that refer to events (in the world or body). Theories of experiential subjectivity must therefore explain how states in the mind can come to explicitly refer to states in the world.

Although distal reference pertains to both percepts and thoughts, much of the literature discussing its functional implications has focused on the perceptual domain.[16] A classical topic that both philosophical and psychological theories of perception address concerns the nature of perceptual content. What do we actually see when we open our eyes? We see, for example, flowers in a meadow or the sun in the sky. Why do we see these things out there—and why don't we "see," for example, the retinal activation patterns or the brain states involved in generating these percepts? To put it in Dretske's terms, the percept "carries information about a distant causal antecedent . . . *without* carrying information about the more proximal members of the causal chain . . . *through which* this information . . . is communicated"; in other words, the percept "as it were, skips over (or 'sees through') the intermediate links in the causal chain in order to represent (carry information about) its more distant causal antecedents."[17]

Distal reference thus goes along with proximal neglect: By focusing on distal things out there, perception neglects proximal things that mediate access to them. Distal reference poses a paradox for perceptual theory: How is it possible for percepts to skip over a number of proximal links in the causal chain of events leading to them, and how is it possible to single out a particular, rather distal link in that chain for representational reference?

As long as we adhere to the classical perspective of focusing on things or events in individual minds there is no obvious way to resolve the paradox. However, a different perspective on distal reference emerges when we go beyond individual minds, assuming that the architecture for mental experience arises from a self-from-others framework as outlined above. As soon as we adopt a framework like this, the paradox goes away. Distal reference now appears to be a natural rather than paradoxical feature of that architecture—a by-product emerging from modeling the self after others.

16. See, e.g., Brunswik (1952); Dretske (1981); Grice (1991); Prinz (1992).
17. Dretske (1981, p. 158).

When the cognitive architecture for self gets modeled after what is perceived to be operating in others, distal reference comes for free. This is because perceivers construe others and their actions to be driven and guided through percepts and thoughts referring to things and events in their environments. Accordingly, the feature of distal reference is from the outset deeply inherent in these construals. Since they interpret others as subjects who experience their environments, they come with a basic distinction between objective states of affairs in the world and subjective knowledge states referring to them. Others are perceived and construed to know (partially, at least) what is going on in their near or far environments. Their private percepts and thoughts (which the external perceiver attributes to them) are understood to refer to the public happenings in the world (to which the perceiver has access as well). Percepts and thoughts are thus construed for the sake of exhibiting representational reference to distal events. It is their proper function to refer to things and events out there, with no links in between mediating that referential relationship.

Dual representation. Perceivers construe what others do in terms of underlying percepts and thoughts. Whereas percepts refer to public things in the current environment (to which perceivers have access as well), thoughts refer to private things (which cannot be accessed in that way). Thoughts, in other words, refer to things and events that are not present in the current situation.[18]

Basically, there are two ways of construing the relationship between percepts and thoughts. One option is to emphasize similarities and transitions from one to the other, yielding what we may call a *sensualist* interpretation of thoughts. This option posits that thoughts that emerge at a given time in a given context must be considered more or less remote derivatives from the individual's perceptual history (pertaining to previously encountered environmental circumstances) and the learning history associated with it. According to this view, thoughts are continuous with percepts: They are seen as arising from remote extensions of previous and current perceptual processing. The other option is to emphasize differences and categorical distinctions, yielding what we may call an *idealist* interpretation of thoughts. This option holds that thoughts follow their own dynamics—dynamics that are internally generated and not derived from, or dictated by, the history of external conditions encountered in the past

---

18. We should remind ourselves that the term *thoughts*, as it is used here, spans a large variety of mental states such as memories, recollections, ideas, deliberations, plans, intentions, etc.

and present. According to this view, there is a deep functional divide between thoughts and percepts since thoughts are understood to lead an internal life of their own—quite independent from the externally grounded life of percepts.

While sensualist/behaviorist and idealist/cognitivist styles of theorizing compete with each other in scientific accounts of architectures for percepts and thoughts, there is no such competition in our folk psychology construals of other people and their behavior. These construals are idealist/cognitivist throughout—not only with respect to our conspecifics but to animals as well. Whenever we watch them acting in ways that we cannot account for in terms of current external circumstances, we construe them as acting spontaneously, that is, driven and guided by internal circumstances. According to these construals, the secret life of their thoughts is quite independent from the public life of their percepts. In other words, we impute them with the capability of entertaining two streams of representation, an exogenous stream referring to things that are present and an endogenous stream referring to things that are absent.

The two modes of operation perceived in others (reactive/spontaneous) and the two implied streams of representation associated with them (exogenous percepts/endogenous thoughts) provide perceivers/imputers with a framework for construing the workings of other minds—a framework that relies on dual representation. The next step goes again from others to self, mediated through the interplay of mutual attribution and appropriation. Once established for construing other minds, this framework will become functional for the workings of their own minds, providing them with an architecture that allows them to maintain two representational streams alongside each other and keep them apart: a stream of percepts pertaining to present things and a stream of thoughts pertaining to absent things.[19]

Adopting a framework like this has two major implications. One is that it makes cognition "smart" since it allows for making absent things present in thought. The other is that it makes volition possible in the first place since it allows for creating endogenous representations like intentions and plans. Again, we may conclude that the self-from-others framework

19. As we saw in chapter 8, this argument also applies to the context of volition: Just as dual representation is entailed by understanding others as perceivers/knowers, it is likewise entailed by understanding them as volitional agents. Dual representation must therefore be seen as a key feature of mentalistic construals of others' behavior—and therefore a key feature of self-construals derived from them.

explains how individuals come to shape their own mental architecture in ways that subserve smart cognition and efficient volition. They do it by using others as blueprints for their selves. Perceiving others (and self through others) delivers to them what they require for building their own mental selves.

Shared reality. Closed-minds approaches in philosophy and psychology have a long tradition of reflections on the issue of how access to other minds is possible at all. How can a (presumably closed) system of one mind come to know what is going on in the (presumably closed) system of other minds? The basic assumption giving rise to this issue is that individual minds, while they do have direct, unmediated access to and knowledge of the streams of their own percepts and thoughts, have no such direct access to streams of mental experience in other individuals. Knowledge about other minds is for them not primarily given but needs to be constructed or reconstructed through secondary inferential operations in which they *project*, as it were, their own mentality onto others. Accordingly, any kind of sharing knowledge with others—knowing what others know and knowing what knowledge they share among each other—for closed-minds approaches must be considered a product of complex operations of inferential reasoning.

By contrast, the self-from-others framework takes an entirely different approach, conceiving minds as open systems designed to build and shape their architectures through interacting and communicating with each other. According to this approach, construing others as selves comes first and lays the foundations for action understanding, whereas construing our own selves comes second and is derivative from interpreting others. It emerges from acts of appropriation through which they *introject*, as it were, the mentality they perceive in others into themselves. On this view, access to other minds emerges from semantic extensions to action interpretation rather than from exercises of inferential reasoning. Adopting this view, one begins to see that the distal world to which percepts and thoughts refer is from the outset a world understood to be shared (or at least shareable) among them.

For the sake of illustration, consider a perceiver watching two individuals interacting with each other. In a scenario like this she will interpret two individual minds whose percepts and thoughts refer to their distal environments. Yet, as is fairly obvious from the perceiver's stance, there is considerable overlap between the two environments. Accordingly, the two individuals' percepts and thoughts will be understood to exhibit such overlap as well, and the perceiver will come to see them as individuals acting and interacting in a common environment and sharing much of their pertinent percepts and thoughts.[20]

While the perceiver may thus begin to understand that others share percepts and thoughts (at least partially), her construals of such shared experiences are, up to this point, limited to others whose actions she is watching and monitoring. Things change profoundly, however, when she begins to appropriate a mental self of her own. At that moment she begins to construe herself as still another player in the game of experiencing subjects acting in a shared environment. In other words, the perceiver is herself incorporated into the community that she has until now interpreted for others: the community of individuals acting and interacting in a shared environment and furnished with shared pertinent representations of things in the environment.

In sum, the self-from-others framework delivers us three things at once: (i) a distal world out there (ii) that we perceive and know and (iii) that we may share with others. No chicken, no egg—and no need for inferential construction of one from the other. The distal world of our percepts is intrinsically shared, and the shared world of our thoughts is intrinsically distal.

20. The present argument emphasizes sharing (i.e., what is being shared), but a full account of the scenario must also consider nonsharing (i.e., what is not being shared). For instance, one thing that is not shared among individuals is the perspective from which they have perceptual access to their common environment. A related aspect in which percepts differ between individuals refers to representations of their bodies. Their own body has for each of them a special representational status, whereas other bodies are things in the environment surrounding their body. A further aspect that a more detailed analysis of sharing/nonsharing must take into account pertains to the ease of assessing shared percepts and thoughts (see this ch., n. 11). Since percepts refer to things that are present in a current scenario, percept sharing is easy to assess: Two individuals are likely to share percepts when they both are part of that scenario. Thought sharing cannot be assessed that way. While streams of percepts are constrained by current scenarios, streams of thoughts are constrained that way to a much lesser degree. As a result, external perceivers will typically have no direct way of assessing others' thought streams. The only way to access them is through communication.

13 Language Crafts

In this concluding chapter we take a look at language and its role in the making and shaping of an architecture for open minds. What do the language faculty and the crafts associated with it contribute to the formation of willing agents and experiencing subjects? Preceding chapters have already incidentally touched on the role of language in social communication and knowledge sharing,[1] without making explicit how that role may have evolved and to what extent language is essential for implementing these functions. Should we think of language as enabling them in the first place—or as building on earlier forms of their implementation and acting to boost their efficiency?

Proponents of a strong role of language in human mentality may be disappointed that the discussion of this topic will be quite brief (covering no more than one chapter) and comes so late (in the very last one). The main reason for being brief is related to the modest aim I am pursuing here. Unlike previous chapters on volition and cognition, the present

---

1. See chapters 8 and 12.

chapter does not aim at outlining an architecture for language and language processing. Instead, it will concentrate on the functional roles that language crafts may play in the building of architectures for volition and cognition as have been outlined above. To put it in terms of functional explanation, most of the chapter will be devoted to an ultimate account of language crafts (i.e., what they may be for). Only in the final section do I come back to some more proximate speculations concerning the machinery carrying them (i.e., how they may work). In other words, I will be brief because I will concentrate on what may be considered preliminaries for a full theory of language and language processing.

The reason for bringing in language so late reflects a crucial feature of the ultimate account I am going to suggest. As will be discussed below, I consider language a late arrival in the natural and cultural history of open minds and their associated architecture. I contend that the outline of this architecture initially evolved before and independently from language and has only then become shaped and restructured by language crafts—in a way, though, that has raised its potential for cognition and volition to an enormously higher power. This view sees language as a late booster of the efficiency of an already-existing architecture, rather than an early enabler of its initial formation. Accordingly, as language comes late, the chapter on language comes late as well.

In the first section, I take a brief look at the notion of ultimate explanation and what it may entail in the language domain. In the second section, I ask more specifically what language can do for open minds. Here I raise the radical claim that language crafts have mainly evolved to boost the efficiency of social control, that is, the social modulation of individual action.[2] In discussing the implications of this claim, I also examine how it relates to classical accounts of language in terms of proper functions such as promoting cognition, communication, and culture. Then, in the con-

2. In fact I do not believe that this claim is overly radical. There are two reasons why it may sound radical. One is that the notion of social control comes with negative and unwanted connotations that are associated with constraining freedom and autonomy. The other is complementary to that: Highly wanted functions seem to be missing here, such as promoting cognition, communication, and culture. Concerning negative connotations, we have no choice but to free ourselves from them: Control goes, by definition, along with constraining degrees of freedom, be it for the good or the bad of the involved systems or individuals. As concerns positive functions, I will discuss below how some of them may be related to the putative prime function of boosting social control.

cluding section I address some rather speculative ideas concerning the roots and the workings of proximate mechanisms for language processing.

What For?

Ultimate explanations provide answers to questions concerning function and purpose. We tend to raise such questions with regard to two major kinds of things: living things (or parts thereof) and artifacts. For instance, we may ask what honey bees are good for or what our lungs do for us. Likewise, we may ask what things like knives and airplanes are good for. Our belief that such questions make sense is grounded in the understanding that these things exhibit design. Unlike nonliving things like stones and stars we understand living things and human-made artifacts as being shaped and designed for instantiating particular functions and purposes. In fact, we may understand them as outcomes of evolutionary processes that have acted to optimize them to subserve these functions and purposes.

Proper Functions

Accordingly, the typical way in which we answer such questions is to specify what we consider a thing's proper function or purpose. Honey bees are for pollinating blossoms, lungs for our oxygen/nitrogen exchange, knives for cutting things, and airplanes for traveling long distances.[3] In the case of artifacts, we attribute purposes to volitional agents acting as intentional designers. In the case of natural things, we consider them outcomes of Darwinian processes. Different as these construals may be, they share the underlying intuition of generative processes that act to tailor the structure of things according to the requirements of the functions they are meant to subserve.

Turning to language and the issue of what may count as its proper function we may, at least for the time being, leave it open and undecided whether we should consider language a natural thing or an artifact. The same crucial question applies in both cases: What may language have evolved for? For what functions may its structure have been optimized?

3. These examples are not meant to provide more than a brief sketch of what the notion of proper function entails. Still, as they indicate, specifying a proper function addresses two questions at a time: why a thing has come into being and why it is like it is (referring to *existence* and *essence*, respectively).

While it is easy to raise a question like this, it is not so easy to tell strong answers from weak ones, let alone find the true one. In fact, the criterion for distinguishing good from worse answers is not related to truth but rather to explanatory power and productivity. For instance, although there is no way for proving or disproving that knives are for cutting, the belief that they are made for cutting is productive in the sense that it explains much of their structure and their use. The belief that lungs are tailored to the needs of gas exchange is productive in precisely the same sense. We evaluate such accounts according to their explanatory power and productivity.

Yet, even if one accepts this criterion, it is often not obvious how to apply it. Consider, for example, the usual suspects that have over centuries competed for the throne of the proper function of language: cognition, communication, and culture. Everybody believes that language supports cognition and is, at least to some extent, tailored to its needs. For instance, as philosophers and linguists have argued and psychologists have shown, concepts may depend on words, and likewise the structure of thought and reasoning may be shaped through the syntax of language.[4] In a similar vein, everybody believes that language is for communication. Languages provide systems of symbolic gestures whose production and perception allows individuals to communicate with each other. Finally, nobody doubts that language is for culture. Through shaping individual cognition and social communication, language provides tools for building and maintaining shared knowledge, which may then act as common ground for the cognitive and normative regulation of individual action.

Transition Scenarios

As mentioned above, my aim here is not to discuss the relative merits of these classical proposals but rather to promote still another one. To get there it may still be helpful to take a brief look at the classical approaches. On the one hand, they seem to address entirely different levels at which the functionality of language and language crafts may be specified. To some extent they are even nested in each other: Cognition subserves communication and communication subserves culture. Accordingly, they are neither independent from each other nor mutually exclusive. On the other hand, they differ deeply with respect to functional goals and implications.

---

4. This touches on the classic issue of in what ways and to what extent the structure of language may shape the structure of thought (as opposed to the commonsense view that thought shapes language). For classic versions of the language-shapes-thought view see, e.g., von Humboldt (1836/1988), Vygotsky (1934/1962), and Whorf (1956).

Each of them highlights its own set of functional key features that the advent of language has putatively enabled and for which the language faculty has presumably been made and shaped in the first place.

A convenient way of looking at these key features is in terms of implied transition scenarios. Each proposal may be seen to imply an initial state of affairs (when certain functions were still lacking), a final state of affairs (when they were in place), and a transition between the two (which takes place for the sake of enabling the novel function). When we adopt that scheme, it becomes apparent that, notwithstanding their mutual interrelations and dependencies, the three classical proposals have three quite distinct transition scenarios in mind. Proposals focusing on cognition envisage a transition from associative to conceptual knowledge and organized thought. Proposals focusing on communication envisage a transition from embodied interaction to symbolic communication. And proposals emphasizing the role of language for culture feature its role for the transition from natural to cultural ways of life.

Thus, whereas proposals for proper functions tend to highlight newly acquired features and functions, transition scenarios address both new states of affairs in which novel features and functions are in place and old states from which the transition has initially departed and in which these functions and features are still lacking. For ultimate accounts, we thus need to specify both proper functions and transition scenarios.

Talking for Control

For the rest of this chapter I am going to examine the heuristic productivity and explanatory power of a single simple idea: that language has evolved for the sake of control, or more specifically, for the sake of social control of individual willing and acting. As previous chapters have outlined, we have good reasons to believe that the human architecture for volition and cognition arises from certain kinds of social interaction and communication—foremost from the interplay of mutual interaction and the mutual attribution and appropriation of mental states that may be associated with such interaction. An architecture like this is open to others in two important senses. One sense, on which previous chapters have focused, is that the basic architecture of individual minds is constructed in and through interaction with others. The other sense, on which we are going to focus now, is that, once an open architecture is in place, individual minds continue to be open to being shaped in and through interactions with others. Human minds thus exhibit an unprecedented potential for social control, that is, for modulation of individual action through others' interactions and communications.

Although they may initially have developed that potential before and independently of the advent of language, they then have come to use language crafts as enormously efficient tools for exploiting that potential and boosting the efficiency of social control to the highest degree. Accordingly, the proper function for which language crafts have been invented, designed, and optimized is to boost the efficiency of social modulation of individual action.[5]

Social Control

Let me briefly reiterate what the notion of social control entails, summarizing earlier discussions on modes and uses of collective control (see chs. 8, 10, and 12) In a broad sense, we may speak of social control if a given individual's action is modulated by others' actions—be they past, present, or anticipated to happen in the future. In a somewhat narrower sense, we may focus on scenarios in which given individuals' actions are modulated through past, present, and future interactions with others. As we have seen, we may classify such scenarios along two basic dimensions: targets of control and modes of communication.

Targets of control. Consider once more a dyadic scenario with two individuals, a controller and a controllee. If the ultimate goal of social control is to modulate the controllee's action, the controller has two ways of getting there: targeting action or knowledge. Targeting action is perhaps the most natural choice. In that case the controller will arrange her own action in a way suited to modulate the controllee's action. For instance, she may demonstrate to him the action he is supposed to take, or she may draw his attention to environmental circumstances that are likely to induce that action. The other option the controller may choose is to target the controllee's knowledge, implying and presupposing that knowing is for acting and that particular pieces of knowledge are therefore likely to induce particular kinds of wanted actions. Targeting knowledge can therefore be considered an indirect way of targeting action.

Modes of communication. Consider furthermore how the two may communicate. One obvious choice is to communicate through physical action and interaction. For instance, the controller may take the controllee from

5. We must not forget that social control of individual acting is always mediated through cognition, volition, and communication. Therefore, if boosting social control counts as the ultimate function, then boosting cognition, volition, and communication must count as subsidiary, penultimate functions.

one place to another, she may point to relevant events in the environment, or she may use her body as an occluder for events that are likely to distract the controllee from what he is supposed to do—basically the repertoire of measures that caretakers may use to constrain and control what babies do. Yet, to the degree the language crafts evolve, acting for control becomes increasingly replaced by talking for control. Talking is a form of acting, too, but it exhibits one particular feature that other kinds of acting cannot achieve: talking can make absent things present. As we will see below, this feature is actually crucial for the role of talking (and related language crafts) as a booster of social control.

Talking for control may take two basic forms: imperative and indicative.[6] Imperative talk addresses what the controllee is supposed to do. It thus reflects a direct route from controllers' talking to controllees' action. As we saw already in previous chapters, imperative talk comes in different guises and flavors, ranging from strict commands over prescriptions and instructions to mild and friendly suggestions. They all have in common that they directly address the actions the controllee is supposed to take. Imperative talk is thus meant to address volitional functions pertaining to action generation. Conversely, indicative talk addresses what the controllee is supposed to know. Still, as knowing is for acting it may also be seen to reflect a route from controllers' talking to controllees' action, though a more indirect one. Whereas imperative talk addresses actions and events that ought to happen in the near or far future, indicative talk addresses events that happened in the past, are happening now, or are likely to happen in the future. Indicative talk is thus meant to address cognitive functions related to event interpretation.

Talking Games

Let us now examine in more detail what the craft of talking entails and why talking is such a powerful tool for social control. Importantly, the

6. The terminology follows Millikan's discussion of two uses of representations (Millikan, 1993, 1995). The distinction between indicative and imperative talk is closely related to the distinction between descriptive and prescriptive communication episodes as discussed in chapter 9. Still, there is an important difference. Whereas that distinction pertained to communication about action, the present distinction is meant to be broader, addressing both actions and nonaction events. Accordingly, while the categories on the imperative/prescriptive side of the two distinctions are coextensional (since both can only be applied to agents and actions), categories on the indicative/descriptive side are not (since indicative talk may apply to all kinds of events, whereas descriptive talk can only apply to actions/agents).

term "talking," as I use it here, is meant to go beyond the narrow sense of speaking to others. It is rather meant to refer to the craft of engaging in scenarios in which individuals take turns at speaking and listening to each other. Talking games provide a natural and a convenient paradigm for studying the pragmatics of language and language use. It is natural because it addresses typical scenarios in and from which language crafts and their precursors may have originally evolved—scenarios in which two or more individuals meet, interact, and communicate. At the same time, it is convenient, since it allows us to examine not only the local games themselves but also study ways in which they are structured and constrained by more global discourses in which they are embedded.

What, then, does people's talking to each other entail for the mutual control of their actions? Since this section aims at elucidating ultimate functions rather than proximate mechanisms, we may start with considering full-fledged talking games. How can we characterize their structure and the potential for social control entailed by them, and what requirements need to be met in order to exploit that potential?

Basic structure. Figure 13.1 depicts the basic constituents of talking games and the way in which they are related to each other. For the sake of simplicity, it faces a dyadic scenario between two talkers who take turns at speaking and listening. The scheme takes a snapshot at a moment at which talker 1 is speaking and talker 2 is listening. The speaker produces an utterance that the listener perceives (e.g., a word, a phrase, a message, an instruction). The entries at the upper level of the scheme stand for the two talkers and the utterance mediating between them; they are part and parcel of the online interaction that is taking place in the current scenario that both talkers share (*Here & Now*). The distinctive feature that turns that interaction into a talking game is derived from the entry at the lower level. Crucially, the utterances that the two talkers exchange refer to events that are themselves *not* part and parcel of the online interaction depicted in the upper line. These events may be happening in the current scenario (so that both talkers have perceptual access to them), or they may be more or less remote in space and time (so that perceptual access is impossible). In any case, these events are entirely decoupled from the utterances representing them (*There & Then*).

Considering the arrows between the top and the bottom line, we may say that talker 1 must somehow have the event in mind in order to be in a position to speak about it, and likewise talker 2 will eventually have the event in mind while listening to the utterance referring to it. Accordingly, we may consider these arrows as reflecting instances of representational

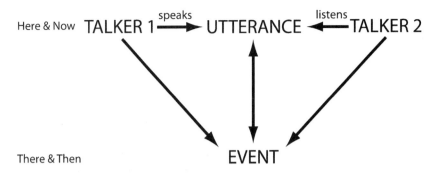

Figure 13.1
A basic scheme for talking games (see text for explanation and discussion).

reference—ordinary intentional relationships between talkers and things they have in mind (be it as percepts or thoughts). Less obvious is what the vertical arrow reflects. Here we may use the same words, but they carry a different meaning. We may say that the utterance represents the event and that the event is represented by the utterance. However, that representational relationship is not intentional (between a person and a thing) but something else (between a thing and a thing). Below we come back to characterizing the nature of this relationship.

Potential for control. How can talking games contribute to social control? As indicated above, we may discern two basic routes, direct/ imperative and indirect/indicative. Whereas the direct route applies to scenarios of prescription in which talkers tell each other what to do, the indicative route applies to scenarios of description in which they exchange knowledge about external happenings. The two routes should not be seen as mutually exclusive. Talking games will often address both ongoing events and desired/intended actions, and the relative contributions of imperative and indicative talk will depend on factors pertaining to the nature of the scenario in which the talking game is embedded (e.g., the aim of the talk, the talkers' social roles, their record of previously talking to each other). Whatever the mix of imperative and indicative contributions may be, they clearly differ in their functional implications. Imperative talk can be seen to reflect an expressway for control, providing a direct impact of talking to others on controlling their actions.[7] By contrast, indicative talk must be seen to reflect a more

7. The expressway metaphor is borrowed from Dijksterhuis and Bargh (2001), who use it to refer to direct, automatic impact of stimuli on action (see ch. 9, n. 5).

indirect way to get there through selective modulation of the knowledge base for their actions.

Since the imperative route can thus be considered to bypass the more complex indicative route, I will here focus on talking games of the indicative kind. Regarding their potential for social control, indicative talking games come with two major assets, one obvious and one less obvious. The obvious asset concerns event knowledge. Talking games provide talkers with knowledge about environmental events that they otherwise may not have and even not be able to access at all. Such knowledge provides representational resources that are from then on available to each talker's private machinery for control, that is, for event interpretation and action generation. The less obvious asset concerns what we may call the social knowledge acquired through engaging in talking games. Here we recall previous discussions on control sharing and knowledge sharing (chs. 8 and 12). While talking games provide knowledge about events, they also, and by implication, provide knowledge about others' knowledge about these events. They combine, in other words, provision of knowledge about *what is the case* with provision of knowledge of *who knows* what is the case.

Who-knowledge may often be less prominent and less salient, but it is certainly no less important for control than is what-knowledge. As we have seen in previous chapters, the craft of keeping track of others' knowing is actually key to any kind of social knowledge and social control. Considering what talking games may contribute to social control, we must further keep in mind that talking scenarios are often much richer and more complex than the simple dyadic scheme in figure 13.1 suggests. For instance, when people chat with their folks about past, present, or future happenings, each of them will, through and after that chat, not only know more about these happenings than he or she had known before (event knowledge/what), but they will also know more about what each of the others knows and thinks about these happenings (social knowledge/who). Whereas what-knowledge is patent and explicit, who-knowledge tends to be latent and implicit. Local talking games are thus always embedded in global discourses in which people learn to know and believe what certain others know and believe, and so on.

Finally, we must not forget that there is still another powerful way in which social knowledge may creep into talking games. This occurs whenever the talk refers to social events. In this case, who-knowledge is not only implicitly provided by the talking game itself but also explicitly addressed through the utterances exchanged in that game. By no means should this case be considered an exceptional scenario. Rather, a great deal of people's everyday talk is actually about people's knowing and doing. Accordingly, talking games may convey social knowledge at two levels: online and implicitly at the level of ongoing games and offline, but explicitly at the level of the events to which they refer.[8]

In sum, since talking games provide listeners with both novel event knowledge and novel knowledge about others' event knowledge, they have the potential to serve as an efficient arena for the social grounding of volition and cognition as we have elaborated in previous chapters. This arena is made for control of volition and action through cognition and knowledge. In this arena, indicative talking games provide talkers with both knowledge of what and knowledge of whom.

Exploiting the potential. What does it take to exploit this potential? What processing architecture and what kinds of representational resources do talking games require in order to be functional and efficient for social control?

Concerning *processing architecture*, the game requires a system designed for dual representation, as we have encountered in previous chapters (chs. 7, 8, and 11). The required architecture must support two parallel streams of transient construction: one pertaining to event interpretation and action generation, including the ongoing talking game (happening here and now) and another one pertaining to understanding the events the game is referring to (happening there and then). While these two streams are related to each other in terms of symbolic reference (i.e., in the sense that the online game entails talk *about* offline events), they are at the same time disjunct from each other since they address two independent and unrelated streams of events. This is one reason for keeping them separate. Another reason derives from what they may contribute to knowledge for control. While representations pertaining to the bottom level of figure 13.1 provide what-knowledge about events, those pertaining to the top level provide who-knowledge about talkers who know these events.[9]

Yet, dual representation implies even more than just keeping talk-related percepts and event-related thoughts separate and shielding them from

8. As I will argue below, talking games that explicitly address people's knowing and doing have played a crucial role for the birth of symbolic reference and the transition from embodied to symbolic communication.

9. As discussed earlier, the primary function of architectures for dual representation is to allow for concurrent maintenance of thoughts and percepts, i.e., for representing absent events without impairing perceptual contact with present events (chs. 7, 8, and 12). Talking games provide—just like intentions and thoughts—examples of functional scenarios requiring such separation.

each other. In virtue of its capacity to keep two concurrent processing streams apart, it lays the ground for creating two separate knowledge bases, one for events and another for social knowledge about events. Assuming that dual representation does not only apply to transient constructions of ongoing processing streams but also extends to the permanent knowledge resources that are built from these constructions, dual representation will eventually deliver a knowledge system in which the knowledge accrued from previous talking games is represented in terms of both a knowledge base for events and another one for knowers of events. As a result, talkers will accumulate the outcomes of previous talking games in a book-keeping system by double entry—one for what is known and another for who knows. This is precisely the kind of knowledge structure that social control requires.

Concerning *representational resources*, the workings of talking games require, and actually presuppose, a functional scenario, as we encountered in the previous chapter: a scenario of individuals who know events that are construed to be happening in their shared environment. As we have seen, this scenario in turn requires a framework for mental experience of others and self (so that both talkers can construe each other and themselves as knowers) and an ontology for intentional relationships between those who know and what is known (so that intentional reference can be established between talkers/knowers and known events).

As we have also seen, these resources, which are essential for getting the talking game started, are likely to have initially become implemented through embodied, language-independent forms of interaction and communication. Accordingly, we may assume that they are likely to be in place for getting the talking game off the ground. However, there is one critical limitation. What participants bring to the talking game are resources for construing themselves as knowers, but not as talkers. They may be prepared for construing self and others as knowers of events but not as talkers exchanging utterances about them.

This is the point at which we may require a miracle—the birth of the craft of talking. As said above, I will here refrain from discussing how that seeming miracle may have occurred. Presupposing that it actually did occur (in a nonmiraculous way), I will briefly focus on the extensions of representational resources that it requires beyond frameworks and ontologies for knowers and ways of knowing.[10]

---

10. Below, to close the chapter, I offer some speculations concerning the birth of talking.

We may discern minor and major extensions. Minor ones pertain to extensions of already existing resources. For instance, the ontology for actions needs to be extended to include acts of speaking as a new brand of human action. Likewise, the framework for mental selves as centers for volition and cognition needs to be extended to accommodate their novel role as centers for exchanging knowledge.

More crucial for the foundation for the emerging craft of talking, and the language faculty instantiated in it, is one major extension of representational resources that the talking game requires: the formation of an ontology for utterances. This ontology needs to address the two sides of utterances, one as action outcomes that talkers produce and perceive in the talking game, and another one as placeholders for external events to which they refer. While this ontology may partially draw on preexisting resources, its structure needs to be created anew, providing permanent resources for transient construction of talk. It serves to provide talkers with knowledge concerning the production and perception of utterances and their placeholder function for external events.

One crucial issue that the new ontology must address concerns the status of utterances and their role in the talking game. As figure 13.1 indicates, a given utterance is, on the one hand, always provided by a given talker while he or she has, on the other hand, a given event in mind. Thus, mediated through the talker/knower's acting and knowing, the utterance is related to the event. This is how the meaning of the utterance is established. Accordingly, the new ontology for utterances needs to furnish them with *symbolic reference* as their most prominent functional feature. Symbolic reference is at the same time both closely related to and fundamentally different from intentional reference. Whereas intentional reference addresses mental subjects having certain things in their minds, symbolic reference addresses utterances as symbolic placeholders referring to those things. In a way, then, we may see the symbolic reference of an utterance as derived from the intentional reference of the talker who has generated it. In any case, the implementation of symbolic reference requires that the new ontology for utterances is built in a way that allows us to link utterances with events to which they refer.

Whereas symbolic reference refers to the semantics of talking, a further important issue that the new ontology needs to take care of is syntax. Syntax in a broad sense may be seen to derive from what we may call the compositional nature of utterances. Natural languages are compositional in the sense that they allow us to generate a large number of different utterances, based on a much smaller repertoire of elementary utterances.

In order to be in a position to address a close-to-infinite number of meaningful utterances, natural languages have developed rules for generating strings of complex and highly specific utterances from less complex and less specific elements (e.g., syllables from phonemes, words from syllables, phonemes from words). Accordingly, ontologies for utterances must provide rules that talkers share for the production and comprehension of well-formed utterances.

Playing the Games

To fully grasp what talking games can do for social control, we need to examine their inherent potential not only at the level of individual games and their associated architectures and resources, but also at the level of ways of playing them and the social and political practices governing the conditions for getting involved in them. To get there, let us briefly study how people play talking games in everyday life, assuming that the requirements for successful participation are fulfilled.

Selectivity. As soon as we shift attention from local games to global practices and policies, entirely new aspects of talking come into view. As long as we keep our focus on individual, isolated games, we envisage two (or more) talkers/knowers engaging in sharing a piece of world knowledge through exchanging pertinent utterances. When we zoom out and look at more global practices of playing and not playing these local games, it becomes apparent that talking games are always highly selective on a number of dimensions. A given talker may, for instance, engage in talk about x but not about y. She may be prone to talk to talker A but not to B. Or she chooses to talk about x to A, but not to B, and about y to C, but not to A and B. She may even choose not to talk at all as long as D and E are part of the talking scenario. And so on.

Of course, there are several further dimensions of selectivity pertaining to, for example, what precisely is being said about x and y (and what not), in what way utterances are being made, at which time or on which occasion an utterance is being made, and so on. In other words, the structure of talking games offers numerous degrees of freedom among which talkers may choose, or need to choose, for designing their games. As a result, the practice of engaging in talking games is in many respects highly selective. Accordingly, while it is true that each local act of talking is an act of sharing knowledge with others, it is also true that the global practice of engaging in such acts is in effect a practice of selective communication—that is, of sharing some knowledge with some others (while at the same time, not sharing some other knowledge with them, and also not sharing this knowledge with other others).

Thus, when we look at talking games from a global perspective, we must conclude that that practice is not tailored to open sharing of everything with everybody but rather to selective sharing of some knowledge items (but not others) with some talkers (but not others). If so, we must conclude that it may be misleading to discuss the proper functions of talking by zooming in on local games. Zooming in on local games fools us into believing that talking is for knowledge sharing. It is only when we zoom out on global practices that we can see that talking is for selective knowledge dissemination rather than open knowledge sharing.[11]

Selective knowledge dissemination is entirely dependent on dual representation and double-entry book-keeping. It requires us to maintain separate streams of representations for scenarios and for contents of talking (for talkers and utterances happening here and now and for events happening there and then, respectively). Further, it requires knowledge integration and accumulation by double entry: one entry for things and events happening there and then (furnished with pointers to talkers/knowers to whom they are known) and another one for knowers/talkers talking here and now (furnished with pointers to things and events that they know).

Criteria. Whereas the structure of local games may be aimed at local control of others' behavior through local knowledge sharing, the structure of global practices of playing them aims at modulating the global dispositions underlying their actions through selective policies for knowledge dissemination. Depending on the context, individuals may address others to whom they apply such selective dissemination as isolated individuals or as members of certain kinds of groups or collectives. When addressed at familiar individuals, for example, one's children, partners, and colleagues, the underlying policies may aim at providing them with knowledge the provider may find useful for directing her actions—useful from

11. The distinction between games and policies for playing them may equally be applied to mirror games and talking games. As we saw in ch. 6, policies for selective mirroring provide powerful tools for social control and differentiation. Likewise, talking games and associated policies provide efficient tools for control and differentiation through selective knowledge dissemination. It should be understood that the present discussion does not intend to give a full account of these practices, but just to hint at their potential for social control. Accordingly, we leave entirely open how individuals acquire their policies and under what conditions their workings are implicit/automatic versus explicit/controlled.

her own perspective and, perhaps, from (her own view of) the providees'
perspectives as well. Yet, when applied to less familiar individuals who
count as members of certain groups or collectives, the criterion of useful-
ness may be complemented or even replaced by the criterion of appropriateness: Providers will selectively disseminate knowledge according to
what they find appropriate for others to know, given the pattern of their
current beliefs and stereotypes concerning those others and their respective
groups and collectives.

Thus, since each individual is both provider and providee, policies for
selective knowledge dissemination will act to shape providees' knowledge
resources for control according to what deems providers useful and appropriate. Talking games may thus be seen as tools for guiding individuals'
knowing and acting according to the way others would like them to know
and to act.[12]

Beyond Control

If it is true that language crafts have evolved to be optimized for social
control, it may still be true that they subserve other important functions
as well—functions that will, in one way or another, be related to their
proper and primary function and the way it is implemented. Here I briefly
address the three suspects mentioned above: cognition, communication,
and culture. Although each of them would require and deserve a chapter
of its own, I confine myself to mentioning some topics concerning ways
in which they are related to issues of social control.[13]

12. Having arrived at this conclusion we may wonder why it has taken such a long
route to get there. One answer is that the claim that talking is a tool for control
diverges from the common opinion that language is, first of all, a tool for knowledge
sharing and communication. A second, more speculative answer suggests that language may even boost the efficiency of social control by hiding that function behind
other, more conspicuous functions. According to that speculation the relative incon-
spicuity of the implications that language has for control may in fact be a prerequisite for efficient performance of that function.
13. Each of these three topics is associated with far-reaching claims concerning the
origins and functions of language and language crafts. For instance, Chomsky and
other linguists have emphasized language-for-cognition over language-for-communication, stressing the role of both language structure and language use for making
and shaping the organization of human cognition and thought (see, e.g., Chomsky,
1995, 2002; Hauser, Chomsky & Fitch, 2002; Levinson, 2003; Slobin, 2007). Conversely, others have emphasized the role of language for supporting communication
as well as the role of communication for shaping language (e.g., Hurford, Studdert-
Kennedy & Knight, 1998; Jackendoff, 2002; Pinker & Jackendoff, 2005; Tomasello,

Concerning *cognition*, we have seen that the novel representational resources that are required for language processing need to be implemented in a way that allows for close functional couplings with the preexisting ontologies for things and events to which the utterances refer. One way of looking at these couplings is in terms of their role in the workings of language, that is, the requirement of mapping utterances to events and events to utterances. This is the perspective we have adopted so far. Another way of looking at the same couplings is in terms of their contribution to cognition proper, that is, their impact on the structure of ontologies for things and events as well as the cognitive operations involved in using them for transient representational construction.

There is a long-standing tradition of discussing the impact of language on knowledge and thought, and a huge literature associated with it.[14] Proposals concerning the nature and the depth of that impact range from weak to strong. Weak proposals may suggest, for example, that words and lexical knowledge help to structure and delimit conceptual knowledge or that verbalization may support visual imagery and help in structuring its time course. Strong proposals may suggest, for instance, that language-based concepts can be addressed by entirely novel kinds of fast and efficient processing operations that do not work for prelinguistic concepts. Even stronger proposals suggest that language-related resources and operations are prerequisites for enabling abstract reasoning in the first place. Proposals along these lines may pertain to simple utterances like words or more complex ones like phrases, and they may address both transient constructions and permanent resources. In any case, these proposals claim that the representational resources for language processing act on cognition proper, boosting the efficiency of knowledge representation and processing.

Concerning *communication*, the scope of language crafts is coextensional with the scope of a narrow reading of that concept. According to that

1999, 2003a,b). Finally, from language-for-cognition and language-for-communication to language-for-culture, it is not a big step. On the cultural perspective, both cognition and communication are seen as proximate instruments for ultimate functions pertaining to the formation and maintenance of cultural values, norms, and traditions (e.g., Boas, 1940; Bruner, 1990, 2003; Lévi-Strauss, 1963; Sapir & Mandelbaum, 1949).

14. For classic proposals, see this ch., n. 4. For more recent linguistic and psychological studies on mutual interactions between language and thought, see, e.g., Boroditsky (2007); Bowerman & Choi (2007); Clark (2003); Gentner and Goldin-Meadow (2003); Gumperz and Levinson (1996); Hunt and Agnoli (1991); Levinson (2003); Lucy (1996); Pinker (1994); Slobin (1996).

reading, its use should be limited to scenarios in which individuals exchange signals on purpose—for the purpose of informing others about internal states or external events. As we have discussed, the major way in which language crafts work for control is through sharing and selective dissemination of knowledge. Accordingly, the scheme in figure 13.1 may also be seen as a scheme for dyadic communication through talking.

Yet, although scopes may be coextensional, associated functions and mechanisms are certainly not. In that regard, the concept of communication is broader than the concept of language. Communication can be achieved through various channels and mechanisms of which language and its crafts figure as just one. Among the various kinds of communication crafts that have evolved in the animal kingdom, language crafts are special in two ways, to which we will return in the concluding section. One is that they rely on symbolic reference between utterances and events. The other is that they rely on speech, that is, utterances carried by gestures generated by the vocal tract.

Accordingly, the common claim that language is for communication is both true and useless. It is true in terms of acknowledging coextensionality of scope, but useless in terms of specifying functions and mechanisms. Subsuming language crafts under the concept of communication does not provide much insight unless one specifies what their proper function is, how they differ from other crafts of communication, and what kind of functional machinery instantiates them.

Concerning *culture*, the crucial role of language for the foundation and promotion of culture is fairly obvious and has been widely recognized.[15] How compatible is the claim that language is for culture with the claim that it is for social control? One fruitful way of looking at culturally coherent collectives of individuals is to view them as systems of shared factual and normative knowledge. That knowledge is shared and communicated

15. On the one hand, there is broad agreement among anthropologists, historians, and philosophers on the constitutive and formative role of language in human culture. Language is understood in that context as the prime medium through which knowledge is transferred within and across generations (see, e.g., Boas, 1940; Lévi-Strauss, 1963; Sapir & Mandelbaum, 1949). On the other hand, this does not necessarily imply that language is a prerequisite for the formation of culture. For instance, as has been convincingly shown for chimpanzees, culture-like frameworks for both instrumental interaction with the environment and social interaction with others can also be established through embodied, nonsymbolic means of communication (see, e.g., Boesch, 1996, 2008; Boesch & Tomasello, 1998; Whiten & Boesch, 2001; Whiten et al., in press).

both synchronically across contemporaries and diachronically across generations. Such systems are, of course, systems of and for social control, offering to individuals both imperative and indicative knowledge resources suited to direct and constrain their behavior.

The cultural perspective on language opens up a much wider horizon for studying the crafts of language than dyadic talking games, on which this chapter has concentrated, can provide. The cultural perspective opens our eyes to the fact that the representational resources on which talking games draw go back to sources far beyond the horizon of their individual participants. While it is always the case that these resources are acquired through learning and socialization procedures in participants' individual lifetimes, their content and structure are shaped not only by what they encounter in their own social and cultural environments but also by the facts and fictions that they encounter in the selection of tales, stories, and histories to which they become exposed and through which they acquire knowledge about actions and events that may have happened long ago and far away.

As we saw above, the practice of engaging in talking games is a practice of sharing/not sharing certain pieces of knowledge with certain others. What the cultural perspective on language adds to the picture is the insight that the dialectics of sharing/not sharing is not only a matter of transient construction but of permanent resources as well. Cultures provide practices for engaging their members in games of talking and storytelling that aim at furnishing them with shared frameworks and ontologies for understanding actions and events that they may encounter in the world—as well as talking about them.

Roots of Talking

In concluding this chapter, I will no longer resist the temptation to add some speculative remarks on the origin of the craft of talking and of the underlying architecture, thus moving a few steps from ultimate function to putative proximate mechanisms. My move will not go into any detail, however. Instead, I will examine, in more general terms, how the open-minds approach that previous chapters have outlined for volition and cognition may constrain evolutionary and psychohistorical scenarios for the origin of language and language crafts.

What does it take to explain the origin of language crafts? To address this question, we may go back to the miracle that we encountered above, trying to reconstruct how it may have occurred in a nonmiraculous way.

The miracle concerns the birth of the craft of talking. At the core of this craft, we may see the notion of utterances. The birth of utterances is the birth of a novel kind of action, associated with novel ways of producing and perceiving them. Utterances, as we know from present-day languages, exhibit two important features in which they differ from ordinary actions: symbolic reference and reliance on vocal gestures. The feature of symbolic reference reflects the placeholder function of utterances—the fact that they refer to events that may be entirely detached from the talking game to which the utterance belongs. The feature of reliance on vocal gestures, or speech, pertains to what we may consider the physical carrier of the utterance, that is, the kind of gestures through which the utterance is expressed. Thus, trying to explain the birth of the craft of talking is tantamount to explaining how speech utterances become possible as a new kind of action for symbolic communication.

How can we get there? Consider, as a hypothetical starting scenario, populations of early humans that are exposed to strong selection pressure concerning their tools for social control. As a result, their fitness and their chances for survival will, at both the population and the individual level, very much depend on the efficacy of the tools they use for mutual control of their acting.

What steps need to be taken to develop and optimize proximate tools suited to instantiate that distal function? I submit that two evolutionary trajectories need to be combined—one that delivers symbolic reference (through converting embodied actions into symbolic utterances) and another that delivers speech (through moving from manual to vocal gestures). A crucial feature of the scenario I am sketching here is that these two transitions follow each other. For reasons that will be explained below, the scenario posits that the acquisition of symbolic reference is initially accomplished in the domain of manual gestures, and then, in a second step, speech is acquired through vocal gestures taking over for manual gestures.[16]

16. On the following pages I speak of manual gestures in a *pars pro toto* mode. I use this term as convenient shorthand for bodily gestures that can be seen by others (and are therefore, at least in principle, suited for communication). Manual gesturing appears to be fairly ubiquitous in humans, perhaps not surprising in view of the fact that our forelimbs have become freed from the burden of locomotion (Corballis, 2003a,b). The enormous potential of manual gestures for communication is also illustrated by the power of sign languages in which manual gestures take over the role of vocal gestures (Duncan, Cassell & Levy, 2007; Goldin-Meadow, 2003, 2007; Kendon, 2004).

Symbolic Reference

How can ordinary actions turn into utterances? By the term *ordinary actions* I refer to segments of bodily activity that are embedded in environmental events that act on them and on which they act back. Utterances are, of course, segments of bodily activity, too, and they are likewise embedded in environmental events like talking games. Yet, on top of being ordinary actions (performed and perceived as interactions with environmental events in the current scenario), utterances are also produced and perceived as placeholders for something else—for things and events that may be entirely detached from that scenario.[17]

How, then, do we get from actions to utterances? I submit that we need three basic steps.

Step 1: Similarity. The first takes us from ordinary to communicative action or, more precisely, to the craft of using ordinary action for communicative purposes. Individuals may, for instance, perform certain actions in order to instruct others what they are supposed or required to do (imperative communication through action demonstration). Likewise, they may perform these actions in order to inform others about previously encountered actions (performed by other others; indicative communication through action simulation). In order to be effective for communication and control, this very first step already requires that individuals adopt a novel understanding of actions that are performed and perceived in the context of communication.

That understanding sees individuals involved in action games—a context in which actions are no longer performed and perceived for their own sake, but for the sake of instructing and/or informing others. Action games may be seen as precursors of talking games, exhibiting the same basic structure. As soon as actions become embedded in such games, they turn from ordinary into communicative actions. Communicative actions differ from ordinary actions in two important respects: They are addressed to other individuals and—most importantly—they refer to something else. For communicative actions to be effective, both of these functional features need to be shared among perceivers and producers: These actions are produced

17. According to the terminology I am using here, an action counts as an utterance if it is produced and perceived to exhibit symbolic reference. The use of that term is therefore not restricted to the domain of speech (i.e., utterances based on vocal tract gestures). Rather, any bodily movement may acquire the status of an utterance if and when it exhibits symbolic reference. Utterances may therefore be carried by both vocal and manual gestures.

and perceived in order to inform others about actions that have been performed or to instruct them about actions that are to be performed.[18]

This step may be seen to provide a powerful tool for action modulation
through embodied communication. Through their own acting each actor
may, on the one hand, prime other actors to mirror his behavior and, on
the other hand, share with others knowledge about what (still other) others
have been doing.[19] Still, there is one crucial limitation to the kind of events
to which communicative action games can refer. Since reference between
communicative actions and those actions to which they refer is based on
similarity, the scope of action games is limited to communication about
short pieces of others' actions—pieces that can easily be reproduced in the
context of action games.

Step 2: Downscaled similarity. Yet, in order to be fast and efficient, communication about more extended events (such as complex actions extended
over hours and days) needs to be much shorter than the events themselves.
Communication about extended action would be pointless (and in any
case inefficient) if actions referring to them took as much time as those to
which they refer. Thus, what is needed for successful communication about
extended actions are procedures for generating what we may call *downscaled similarity*. These procedures allow us to generate small-scale actions
whose structure exhibits a downscaled similarity relationship with the
large-scale actions to which they refer.

Such downscaling will first of all pertain to the time course, but it may
pertain to a variety of other features of the action as well. As a result, communicative action may take the shape of more or less compressed and
condensed sketches of the actions to which they refer. Since such compres-
sion/condensation leaves the basic representational dimensions unaffected, represented and representing action will still share the same basic
dimensionality and the referential relationship between the two may still
be based on similarity. Yet, the stronger the required downscaling is, the
weaker and the less conspicuous will be the resulting similarity relation-

18. This is what so-called pedagogical scenarios are about (Csibra & Gergely, 2006;
Gergely & Csibra, 2005). They aim at creating situations in which the child understands that the adult's talking and acting refers to something beyond the ongoing
action/talking games themselves.
19. Action modulation through embodied communication can only be effective if
two further conditions are met: (i) participants need to agree on the nature of the
ongoing communicative act (i.e., imperative vs. indicative), and (ii) in the indicative
case, they need to have means to identify the third-party agent to whose actions
the ongoing communication refers.

ship. Importantly, the second step broadens the scope of actions to which communicative action may refer: Downscaled similarity allows for short-lived communications about long-lived actions.

Step 3: Symbolic reference. Although downscaling of similarity extends the scope of communication from small to big actions, there is another limitation of scope that downscaling cannot overcome: Communication is up to this point limited to communication about actions, that is, to representing actions exhibiting the same dimensionality as the events that are being represented. On the one hand, the limitation to actions reflects the fact that embodied communication is intimately linked to action perception and control and has actually emerged to subserve the social control of action. From this perspective, it appears to be natural that in embodied action games others and their acting play two roles at a time: the procedural role of being partners in the game and the declarative role of being actors addressed by the game. On the other hand, the similarity requirement is clearly a limiting factor for communication. It limits the scope of communication to actions, that is, to to-be-represented events that may exhibit (full or downscaled) similarity with elements from the repertoire of possible actions representing them.

The obvious next step from here is to abandon similarity and replace it with symbolic reference as the functional basis for the relationship between representing actions and represented events. When that step is taken, communication turns from embodied to symbolic. From then on, gestures of communicative action need no longer bear resemblance to the actions and events to which they refer. As a consequence, the scope of such events is now entirely unlimited. Symbolic reference can, in principle, be established between any kind of communicative gesture and any kind of event to be addressed. Still, the downside of taking this step is that symbolic communication depends on prior acquisition of symbol systems and the referential relationships associated with them. Symbolic communication can, in other words, only work for communities that share given symbol systems.[20]

20. When seen from a functionalist perspective, the consequences of this limitation are often more beneficial than detrimental. Symbol systems may be seen as convenient tools for delimiting collectives of individuals that share certain pieces of knowledge from other individuals and collectives who don't share them. Symbol systems thus act to strengthen the dialectics of knowledge sharing/nonsharing that is constitutive for all kinds of deliberate communication. They carry on, at the level of cultural differentiation, what action games and talking games establish at the level of interindividual communication.

In sum, these three steps take us from ordinary (embodied) actions to (symbolic) utterances. While ordinary actions are perceived and produced as (nothing but) actions, utterances are perceived and produced as actions that refer to other actions or events. Our hypothetical scenario places the transition from one to the other in the context of communication about others' actions. At the outset, that communication is entirely based on similarity between representing and represented action. Then, in the interest of extending the scope of communication, similarity becomes increasingly weaker, and eventually the role of similarity in grounding the referential relationship between representing and represented events is entirely taken over by symbolic reference. At that stage embodied turns into symbolic communication, and communicative actions acquire the status of utterances as we have depicted and discussed them with reference to figure 13.1.

Vocal Gestures

Up to this point, our scenario has addressed the transition from embodied to symbolic communication without being explicit concerning the bodily gestures that carry that communication. Still, the way in which I have sketched the putative transition from ordinary actions to utterances was meant to suggest that that transition may have taken place in the domain of bodily movements for which we may use the *pars pro toto* term *manual gestures*. When the notion of utterance is applied to that domain it thus refers to body language, not spoken language. Yet, our transition scenario is aiming to account for the roots of spoken language. To understand how talking games may have evolved from action games, we therefore need to consider another putative transition that takes us from manual gestures to vocal tract gestures and, hence, from body movements to speech.

In recent years, the idea that speech has evolved from vocal tract gestures taking over communicative functions that were initially instantiated in manual and bodily gestures has gained considerable interest and support.[21] When this idea is placed in the context of the present framework

21. Support for the idea that manual gestures may have played an important role in the early evolution of human language comes from studies on the ontogenetic and phylogenetic development of gesturing proper (see, e.g., Corballis, 2003a,b; Goldin-Meadow, 2006, 2007; Klima & Bellugi, 1979; but see Fitch, 2010; MacNeilage, 2003, 2008; MacNeilage & Davis, 2005, for critical discussions). Further support for this notion has recently been derived from experiments and models on mirror neurons and mirror systems (see, e.g., Arbib, 2005, 2006; Bellugi & Klima, 2000; Emmorey, 2006; Rizzolatti & Arbib, 1998; Rizzolatti & Sinigaglia, 2008; see also Fogassi & Ferrari, 2007; Gentilucci & Corballis, 2006; Wargo, 2008).

for the transition from embodied to symbolic communication, it proves to be particularly attractive because it splits a hard problem into two less hard and more tractable ones. The hard problem is to understand how speech processing becomes possible, that is, how vocal tract gestures can become carriers of meaningful utterances in talking games. That problem is hard because it poses two questions at a time: how symbolic reference can become possible, and how vocal tract gestures can become carriers of utterances exhibiting such reference. Now, when we assume that utterances exhibiting symbolic reference initially evolved in the domain of manual gestures and that only later did vocal tract gestures take over from these gestures, we can address the two questions one after the other, rather than answering both at once. The claim that symbolic reference initially evolved in the domain of manual gestures is particularly attractive because it concentrates the burden of explanation of the embodied-symbolic transition entirely on these gestures. In that domain, it appears to be relatively easy to establish a transition from similarity-based to symbolic reference—certainly much easier than it would be in the domain of vocal tract gestures.

The first problem is thus solved through the transition from embodied to symbolic manual gestures. This transition explains how symbolic reference becomes possible. The second problem needs to be solved by the putative transition from manual to vocal tract gestures. This transition helps us to understand how speech has taken on the role of the chief carrier of symbolic utterances. Taking both steps together provides us with a non-miraculous explanation of the birth of talking.

How can we proceed from manual to vocal tract gestures? While different proposals have been advanced concerning the evolutionary trajectories that may underlie the putative transition from one to the other kind of gesture, they all agree in two major respects concerning the functional and structural implications of that transition.

Functional implications pertain to fitness advantages that may be associated with the transition. One such advantage is closely associated with an important functional difference between vision and audition. As long as symbolic communication depends on utterances carried by manual gestures, communication is entirely dependent on the visual modality and the attentional limitations entailed by it. The efficiency of visual communication is for obvious reasons much more dependent on the communicators' strategies for attentional deployment than is auditory communication. This is why speech gestures offer themselves as more efficient carriers of symbolic utterances. Further functional advantages associated with moving from manual to vocal gestures may be entailed by relieving the control system for ordinary bodily and manual gestures of the function of carrying communicative gestures, thus keeping it ready and available for other kinds of noncommunicative action. According to this view, delegating communicative functions to vocal tract gestures may be seen to instantiate a dual-systems architecture that allows for parallel (i.e., more or less interference-free) control of instrumental action and communicative action through hand and mouth, respectively.[22]

Structural implications pertain to the systematic relationship between bodily movements and vocal gestures and their underlying representational resources. The terms in which we have so far addressed the trajectory that leads from one to the other may be misleading because it suggests two disjunct domains of gesturing, one taking over functions from the other. For a more adequate picture we need to acknowledge that vocal tract gestures must be considered a specific subset of general bodily gestures and that we must therefore characterize the evolutionary trajectory from movements to speech as a process of concentrating the instantiation of communicative functions on a specific subset of bodily gestures. Thus, rather than talking about transferring that function from movements to speech, or from manual to vocal gestures, we need to talk about an evolutionary trajectory of zooming in from a total set onto a specific subset of gestures that qualify as efficient carriers of symbolic utterances. That subset of specialized gestures may from then on coexist alongside others that qualify as likewise efficient carriers of instrumental interactions with the environment.

Language from Action

To conclude, it should be noted that our scenario derives language crafts from action crafts—and even does so in two independent though interrelated senses. On the one hand, it claims that language crafts initially emerged as tools for *communication about action*. According to this claim, language crafts have evolved from crafts for action perception and representation. On the other hand, it claims that language crafts rely on *communication through action*, be it in the general domain of bodily gestures or the specific domain of vocal gestures. According to this claim, language crafts are seen to have evolved from crafts for action planning and control.

If these claims are true, we should not be surprised to find the crafts for perception and production of speech still bearing marks of the underlying

22. The hand–mouth terminology follows Corballis (2003a,b).

crafts for perception and control of action. If such marks exist and if they really reflect deep, genuine features of the human language faculty, they should be common to most if not all languages that humans have brought forth.[23] Accordingly, if language universals exist, some of them should bear marks of the grounding of language in action.

To close our speculations on the roots of speech, we may in fact discern such marks. While some, which pertain to the semantic side of language, seem to reflect the fact that languages have evolved as tools for communication *about* action, others, which pertain to the syntactical side, seem to reflect basic structural features of the organization of the actions *through* which that communication is achieved.[24] Taken together, these observations lend support to the notion that language crafts are rooted in action crafts.

23. The idea of language universals is as old as philosophical deliberation and scientific theorizing about the nature and the origin of human language. It reflects the assumption, belief, or even hope that behind and atop the (rather conspicuous) diversity of human languages, some hidden (perhaps rather inconspicuous) commonalities must exist that reflect innate foundations of the language faculty (see, e.g., Chomsky, 1995, 2002; Comrie, 1989; Pinker, 1994; Pinker & Bloom, 1990). For a challenge of "the myth of language universals," see Evans and Levinson (2009). On innate, biological foundations of syntax, see Bickerton and Szathmáry (2009); but see Kirby, Christiansen, and Chater (2009) and Steels (2009) for challenges to a leading role for biological factors.

24. For instance, as has been shown on the semantic side, categories like actorhood, agency, and animacy may play an important role in semantic disambiguation of grammatical structure (see, e.g., Andrews, 2007; Comrie, 1989; Fillmore, 1972; Foley, 2007). The same applies to production and comprehension of speech and language in real time (see, e.g., Bornkessel & Schlesewsky, 2006; Bornkessel-Schlesewsky & Schlesewsky, 2009). These studies show that prominent semantic roles like actorhood not only help speakers–listeners to organize the structure of what is being said but also determine the organization of the utterances through which communication is conveyed. In a similar vein it has been argued, on the syntactic side, that the feature of recursion that some authors have elevated to the status of the hallmark and most distinctive feature of human language (e.g., Hauser, Chomsky & Fitch, 2002; cf. van der Hulst, 2010) may in fact be derived and imported from the hierarchical, recursive structure inherent in human action (see, e.g., Humphreys, Forde, & Riddoch, 2001; Humphreys & Riddoch, 2006; Miller, Galanter & Pribram, 1960). Since competencies for negotiating recursion in action are much older than related competencies in the language domain, it is tempting to consider recursion in language a functional derivative of recursion in action (see, e.g., Jackendoff, 2007, ch. 4).

Epilogue

And the Lord God took the man,
and put him into the garden of Eden to dress it and to keep it.
And the Lord God commanded the man,
saying, Of every tree of the garden thou mayest freely eat:
But of the tree of the knowledge of good and evil, thou shalt not eat of it.
. . .
And when the woman saw that the tree was good for food,
and that it was pleasant to the eyes,
and a tree to be desired to make one wise,
she took of the fruit thereof, and did eat,
and gave also unto her husband with her; and he did eat.
And the eyes of them both were opened. . . .
—Genesis

The Garden of Eden

To conclude, let us take another brief look at ancient ideas concerning human autonomy and see in what ways they preempt ideas and notions entailed by the foregoing discussion on open minds. Back in the fifteenth century when the philosopher Pico della Mirandola came up with his new ideas on the dignity of man and his mission to create and design himself, his views were not well received by the authorities of the Catholic church. A commission appointed by the pope condemned his central theses as heretical readings of what the Bible truly entails.

When we compare Pico's enthusiastic story about God giving man autonomy for a present with what Genesis has to tell us about the human condition and man's mission in the world, we may see that Pico's interpretation is in fact quite idiosyncratic and selective and, for that matter, perhaps heretical. The biblical tale of the Garden of Eden is much leaner and less verbose than Pico's story is. Most importantly, while it does mention that God gives man dominion over all living things, there is no explicit mention whatsoever of man's mission or capacity to make and mold himself.

Man's autonomy is, on the contrary, quite limited and constrained. According to Genesis, God takes man and puts him in the Garden of Eden. Fairly obviously, that garden is a golden cage, which has two sides. On the one side it is a paradise, providing Adam and Eve with trees that are pleasant to look at and that provide good food, allowing them a life of ease. Yet, on the other side, it limits and constrains the range of their actions and the freedom of their choices. The constraints are both implicit and explicit. More implicit constraints derive from the fact that the garden is segregated and secluded from the rest of the world. Therefore, since God has ordained that they live in the garden, its borders must act to constrain their freedom. More explicit is the taboo under which God puts the Tree of the Knowledge of Good and Evil, punishing its violation by man by the threat of death.

Thus, whereas Pico sees God granting man autonomy, Genesis sees God constraining man's range of action through the confines and taboos he sets for him. According to Genesis, Adam's mission in the world is to be obedient to God. So, if there is any autonomy left at all, it is limited by God-set confines. Obviously, this picture is quite different from Pico's view, and with hindsight this difference may explain why Pico's reading of Genesis was considered heretical.

Self-made Autonomy

Still, a few lines later, the tale of Genesis discusses autonomy, too. However, in that tale, autonomy is not granted by God but self-made through Eve's and Adam's own actions. After a while living in the garden, and following a remarkable conversation with a serpent, we find them violating God's taboo and eating a fruit from the Tree of the Knowledge of Good and Evil. Importantly, as the serpent had told them beforehand (and God later acknowledges, too), they become, through that deed, endowed with the God-like property of knowing good and evil.

Accordingly, if we take the knowledge of good and evil as a metaphor for the autonomy entailed by making choices and decisions, it becomes apparent that the fall of man is, at the same time, the rise of the will. As long as Adam and Eve had not eaten from the Tree of the Knowledge of Good and Evil, their behavior was governed by obedience to God's laws.

Yet, once they violated these laws, they acquired, through that very deed, the God-like capacity of making their own choices.

Thus, whereas Pico's story holds that God grants man autonomy through an act of grace, Genesis implies that man gains self-made autonomy through an act of disobedience to God's law. Taking both views together and rephrasing them in terms of ideas laid out above, we may say that Pico's and the Bible's tales stress attribution and appropriation of autonomy, respectively.

It should not go unnoticed that the reading I am suggesting here for the biblical tale about Adam and Eve in the Garden of Eden is fairly different from the usual reading—probably a heretical one as well. Being disobedient to God's law is, from a moral theology point of view, one of the most evil things that man can do. Yet, from the point of view of our mental history, it is, at the same time, one of the best things that man can do in order to become an autonomous agent.[1] The biblical tale from ancient times seems to preempt a lesson that humans have since learned over and over again. The lesson says that the sole reliable way through which they can acquire autonomy is through destroying the golden cages that thrones and altars erect for them.

1. In Jaynes's psychohistorical scenario, this is in fact the key point at which the bicameral mind breaks down: Consciousness emerges when the role of God's voice is taken over by man's own voice (Jaynes, 1976).

References

Aarts, H., & Elliot, A. (Eds.). (2011). *Goal-directed behavior*. Philadelphia: Psychology Press.

Aarts, H., Gollwitzer, P. M., & Hassin, R. R. (2004). Goal contagion: Perceiving is for pursuing. *Journal of Personality and Social Psychology, 87*(1), 23–37.

Aarts, H., & Hassin, R. R. (2005). Automatic goal inference and contagion: On pursuing goals one perceives in other people's behavior. In J. P. Forgas, K. D. William, & S. M. Laham (Eds.), *Social motivation: Conscious and unconscious processes* (pp. 153–167). Cambridge: Cambridge University Press.

Ach, N. (1905). *Über die Willenstätigkeit und das Denken*. Göttingen: Vandenhoeck & Ruprecht.

Ach, N. (1910). *Über den Willensakt und das Temperament*. Leipzig: Quelle & Meyer.

Achtziger, A., & Gollwitzer, P. M. (2008). Motivation and volition in the course of action. In J. Heckhausen & H. Heckhausen (Eds.), *Motivation and action* (pp. 272–295). New York: Cambridge University Press.

Adolph, K. E. (2008). The growing body in action: What infant locomotion tells us about perceptually guided action. In R. L. Klatzky, B. MacWhinney, & M. Behrmann (Eds.), *Embodiment, ego-space, and action* (pp. 275–321). New York: Psychology Press.

Agnetta, B., & Rochat, P. (2004). Imitative games by 9-, 14-, and 18-month-old infants. *Infancy, 6*(1), 1–36.

Aguilar, J. H., & Buckareff, A. A. (2010). The causal theory of action: Origins and issues. In J. H. Aguilar & A. A. Buckareff (Eds.), *Causing human actions* (pp. 1–26). Cambridge, MA: MIT Press.

Ainslie, G. (2001). *Breakdown of will*. Cambridge: Cambridge University Press.

Albright, T. D., Kandel, E. R., & Posner, M. I. (2000). Cognitive neuroscience. *Current Opinion in Neurobiology, 10*(5), 612–624.

Amsterdam, B. (1972). Mirror self-image reactions before age two. *Developmental Psychobiology, 5*(4), 297–305.

Anderson, J. R. (1983). *The architecture of cognition* (Vol. 5). Cambridge, MA: Harvard University Press.

Andrews, A. D. (2007). The major functions of the noun phrase. In T. Shopen (Ed.), *Language typology and syntactic description* (pp. 132–223). Cambridge: Cambridge University Press.

Anisfeld, M. (2005). No compelling evidence to dispute Piaget's timetable of the development of representational imitation in infancy. In S. Hurley & N. Chater (Series Ed.), *Perspectives on imitation: From neuroscience to social science*, Vol. 2: *Imitation, human development, and culture* (pp. 107–131). Cambridge, MA: MIT Press.

Anisfeld, M., Turkewitz, G., Rose, S. A., Rosenberg, F. R., Sheiber, F. J., Couturier-Fagan, D. A., et al. (2001). No compelling evidence that newborns imitate oral gestures. *Infancy, 2*(1), 111–122.

Aquila, R. E. (1977). *Intentionality: A study of mental acts*. University Park: Pennsylvania State University Press.

Arbib, M. A. (2005). From monkey-like action recognition to human language: An evolutionary framework for neurolinguistics. *Behavioral and Brain Sciences, 28*(2), 105–167.

Arbib, M. A. (2006). The mirror system hypothesis on the linkage of action and languages. In M. A. Arbib (Ed.), *Action to language via the mirror neuron system* (pp. 3–47). Cambridge: Cambridge University Press.

Armel, K. C., & Ramachandran, V. S. (2003). Projecting sensations to external objects: Evidence from skin conductance response. *Proceedings of the Royal Society of London: B, Biological Sciences, 270*(1523), 1499–1506.

Atkinson, J. W. (1964). *An introduction to motivation*. Princeton: Van Nostrand.

Avenanti, A., Bueti, D., Galati, G., & Aglioti, S. M. (2005). Transcranial magnetic stimulation highlights the sensorimotor side of empathy for pain. *Nature Neuroscience, 8*(7), 955–960.

Baars, B. J. (1986). *The cognitive revolution in psychology*. New York: Guilford Press.

Baars, B. J. (1988). *A cognitive theory of consciousness*. Cambridge: Cambridge University Press.

Baars, B. J. (1997). *In the theater of consciousness: The workspace of the mind*. Oxford: Oxford University Press.

Baars, B. J. (2002). The conscious access hypothesis: Origins and recent evidence. *Trends in Cognitive Sciences, 6*, 47–52.

Babcock, M. K., & Freyd, J. J. (1988). The perception of dynamic information in static handwritten forms. *American Journal of Psychology, 101*(1), 111–130.

Baddeley, A. D. (2007). *Working memory, thought, and action.* Oxford: Oxford University Press.

Baillargeon, R. (2001). Infants' physical knowledge: Of acquired expectations and core principles. In E. Dupoux (Ed.), *Language, brain, and cognitive development: Essays in honor of Jacques Mehler* (pp. 341–361). Cambridge, MA: MIT Press.

Balensiefen, L. (1990). *Die Bedeutung des Spiegelbildes als ikonographisches Motiv in der antiken Kunst.* Tübingen: Wasmuth.

Baltes, P. B., Reuter-Lorenz, P. A., & Rösler, F. (Eds.). (2006). *Lifespan development and the brain.* Cambridge: Cambridge University Press.

Baltes, P. B., Rösler, F., & Reuter-Lorenz, P. A. (2006). Prologue: Biocultural co-constructivism as a theoretical metascript. In P. B. Baltes, P. A. Reuter-Lorenz, & F. Rösler (Eds.), *Lifespan development and the brain* (pp. 3–39). Cambridge: Cambridge University Press.

Bargh, J. A. (1989). Conditional automaticity: Varieties of automatic influence in social perception and cognition. In J. S. Uleman & J. A. Bargh (Eds.), *Unintended thought* (pp. 3–51). New York: Guilford Press.

Bargh, J. A. (1990). Auto-motives: Preconscious determinants of social interaction. In E. T. Higgins & R. M. Sorrentino (Eds.), *Handbook of motivation and cognition: Foundations of social behavior* (Vol. 2, pp. 93–130). New York: Guilford Press.

Bargh, J. A. (2005). Bypassing the will: Towards demystifying the nonconscious control of social behavior. In R. R. Hassin, J. S. Uleman, & J. A. Bargh (Eds.), *The new unconscious* (pp. 37–58). New York: Oxford University Press.

Bargh, J. A. (2006). Agenda 2006: What have we been priming all these years? On the development, mechanisms, and ecology of nonconscious social behavior. *European Journal of Social Psychology, 36*(2), 147–168.

Bargh, J. A., & Morsella, E. (2008). The unconscious mind. *Perspectives on Psychological Science, 3*(1), 73–79.

Barker, R. G. (1963). The stream of behavior as an empirical problem. In R. G. Barker (Ed.), *The stream of behavior: Explorations of its structure & content* (pp. 1–22). New York: Appleton-Century-Crofts.

Barkley, R. A. (2001). The executive functions and self-regulation: An evolutionary neuropsychological perspective. *Neuropsychology Review, 11*(1), 1–29.

Barnes, B. (2000). *Understanding agency: Social theory and responsible action.* London: SAGE.

Baron-Cohen, S., Tager-Flusberg, H., & Cohen, D. J. (Eds.). (1993). *Understanding other minds: Perspectives from autism*. Oxford: Oxford University Press.

Barresi, J., & Moore, C. (1996). Intentional relations and social understanding. *Behavioral and Brain Sciences*, *19*, 107–154.

Barsalou, L. W., Simmons, W. K., Barbey, A. K., & Wilson, C. D. (2003). Grounding conceptual knowledge in modality-specific systems. *Trends in Cognitive Sciences*, *7*(2), 84–91.

Bavelas, J. B. (2007). Face-to-face dialogue as a micro-social context. In S. D. Duncan, J. Cassell, & E. T. Levy (Eds.), *Gesture and the dynamic dimension of language* (pp. 127–146). Amsterdam: John Benjamins.

Bavelas, J. B., & Chovil, N. (2006). Hand gestures and facial displays as part of language use in face-to-face dialogue. In V. Manusov & M. Patterson (Eds.), *Handbook of nonverbal communication* (pp. 97–115). Thousand Oaks: SAGE.

Bavelas, J. B., & Gerwing, J. (2007). Conversational hand gestures and facial displays in face-to-face dialogue. In K. Fiedler (Ed.), *Social communication* (pp. 283–308). New York: Psychology Press.

Bayne, T., & Chalmers, D. J. (2003). What is the unity of consciousness? In A. Cleeremans (Ed.), *The unity of consciousness: Binding, integration, and dissociation* (pp. 23–58). Oxford: Oxford University Press.

Beckermann, A. (1992). Supervenience, emergence, and reduction. In A. Beckermann, H. Flohr, & J. Kim (Eds.), *Emergence or reduction? Essays on the prospects of nonreductive physicalism* (pp. 94–118). Berlin: Walter de Gruyter.

Bekkering, H., & Prinz, W. (2002). Goal representations in imitative actions. In K. Dautenhahn & C. L. Nehaniv (Eds.), *Imitation in animals and artifacts* (pp. 555–572). Cambridge, MA: MIT Press.

Bekkering, H., & Wohlschläger, A. (2002). Action perception and imitation: A tutorial. In W. Prinz & B. Hommel (Eds.), *Common mechanisms in perception and action: Attention and performance XIX* (pp. 294–314). Oxford: Oxford University Press.

Bellugi, U., & Klima, E. (2000). *The signs of language revisited*. Mahwah: Erlbaum.

Berger, P. L., & Luckmann, T. (1966). *The social construction of reality: A treatise in the sociology of knowledge*. Garden City: Doubleday.

Bermúdez, J. L., Marcel, A. J., & Eilan, N. (1995). *The body and the self*. Cambridge, MA: MIT Press.

Bertenthal, B. I., & Longo, M. R. (2008). Motor knowledge and action understanding: A developmental perspective. In R. L. Klatzky, B. MacWhinney, & M. Behrmann (Eds.), *Embodiment, ego-space, and action* (pp. 323–368). New York: Psychology Press.

Bickerton, D., & Szathmáry, E. (Eds.). (2009). *Biological foundations and origin of syntax*. Cambridge, MA: MIT Press.

Bingham, G. P., & Wickelgren, E. A. (2008). Events and actions as dynamically molded spatiotemporal objects: A critique of the motor theory of biological motion perception. In T. F. Shipley & J. M. Zacks (Eds.), *Understanding events: From perception to action* (pp. 255–285). New York: Oxford University Press.

Bischof-Köhler, D. (1989). *Spiegelbild und Empathie*. Bern: Huber.

Blakemore, S.-J. (2006). When the other influences the self: Interference between perception and action. In G. Knoblich, I. M. Thornton, M. Grosjean, & M. Shiffrar (Eds.), *Human body perception from the inside out* (pp. 413–425). Oxford: Oxford University Press.

Blakemore, S.-J., Frith, C. D., & Wolpert, D. (2002). Abnormalities in the awareness of action. *Trends in Cognitive Sciences*, *6*, 237–242.

Block, N., Flanagan, O., & Güzeldere, G. (1997). *The nature of consciousness: Philosophical debates*. Cambridge, MA: MIT Press.

Boas, F. (1940). *Race, language, and culture*. New York: Macmillan.

Boesch, C. (1996). The question of culture: News and views. *Nature*, *379*(6562), 207–208.

Boesch, C. (2008). Culture in evolution: Towards an integration of chimpanzee and human culture. In M. J. Brown (Ed.), *Explaining culture scientifically* (pp. 37–54). Washington: University of Washington Press.

Boesch, C., & Tomasello, M. (1998). Chimpanzee and human cultures. *Current Anthropology*, *39*(5), 591–614.

Bogdan, R. J. (1991). *Mind and common sense: Philosophical essays on commonsense psychology*. Cambridge: Cambridge University Press.

Bogdan, R. J. (1997). *Interpreting minds: The evolution of a practice*. Cambridge, MA: MIT Press.

Bogdan, R. J. (2000). *Minding minds: Evolving a reflexive mind by interpreting others*. Cambridge, MA: MIT Press.

Bogdan, R. J. (2007). Inside loops: Developmental premises of self-ascriptions. *Synthese*, *159*(2), 235–251.

Bogdan, R. J. (2009). *Predicative minds: The social ontogeny of propositional thinking*. Cambridge, MA: MIT Press.

Bogdan, R. J. (2010). *Our own minds: Sociocultural grounds for self-consciousness*. Cambridge, MA: MIT Press.

Boring, E. G. (1942). *Sensation and perception in the history of experimental psychology.* New York: Appleton-Century-Crofts.

Boring, E. G. (1957). *A history of experimental psychology* (2nd ed.). New York: Appleton-Century-Crofts.

Bornkessel, I., & Schlesewsky, M. (2006). The extended argument dependency model: A neurocognitive approach to sentence comprehension across languages. *Psychological Review, 113*(4), 787–821.

Bornkessel-Schlesewsky, I., & Schlesewsky, M. (2009). The role of prominence information in the real time comprehension of transitive constructions: A cross-linguistic approach. *Language and Linguistics Compass, 3*(1), 19–58.

Boroditsky, L. (2007). Does language shape thought? English and Mandarin speakers' conceptions of time. In V. Evans, B. K. Bergen, & J. Zinken (Eds.), *The cognitive linguistics reader* (pp. 880–901). London: Equinox.

Botvinick, M., & Cohen, J. (1998). Rubber hands "feel" touch that eyes see. *Nature, 391*(6669), 756.

Bowerman, M., & Choi, S. (2007). Space under construction: Language-specific spatial categorization in first language acquisition. In V. Evans, B. K. Bergen, & J. Zinken (Eds.), *The cognitive linguistics reader* (pp. 849–879). London: Equinox.

Brass, M., Bekkering, H., & Prinz, W. (2001). Movement observation affects movement execution in a simple response task. *Acta Psychologica, 106*(1–2), 3–22.

Brass, M., Bekkering, H., Wohlschläger, A., & Prinz, W. (2000). Compatibility between observed and executed finger movements: Comparing symbolic, spatial, and imitative cues. *Brain and Cognition, 44*(2), 124–143.

Brass, M., & Heyes, C. (2005). Imitation: Is cognitive neuroscience solving the correspondence problem? *Trends in Cognitive Sciences, 9,* 489–495.

Bråten, S. (1998). Infant learning by altercentric participation: The reverse of egocentric observation in autism. In S. Bråten (Ed.), *Intersubjective communication and emotion in early ontogeny* (pp. 105–124). Cambridge: Cambridge University Press.

Braver, T. S., & Ruge, H. (2006). Functional neuroimaging of executive functions. In R. Cabeza & A. Kingstone (Eds.), *Handbook of functional neuroimaging of cognition* (2nd ed., pp. 307–348). Cambridge, MA: MIT Press.

Brazelton, T. B. (1976). Early parent-infant reciprocity. In V. C. Vaughan & T. B. Brazelton (Eds.), *The family, can it be saved?* (pp. 133–142). Chicago: Yearbook Medical Publishers.

Brazelton, T. B., & Cramer, B. G. (1991). *The earliest relationship: Parents, infants and the drama of early attachment.* London: Karnac Books.

Brentano, F. (1874/1924). *Psychologie vom empirischen Standpunkt.* (O. Kraus, Ed.) Leipzig: Meiner.

Broad, C. D. (1925). *The mind and its place in nature.* London: Kegan Paul.

Brugger, P. (2002). Reflective mirrors: Perspective-taking in autoscopic phenomena. *Cognitive Neuropsychiatry, 7*(3), 179–194.

Brugger, P. (2006). From phantom limb to phantom body: Varieties of extracorporal awareness. In G. Knoblich, I. M. Thornton, M. Grosjean, & M. Shiffrar (Eds.), *Human body perception from the inside out* (pp. 171–209). Oxford: Oxford University Press.

Brugger, P., Kollias, S. S., Müri, R. M., Crelier, G., Hepp-Reymond, M.-C., & Regard, M. (2000). Beyond re-membering: Phantom sensations of congenitally absent limbs. *Proceedings of the National Academy of Sciences of the United States of America, 97*(11), 6167–6172.

Brugger, P., Regard, M., & Landis, T. (1997). Illusory reduplication of one's own body: Phenomenology and classification of autscopic phenomena. *Cognitive Neuropsychiatry, 2*(1), 19–38.

Bruner, J. S. (1957). On perceptual readiness. *Psychological Review, 64,* 123–152.

Bruner, J. S. (1990). *Acts of meaning.* Cambridge, MA: Harvard University Press.

Bruner, J. S. (2003). *Making stories: Law, literature, life.* Cambridge, MA: Harvard University Press.

Brunswik, E. (1944). Distal focussing of perception: Size constancy in a representative sample of situations. *Psychological Monographs, 56*(1), 1–49.

Brunswik, E. (1952). The conceptual framework of psychology. In O. Neurath, R. Carnap, & C. Morris (Eds.), *International encyclopedia of united science* (Vol. 1). Chicago: University of Chicago Press.

Brunswik, E. (1955). Representative design and probabilistic theory in a functional psychology. *Psychological Review, 62,* 193–217.

Buccino, G., Binkofski, F., Fink, G., Fadiga, L., Fogassi, L., Gallese, V., et al. (2001). Action observation activates premotor and parietal areas in a somatotopic manner: An fMRI study. *European Journal of Neuroscience, 13*(2), 400–404.

Butterworth, G. (1995). An ecological perspective on the origins of self. In J. L. Bermúdez, A. J. Marcel, & N. Eilan (Eds.), *The body and the self* (pp. 87–105). Cambridge, MA: MIT Press.

Calder, A. J., Keane, J., Manes, F., Antoun, N., & Young, A. W. (2000). Impaired recognition and experience of disgust following brain injury. *Nature Neuroscience, 3,* 1077–1078.

Call, J., & Tomasello, M. (2005). What chimpanzees know about seeing revisited. An explanation of the third kind. In N. Eilan, C. Hoerl, T. McCormack, & J. Roessler

(Eds.), *Joint attention: Communication and other minds* (pp. 45–64). Oxford: Oxford University Press.

Call, J., & Tomasello, M. (2007). *The gestural communication of apes and monkeys.* Mahwah: Erlbaum.

Candidi, M., Urgesi, C., Ionta, S., & Aglioti, S. M. (2008). Virtual lesion of ventral premotor cortex impairs visual perception of biomechanically possible but not impossible actions. *Social Neuroscience, 3*(3–4), 388–400.

Carey, S. (2009). *The origin of concepts.* Oxford: Oxford University Press.

Carey, S., & Spelke, E. (1994). Domain-specific knowledge and conceptual change. In L. A. Hirshfeld & S. A. Gelman (Eds.), *Mapping the mind: Domain specificity in cognition and culture* (pp. 169–200). Cambridge: Cambridge University Press.

Caro, T. M., & Hauser, M. D. (1992). Is there teaching in nonhuman animals? *Quarterly Review of Biology, 67*(2), 151–174.

Carruthers, P. (2009). How we know our own minds: The relationship between mindreading and metacognition. *Behavioral and Brain Sciences, 32*(2), 121–182.

Chaminade, T., Meltzoff, A. N., & Decety, J. (2002). Does the end justify the means? A PET exploration of the mechanisms involved in human imitation. *NeuroImage, 15*(2), 318–328.

Chartrand, T. L., & Bargh, J. A. (1999). The chameleon effect: The perception-behavior link and social interaction. *Journal of Personality and Social Psychology, 76,* 893–910.

Chartrand, T. L., & Dalton, A. N. (2009). Mimicry: Its ubiquity, importance, and functionality. In E. Morsella, J. A. Bargh, & P. M. Gollwitzer (Eds.), *Oxford handbook of human action* (pp. 458–486). New York: Oxford University Press.

Chisholm, R. M. (1967). Intentionality. In P. Edwards (Ed.), *Encyclopedia of philosophy* (pp. 201–204). London: Macmillan.

Chomsky, N. (1995). *The minimalist program.* Cambridge, MA: MIT Press.

Chomsky, N. (2002). *On nature and language.* Cambridge: Cambridge University Press.

Chouinard, M. M., & Clark, E. V. (2003). Adult reformulations of child errors as negative evidence. *Journal of Child Language, 30,* 637–669.

Churchland, P. M. (1970). Logical character of action-explanations. *Philosophical Review, 79,* 214–236.

Churchland, P. M. (1991). Folk psychology and the explanation of human behavior. In J. D. Greenwood (Ed.), *The future of folk psychology: Intentionality and cognitive science* (pp. 51–69). Cambridge: Cambridge University Press.

Clark, E. V. (2003). Languages and representations. In D. Gentner & S. Goldin-Meadow (Eds.), *Language in mind: Advances in the study of language and thought* (pp. 17–24). Cambridge, MA: MIT Press.

Clark, E. V. (2007). Young children's uptake of new words in conversation. *Language in Society, 36*, 157–182.

Cleeremans, A. (2003). *The unity of consciousness: Binding, integration, and dissociation.* New York: Oxford University Press.

Cleeremans, A. (2008). Consciousness: The radical plasticity thesis. In R. Banerjee & B. K. Chakrabarti (Eds.), *Models of brain and mind: Physical, computational and psychological approaches* (Vol. 168, pp. 19–34). Amsterdam: Elsevier.

Cleeremans, A., Timmermans, B., & Pasquali, A. (2007). Consciousness and meta-representation: A computational sketch. *Neural Networks, 20*(9), 1032–1039.

Coe, W. C. (1989). Posthypnotic amnesia: Theory and research. In N. P. Spanos & J. F. Chaves (Eds.), *Hypnosis: The cognitive-behavioral perspective* (pp. 110–148). Buffalo: Prometheus Books.

Cohen, J. D., & Schooler, J. W. (Eds.). (1997). *Scientific approaches to consciousness.* Hillsdale: Erlbaum.

Cole, M. (1996). *Cultural psychology: A once and future discipline.* Cambridge, MA: Harvard University Press.

Comrie, B. (1989). *Language universals and linguistic typology: Syntax and morphology* (2nd ed.). Oxford: Blackwell.

Confer, W. N., & Ables, B. S. (1983). *Multiple personality: Etiology, diagnosis, and treatment.* New York: Human Sciences Press.

Corballis, M. C. (2003a). *From hand to mouth: The origins of language.* Princeton: Princeton University Press.

Corballis, M. C. (2003b). From mouth to hand: Gesture, speech, and the evolution of right-handedness. *Behavioral and Brain Sciences, 26*(2), 199–260.

Cosmides, L., & Tooby, J. (2000). Consider the source: The evolution of adaptations for decoupling and metarepresentation. In D. Sperber (Ed.), *Metarepresentations: A multidisciplinary perspective* (pp. 53–115). Oxford: Oxford University Press.

Costantini, M., Galati, G., Ferretti, A., Caulo, M., Tartaro, A., Romani, G. L., et al. (2005). Neural systems underlying observation of humanly impossible movements: An fMRI study. *Cerebral Cortex, 15*(11), 1761–1767.

Craighero, L., Bello, A., Fadiga, L., & Rizzolatti, G. (2002). Hand action preparation influences the processing of hand pictures. *Neuropsychologia, 40*(5), 492–502.

Csibra, G. (2007). Action mirroring and action understanding: An alternative account. In P. Haggard, Y. Rosetti, & M. Kawato (Eds.), *Sensorimotor foundations of higher cognition: Attention and performance XXII* (pp. 435–459). Oxford: Oxford University Press.

Csibra, G., & Gergely, G. (1998). The teleological origins of mentalistic action explanations: A developmental hypothesis. *Developmental Science, 1*(2), 255–259.

Csibra, G., & Gergely, G. (2006). Social learning and social cognition. The case for pedagogy. In Y. Munakata & M. H. Johnson (Eds.), *Processes of change in brain and cognitive development: Attention and performance XXI* (pp. 249–274). Oxford: Oxford University Press.

Danziger, K. (1990). *Constructing the subject: Historical origins of psychological research.* Cambridge: Cambridge University Press.

Daprati, E., Pranck, N., Georgieff, N., Proust, J., Pacherie, E., Dalery, J., et al. (1997). Looking for the agent: An investigation into consciousness of action and self-consciousness in schizophrenic patients. *Cognition, 65,* 71–86.

Daum, M. M., Sommerville, J., & Prinz, W. (2009). Becoming a social agent: Developmental foundations of an embodied social psychology. *European Journal of Social Psychology, 39,* 1196–1206.

Dautenhahn, K., & Nehaniv, C. L. (Eds.). (2002). *Imitation in animals and artifacts.* Cambridge, MA: MIT Press.

Decety, J., & Chaminade, T. (2003). When the self represents the other: A new cognitive neuroscience view on psychological identification. *Consciousness and Cognition, 12*(4), 577–596.

Decety, J., & Chaminade, T. (2005). The neurophysiology of imitation and intersubjectivity. In S. Hurley & N. Chater (Eds.), *Mechanisms of imitation and imitation in animals* (Vol. 1, pp. 119–140). Cambridge, MA: MIT Press.

Decety, J., & Grèzes, J. (1999). Neural mechanisms subserving the perception of human actions. *Trends in Cognitive Sciences, 3*(5), 172–178.

Decety, J., & Jackson, P. L. (2004). The functional architecture of human empathy. *Behavioral and Cognitive Neuroscience Reviews, 3*(2), 71–100.

Decety, J., & Jackson, P. L. (2006). A social-neuroscience perspective on empathy. *Current Directions in Psychological Science, 15*(2), 54–58.

Decety, J., & Sommerville, J. A. (2003). Shared representations between self and other: A social cognitive neuroscience view. *Trends in Cognitive Sciences, 7*(12), 527–533.

de Maeght, S., & Prinz, W. (2004). Action induction through action observation. *Psychological Research, 68*(2–3), 97–114.

Dennett, D. C. (1978). *Brainstorms: Philosophical essays on mind and psychology.* Montgomery: Bradford Books.

Dennett, D. C. (1987). *The intentional stance.* Cambridge, MA: MIT Press.

Dennett, D. C. (1990). *The origin of selves.* Bielefeld: Research Group on Cognition and the Brain, Center for Interdisciplinary Research (ZiF), University of Bielefeld.

Dennett, D. C. (1991). Two contrasts: Folk craft versus folk science, and belief versus opinion. In J. D. Greenwood (Ed.), *The future of folk psychology: Intentionality and cognitive science* (pp. 135–148). Cambridge: Cambridge University Press.

Dennett, D. C. (1992). The self as the center of narrative gravity. In F. S. Kessel, P. M. Cole, & D. L. Johnson (Eds.), *Self and consciousness: Multiple perspectives* (pp. 103–115). Hillsdale: Erlbaum.

Descartes, R. [1641] (1990). *Meditations on first philosophy = Meditationes de prima philosophia: A bilingual edition* (G. Heffernan, Trans.). Notre Dame: University of Notre Dame Press.

de Vignemont, F., & Fourneret, P. (2004). The sense of agency: A philosophical and empirical review of the "who" system. *Consciousness and Cognition, 13*(1), 1–19.

de Vignemont, F., & Singer, T. (2006). The empathic brain: How, when, and why? *Trends in Cognitive Sciences, 10,* 435–441.

de Wit, S., Niry, D., Wariyar, R., Aitken, M. R. F., & Dickinson, A. (2007). Stimulus-outcome interactions during instrumental discrimination, learning by rats and humans. *Journal of Experimental Psychology. Animal Behavior Processes, 33*(1), 1–11.

Dickinson, A. (1985). Actions and habits: The development of behavioral autonomy. *Philosophical Transactions of the Royal Society of London: Series B, Biological Sciences, 308*(1135), 67–78.

Dickinson, A. (1989). Expectancy theory in animal conditioning. In S. B. Klein & R. R. Mowrer (Eds.), *Contemporary learning theories: Pavlovian conditioning and the status of traditional learning theory* (pp. 279–308). Hillsdale: Erlbaum.

Dijksterhuis, A., & Bargh, J. A. (2001). The perception-behavior expressway: Automatic effects of social perception on social behavior. In M. P. Zanna (Ed.), *Advances in experimental social psychology* (Vol. 33, pp. 1–40). San Diego: Academic Press.

Dijksterhuis, A., & Nordgren, L. F. (2006). A theory of unconscious thought. *Perspectives on Psychological Science, 1*(2), 95–109.

di Pellegrino, G., Fadiga, L., Fogassi, L., Gallese, V., & Rizzolatti, G. (1992). Understanding motor events: A neurophysiological study. *Experimental Brain Research, 91*(1), 176–180.

Dokic, J., & Proust, J. (Eds.). (2002). *Simulation and knowledge of action*. Amsterdam: John Benjamins.

Donald, M. (2001). *A mind so rare: The evolution of human consciousness*. New York: Norton.

Donders, F. C. (1868/1969). On the speed of mental processes. In W. G. Koster (Ed.), *Proceedings of the Donders Centenary Symposium on Reaction Time: Attention and performance II* (pp. 412–431). Amsterdam: North-Holland.

Dretske, F. I. (1981). *Knowledge and the flow of information*. Cambridge, MA: MIT Press.

Dretske, F. I. (1995). *Naturalizing the mind*. Cambridge, MA: MIT Press.

Duncan, S. D., Cassell, J., & Levy, E. T. (Eds.). (2007). *Gesture and the dynamic dimension of language*. Amsterdam: John Benjamins.

Dupuy, J.-P. (2009). *On the origins of cognitive science: The mechanization of the mind*. Cambridge, MA: MIT Press.

Echterhoff, G. (2010). Shared reality: Antecedents, processes, consequences. *Social Cognition, 28*(3), 273–276.

Echterhoff, G., Higgins, E. T., & Levine, J. M. (2009). Shared reality: Experiencing commonality with others' inner states about the world. *Perspectives on Psychological Science, 4*(5), 496–521.

Edelman, G. M. (1989). *The remembered present: A biological theory of consciousness*. New York: Basic Books.

Eilan, N., Marcel, A., & Bermúdez, J. L. (1995). Self-consciousness and the body: An interdisciplinary introduction. In J. L. Bermúdez, A. J. Marcel, & N. Eilan (Eds.), *The body and the self* (pp. 1–28). Cambridge, MA: MIT Press.

Elias, N. [1939] (2000). *The civilizing process. Sociogenetic and psychogenetic investigations* (2nd ed.). Malden: Blackwell.

Elsner, B. (2000). *Der Erwerb kognitiver Handlungsrepräsentationen*. [The acquisition of cognitive representations of action.] Berlin: Wissenschaftlicher Verlag.

Elsner, B., & Hommel, B. (2001). Effect anticipation and action control. *Journal of Experimental Psychology. Human Perception and Performance, 27*(1), 229–240.

Elsner, B., & Hommel, B. (2004). Contiguity and contingency in action-effect learning. *Psychological Research, 68*(2–3), 138–154.

Emmorey, K. (2006). The signer as an embodied mirror neuron system: Neural mechanisms underlying sign language and action. In M. A. Arbib (Ed.), *Action to language via the mirror neuron system* (pp. 110–135). Cambridge: Cambridge University Press.

Epstein, W. (1973). The process of "taking-into-account" in visual perception. *Perception, 2*(3), 267–285.

Epstein, W. (Ed.). (1977). *Stability and constancy in visual perception: Mechanisms and processes.* New York: Wiley.

Evans, N., & Levinson, S. C. (2009). The myth of language universals: Language diversity and its importance for cognitive science. *Behavioral and Brain Sciences, 32*(5), 429–492.

Farrer, C., Franck, N., d'Amato, T., & Jeannerod, M. (2004). Neural correlates of action attribution in schizophrenia. *Psychiatry Research: Neuroimaging, 131,* 31–44.

Feldman, R. (2007). Parent-infant synchrony: Biological foundations and developmental outcomes. *Current Directions in Psychological Science, 16*(6), 340–345.

Fernandez-Duque, D., Baird, J. A., & Posner, M. I. (2000). Executive attention and metacognitive regulation. *Consciousness and Cognition, 9*(2), 288–307.

Fillmore, C. J. (1972). Subjects, speakers, and roles. In D. Davidson & G. Harman (Eds.), *Semantics of natural language* (pp. 1–24). Dordrecht: Reidel.

Fischer, R., Dreisbach, G., & Goschke, T. (2008). Context-sensitive adjustments of cognitive control: Conflict-adaption effects are modulated by processing demands of the ongoing task. *Journal of Experimental Psychology, 34*(3), 712–718.

Fitch, W. T. (2010). *The evolution of language.* Cambridge: Cambridge University Press.

Flach, R., Knoblich, G., & Prinz, W. (2003). Off-line authorship effects in action perception. *Brain and Cognition, 53*(3), 503–513.

Fodor, J. A. (1975). *Language of thought.* Cambridge, MA: Harvard University Press.

Fodor, J. A. (1981). *Representations: Philosophical essays on the foundations of cognitive science.* Cambridge, MA: MIT Press.

Fodor, J. A. (1987). *Psychosemantics: The problem of meaning in the philosophy of mind.* Cambridge, MA: MIT Press.

Fodor, J. A. (1992). *A theory of content and other essays.* Cambridge, MA: MIT Press.

Fogassi, L., & Ferrari, P. F. (2007). Mirror neurons and the evolution of embodied language. *Current Directions in Psychological Science, 16*(3), 136–141.

Fogassi, L., & Gallese, V. (2002). The neural correlates of action understanding in non-human primates. In M. I. Stamenov & V. Gallese (Eds.), *Mirror neurons and the evolution of brain and language* (pp. 13–36). Amsterdam: John Benjamins.

Foley, W. A. (2007). A typology of information packaging in the clause. In T. Shopen (Series Ed.), *Language typology and syntactic description*, Vol. 1: *Clause structure* (pp. 362–446). Cambridge: Cambridge University Press.

Fonagy, P., Gergely, G., Jurist, E. L., & Target, M. (2004). *Affect regulation, mentalization, and the development of self*. London: Karnac.

Foucault, M. (1988). Technologies of the self. In L. H. Martin, J. H. Gutman, & P. H. Hutton (Eds.), *Technologies of the self: A seminar with Michel Focault* (pp. 16–49). Amherst: University of Massachusetts Press.

Frankish, K. (2004). *Mind and supermind*. Cambridge: Cambridge University Press.

Freud, S. (1922). *Introduction lectures on psycho-analysis. A course of twenty-eight lectures delivered at the University of Vienna* (J. Riviere, Trans.). London: Allen & Unwin.

Freyd, J. J. (1983). The mental presentation of movement when static stimuli are viewed. *Perception & Psychophysics, 33*(6), 575–581.

Freyd, J. J. (1987). Dynamic mental representations. *Psychological Review, 94*(4), 427–438.

Frie, R. (Ed.). (2008). *Psychological agency: Theory, practice, and culture*. Cambridge, MA: MIT Press.

Frith, C. (1994). Theory of Mind in schizophrenia. In A. S. David & J. C. Cutting (Eds.), *The neuropsychology of schizophrenia* (pp. 147–161). Hove: Erlbaum.

Frith, C. D. (1992). *Essays in cognitive psychology: The cognitive neuropsychology of schizophrenia*. Hove: Erlbaum.

Frith, C. D., Blakemore, S.-J., & Wolpert, D. M. (2000). Abnormalities in the awareness and control of action. *Philosophical Transactions of the Royal Society of London: Series B, Biological Sciences, 355*(1404), 1771–1788.

Frith, C. D., & Done, D. J. (1989). Experiences of alien control in schizophrenia reflect a disorder in the central monitoring of action. *Psychological Medicine, 19*, 359–363.

Frith, C. D., & Frith, U. (2006). How we predict what other people are going to do. *Brain Research, 1079*, 36–46.

Frith, C. D., & Singer, T. (2008). The role of social cognition in decision making. *Philosophical Transactions of the Royal Society of London: Series B, Biological Sciences, 363*, 3875–3886.

Frith, C. D., & Wolpert, D. M. (2004). *The neuroscience of social interaction: Decoding, imitating, and influencing the actions of others*. New York: Oxford University Press.

Galantucci, B., Fowler, C. A., & Turvey, M. T. (2006). The motor theory of speech perception reviewed. *Psychonomic Bulletin & Review, 13*(3), 361–377.

Gallagher, S. (1986). Body image and body schema: A conceptual clarification. *Journal of Mind and Behavior, 7*(4), 541–554.

Gallagher, S. (1995). Body schema and intentionality. In J. L. Bermúdez, A. J. Marcel, & N. Eilan (Eds.), *The body and the self* (pp. 225–244). Cambridge, MA: MIT Press.

Gallagher, S. (2001). The practice of mind: Theory, simulation, or primary interaction? *Journal of Consciousness Studies, 8*(5–7), 83–108.

Gallagher, S. (2005). *How the body shapes the mind.* Oxford: Oxford University Press.

Gallagher, S., & Meltzoff, A. W. (1996). The earliest sense of self and others: Merleau-Ponty and recent developmental studies. *Philosophical Psychology, 9*(2), 211–233.

Gallese, V. (2003). The manifold nature of interpersonal relations: The quest for a common mechanism. *Philosophical Transactions of the Royal Society of London: Series B, Biological Sciences, 358*(1431), 517–528.

Gallese, V. (2005a). "Being like me": Self-other identity, mirror neurons, and empathy. In S. Hurley & N. Chater (Eds.), *Mechanisms of imitation and imitation in animals* (Vol. 1, pp. 101–118). Cambridge, MA: MIT Press.

Gallese, V. (2005b). Embodied simulation: From neurons to phenomenal experience. *Phenomenology and the Cognitive Sciences, 4*(1), 23–48.

Gallese, V., Fadiga, L., Fogassi, L., & Rizzolatti, G. (1996). Action recognition in the premotor cortex. *Brain, 119,* 593–609.

Gallese, V., Fadiga, L., Fogassi, L., & Rizzolatti, G. (2002). Action representation and the inferior parietal lobule. In W. Prinz & B. Hommel (Eds.), *Common mechanisms in perception and action: Attention and performance XIX* (pp. 334–355). Oxford: Oxford University Press.

Gallese, V., & Goldman, A. I. (1998). Mirror neurons and the simulation theory of mind-reading. *Trends in Cognitive Sciences, 2*(12), 493–501.

Gallup, G. G. (1968). Mirror-image stimulation. *Psychological Bulletin, 70,* 782–793.

Gallup, G. G. (1970). Chimpanzees: Self-recognition. *Science, 167*(3914), 86–87.

Gallup, G. G., McClure, M. K., Hill, S. D., & Bundy, R. A. (1971). Capacity for self-recognition in differentially reared chimpanzees. *Psychological Record, 21,* 69–74.

Gao, T., McCarthy, G., & Scholl, B. J. (in press). The wolfpack effect: Perception of animacy irresistibly influences interactive behavior. *Psychological Science.*

Gao, T., Newman, G. E., & Scholl, B. J. (2009). The psychophysics of chasing: A case study in the perception of animacy. *Cognitive Psychology, 59,* 154–179.

Garner, W. R. (1966). To perceive is to know. *American Psychologist, 21,* 11–19.

Gattis, M., Bekkering, H., & Wohlschläger, A. (2002). Goal-directed imitation. In A. N. Meltzoff & W. Prinz (Eds.), *The imitative mind: Development, evolution, and brain bases* (pp. 183–205). Cambridge: Cambridge University Press.

Gazzaniga, M. S., & Smylie, C. S. (1984). What does language do for a right hemisphere? In M. S. Gazzaniga (Ed.), *Handbook of cognitive neuroscience* (pp. 199–209). New York: Plenum Press.

Gentilucci, M., & Corballis, M. C. (2006). From manual gesture to speech: A gradual transition. *Neuroscience and Biobehavioral Reviews, 30*(7), 949–960.

Gentner, D., & Goldin-Meadow, S. (Eds.). (2003). *Language in mind: Advances in the study of language and thought.* Cambridge, MA: MIT Press.

Gergely, G., & Csibra, G. (2005). The social construction of the cultural mind: Imitative learning as a mechanism of human pedagogy. *Interaction Studies: Social Behaviour and Communication in Biological and Artificial Systems, 6*(3), 463–481.

Gergely, G., & Watson, J. S. (1996). The social biofeedback theory of parental affect-mirroring: The development of emotional self-awareness and self-control in infancy. *International Journal of Psycho-Analysis, 77,* 1–31.

Gergen, K. J., & Davis, K. E. (Eds.). (1985). *The social construction of the person.* New York: Springer.

Gibson, J. J. (1986). *The ecological approach to visual perception.* Hillsdale: Erlbaum.

Gigerenzer, G. (2004). Fast and frugal heuristics: The tools of bounded rationality. In D. J. Koehler & N. Harvey (Eds.), *Blackwell handbook of judgement and decision making* (pp. 62–88). Oxford: Blackwell.

Gigerenzer, G. (2008). *Rationality for mortals: How people cope with uncertainty.* Oxford: Oxford University Press.

Giummarra, M. J., Gibson, S. J., Georgiou-Karistianis, N., & Bradshaw, J. L. (2008). Mechanisms underlying embodiment, disembodiment and loss of embodiment. *Neuroscience and Biobehavioral Reviews, 32*(1), 143–166.

Gleissner, B., Meltzoff, A. N., & Bekkering, H. (2000). Children's coding of human action: Cognitive factors influencing imitation in 3-year-olds. *Developmental Science, 3*(4), 405–414.

Goldin-Meadow, S. (2003). *The resilience of language: What gesture creation in deaf children can tell us about how all children learn language.* New York: Psychology Press.

Goldin-Meadow, S. (2006). Talking and thinking with our hands. *Current Directions in Psychological Science, 15*(1), 34–39.

Goldin-Meadow, S. (2007). Gesture with speech and without it. In S. D. Duncan, J. Cassell, & E. T. Levy (Eds.), *Gesture and dynamic dimension of language: Essays in honor of David McNeill* (pp. 31–50). Amsterdam: John Benjamins.

Goldman, A. I. (1993). The psychology of folk psychology. *Behavioral and Brain Sciences*, *16*(1), 15–28.

Goldman, A. I. (1995). Interpretation psychologized. In M. Davies & T. Stone (Eds.), *Folk psychology* (pp. 74–99). Oxford: Blackwell.

Goldman, A. I. (2002). Simulation theory and mental concepts. In J. Dokic & J. Proust (Eds.), *Simulation and knowledge of action* (pp. 1–19). Amsterdam: John Benjamins.

Goldman, A. I. (2005). Imitation, mind reading, and simulation. In S. Hurley & N. Chater (Eds.), *Imitation, human development, and culture* (Vol. 2, pp. 79–93). Cambridge, MA: MIT Press.

Goldman, A. I. (2006). *Simulating minds: The philosophy, psychology, and neuroscience of mindreading*. New York: Oxford University Press.

Gollwitzer, P. M. (1990a). *Abwägen und Planen*. Göttingen: Hogrefe.

Gollwitzer, P. M. (1990b). Action phases and mind-sets. In E. T. Higgins & R. M. Sorrentino (Eds.), *Handbook of motivation and cognition* (Vol. 2, pp. 53–92). New York: Guilford Press.

Gollwitzer, P. M. (1999). Implementation intentions: Strong effects of simple plans. *American Psychologist*, *54*(7), 493–503.

Gollwitzer, P. M., & Bargh, J. A. (Eds.). (1996). *The psychology of action: Linking cognition and motivation to behavior*. New York: Guilford Press.

Gollwitzer, P. M., & Bargh, J. A. (2005). Automaticity in goal pursuit. In A. Elliot & C. Dweck (Eds.), *Handbook of competence and motivation* (pp. 624–646). New York: Guilford Press.

Gollwitzer, P. M., & Moskowitz, G. B. (1996). Goal effects on action and cognition. In E. T. Higgins & A. W. Kruglanski (Eds.), *Social psychology: Handbook of basic principles* (pp. 361–399). New York: Guilford Press.

Gopnik, A., & Meltzoff, A. N. (1997). *Words, thoughts, and theories*. Cambridge, MA: MIT Press.

Gopnik, A., & Wellmann, H. M. (1994). The theory theory. In L. A. Hirschfeld & S. A. Gelman (Eds.), *Mapping the mind: Domain specificity in cognition and culture* (pp. 257–293). Cambridge: Cambridge University Press.

Gordon, R. M. (1995a). Folk psychology as simulation. In M. Davies & T. Stone (Eds.), *Folk psychology: The theory of mind debate* (pp. 60–73). Oxford: Blackwell.

Gordon, R. M. (1995b). Simulation without introspection or inference from me to you. In M. Davies & T. Stone (Eds.), *Mental simulation: Evaluations and applications* (pp. 53–67). Oxford: Blackwell.

Gordon, R. M. (1996). "Radical" simulationism. In P. Carruthers & P. K. Smith (Eds.), *Theories of theories of mind* (pp. 11–21). Cambridge: Cambridge University Press.

Gordon, R. M. (2001). Simulation and reason explanation: The radical view. *Philosophical Topics, 29,* 175–192.

Goschke, T. (2003). Voluntary action and cognitive control from a cognitive neuroscience perspective. In S. Maasen, W. Prinz, & G. Roth (Eds.), *Voluntary action: Brains, minds, and sociality* (pp. 49–85). Oxford: Oxford University Press.

Grabes, H. (1973). *Speculum, Mirror und Looking-Glass: Kontinuität und Originalität der Spiegelmetapher in den Buchtiteln des Mittelalters und der englischen Literatur des 13. bis 17. Jahrhunderts.* Tübingen: Niemeyer.

Graf, M., Schütz-Bosbach, S., & Prinz, W. (2010). Motor representations in the perception of actions and objects: Similarity and complementarity. In G. Echterhoff & G. R. Semin (Eds.), *Grounding sociality: Neurons, mind, and culture* (pp. 17–42). Hove: Psychology Press.

Grammont, F., Legrand, D., & Livet, P. (Eds.). (2010). *Naturalizing intention in action.* Cambridge, MA: MIT Press.

Gray, J. (2004). *Consciousness: Creeping up on the hard problem.* Oxford: Oxford University Press.

Graziano, M. S. A., & Botvinick, M. M. (2002). How the brain represents the body: Insights from neurophysiology and psychology. In B. Hommel (Ed.), *Common mechanisms in perception and action: Attention and performance XIX* (pp. 136–157). Oxford: Oxford University Press.

Greaves, G. B. (1993). History of multiple personality disorder. In R. P. Kluft & C. G. Fine (Eds.), *Clinical perspectives on multiple personality disorder* (pp. 355–380). Washington, D.C.: American Psychiatric Press.

Greenwald, A. G. (1970). Sensory feedback mechanisms in performance control: With special reference to the ideomotor mechanism. *Psychological Review, 77*(2), 73–99.

Greenwald, A. G. (1972). On doing two things at once: Time sharing as a function of ideomotor compatibility. *Journal of Experimental Psychology, 94,* 52–57.

Greenwood, J. D. (Ed.). (1991). *The future of folk psychology: Intentionality and cognitive science.* Cambridge: Cambridge University Press.

Gregory, R. (1996). *Mirrors in mind.* New York: Freeman.

Grèzes, J., & de Gelder, B. (2005). Contagion motrice et contagion émotionelle. In C. Andrès, C. Barthélémy, A. Berthoz, J. Massion & B. Rogé (Eds.), *Autisme, cerveau et développement: De la recherche à la pratique* (pp. 293–318). Paris: Éditions Odile Jacob.

Grice, P. (1991). *Studies in the way of words.* Cambridge, MA: Harvard University Press.

Grosjean, M., Zwickel, J., & Prinz, W. (2009). Acting while perceiving: Assimilation precedes contrast. *Psychological Research, 73*(1), 3–13.

Grossmann, K. E., & Grossmann, K. (2005). Universality of human social attachment as an adaptive process. In C. S. Carter, L. Ahnert, K. E. Grossmann, S. B. Hrdy, M. E. Lamb, S. W. Porges, et al. (Eds.), *Attachment and bonding: A new synthesis* (pp. 199–228). Cambridge, MA: MIT Press.

Gumperz, J. J., & Levinson, S. C. (1996). Introduction to part I. In J. J. Gumperz & S. C. Levinson (Eds.), *Rethinking linguistic relativity* (pp. 21–35). Cambridge: Cambridge University Press.

Gurwitsch, A. (1941). A non-egological conception of consciousness. *Philosophy and Phenomenological Research, 1,* 325–338.

Häberle, A., Schütz-Bosbach, S., Laboissière, R., & Prinz, W. (2008). Ideomotor action in cooperative and competitive settings. *Social Neuroscience, 3*(1), 26–36.

Haggard, P. (2006). Conscious intention and the sense of agency. In N. Sebanz & W. Prinz (Eds.), *Disorders of volition* (pp. 69–86). Cambridge, MA: MIT Press.

Haggard, P., & Tsakiris, M. (2009). The experience of agency: Feelings, judgments, and responsibility. *Current Directions in Psychological Science, 18,* 242–246.

Halligan, P. W. (2002). Phantom limbs: The body in mind. *Cognitive Neuropsychiatry, 7*(3), 251–269.

Hamilton, A., Wolpert, D., & Frith, U. (2004). Your own action influences how you perceive another person's action. *Current Biology, 14*(6), 493–498.

Hamilton, A., Wolpert, D. M., Frith, U., & Grafton, S. T. (2006). Where does your own action influence your perception of another person's action in the brain? *NeuroImage, 29*(2), 524–535.

Harbison, C. (1995). *The mirror of the artist: Northern Renaissance art in its historical context.* New York: Abrams.

Harris, P. L. (1991). The work of imagination. In A. Whiten (Ed.), *Natural theories of mind: Evolution, development and simulation of everyday mindreading* (pp. 283–304). Cambridge, MA: Blackwell.

Hassin, R. R., Aarts, H., Eitam, B., Custers, R., & Kleiman, T. (2009). Non-conscious goal pursuit and the effortful control of behavior. In E. Morsella, J. A. Bargh, & P. M. Gollwitzer (Eds.), *Oxford handbook of the psychology of action* (pp. 549–568). New York: Oxford University Press.

Hastie, R., & Dawes, R. M. (2001). *Rational choice in an uncertain world: An introduction to judgement and decision making.* London: SAGE.

Hauf, P., & Försterling, F. (Eds.). (2007). *Making minds: The shaping of human minds through social context.* Amsterdam: John Benjamins.

Hauf, P., & Prinz, W. (2005). The understanding of own and others' actions during infancy: "You-like-Me" or "Me-like-You"? *Interaction Studies: Social Behaviour and Communication in Biological and Artificial Systems, 6,* 429–445.

Hauser, M. D., Chomsky, N., & Fitch, W. T. (2002). The faculty of language: What is it, who has it, and how did it evolve? *Science, 298*(5598), 1569–1579.

Hayes-Roth, B., & Hayes-Roth, F. (1988). A cognitive model of planning. In A. M. Collins & E. E. Smith (Eds.), *Readings in cognitive science: A perspective from psychology and artificial intelligence* (pp. 496–513). San Mateo: Morgan Kaufman.

Head, H. (1920). *Studies in neurology.* London: Frowde & Hodder.

Heberlein, A. S. (2008). Animacy and intention in the brain: Neuroscience of social event perception. In T. F. Shipley & J. M. Zacks (Eds.), *Understanding events: From perception to action* (pp. 363–390). Oxford: Oxford University Press.

Heckhausen, H. (2008). Historical trends in motivation research. In J. Heckhausen & H. Heckhausen (Eds.), *Motivation and action* (pp. 10–41). New York: Cambridge University Press.

Heckhausen, H., & Gollwitzer, P. M. (1987). Thought contents and cognitive functioning in motivational versus volitional states of mind. *Motivation and Emotion, 11,* 101–120.

Heckhausen, J., & Heckhausen, H. (Eds.). (2008). *Motivation and action.* New York: Cambridge University Press.

Hegel, G. W. F. [1802] (1967). *System der Sittlichkeit.* G. Lasson (Ed.). Hamburg: Felix Meiner.

Heider, F. (1944). Social perception and phenomenal causality. *Psychological Review, 51,* 358–374.

Heider, F. (1958). *The psychology of interpersonal relations.* New York: Wiley.

Heider, F. (1967). On social cognition. *American Psychologist, 22*(1), 25–31.

Heider, F., & Simmel, M. (1944). An experimental study of apparent behavior. *American Journal of Psychology, 57,* 243–259.

Held, R. (1968). Action contingent development of vision in neonatal animals. In D. B. Kimble (Ed.), *Experience and capacity* (pp. 31–111). New York: New York Academy of Sciences.

Held, R., & Hein, A. (1963). Movement-produced stimulation in the development of visually guided behavior. *Journal of Comparative and Physiological Psychology, 56*(5), 872–876.

Helmholtz, H. von (1866). *Handbuch der physiologischen Optik*. Leipzig, Hamburg: Voss.

Helmholtz, H. von (1924/1925). *Helmholtz's treatise on physiological optics* (J. P. C. Southall, Trans.). New York: The Optical Society of America.

Heptulla-Chatterjee, S., Freyd, J. J., & Shiffrar, M. (1996). Configural processing in the perception of apparent biological motion. *Journal of Experimental Psychology. Human Perception and Performance, 22*(4), 916–929.

Hershberger, W. A. (1989). The synergy of voluntary and involuntary action. In W. A. Hershberger (Ed.), *Volitional action: Conation and control* (pp. 3–20). Amsterdam: Elsevier.

Heyes, C. (2001). Causes and consequences of imitation. *Trends in Cognitive Sciences, 5*, 253–261.

Higgins, E. T. (2010). Sharing inner states: A defining feature of human motivation. In G. R. Semin & G. Echterhoff (Eds.), *Grounding sociality: Neurons, mind, and culture* (pp. 139–164). New York: Psychology Press.

Higgins, E. T., & Pittman, T. S. (2008). Motives of the human animal: Comprehending, managing, and sharing inner states. *Annual Review of Psychology, 59*, 361–385.

Hilgard, E. R. (1965). *Hypnotic susceptibility*. New York: Harcourt, Brace & World.

Hilgard, E. R. (1977). *Divided consciousness: Multiple controls in human thought and action*. New York: Wiley.

Hommel, B., Müsseler, J., Aschersleben, G., & Prinz, W. (2001). The theory of event coding (TEC): A framework for perception and action planning. *Behavioral and Brain Sciences, 24*, 849–878.

Hommel, B., & Prinz, W. (Eds.). (1997). *Theoretical issues in stimulus-response compatibility: Editors' introduction* (Vol. 118). Amsterdam: North-Holland.

Honneth, A. (1996). *The struggle for recognition: The moral grammar of social conflicts*. Cambridge, MA: MIT Press.

Howard, I. P. (1986). The perception of posture, self motion, and the visual vertical. In K. R. Boff, L. Kaufman, & J. P. Thomas (Eds.), *Handbook of perception and human performance* (Vol. 1, pp. 18.01–18.62). New York: Wiley.

Howard, I. P., & Templeton, W. B. (1966). *Human spatial orientation*. New York: Wiley.

Hull, C. L. (1943). *Principles of behavior: An introduction to behavior theory*. New York: Appleton-Century-Crofts.

Humboldt, W. v. [1836] (1988). *On language: The diversity of human language-structure and its influence on the mental development of mankind* (Heath, P. L., Trans.). Cambridge: Cambridge University Press.

Humphreys, G. W., Forde, E. M. E., & Riddoch, M. J. (2001). The planning and execution of everyday actions. In B. Rapp (Ed.), *The handbook of cognitive neuropsychology: What deficits reveal about the human mind* (pp. 565–589). Philadelphia: Psychology Press.

Humphreys, G. W., & Riddoch, M. J. (2006). Features, objects, action: The cognitive neuropsychology of vision from 1984–2004. *Cognitive Neuropsychology, 23*, 156–183.

Hunt, E., & Agnoli, F. (1991). The Whorfian hypothesis: A cognitive psychology perspective. *Psychological Review, 98*(3), 377–389.

Hurford, J. R., Studdert-Kennedy, M., & Knight, C. (Eds.). (1998). *Approaches to the evolution of language: Social and cognitive bases*. Cambridge: Cambridge University Press.

Hurley, S. (1998). *Consciousness in action*. Cambridge, MA: Harvard University Press.

Hurley, S. (2005). The shared circuits hypothesis: A unified functional architecture for control, imitation, and simulation. In S. Hurley and N. Chater (Eds.), *Perspectives on imitation: From neuroscience to social science*, Vol. 1: *Mechanisms of imitation and imitation in animals* (pp. 177–193). Cambridge, MA: MIT Press.

Hurley, S. (2008). The shared circuits model (SCM): How control, mirroring, and simulation can enable imitation, deliberation, and mindreading. *Behavioral and Brain Sciences, 31*, 1–58.

Hurley, S., & Chater, N. (Eds.). (2005). *Mechanisms of imitation and imitation in animals* (Vol. 1). Cambridge, MA: MIT Press.

Hutto, D. D. (2004). The limits of spectatorial folk psychology. *Mind & Language, 19*, 548–573.

Hutto, D. D. (2008). *Folk psychological narratives: The sociocultural basis of understanding reasons*. Cambridge, MA: MIT Press.

Iacoboni, M. (2005). Understanding others: Imitation, language, and empathy. In S. Hurley & N. Chater (Eds.), *Mechanisms of imitation and imitation in animals* (Vol. 1, pp. 77–99). Cambridge, MA: MIT Press.

Iacoboni, M. (2008). *Mirroring people: The new science on how we connect with others*. New York: Farrar, Straus & Giroux.

Iacoboni, M., Molnar-Szakacs, I., Gallese, V., Buccino, G., Mazziotta, J. C., & Rizzolatti, G. (2005). Grasping the intentions of others with one's own mirror neuron system. *PLoS Biology, 3*(3), 529–535.

Jackendoff, R. (2002). *Foundations of language: Brain, meaning, grammar, evolution.* Oxford: Oxford University Press.

Jackendoff, R. (Ed.). (2007). *Language, consciousness, culture.* Cambridge, MA: MIT Press.

Jacob, P. (2002). The scope and limits of mental simulation. In J. Dokic & J. Proust (Eds.), *Simulation and knowledge of action* (pp. 87–109). Amsterdam: John Benjamins.

Jacob, P., & Jeannerod, M. (2005). The motor theory of social cognition: A critique. *Trends in Cognitive Sciences, 9*(1), 21–25.

Jacobs, A., & Shiffrar, M. (2005). Walking perception by walking observers. *Journal of Experimental Psychology: Human Perception and Performance, 31*(1), 157–169.

James, W. (1890). *The principles of psychology.* New York: Holt.

Jaynes, J. (1976). *The origin of consciousness in the breakdown of the bicameral mind.* Boston: Houghton Mifflin.

Jeannerod, M. (1997). *The cognitive neuroscience of action.* Oxford: Blackwell.

Jeannerod, M. (1999). To act or not to act: Perspectives on the representation of actions. *Quarterly Journal of Experimental Psychology, 52A*, 1–29.

Jeannerod, M. (2001). Neural simulation of action: A unifying mechanism for motor cognition. *NeuroImage, 14*(1), S103–S109.

Jeannerod, M. (2003a). Consciousness of action and self-consciousness. A cognitive neuroscience approach. In J. Roessler & N. Eilan (Eds.), *Agency and self-awareness: Issues in philosophy and psychology* (pp. 128–149). New York: Oxford University Press.

Jeannerod, M. (2003b). The mechanisms of self-recognition in humans. *Behavioural Brain Research, 142*(1–2), 1–15.

Jeannerod, M. (2005). How do we decipher others' minds. In J.-M. Fellous & M. A. Arbib (Eds.), *Who needs emotions? The brain meets the robot* (pp. 147–169). Oxford: Oxford University Press.

Jeannerod, M. (2006). *Motor cognition: What actions tell the self.* New York: Oxford University Press.

Jeannerod, M., Farrer, C., Pranck, N., Fourneret, P., Daprati, E., & Georgieff, N. (2003). Recognition of action in normal and schizophrenic subjects. In T. Kircher & A. David (Eds.), *The self in neuroscience and psychiatry* (pp. 380–406). Cambridge: Cambridge University Press.

Jeannerod, M., & Pacherie, E. (2004). Agency, simulation, and self-identification. *Mind & Language, 19*, 113–146.

Jellema, T., Baker, C. I., Oram, M. W., & Perrett, D. I. (2002). Cell populations in the banks of the superior temporal sulcus of the macaque and imitation. In A. N. Meltzoff & W. Prinz (Eds.), *The imitative mind: Development, evolution, and brain bases* (pp. 267–290). Cambridge: Cambridge University Press.

Jellema, T., Baker, C. I., Wicker, B., & Perrett, D. I. (2000). Neural representation for the perception of intentionality of actions. *Brain and Cognition, 44*(2), 280–302.

Jellema, T., & Perrett, D. (2002). Coding of visible and hidden action. In W. Prinz & B. Hommel (Eds.), *Common mechanisms in perception and action: Attention and performance XIX* (pp. 267–290). Oxford: Oxford University Press.

Joas, H. (1983). The intersubjective constitution of the body-image. *Human Studies, 6*(2), 197–204.

Johnson, S. C. (2000). The recognition of mentalistic agents in infancy. *Trends in Cognitive Sciences, 4*(1), 22–28.

Jones, S. S. (1996). Imitation or exploration: Young infants' matching of adults' oral gestures. *Child Development, 67*(5), 1952–1969.

Jordan, M. I. (1996). Computational aspects of motor control and motor learning. In H. Heuer & S. W. Keele (Eds.), *Motor skills* (Vol. 2, pp. 71–118). New York: Academic Press.

Kandel, S., Orliaguet, J.-P., & Boë, L.-J. (1995). Visual perception of motor anticipation in handwriting: Influence of letter size and movement velocity. In B. G. Bardy, R. J. Bootsma, & Y. Guiard (Eds.), *Studies on perception and action* (Vol. 3, pp. 347–350). Hillsdale: Erlbaum.

Kandel, S., Orliaguet, J.-P., & Boë, L.-J. (2000). Detecting anticipatory events in handwriting movements. *Perception & Psychophysics, 29*(8), 953–964.

Kandel, S., Orliaguet, J.-P., & Viviani, P. (2000). Perceptual anticipation in handwriting: The role of implicit motor competence. *Perception & Psychophysics, 62*(4), 706–716.

Kant, I. (1996). *Critique of pure reason* (W. S. Pluhar, Trans. Unified ed., with all variants from the 1781 and 1787 eds.). Indianapolis: Hackett.

Karmiloff-Smith, A. (1992). *Beyond modularity: A developmental perspective on cognitive science.* Cambridge, MA: MIT Press.

Karmiloff-Smith, A. (1994). Précis of beyond modularity: A developmental perspective on cognitive science. *Behavioral and Brain Sciences, 17*(4), 639–706.

Keenan, J. P., Gallup, G. G. J., & Falk, D. (2003). *The face in the mirror: How we know who we are.* New York: Ecco.

Keil, F. C., Smith, W. C., Simons, D. J., & Levin, D. T. (1998). Two dogmas of conceptual empiricism: Implications for hybrid models of the structure of knowledge. *Cognition, 65,* 103–135.

Kendon, A. (2004). *Gesture: Visible action as utterance.* Cambridge: Cambridge University Press.

Keysers, C., Wicker, B., Gazzola, V., Anton, J., & Fogassi, L. (2004). A touching sight: SII/PV activation during the observation and experience of touch. *Neuron, 42*(2), 335–346.

Kiefer, M., Sim, E.-J., Herrnberger, B., Grothe, J., & Hoenig, K. (2008). The sound of concepts: Four markers for a link between auditory and conceptual brain systems. *Journal of Neuroscience, 28,* 12224–12230.

Kiefer, M., Sim, E.-J., Liebich, S., Hauk, O., & Tanaka, J. (2007). Experience-dependent plasticity of conceptual representations in human sensory-motor areas. *Journal of Cognitive Neuroscience, 19*(3), 525–542.

Kihlstrom, J. F. (1985). Hypnosis. *Annual Review of Psychology, 36,* 385–418.

Kilner, J., Hamilton, A., & Blakemore, S.-J. (2007). Interference effect of observed human movement on action is due to velocity profile of biological motion. *Social Neuroscience, 2*(3–4), 158–166.

Kinsbourne, M. (1995). Awareness of one's own body: An attentional theory of its nature, development, and brain basis. In J. L. Bermúdez, A. J. Marcel, & N. Eilan (Eds.), *The body and the self* (pp. 205–224). Cambridge, MA: MIT Press.

Kirby, S., Christiansen, M. H., & Chater, N. (2009). Syntax as an adaption to the learner. In D. Bickerton & E. Szathmáry (Eds.), *Biological foundations and origin of syntax* (pp. 325–344). Cambridge, MA: MIT Press.

Klatzky, R. L., MacWhinney, B., & Behrmann, M. (Eds.). (2008). *Embodiment, egospace, and action.* New York: Psychology Press.

Klima, E., & Bellugi, U. (1979). *The signs of language.* Cambridge, MA: Harvard University Press.

Klossek, U. M. H., Russell, J., & Dickinson, A. (2008). The control of instrumental action following outcome devaluation in young children aged between 1 and 4 years. *Journal of Experimental Psychology, 137*(1), 39–51.

Kluft, R. P. (1993). Clinical approaches to the integration of personalities. In R. P. Kluft & C. G. Fine (Eds.), *Clinical perspectives on multiple personality disorders* (pp. 101–133). Washington, D.C.: American Psychiatric Press.

Knoblich, G., & Flach, R. (2001). Predicting the effects of actions: Interactions of perception and action. *Psychological Science, 12*(6), 467–472.

Knoblich, G., & Flach, R. (2003). Action identity: Evidence from self-recognition, prediction, and coordination. *Consciousness and Cognition, 12*(4), 620–632.

Knoblich, G., & Prinz, W. (2001). Recognition of self-generated actions from kinematic displays of drawing. *Journal of Experimental Psychology: Human Perception and Performance, 27*(2), 456–465.

Knoblich, G., Seigerschmidt, E., Flach, R., & Prinz, W. (2002). Authorship effects in the prediction of handwriting strokes: Evidence for action simulation during action perception. *Quarterly Journal of Experimental Psychology, 55A*(3), 1027–1046.

Knoblich, G., Thornton, I. M., Grosjean, F., & Shiffrar, M. (Eds.). (2006). *Human body perception from the inside out*. Oxford: Oxford University Press.

Knuf, L., Aschersleben, G., & Prinz, W. (2001). An analysis of ideomotor action. *Journal of Experimental Psychology: General, 130*(4), 779–798.

Koch, I., Keller, P., & Prinz, W. (2004). The ideomotor approach to action control: Implications for skilled performance. *International Journal of Sport and Exercise Psychology, 2*(4), 362–375.

Koch, I., & Prinz, W. (2005). Response preparation and code overlap in dual tasks. *Memory & Cognition, 33*(6), 1085–1095.

Koehler, D. J., & Harvey, N. (Eds.). (2004). *Blackwell handbook of judgement and decision making*. Malden: Blackwell.

Kögler, H. H., & Stueber, K. R. (Eds.). (2000). *Empathy and agency*. Boulder: Westview Press.

Köhler, W. (1924). *Die physischen Gestalten in Ruhe und im stationären Zustand*. Erlangen: Verlag der Philosophischen Akademie.

Köhler, W. (1947). *Gestalt psychology: an introduction to new concepts in modern psychology*. New York: Liveright.

Kohut, H. (1971). *The analysis of the self: A systematic approach to the psychoanalytic treatment of narcissistic personality disorders*. Guilford: International University Press.

Kohut, H. (1985). *Self psychology and the humanities: Reflections on a new psychoanalytic approach*. New York: Norton.

Kriegel, U., & Williford, K. (Eds.). (2006). *Self-representational approaches to consciousness*. Cambridge, MA: MIT Press.

Kruglanski, A. W., Shah, J. Y., Fishbach, A., Friedman, R., Chun, W. Y., & Sleeth-Keppler, D. (2002). A theory of goal systems. In M. P. Zanna (Ed.), *Advances in experimental social psychology* (pp. 331–378). New York: Academic Press.

Kunde, W. (2001). Response-effect compatibility in manual choice-reaction tasks. *Journal of Experimental Psychology. Human Perception and Performance, 27*(2), 387–394.

Kunde, W. (2003). Temporal response-effect compatibility. *Psychological Research, 67*(3), 153–159.

Kunde, W., Koch, I., & Hoffmann, J. (2004). Anticipated action effects affect the selection, initiation, and execution of actions. *Quarterly Journal of Experimental Psychology, 57A*(1), 87–106.

Kusch, M. (1997). The sociophilosophy of folk psychology. *Studies in History and Philosophy of Science, 28*(1), 1–25.

Kusch, M. (1999). *Psychological knowledge: A social history and philosophy*. London: Routledge.

Kusch, M. (2005). How minds and selves are made: Some conceptual preliminaries. *Interaction Studies: Social Behaviour and Communication in Biological and Artificial Systems, 6*(1), 21–34.

Lacan, J. (1949/1977). The mirror stage as formative of the function of the I as reavealed in psychoanalytic experience. (A. Sheridan, Trans.) *Écrits: A selection* (pp. 3–9). New York: Norton.

Laycock, S. W. (1994). *Mind as mirror and the mirroring of mind: Buddhist reflections on western phenomenology*. Albany: State University of New York Press.

Leslie, A. M. (1987). Pretense and representation: The origins of "theory of mind." *Psychological Review, 94*, 412–426.

Levinson, S. C. (2003). *Space in language and cognition: Explorations in cognitive diversity*. Cambridge: Cambridge University Press.

Lévi-Strauss, C. (1963). Structural analysis in linguistics and in anthropology. In C. Lévi-Strauss (Ed.), *Structural anthropology* (pp. 31–54). New York: Basic Books.

Liberman, A. M., Cooper, F. S., Shankweiler, D. P., & Studdert-Kennedy, M. (1967). Perception of speech code. *Psychological Review, 74*(6), 431–461.

Libet, B. (1985). Unconscious cerebral initiative and the role of conscious will in voluntary action. *Behavioral and Brain Sciences, 8*(4), 529–566.

Libet, B. (1993). The neural time factor in conscious and unconscious events. In G. R. Bock & J. Marsh (Eds.), *Experimental and theoretical studies of consciousness* (pp. 123–146). Chichester: Wiley.

Libet, B. (1996). Neural processes in the production of conscious experience. In M. Velmans (Ed.), *The science of consciousness: Psychological, neuropsychological, and clinical reviews* (pp. 96–117). London: Routledge.

Logan, G. D. (2009). The role of memory in the control of action. In E. Morsella, J. A. Bargh, & P. M. Gollwitzer (Eds.), *Oxford handbook of human action* (pp. 427–441). Oxford: Oxford University Press.

Logan, G. D., & Bundesen, C. (2003). Clever homunculus: Is there an endogenous act of control in the explicit task-cuing procedure? *Journal of Experimental Psychology: Human Perception and Performance, 29*(3), 575–599.

Logan, G. D., & Bundesen, C. (2004). Very clever homunculus: Compound stimulus strategies for the explicit task-cuing procedure. *Psychonomic Bulletin & Review, 11*(5), 832–840.

Logan, G. D., Schneider, D. W., & Bundesen, C. (2007). Still clever after all these years: Searching for the homunculus in explicitly cued task switching. *Journal of Experimental Psychology: Human Perception and Performance, 33*(4), 978–994.

Longo, M. R., Schüür, F., Kammers, M. P. M., Tsakiris, M., & Haggard, P. (2008). What is embodiment? A psychometric approach. *Cognition, 107*(3), 978–998.

Loomis, J. M., & Philbeck, J. W. (2008). Measuring spatial perception with spatial updating and action. In R. L. Klatzky, B. MacWhinney, & M. Behrmann (Eds.), *Embodiment, ego-space, and action* (pp. 1–43). New York: Psychology Press.

Lotze, R. H. (1852). *Medicinische Psychologie oder Physiologie der Seele.* Leipzig: Weidmann.

Lucy, J. A. (1996). The scope of linguistic relativity: An analysis and review of empirical research. In J. J. Gumperz & S. C. Levinson (Eds.), *Rethinking linguistic relativity* (pp. 37–69). Cambridge: Cambridge University Press.

Luhmann, N. (1995). *Social systems* (J. Bednarz & D. Baecker, Trans.). Stanford: Stanford University Press.

Lycan, W. G. (1996). *Consciousness and experience.* Cambridge, MA: MIT Press.

Lycan, W. G. (1999). Intentionality. In R. A. Wilson & F. C. Keil (Eds.), *The MIT encyclopedia of the cognitive sciences* (pp. 413–415). Cambridge, MA: MIT Press.

Maasen, S., Prinz, W., & Roth, G. (Eds.). (2003). *Voluntary action: Brains, minds, and sociality.* Oxford: Oxford University Press.

Maasen, S., & Sutter, B. (Eds.). (2007). *On willing selves: Neoliberal politics vis-à-vis the neuroscientific challenge.* New York: Macmillan.

Mach, E. [1897] (1959). *The analysis of sensations, and the relation of the physical to the psychical* (C. M. Williams & S. Waterlow, Trans.). New York: Dover.

Macho, T. (2004). Narziß und der Spiegel: Selbstrepräsentation in der Geschichte der Optik. In W. Braungart, K. Ridder, & F. Apel (Eds.), *Wahrnehmen und Handeln: Perspektiven einer Literaturanthropologie* (pp. 231–246). Bielefeld: Aisthesis.

MacKay, D. (1987). *The organization of perception and action: A theory for language and other cognitive skills*. Berlin: Springer.

MacNeilage, P. F. (2003). Mouth to hand and back again: Could language have made those journeys? *Behavioral and Brain Sciences, 26*(2), 233–234.

MacNeilage, P. F. (2008). *The origin of speech*. Oxford: Oxford University Press.

MacNeilage, P. F., & Davis, B. L. (2005). Evolution of language. In D. M. Buss (Ed.), *Handbook of evolutionary psychology* (pp. 698–723). Hoboken: Wiley.

Makin, T. R., Holmes, N. P., & Ehrsson, H. H. (2008). On the other hand: Dummy hands and peripersonal space. *Behavioural Brain Research, 191*(1), 1–10.

Malle, B. F. (2004). *How the mind explains behavior: Folk explanations, meaning, and social interaction*. Cambridge, MA: MIT Press.

Malle, B. F., Moses, L. J., & Baldwin, D. A. (2001). *Intentions and intentionality: Foundations of social cognition*. Cambridge, MA: MIT Press.

Mandler, G. (1998). Consciousness and mind as philosophical problems and psychological issues. In J. Hochberg (Ed.), *Perception and cognition at century's end* (2nd ed., pp. 45–65). San Diego: Academic Press.

Maravita, A. (2006). From "body in the brain" to "body in space": Sensory and intentional components of body representation. In G. Knoblich, I. M. Thornton, M. Grosjean, & M. Shiffrar (Eds.), *Human body perception from the inside out* (pp. 65–88). Oxford: Oxford University Press.

Marcel, A. J., & Bisiach, E. (1988). *Consciousness in contemporary science*. Oxford: Clarendon Press.

Markus, H. R., Kitayama, S., & Heiman, R. J. (1996). Culture and "basic" psychological principles. In E. T. Higgins & A. W. Kruglanski (Eds.), *Social psychology: Handbook of basic principles* (pp. 857–913). New York: Guilford Press.

Mead, G. H. (1934). *Mind, self, & society: From the standpoint of a social behaviorist*. Chicago: University of Chicago Press.

Mead, G. H. (1938). *The philosophy of the act*. Chicago: University of Chicago Press.

Mead, G. H. (1980). Der Mechanismus des sozialen Bewusstseins. In H. Joas (Ed.), *George H. Mead: Gesammelte Aufsätze* (Vol. 1, pp. 232–240). Frankfurt: Suhrkamp.

Melchior-Bonnet, S. (2002). *The mirror: A history* (K. H. Jewett, Trans.). New York: Routledge.

Meltzoff, A. N. (1990). Foundations for developing a concept of self: The role of imitation in relating self to other and the value of social mirroring, social modeling, and self-practice in infancy. In D. Cicchetti & M. Beeghly (Eds.), *The self in transition: Infancy to childhood* (pp. 139–164). Chicago: University of Chicago Press.

Meltzoff, A. N. (2002). Elements of a developmental theory of imitation. In A. N. Meltzoff & W. Prinz (Eds.), *The imitative mind* (pp. 19–41). Cambridge: Cambridge University Press.

Meltzoff, A. N. (2005). Imitation and other minds: The "like me" hypothesis. In S. Hurley & N. Chater (Eds.), *Imitation, human development, and culture* (Vol. 2, pp. 55–77). Cambridge, MA: MIT Press.

Meltzoff, A. N. (2007). The "like me" framework for recognizing and becoming an intentional agent. *Acta Psychologica, 124*(1), 26–43.

Meltzoff, A. N., & Gopnik, A. (1993). The role of imitation in understanding persons and developing a theory of mind. In S. Baron-Cohen, H. Tager-Flusberg, & D. J. Cohen (Eds.), *Understanding other minds: Perspectives from autism* (pp. 335–366). Oxford: Oxford University Press.

Meltzoff, A. N., & Moore, M. K. (1977). Imitation of facial and manual gestures by human neonates. *Science, 198*(4312), 75–78.

Meltzoff, A. N., & Moore, M. K. (1983). Newborn infants imitate adult facial gestures. *Child Development, 54*(3), 702–709.

Meltzoff, A. N., & Moore, M. K. (1989). Imitation in newborn infants: Exploring the range of gestures imitated and the underlying mechanisms. *Developmental Psychology, 25*(6), 954–962.

Meltzoff, A. N., & Moore, M. K. (1995a). A theory of the role of imitation in the emergence of self. In P. Rochat (Ed.), *The self in infancy: Theory and research* (pp. 73–93). Amsterdam: Elsevier.

Meltzoff, A. N., & Moore, M. K. (1995b). Infants' understanding of people and things: From body imitation to folk psychology. In J. L. Bermúdez, A. J. Marcel & N. Eilan (Eds.), *The body and the self* (pp. 43–69). Cambridge, MA: MIT Press.

Meltzoff, A. N., & Prinz, W. (Eds.). (2002). *The imitative mind: Development, evolution and brain bases*. Cambridge: Cambridge University Press.

Melzack, R. (1990). Phantoms limbs and the concept of a neuromatrix. *Trends in Neurosciences, 13*, 88–92.

Melzack, R. (1992). Phantom limbs. *Scientific American, 266*(4), 120–126.

Mercier, P. (2008). *Night train to Lisbon* (B. Harshav, Trans.). New York: Grove Press.

Merker, B. (2007). Consciousness without a cerebral cortex: A challenge for neuroscience and medicine. *Behavioral and Brain Sciences, 30*(1), 63–134.

Merleau-Ponty, M. [1945] (2003). *Phenomenology of perception* (C. Smith, Trans.). London: Routledge.

Metzinger, T. (1993). *Subjekt und Selbstmodell. Die Perspektivität phänomenalen Bewußt-seins vor dem Hintergrund einer naturalistischen Theorie mentaler Repräsentation.* Pader-born: Schöningh.

Metzinger, T. (2003). *Being no one: The self-model theory of subjectivity.* Cambridge, MA: MIT Press.

Miall, R. C., & Wolpert, D. M. (1996). Forward models for physiological motor control. *Neural Networks, 9*(8), 1265–1279.

Michotte, A. (1946). *La perception de la causalité.* Louvain: Editions de l'Institut Superieur de Philosophie.

Michotte, A. (1962). *Causalité, permanence et réalité phénoménales: Études de psycholo-gie expérimentale.* Louvain: Publications University.

Michotte, A. (1963). *The perception of causality* (T. R. Miles & E. Miles, Trans.). New York: Basic Books.

Miller, G. A., Galanter, E., & Pribram, K. H. (1960). *Plans and the structure of behavior.* London: Holt, Rinehart & Winston.

Millikan, R. G. (1993). *White queen psychology and other essays for Alice.* Cambridge, MA: MIT Press.

Millikan, R. G. (1995). Pushmi-pullyu representations. *Philosophical Perspectives, 9,* 185–200.

Mithen, S. (1996). *The prehistory of the mind: A search for the origins of art, religion, and science.* London: Thames & Hudson.

Monsell, S. (2003). Task switching. *Trends in Cognitive Sciences, 7*(3), 134–140.

Monsell, S., & Driver, J. (2000a). Banishing the control homunculus. In S. Monsell & J. Driver (Eds.), *Control of cognitive processes: Attention and performance XVIII* (pp. 3–32). Cambridge, MA: MIT Press.

Monsell, S., & Driver, J. (Eds.). (2000b). *Control of cognitive processes: Attention and performance XVIII.* Cambridge, MA: MIT Press.

Morsella, E. (2005). The function of phenomenal states: Supramodular interaction theory. *Psychological Review, 112*(4), 1000–1021.

Morsella, E., Bargh, J. A., & Gollwitzer, P. M. (Eds.). (2009). *Oxford handbook of human action.* Oxford: Oxford University Press.

Morsella, E., Krieger, S. C., & Bargh, J. A. (2009). The primary function of conscious-ness: Why skeletal muscles are "voluntary" muscles. In E. Morsella, J. A. Bargh, & P. M. Gollwitzer (Eds.), *Oxford handbook of human action* (pp. 625–634). Oxford: Oxford University Press.

Mundy, P., & Newell, L. (2007). Attention, joint attention, and social cognition. *Current Directions in Psychological Science, 16*(5), 269–274.

Mundy, P. C., & Acra, C. F. (2006). Joint attention, social engagement, and the development of social competence. In P. J. Marshall & N. A. Fox (Eds.), *The development of social engagement: Neurobiological perspectives* (pp. 81–117). Oxford: Oxford University Press.

Münsterberg, H. (1888). *Die Willenshandlung: Ein Beitrag zur physiologischen Psychologie.* Freiburg: Mohr.

Müsseler, J., & Hommel, B. (1997a). Blindness to response-compatible stimuli. *Journal of Experimental Psychology: Human Perception and Performance, 23*(3), 861–872.

Müsseler, J., & Hommel, B. (1997b). Detecting and identifying response-compatible stimuli. *Psychonomic Bulletin & Review, 4*(1), 125–129.

Nadel, J. (2002). Imitation and imitation recognition: Functional use in preverbal infants and nonverbal children with autism. In A. N. Meltzoff & W. Prinz (Eds.), *The imitative mind: Development, evolution, and brain bases* (pp. 42–62). Cambridge: Cambridge University Press.

Nadel, J., & Butterworth, G. (Eds.). (1999). *Imitation in infancy.* Cambridge: Cambridge University Press.

Nadel, J., Guérini, C., Pezé, A., & Rivet, C. (1999). The evolving nature of imitation as a format for communication. In J. Nadel & G. Butterworth (Eds.), *Imitation in infancy* (pp. 209–234). Cambridge: Cambridge University Press.

Nadel, L. (2003). *What is cognitive science? Encyclopedia of cognitive science* (Vol. 1, pp. xiii–xli). London: Nature Publishing Group.

Nadel, L., & Piatelli-Palmarini, M. (2003). What is cognitive science. In L. Nadel (Ed.), *Encyclopedia of cognitive science* (Vol. 1). London: Nature Publishing Group.

Nagy, E. (2006). From imitation to conversation: The first dialogues with human neonates. *Infant and Child Development, 15*(3), 223–232.

Nagy, E., & Molnar, P. (2004). Homo imitans or homo provocans? Human imprinting model of neonatal imitation. *Infant Behavior and Development, 27*(1), 54–63.

Neisser, U. (1967). *Cognitive psychology.* New York: Appleton-Century-Crofts.

Neisser, U. (Ed.). (1993). *The perceived self: Ecological and interpersonal sources of self-knowledge.* Cambridge: Cambridge University Press.

Neisser, U., & Jopling, D. A. (Eds.). (1997). *The conceptual self in context: Culture, experience, self-understanding.* Cambridge: Cambridge University Press.

Neumann, O. (1990). Visual attention and action. In O. Neumann & W. Prinz (Eds.), *Relationships between perception and action: Current approaches* (pp. 227–267). Berlin: Springer.

Neumann, O., & Prinz, W. (1987). Kognitive Antezedenzien von Willkürhandlungen. In H. Heckhausen, P. M. Gollwitzer, & F. E. Weinert (Eds.), *Jenseits des Rubikon: Der Wille in den Humanwissenschaften* (pp. 195–215). Berlin: Springer.

Neumann, O., & Prinz, W. (Eds.). (1990). *Relationships between perception and action: Current approaches*. Berlin: Springer.

Newtson, D. (1976). Foundation of attribution: The perception of ongoing behavior. In J. H. Harvey, W. J. Ickes, & R. F. Kidd (Eds.), *New Directions in Attribution Research* (Vol. 1, pp. 223–247). Hillsdale: Erlbaum.

Niedenthal, P. M., Mermillod, M., Maringer, M., & Hess, U. (2010). The simulation of smiles (SIMS) model: Embodied simulation and the meaning of facial expression. *Behavioral and Brain Sciences, 33,* 417–480.

Noë, A. (2004). *Action in perception.* Cambridge, MA: MIT Press.

Norman, D. A., & Shallice, T. (1980). *Attention to action: Willed and automatic control of behavior.* La Jolla: Center for Human Information Processing, University of California.

Norman, D. A., & Shallice, T. (1986). Attention to action: Willed and automatic control of behavior. In R. J. Davidson, G. E. Schwartz, & D. Shapiro (Eds.), *Consciousness and self-regulation* (Vol. 4, pp. 1–18). New York: Plenum Press.

Olson, D. R., & Kamawar, D. (1999). The theory of ascriptions. In P. D. Zelazo, J. W. Astington, & D. R. Olson (Eds.), *Developing theories of intention: Social understanding and self-control* (pp. 153–166). Mahwah: Erlbaum.

O'Reilley, R. C., Braver, T. S., & Cohen, J. D. (1999). A biologically based computational model of working memory. In A. Miyake & P. Shah (Eds.), *Models of working memory: Mechanisms of active maintenance and executive control* (pp. 375–411). Cambridge: Cambridge University Press.

Ovid [Publius Ovidius Naso]. (2005). *Metamorphoses* (C. Martin, Trans.). New York: Norton.

Pashler, H. (2000). Task switching and multitask performance. In S. Monsell & J. Driver (Eds.), *Control of cognitive processes: Attention and performance XVIII* (pp. 277–307). Cambridge, MA: MIT Press.

Pearce, J. M. (1997). *Animal learning & cognition: An introduction* (2nd ed.). Hove: Psychology Press.

Pendergrast, M. (2003). *Mirror, mirror: A history of the human love affair with reflection.* New York: Basic Books.

Perner, J. (1991). *Understanding the representational mind.* Cambridge, MA: MIT Press.

Perrett, D. I., & Emery, N. J. (1994). Understanding the intentions of others from visual signals: Neurophysiological evidence. *Current Psychological Cognition, 13*(5), 683–694.

Perrett, D. I., Harries, M., Bevan, R., Thomas, S., Benson, P., Mistlin, A., et al. (1989). Frameworks of analysis for the neuronal representation of animate objects and actions. *Journal of Experimental Biology, 146,* 87–113.

Perrett, D. I., Harries, M., Mistlin, A., Hietanen, J., Benson, P., Bevan, R., et al. (1990). Social signals analyzed at the single cell level: Someone is looking at me, something touched me, something moved! *International Journal of Comparative Psychology, 4*(1), 25–55.

Perry, J. (1994). Intentionality. In S. Guttenplan (Ed.), *A companion to the philosophy of mind* (pp. 386–395). Oxford: Blackwell.

Pfeifer, R., & Bongard, J. (2007). *How the body shapes the way we think: A new view of intelligence.* Cambridge, MA: MIT Press.

Piaget, J. (1954). *The construction of reality in the child.* New York: Basic Books.

Pico della Mirandola, G. (1486/1948). Oration on the dignity of man (E. Livermore Forbes, Trans.). In E. Cassirer, P. O. Kristeller & J. H. Randall (Eds.), *The Renaissance philosophy of man* (pp. 223–254). Chicago: University of Chicago Press.

Pineda, J. A. (Ed.). (2009). *Mirror neuron systems: The role of mirroring processes in social cognition.* New York: Humana Press.

Pinker, S. (1994). *The language instinct.* New York: Morrow.

Pinker, S., & Bloom, P. (1990). Natural language and natural selection. *Behavioral and Brain Sciences, 13*(4), 707–726.

Pinker, S., & Jackendoff, R. (2005). The faculty of language: What's special about it? *Cognition, 95*(2), 201–236.

Pockett, S., Banks, W. P., & Gallagher, S. (Eds.). (2006). *Does consciousness cause behavior?* Cambridge, MA: MIT Press.

Porter, R. (Ed.). (1997). *Rewriting the self: Histories from the Renaissance to the present.* London: Routledge.

Posner, M. I. (Ed.). (1989). *Foundations of cognitive science.* Cambridge, MA: MIT Press.

Powers, W. T. (1973). *Behavior: The control of perception.* New York: Aldine.

Powers, W. T. (1978). Quantitative analysis of purposive systems—some spadework at the foundations of scientific psychology. *Psychological Review, 85*(5), 417–435.

Powers, W. T. (1989). Volition: A semi-scientific essay. In W. A. Hershberger (Ed.), *Volitional action: Conation and control* (pp. 21–37). Amsterdam: Elsevier.

Prinz, W. (1983). *Wahrnehmung und Tätigkeitssteuerung*. Berlin: Springer.

Prinz, W. (1984). Modes of linkage between perception and action. In W. Prinz & A. F. Sanders (Eds.), *Cognition and motor processes* (pp. 185–193). Berlin: Springer.

Prinz, W. (1987). Ideo-motor action. In H. Heuer & A. F. Sanders (Eds.), *Perspectives on perception and action* (pp. 47–76). Hillsdale: Erlbaum.

Prinz, W. (1990). A common coding approach to perception and action. In O. Neumann & W. Prinz (Eds.), *Relationships between perception and action: Current approaches* (pp. 167–201). Berlin: Springer.

Prinz, W. (1992). Why don't we perceive our brain states? *European Journal of Cognitive Psychology, 4*(1), 1–20.

Prinz, W. (1997). Perception and action planning. *European Journal of Cognitive Psychology, 9*(2), 129–154.

Prinz, W. (2002). Experimental approaches to imitation. In A. N. Meltzoff & W. Prinz (Eds.), *The imitative mind: Development, evolution and brain bases* (pp. 143–162). Cambridge: Cambridge University Press.

Prinz, W. (2003). Emerging selves: Representational foundations of subjectivity. *Consciousness and Cognition, 12*, 515–528.

Prinz, W. (2005). An ideomotor approach to imitation. In S. Hurley & N. Chater (Eds.), *Mechanisms of imitation and imitation in animals* (Vol. 1, pp. 141–156). Cambridge, MA: MIT Press.

Prinz, W. (2006a). Free will as a social institution. In S. Pockett, W. P. Banks, & S. Gallagher (Eds.), *Does consciousness cause behavior?* (pp. 257–276). Cambridge, MA: MIT Press.

Prinz, W. (2006b). What re-enactment earns us. *Cortex, 42*(4), 515–517.

Prinz, W. (2008). Mirrors for embodied communication. In I. Wachsmuth, M. Lenzen, & G. Knoblich (Eds.), *Embodied communication in humans and machines* (pp. 111–128). Oxford: Oxford University Press.

Prinz, W. (2009). Selbst im Spiegel. Kognitive Mechanismen und soziale Praktiken der Selbst-Konstitution. In J. Ehmer & O. Höffe (Eds.), *Bilder des Alterns im Wandel: Historische, interkulturelle, theoretische und aktuelle Perspektiven* (pp. 117–137). Stuttgart: Wissenschaftliche Verlagsgesellschaft mbH.

Prinz, W. (in press). Common coding. In H. Pashler, F. Ferreira, M. Kinsbourne, & R. Zemel (Eds.), *The encyclopedia of the mind*. Los Angeles: SAGE.

Prinz, W., Aschersleben, G., & Koch, I. (2009). Cognition and action. In E. Morsella, J. A. Bargh, & P. M. Gollwitzer (Eds.), *Oxford handbook of human action* (pp. 35–71). Oxford: Oxford University Press.

Prinz, W., de Maeght, S., & Knuf, L. (2005). Intention in action. In G. W. Humphreys & M. J. Riddoch (Eds.), *Attention in action: Advances from cognitive neuroscience* (pp. 93–107). Hove: Psychology Press.

Prinz, W., Försterling, F., & Hauf, P. (2007). Of minds and mirrors: An introduction to the social making of minds. In F. Försterling & P. Hauf (Eds.), *Making minds: The shaping of human minds through social context* (pp. 1–16). Amsterdam: John Benjamins.

Prinz, W., & Hommel, B. (Eds.). (2002). *Common mechanisms in perception and action: Attention and performance XIX*. Oxford: Oxford University Press.

Proctor, R. W., & Reeve, T. G. (Eds.). (1990). *Stimulus-response compatibility: An integrated perspective*. Amsterdam: North-Holland.

Proffitt, D. R. (2008). An action-specific approach to spatial perception. In R. L. Klatzky, B. MacWhinney, & M. Behrmann (Eds.), *Embodiment, ego-space, and action* (pp. 179–202). New York: Psychology Press.

Proust, J. (2002). Can "radical" simulation theories explain psychological concept acquisition? In J. Dokic & J. Proust (Eds.), *Simulation and knowledge of action* (pp. 201–228). Amsterdam: John Benjamins.

Pulvermüller, F. (2001). Brain reflections of words and their meaning. *Trends in Cognitive Sciences, 5*(12), 517–524.

Pulvermüller, F. (2007). Word processing in the brain revealed by neurophysiological imaging using EEG and MEG. In G. Gaskell (Ed.), *The Oxford handbook of psycholinguistics* (pp. 119–138). Oxford: Oxford University Press.

Pylyshyn, Z. W. (1986). *Computation and cognition. Toward a foundation for cognitive science*. Cambridge, MA: MIT Press.

Ramachandran, V. S., & Blakeslee, S. (1998). *Phantoms in the brain: Human nature and the architecture of the mind*. London: Fourth Estate.

Ramachandran, V. S., & Hirstein, W. (1998). The perception of phantom limbs: The D. O. Hebb lecture. *Brain, 121*, 1603–1630.

Raphael-Leff, J. (Ed.). (2003). *Parent-infant psychodynamics: Wild things, mirrors, and ghosts*. London: Whurr.

Redding, G. M., & Wallace, B. (1997). *Adaptive spatial alignment*. Mahwah: Erlbaum.

Rescorla, R. A. (1998). Instrumental learning: Nature and persistence. In M. Sabourin, F. Craik, & M. Robert (Eds.), *Biological and cognitive aspects* (Vol. 2, pp. 239–257). Hove: Psychology Press.

Rescorla, R. A., & Wagner, A. R. (1972). A theory of Pavlovian conditioning: Variations on the effectiveness of reinforcement and nonreinforcement. In A. H. Black & W. F. Prokasy (Eds.), *Classical conditioning II: Current research and theory* (pp. 64–99). New York: Appleton-Century-Crofts.

Reznick, J. S. (1999). Influences on maternal attribution of infant intentionality. In P. D. Zelazo, J. W. Astington, & D. R. Olson (Eds.), *Developing theories of intention: Social understanding and self-control* (pp. 243–267). Mahwah: Erlbaum.

Ricoeur, P. (2005). *The course of recognition.* Cambridge, MA: Harvard University Press.

Rizzolatti, G. (2005). The mirror neuron system and imitation. In S. Hurley & N. Chater (Eds.), *Mechanisms of imitation and imitation in animals* (Vol. 1, pp. 55–76). Cambridge, MA: MIT Press.

Rizzolatti, G., & Arbib, M. A. (1998). Language within our grasp. *Trends in Neurosciences, 21*(5), 188–194.

Rizzolatti, G., Craighero, L., & Fadiga, L. (2002). The mirror system in humans. In M. I. Stamenov & V. Gallese (Eds.), *Mirror neurons and the evolution of brain and language* (pp. 37–59). Amsterdam: John Benjamins.

Rizzolatti, G., Fadiga, L., Fogassi, L., & Gallese, V. (2002). From mirror neurons to imitation: Facts and speculations. In A. N. Meltzoff & W. Prinz (Eds.), *The imitative mind: Development, evolution, and brain bases* (pp. 247–266). Cambridge: Cambridge University Press.

Rizzolatti, G., Fadiga, L., Gallese, V., & Fogassi, L. (1996). Premotor cortex and the recognition of motor actions. *Brain Research. Cognitive Brain Research, 3*(2), 131–141.

Rizzolatti, G., Fogassi, L., & Gallese, V. (2000). Cortical mechanisms subserving object grasping and action recognition: A new view on the cortical motor functions. In M. S. Gazzaniga (Ed.), *The cognitive neurosciences* (pp. 539–552). Cambridge, MA: MIT Press.

Rizzolatti, G., Fogassi, L., & Gallese, V. (2001). Neurophysiological mechanisms underlying the understanding and imitation of action. *Nature Reviews. Neuroscience, 2*(9), 661–670.

Rizzolatti, G., & Sinigaglia, C. (2008). *Mirrors in the brain: How our minds share actions and emotions* (F. Anderson, Trans.). Oxford: Oxford University Press.

Rochat, P. (Ed.). (1999). *Early social cognition: Understanding others in the first months of life.* Mahwah: Erlbaum.

Rochat, P. (2009). Commentary: Mutual recognition as a foundation of sociality and social comfort. In T. Striano & V. M. Reid (Eds.), *Social cognition: Development, neuroscience, and autism* (pp. 303–317). Chichester: Wiley-Blackwell.

Rochat, P., & Passos-Ferreira, C. (2009). From imitation to reciprocation and mutual recognition. In J. A. Pineda (Ed.), *Mirror neuron systems: The role of mirroring processes in social cognition* (pp. 191–212). New York: Humana Press.

Rock, I. (1966). *The nature of perceptual adaptation.* New York: Basic Books.

Roessler, J., & Eilan, N. (Eds.). (2003). *Agency and self-awareness.* New York: Oxford University Press.

Rogers, C. R. (1951). *Client-centered therapy: Its current practice, implications, and theory.* Boston: Houghton Mifflin.

Rogers, C. R. (1959). A theory of therapy, personality, and interpersonal relationships as developed in the client-centered framework. In S. Koch (Ed.), *Formulations of the person and the social context* (pp. 184–256). New York: McGraw-Hill.

Romani, M., Cesari, P., Urgesi, C., Facchini, S., & Aglioti, S. M. (2005). Motor facilitation of the human cortico-spinal system during observation of bio-mechanically impossible movements. *NeuroImage, 26*(3), 755–763.

Rose, N. (1990). *Governing the soul: The shaping of the private self.* London: Routledge.

Rose, N. (1996). *Inventing our selves: Psychology, power, and personhood.* Cambridge: Cambridge University Press.

Ross, D., Spurrett, D., Kincaid, H., & Stephens, G. L. (Eds.). (2007). *Distributed cognition and the will: Individual volition and social context.* Cambridge, MA: MIT Press.

Rowlands, M. (2006). *Body language: Representation in action.* Cambridge, MA: MIT Press.

Rowlands, M. (2010). *The new science of the mind: From extended mind to embodied phenomenology.* Cambridge, MA: MIT Press.

Roy, J.-M., Petitot, J., Pachoud, B., & Varela, F. J. (1999). Beyond the gap: An introduction to naturalizing phenomenology. In J. Petitot, F. J. Varela, B. Pachoud, & J.-M. Roy (Eds.), *Naturalizing phenomenology and cognitive science: Issues in contemporary phenomenology and cognitive science* (pp. 1–82). Stanford: Stanford University Press.

Ruby, P., & Decety, J. (2001). Effect of subjective perspective taking during simulation of action: A PET investigation of agency. *Nature Neuroscience, 4*(5), 546–550.

Ruby, P., & Decety, J. (2003). What you believe versus what you think they believe: A neuroimaging study of conceptual perspective-taking. *European Journal of Neuroscience, 17*(11), 2475–2480.

Ruby, P., & Decety, J. (2004). How would you feel versus how do you think she would feel? A neuroimaging study of perspective-taking. *European Journal of Neuroscience, 16*(6), 988–999.

Runeson, S., & Frykholm, G. (1981). Visual perception of lifted weight. *Journal of Experimental Psychology: Human Perception and Performance, 7*(4), 733–740.

Russell, J. (1996). *Agency: Its role in mental development.* Hove: Erlbaum.

Sapir, E., & Mandelbaum, D. G. (Eds.). (1949). *Selected writings of Edward Sapir in language, culture, personality.* Berkeley: University of California Press.

Schacter, D. L., Wagner, A. D., & Buckner, R. L. (2000). Memory systems of 1999. In E. Tulving & F. I. M. Craik (Eds.), *The Oxford handbook of memory* (pp. 627–643). Oxford: Oxford University Press.

Schilder, P. F. (1935). *The image and appearance of the human body: Studies in the constructive energies of the psyche* (Vol. 4). London: Kegan Paul, Trench, Trubner & Co.

Schmidt, G. (2001). *Mirror image and therapy: Dialectics of criticism and culture.* Oxford: Lang.

Schubö, A., Aschersleben, G., & Prinz, W. (2001). Interactions between perception and action in a reaction task with overlapping S-R assignments. *Psychological Research, 65*(3), 145–157.

Schubö, A., Prinz, W., & Aschersleben, G. (2004). Perceiving while acting: Action affects perception. *Psychological Research, 68*(4), 208–215.

Schütz-Bosbach, S., & Prinz, W. (2007a). Perceptual resonance: Action-induced modulation of perception. *Trends in Cognitive Sciences, 11*(8), 349–355.

Schütz-Bosbach, S., & Prinz, W. (2007b). Prospective coding in event representation. *Cognitive Processing, 8*(2), 93–102.

Schütz-Bosbach, S., Tausche, P., & Weiss, C. (2009). Roughness perception during the rubber hand illusion. *Brain and Cognition, 70*(1), 136–144.

Searle, J. R. (1983). *Intentionality: An essay in the philosophy of mind.* Cambridge: Cambridge University Press.

Searle, J. R. (1994). Intentionality. In S. Guttenplan (Ed.), *A companion to the philosophy of mind* (pp. 379–386). Oxford: Blackwell.

Sebanz, N., & Prinz, W. (Eds.). (2006). *Disorders of volition.* Cambridge, MA: MIT Press.

Sedgwick, H. A. (1986). Space perception. In K. R. Boff, L. Kaufman, & J. P. Thomas (Eds.), *Handbook of perception and human performance* (Vol. 1, pp. 21.01–21.57). New York: Wiley.

Sellars, W. (1956). Empiricism and the philosophy of mind. In H. Feigl & M. Scriven (Eds.), *The foundations of science and the concepts of psychology and psychoanalysis* (Vol. 1, pp. 253–329). Minneapolis: University of Minnesota Press.

Semin, G. R., & Cacioppo, J. T. (2008). Grounding social cognition: Synchronization, coordination, and co-regulation. In G. R. Semin & E. R. Smith (Eds.), *Embodied grounding: Social, cognitive, affective, and neuroscientific approaches* (pp. 119–147). Cambridge: Cambridge University Press.

Shah, J. Y. (2005). The automatic pursuit and management of goals. *American Psychological Society, 14*(1), 10–13.

Sharpe, R. A. (1990). *Making the human mind.* London: Routledge.

Shear, J. (1995). *Explaining consciousness: The "hard problem."* Cambridge, MA: MIT Press.

Shiffrar, M. (2001). Movement and event perception. In E. B. Goldstein (Ed.), *The Blackwell handbook of perception* (pp. 237–271). Oxford: Blackwell.

Shiffrar, M., & Freyd, J. J. (1990). Apparent motion of the human body. *Psychological Science, 1*(4), 257–264.

Shiffrar, M., & Freyd, J. J. (1993). Timing and apparent motion path choice with human body photographs. *Psychological Science, 4*(6), 379–384.

Shiffrar, M., & Pinto, J. (2002). The visual analysis of bodily motion. In W. Prinz & B. Hommel (Eds.), *Common mechanisms in perception and action: Attention and performance XIX* (pp. 381–399). Oxford: Oxford University Press.

Shipley, T. F., & Zacks, J. M. (Eds.). (2008). *Understanding events: From perception to action.* New York: Oxford University Press.

Shoemaker, S. (1996). *The first-person perspective and other essays.* Cambridge: Cambridge University Press.

Singer, T., & Decety, J. (in press). Empathy. In J. Decety & J. T. Cacioppo (Eds.), *Handbook of social neuroscience.* New York: Oxford University Press.

Singer, T., & Lamm, C. (2009). The social neuroscience of empathy. The Year in Cognitive Neuroscience 2009. *Annals of the New York Academy of Sciences, 1156,* 81–96.

Singer, T., Seymour, B., O'Doherty, J., Kaube, H., Dolan, R. J., & Frith, C. D. (2004). Empathy for pain involves the affective but not sensory components of pain. *Science, 303*(5661), 1157–1162.

Skinner, B. F. (1953). *Science and human behavior.* New York: Macmillan.

Skinner, B. F. (1972). *Beyond freedom and dignity.* New York: Knopf.

Slobin, D. I. (1996). From "thought and language" to "thinking for speaking". In J. J. Gumperz & S. C. Levinson (Eds.), *Rethinking linguistic relativity* (pp. 70–96). Cambridge: Cambridge University Press.

Slobin, D. I. (2007). Language and thought online: Cognitive consequences of linguistic relativity. In V. Evans, B. K. Bergen, & J. Zinken (Eds.), *The cognitive linguistics reader* (pp. 902–928). London: Equinox.

Sloman, S. A. (1996). The empirical case for two systems of reasoning. *Psychological Bulletin, 119*, 3–22.

Sloman, S. A., & Rips, L. J. (1998). Similarity as an explanatory construct. *Cognition, 65*, 87–101.

Smith, A. [1759] (1976). *The theory of moral sentiments* (Vol. 1). Oxford: Clarendon Press.

Smith, D. W. (1999). Intentionality naturalized? In J. Petitot, F. J. Varela, B. Pachoud, & J.-M. Roy (Eds.), *Naturalizing phenomenology: Issues in contemporary phenomenology and cognitive science* (pp. 83–110). Stanford: Stanford University Press.

Sommerville, J. A., & Decety, J. (2006). Weaving the fabric of social interaction: Articulating developmental psychology and cognitive neuroscience in the domain of motor cognition. *Psychonomic Bulletin & Review, 13*(2), 179–200.

Sonnby-Borgström, M. (2002). Automatic mimicry reactions as related to differences in emotional empathy. *Scandinavian Journal of Psychology, 43*(5), 433–443.

Spelke, E. S., & Newport, E. L. (1998). Nativism, empiricism, and the development of knowledge. In R. M. Lerner (Ed.), *Handbook of child psychology: Theoretical models of human development* (Vol. 1, pp. 275–340). New York: Wiley.

Spencer, H. (1899). *The principles of psychology*. London: Williams & Norgate.

Sperber, D. (Ed.). (2000). *Metarepresentations: A multidisciplinary perspective*. Oxford: Oxford University Press.

Spiegel, D. (1993). Multiple posttraumatic personality disorders. In R. P. Kluft & C. G. Fine (Eds.), *Clinical perspectives on multiple personality disorders* (pp. 87–99). Washington, D.C.: American Psychiatric Press.

Stanovich, K. E. (2004). *The robot's rebellion: Finding meaning in the age of Darwin*. Chicago: University of Chicago Press.

Steels, L. (2009). Cognition and social dynamics play a major role in the formation of grammar. In D. Bickerton & E. Szathmáry (Eds.), *Biological foundations and origin of syntax* (pp. 345–368). Cambridge, MA: MIT Press.

Stephan, A. (1992). Emergence: A systematic view on its historical facets. In A. Beckermann (Ed.), *Emergence or reduction? Essays on the prospects of nonreductive physicalism* (pp. 25–48). Berlin: de Gruyter.

Stevens, J. A., Fonlupt, P., Shiffrar, M., & Decety, J. (2000). New aspects of motion perception: Selective neural encoding of apparent human movements. *Neuroreport, 11*(1), 109–115.

Stich, S. P. (1983). *From folk psychology to cognitive science: The case against belief.* Cambridge, MA: MIT Press.

Stigler, J. W., Shweder, R. A., & Herdt, G. H. (Eds.). (1990). *Cultural psychology: Essays on comparative human development.* Cambridge: Cambridge University Press.

Stiles-Davis, J., Kritchevsky, M., & Bellugi, U. (Eds.). (1988). *Spatial cognition: Brain bases and development.* Hillsdale: Erlbaum.

Stock, A., & Hoffmann, J. (2002). Intentional fixation of behavioural learning, or how R-O learning blocks S-R learning. *European Journal of Cognitive Psychology, 14*(1), 127–153.

Stoet, G., & Snyder, L. H. (2007). Task-switching in human and non-human primates: Understanding rule encoding and control from behavior to single neurons. In S. A. Bunge & J. D. Wallis (Eds.), *The neuroscience of rule-guided behavior* (pp. 227–254). Oxford: Oxford University Press.

Stoet, G., & Snyder, L. H. (2009). Neural correlates of executive control functions in the monkey. *Trends in Cognitive Sciences, 13*(5), 228–234.

Stränger, J., & Hommel, B. (1995). The perception of action and movement. In W. Prinz & B. Bridgeman (Eds.), *Handbook of perception and action* (Vol. 1, pp. 397–451). London: Academic Press.

Striano, T., & Reid, V. M. (2006). Social cognition in the first year. *Trends in Cognitive Sciences, 10*(10), 471–476.

Stueber, K. R. (2006). *Rediscovering empathy: Agency, folk psychology, and the human sciences.* Cambridge, MA: MIT Press.

Stumpf, C. (1906). *Erscheinungen und psychische Funktionen.* Berlin: Verlag der Königlichen Akademie der Wissenschaften.

Stürmer, B., Aschersleben, G., & Prinz, W. (2000). Correspondence effects with manual gestures and postures: A study of imitation. *Journal of Experimental Psychology: Human Perception and Performance, 26*(6), 1746–1759.

Synofzik, M., Vosgerau, G., & Newen, A. (2008). Beyond the comparator model: A multifactorial two-step account of agency. *Consciousness and Cognition, 17*(1), 219–239.

Taylor, C. (1989). *Sources of the self: The making of the modern identity.* Cambridge, MA: Harvard University Press.

Thines, G., Costall, A., & Butterworth, G. (Eds.). (1991). *Michotte's experimental phenomenology of perception.* Hillsdale: Erlbaum.

Thorndike, E. L. (1911). *Animal intelligence: Experimental studies.* New York: Macmillan.

Tolman, E. C. (1932). *Purposive behavior in animals and men.* New York: Century.

Tomasello, M. (1999). *The cultural origins of human cognition.* Cambridge, MA: Harvard University Press.

Tomasello, M. (2003a). *Constructing a language: A usage-based theory of language acquisition.* Cambridge, MA: Harvard University Press.

Tomasello, M. (2003b). The key is social cognition. In D. Gentner & S. Goldin-Meadow (Eds.), *Language in mind: Advances in the study of language and thought* (pp. 47–58). Cambridge, MA: MIT Press.

Tomasello, M. (2008). *Origins of human communication.* Cambridge, MA: MIT Press.

Tomasello, M., & Call, J. (1997). *Primate cognition.* Oxford: Oxford University Press.

Tomasello, M., Carpenter, M., Call, J., Behne, T., & Moll, H. (2005). Understanding and sharing intentions: The origins of cultural cognition. *Behavioral and Brain Sciences, 28*(5), 675–691.

Tomasello, M., & Herrmann, E. (2010). Ape and human cognition: What's the difference? *Current Directions in Psychological Science, 19,* 3–8.

Trevarthen, C. (1993). The self born in intersubjectivity: The psychology of an infant communicating. In U. Neisser (Ed.), *The perceived self: Ecological and interpersonal sources of self knowledge* (pp. 121–173). Cambridge: Cambridge University Press.

Trevarthen, C. (1998). The concept and foundations of infant intersubjectivity. In S. Bråten (Ed.), *Intersubjective communication and emotion in early ontogeny* (pp. 15–46). Cambridge: Cambridge University Press.

Trevarthen, C. (2005). "Stepping away from the mirror: Pride and shame in adventures of companionship." Reflections on the nature and emotional needs of infant intersubjectivity. In C. S. Carter, L. Ahnert, K. E. Grossmann, S. B. Hrdy, M. E. Lamb, S. W. Porges, et al. (Eds.), *Attachment and bonding* (pp. 55–84). Cambridge, MA: MIT Press.

Trevarthen, C., Kokkinaki, T., & Fiamenghi, G. A. J. (1999). What infants' imitations communicate: With mothers, with fathers and with peers. In J. Nadel & G. Butterworth (Eds.), *Imitation in infancy* (pp. 127–185). Cambridge: Cambridge University Press.

Tsakiris, M., & Haggard, P. (2005). The rubber hand illusion revisited: Visuotactile integration and self-attribution. *Journal of Experimental Psychology: Human Perception and Performance, 31*(1), 80–91.

Tulving, E. (1983). *Elements of episodic memory.* Oxford: Clarendon Press.

Tversky, A. (1977). Features of similarity. *Psychological Review, 84,* 327–352.

Vallacher, R. R., & Wegner, D. M. (Eds.). (1985). *A theory of action identification.* Hillsdale: Erlbaum.

Vallacher, R. R., & Wegner, D. M. (1989). Levels of personal agency: Individual variation in action identification. *Journal of Personality and Social Psychology, 57*(4), 600–671.

van der Hulst, H. G. (Ed.). (2010). *Recursion and human language.* Berlin: de Gruyter.

Vetter, R. J., & Weinstein, S. (1967). The history of the phantom in congenitally absent limbs. *Neuropsychologia, 5*(4), 335–338.

Vico, G. [1710] (1988). *On the most ancient wisdom of the Italians: Unearthed from the origins of the Latin language; Including the disputation with the "Giornale de' letterati d'Italia"* (L. M. Palmer, Trans.). Ithaca: Cornell University Press.

Viviani, P. (2002). Motor competence in the perception of dynamic events: A tutorial. In W. Prinz & B. Hommel (Eds.), *Common mechanisms in perception and action: Attention and performance XIX* (pp. 406–442). Oxford: Oxford University Press.

Viviani, P., Baud-Bovy, G., & Redolfi, M. (1997). Perceiving and tracking kinesthetic stimuli: Further evidence of motor-perceptual interactions. *Journal of Experimental Performance: Human Perception & Performance, 23*(4), 1232–1252.

Viviani, P., & Stucchi, N. (1989). The effect of movement velocity on form perception: Geometric illusions in dynamic displays. *Perception & Psychophysics, 46*(3), 266–274.

Viviani, P., & Terzuolo, C. (1982). Trajectory determines movement dynamics. *Neuroscience, 7*(2), 431–437.

Vogeley, K., & Fink, G. (2003). Neural correlates of the first-person-perspective. *Trends in Cognitive Sciences, 7*(1), 38–42.

Vogeley, K., May, M., Ritzl, A., Falkai, P., Zilles, K., & Fink, G. (2004). Neural correlates of first-person perspective as one constituent of human self-consciousness. *Journal of Cognitive Neuroscience, 16*(5), 817–827.

von Holst, E., & Mittelstädt, H. (1950). Das Reafferenzprinzip. *Naturwissenschaften, 37*(40), 464–476.

Vygotsky, L. S. (1934/1962). *Thought and language.* Cambridge, MA: MIT Press.

Vygotsky, L. S. (1979). The genesis of higher mental functions. In J. V. Wertsch (Ed.), *The concept of activity in Soviet psychology* (pp. 144–188). Armonk: Sharpe.

Wargo, E. (2008). Talk to the hand: New insights into the evolution of language and gesture. *Observer, 21*(5), 16–22.

Warren, R., & Wertheim, A. H. (Eds.). (1990). *Perception & control of self-motion.* Hillsdale: Erlbaum.

Wegner, D. M. (2002). *The illusion of conscious will*. Cambridge, MA: MIT Press.

Wegner, D. M., & Barg, J. A. (1998). Control and automaticity in social life. In D. T. Gilbert, S. T. Fiske, & G. Lindzey (Eds.), *The handbook of social psychology* (Vol. 1). Boston: McGraw-Hill.

Wegner, D. M., & Erber, R. (1993). Social foundations of mental control. In D. M. Wegner & J. W. Pennebaker (Eds.), *Handbook of mental control*. Englewood Cliffs: Prentice Hall.

Wegner, D. M., & Vallacher, R. R. (1986). Action identification. In E. T. Higgins & R. M. Sorrentino (Eds.), *Handbook of motivation and cognition: Foundations of social behavior* (Vol. 1, pp. 550–582). Chichester: Wiley.

Weinstein, S., & Sersen, E. A. (1961). Phantoms in cases of congenital absence of limbs. *Neurology, 11*(10), 905–911.

Weinstein, S., Sersen, E. A., & Vetter, R. J. (1964). Phantoms and somatic sensation in cases of congenital aplasia. *Cortex, 1*, 276–290.

Welch, R. B. (1978). *Perceptual modification: Adapting to altered sensory environments*. New York: Academic Press.

Welch, R. B. (1986). Adaption of space perception. In K. R. Boff, L. Kaufman, & J. P. Thomas (Eds.), *Handbook of perception and human performance* (Vol. 1, pp. 24.01–24.45). New York: Wiley.

Wertsch, J. V. (1985). *Vygotsky and the social formation of mind*. Cambridge, MA: Harvard University Press.

Whitehead, C. (2001). Social mirrors and shared experiential worlds. *Journal of Consciousness Studies, 8*, 3–36.

Whiten, A., & Boesch, C. (2001). The cultures of chimpanzees. *Scientific American, 284*(1), 60–67.

Whiten, A., Hinde, R. A., Laland, K. N., & Stringer, C. B. (in press). Culture evolves. *Philosophical Transactions of the Royal Society of London: Series B, Biological Sciences*.

Whorf, B., & Carroll, J. B. (1956). *Language, thought, and reality: Selected writings of Benjamin Lee Whorf*. Cambridge, MA: MIT Press.

Wilkes, K. V. (1984). Pragmatics in science and theory in commonsense. *Inquiry, 27*(4), 339–361.

Wilkes, K. V. (1991). The relationship between scientific psychology and common sense psychology. *Synthese, 89*(1), 15–39.

Wilson, M. (2002). Six views of embodied cognition. *Psychonomic Bulletin & Review, 9*(4), 625–636.

Wilson, M. (2006). Covert imitation: How the body schema acts as a prediction device. In G. Knoblich, I. M. Thornton, F. Grosjean, & M. Shiffrar (Eds.), *Human body perception from the inside out* (pp. 211–228). Oxford: Oxford University Press.

Wilson, R. A., & Keil, F. C. (Eds.). (1999). *The MIT encyclopedia of the cognitive sciences.* Cambridge, MA: MIT Press.

Winnicott, D. W. (1971). Mirror role of mother and family in child development. In D. W. Winnicott (Ed.), *Playing and reality* (pp. 111–118). London: Tavistock.

Wittgenstein, L. (1980). *Remarks on the philosophy of psychology* (Anscombe, G. E. M., Trans.). Chicago: University of Chicago Press.

Wohlschläger, A. (2000). Visual motion priming by invisible actions. *Vision Research, 40*(8), 925–930.

Wolff, P. (2008). Dynamics and the perception of causal events. In T. F. Shipley & J. M. Zacks (Eds.), *Understanding events: From perception to action* (pp. 555–588). New York: Oxford University Press.

Wolpert, D. M., & Flanagan, J. R. (2001). Motor prediction. *Current Biology, 11*(18), R729–R732.

Wolpert, D. M., Ghahramani, Z., & Jordan, M. I. (1995). An internal model for sensorimotor integration. *Science, 269*(5232), 1880–1882.

Wolpert, D. M., & Kawato, M. (1998). Multiple paired forward and inverse models for motor control. *Neural Networks, 11*(8), 1317–1329.

Woodward, A. L., Sommerville, J. A., & Guajardo, J. J. (2001). How infants make sense of intentional action. In B. F. Malle, L. J. Moses, & D. A. Baldwin (Eds.), *Intentions and intentionality: Foundations of social cognition* (pp. 149–170). Cambridge, MA: MIT Press.

Wright, K. (2003). Face and façade—the mother's face as the baby's mirror. In J. Raphael-Leff (Ed.), *Parent-infant psychodynamics: Wild things, mirrors & ghosts* (pp. 5–17). London: Whurr.

Wulf, G., & Prinz, W. (2001). Directing attention to movement effects enhances learning: A review. *Psychonomic Bulletin & Review, 8*(4), 648–660.

Wundt, W. (1902/1903). *Grundzüge der physiologischen Psychologie* (5th ed., Vol. 1–4). Leipzig: Engelmann.

Zahavi, D. (2005). *Subjectivity and selfhood: Investigating the first-person perspective.* Cambridge, MA: MIT Press.

Zaidel, E. (1990). Language functions in the two hemispheres following complete cerebral commissurotomy and hemispherectomy. In F. Boller & J. Grafman (Eds.), *Handbook of neuropsychology* (Vol. 4, pp. 115–150). Amsterdam: Elsevier.

Zwickel, J., Grosjean, M., & Prinz, W. (2007). Seeing while moving: Measuring the online influence of action on perception. *Quarterly Journal of Experimental Psychology, 60*(8), 1063–1071.

Zwickel, J., Grosjean, M., & Prinz, W. (2008). A contrast effect between the concurrent production and perception of movement directions. *Visual Cognition, 16*(7), 953–978.

Zwickel, J., Grosjean, M., & Prinz, W. (2010). On interference effects in concurrent perception and action. *Psychological Research, 74*(2), 152–171.

Name Index

Subject Index